WHOSE BOOK IS IT ANYWAY?

Whose Book is it Anyway?

A View from Elsewhere on Publishing, Copyright and Creativity

*Edited by Janis Jefferies
and Sarah Kember*

https://www.openbookpublishers.com

© 2019 Janis Jefferies and Sarah Kember. Copyright of individual chapters is maintained by the chapter's author.

This work is licensed under a Creative Commons Attribution 4.0 International license (CC BY 4.0). This license allows you to share, copy, distribute and transmit the work; to adapt the work and to make commercial use of the work providing attribution is made to the authors (but not in any way that suggests that they endorse you or your use of the work). Attribution should include the following information:

Janis Jefferies and Sarah Kember (eds.), *Whose Book is it Anyway? A View from Elsewhere on Publishing, Copyright and Creativity*. Cambridge, UK: Open Book Publishers, 2019, https://doi.org/10.11647/OBP.0159

Copyright and permissions for the reuse of many of the images included in this publication differ from the above. Copyright and permissions information for images is provided separately in the List of Illustrations.
Every effort has been made to identify and contact copyright holders and any omission or error will be corrected if notification is made to the publisher.

In order to access detailed and updated information on the license, please visit https://www.openbookpublishers.com/product/925#copyright

Further details about CC BY licenses are available at http://creativecommons.org/licenses/by/4.0/

All external links were active at the time of publication unless otherwise stated and have been archived via the Internet Archive Wayback Machine at https://archive.org/web

Digital material and resources associated with this volume are available at https://www.openbookpublishers.com/product/925#resources

Every effort has been made to identify and contact copyright holders and any omission or error will be corrected if notification is made to the publisher.

ISBN Paperback: 978-1-78374-648-4
ISBN Hardback: 978-1-78374-649-1
ISBN Digital (PDF): 978-1-78374-650-7
ISBN Digital ebook (epub): 978-1-78374-651-4
ISBN Digital ebook (mobi): 978-1-78374-652-1
ISBN Digital (XML): 978-1-78374-653-8
DOI: 10.11647/OBP.0159

Cover image: Photo by Toa Heftiba on Unsplash at https://unsplash.com/photos/DakDfhDHMSA Cover design by Anna Gatti.

All paper used by Open Book Publishers is SFI (Sustainable Forestry Initiative) and PEFC (Programme for the Endorsement of Forest Certification Schemes) Certified.

Contents

Notes on Contributors ... ix

Introduction: Whose Book is it Anyway? A View from Elsewhere on Publishing, Copyright and Creativity ... 1
Janis Jefferies and Sarah Kember

PART I: ... 19
Opening out the Copyright Debate: Open Access, Ethics and Creativity

1. A Statement by *The Readers Project* Concerning Contemporary Literary Practice, Digital Mediation, Intellectual Property, and Associated Moral Rights ... 21
   John Cayley and Daniel C. Howe

2. London-Havana Diary: Art Publishing, Sustainability, Free Speech and Free Papers ... 33
   Louise O'Hare

3. The Ethics of Emergent Creativity: Can We Move Beyond Writing as Human Enterprise, Commodity and Innovation? ... 65
   Janneke Adema

4. Are Publishers Worth It? Filtering, Amplification and the Value of Publishing ... 91
   Michael Bhaskar

5. Who Takes Legal Responsibility for Published Work? Why Both an Understanding and Lived Experience of Copyright Are Becoming Increasingly Important to Writers 105

   Alison Baverstock

6. Telling Stories or Selling Stories: Writing for Pleasure, Writing for Art or Writing to Get Paid? 129

   Sophie Rochester

7. Copyright in the Everyday Practice of Writers 141

   Smita Kheria

8. Comics, Copyright and Academic Publishing: The Deluxe Edition 181

   Ronan Deazley and Jason Mathis

PART II:
Views from Elsewhere 227

9. Diversity or die: How the Face of Book Publishing Needs to Change if it is to Have a Future 229

   Danuta Kean

10. Writing on the Cusp of Becoming Something Else 243

    J. R. Carpenter

11. Confronting Authorship, Constructing Practices (How Copyright is Destroying Collective Practice) 267

    Eva Weinmayr

12. Ethical Scholarly Publishing Practices, Copyright and Open Access: A View from Ethnomusicology and Anthropology 309

    Muriel Swijghuisen Reigersberg

13. Show me the Copy! How Digital Media (Re)Assert Relational Creativity, Complicating Existing Intellectual Property and Publishing Paradigms   347
    Joseph F. Turcotte

14. Redefining Reader and Writer, Remixing Copyright: Experimental Publishing at if:book Australia   379
    Simon Groth

APPENDIX: 403
CREATe Position Papers

1. Publishing Industry   405
   Janis Jefferies

2. Is the Current Copyright Framework fit for Purpose in Relation to Writing, Reading and Publishing in the Digital Age?   415
   Laurence Kaye

3. Is the Current Copyright Framework fit for Purpose in Relation to Writing, Reading, and Publishing in the Digital Age?   417
   Richard Mollet

4. History of Copyright Changes 1710–2013   423
   Rachel Calder

5. Is the Current Copyright Framework fit for Purpose in Relation to Writing, Reading, and Publishing in the Digital Age?   427
   Max Whitby

List of Illustrations   429

Index   431

Notes on Contributors

Janneke Adema is a Research Fellow at the Centre for Postdigital Cultures at Coventry University. In her research, she explores the future of scholarly communication and experimental forms of knowledge production, where her work incorporates processual and performative publishing, radical open access, scholarly poethics, media studies, book history, cultural studies, and critical theory. She explores these issues in depth in her various publications, but also by supporting a variety of scholar-led, not-for-profit publishing projects, including the Radical Open Access Collective, Open Humanities Press, and Post Office Press (POP).

Alison Baverstock is a publisher and pioneer of publishing education and profession-orientated education within universities. She co-founded MA Publishing at Kingston University in 2006 and has researched and written widely about publishing. *How to Market Books*, first published in 1990 and now in its seventh edition, has been widely licensed for translation and is an international bedrock of publisher education, within both the academy and the profession. She is a champion of the widening of literacy and the value of shared-reading: Well Worth Reading won an arts and industry award and since then she has founded both www.readingforce.org.uk and The Kingston University Big Read, which won the 2017 Times Higher Award for Widening Participation. In 2007 she received the Pandora Award for a significant contribution to the industry.

Michael Bhaskar is a writer and publisher based in London and Oxford. He is co-founder of Canelo, a new digital publisher, and Writer in

Residence at DeepMind, the world's leading AI research lab. Previously he has been a digital publisher, economist, agent and start-up founder amongst other things. He is author of *The Content Machine* (2013) and *Curation: The Power of Selection in a World of Excess* (2016) and is co-editor of the forthcoming *Oxford Handbook of Publishing* (2019). He regularly speaks and writes about the future of publishing, media, culture and society.

J. R. Carpenter is an artist, writer, researcher, and lecturer working across print, digital, and live performance. Her pioneering works of digital literature have been presented in journals, museums, galleries, and festivals around the world. Her recent web-based work *The Gathering Cloud* won the New Media Writing Prize 2016. A print book by the same name was published in 2017. Her debut poetry collection *An Ocean of Static* (*Penned in the Margins*) was highly commended for the Forward Prize 2018.

John Cayley is a writer, theorist, and pioneering maker of language art in programmable media. Apart from more or less conventional poetry and translation, he has explored dynamic and ambient poetics, text generation, transliteral morphing, aestheticized vectors of reading, and transactive synthetic language. Today, he composes as much for reading in aurality as in visuality. *Grammalepsy: Essays on Digital Language Art* was published in 2018. Professor of Literary Arts at Brown University, he directs a graduate program in Digital Language Arts. https://programmatology.shadoof.net

Ronan Deazley is the Professor of Copyright Law at Queen's University Belfast. His current research addresses the way the copyright regime impacts how memory institutions enable access to and use of our shared cultural heritage, online and across borders. In addition, he develops copyright education tools and materials for cultural heritage practitioners, information and media professionals, students and the wider public. He was the General Editor of the *Copyright User* initiative between 2013–2016 (copyrightuser.org), launched the *Copyright Cortex* in June 2017 (copyrightcortex.org), and is the co-creator of *The Game is On!* (2015–2018) an award-winning series of six animated films exploring copying, creativity and limits of lawful appropriation and reuse.

Simon Groth is a writer and editor whose works include *Off the Record: 25 Years of Music Street Press* (with Sean Sennett, 2010), *Hunted Down and Other Tales* (with Marcus Clarke, 2016), and *Infinite Blue* (with Darren Groth, 2018). With if:book Australia, Simon created a series of award-winning experimental works including the 24-Hour Book, live writing events at writers festivals around the world, and works of literary remix. His reporting on digital publishing has seen him travel the globe to discuss and explore the challenges and opportunities for writers and readers in a digital world. He is currently an editor at The Writing Platform.

Daniel C. Howe is an artist and coder whose work focuses on the relationships between networks, language and politics. His hybrid practice explores the impact of computational technologies on human values such as diversity, privacy and freedom. He has been an open-source advocate and contributor to dozens of socially-engaged software projects over the past two decades. His outputs include software interventions, art installations, algorithmically-generated text and sound, and tools for artists. He currently serves as Associate Professor in the School of Creative Media Hong Kong.

Janis Jefferies is professor emerita of Visual Arts, Goldsmiths, University of London, UK. She has edited numerous books and chapter contributions on textiles, technology, performance and practice research, most recently *TECHSTYLE Series 2.0: Ariadne's Thread* (2017) and *A Reader TEXTYLE 2.0 FabPublic, Talking about Textiles, Community and Public Space both for CHAT/MILL6 Foundation. Hong Kong* (2018). The Enchantment of Textiles research project with Professor Barbara Layne, Concordia University documents twenty years of their collaborative, textile and technology based research. The exhibition will be shown at the ASM Expression Gallery. Art Science Museum, Singapore in 2019. She is contributing 'Art, Craft & Design technologies' to Charlie Gere and Francesca Franco's three-volume *Bloomsbury Encyclopedia of New Media Art*, to be published in 2022.

Danuta Kean writes for *The Guardian* and is books editor at *Mslexia*. She has edited three reports on diversity within UK publishing, including *Writing the Future* (2016) and *Free Verse* (2006), which have resulted in significant initiatives to improve inclusivity within the worlds of poetry and books. In 2017 she edited *Centre Stage* for the Andrew Lloyd Webber Foundation, which has also led to significant initiatives to improve diversity within the theatrical professions. She is a regular speaker on the radio and at festivals, revealing the inner workings of a trade that seems opaque to many, and has taught publishing and journalism on the Creative Writing MA at Brunel University.

Sarah Kember is a writer and academic. She is Professor of New Technologies of Communication at Goldsmiths, University of London and Director of Goldsmiths Press. Her work incorporates new media, photography and feminist cultural approaches to science and technology. Publications include a novel and a short story *The Optical Effects of Lightning* (2011) and 'The Mysterious Case of Mr Charles D. Levy' (2010). Experimental work includes an edited open access electronic book entitled *Astrobiology and the Search for Life on Mars* (2011) and 'Media, Mars and Metamorphosis' (*Culture Machine*, Vol. 11). Recent monographs include a feminist critique of smart media: *iMedia: The Gendering of Objects, Environments and Smart Materials* (2016) and, with Joanna Zylinska, *Life after New Media: Mediation as a Vital Process* (2012). Sarah co-edits the journal *Feminist Theory*. Previous publications include: *Virtual Anxiety. Photography, New Technologies and Subjectivity* (1998); *Cyberfeminism and Artificial Life* (2003) and the co-edited volume *Inventive Life. Towards the New Vitalism* (2006). Current work includes a novel, provisionally entitled *A Day in The Life of Janet Smart*. With Janis Jefferies, Sarah Kember was co-PI of an RCUK funded project on digital publishing ('Whose Book Is It Anyway?' 2012–2016), part of CREATe (Centre for Creativity, Copyright, Regulation, Enterprise and Technology).

Smita Kheria is a Senior Lecturer in Intellectual Property Law at the University of Edinburgh. She is also a member of SCRIPT, a law and technology research centre in Edinburgh Law School. She combines legal expertise in copyright and related rights with socio-legal research on intellectual property law in the real world. Her research has examined how copyright intersects with the everyday lives and creative practices of digital artists, online creative communities, arts and humanities researchers, and professional creators and performers. Smita was PI on two RCUK funded projects (Copyright and Individual Creators;

Copyright policy and Creators' Organisations) as part of CREATe. She is a co-author of the textbook *Contemporary Intellectual Property: Law and Policy* (2013, 2016, 2019). She promotes IP awareness through speaking to creative communities and is active in public engagement events (Edinburgh Festival Fringe shows 2017–2019).

Jason Mathis is a Calgary-based artist whose work focuses primarily on comics. He studied at the Alberta College of Art & Design for his BFA, and at the Glasgow School of Art for his MFA. Jason's work can be found in small-press publications across North America and the UK. He also paints occasionally and loves to cook.

Louise O'Hare founded the London Bookshop Map in 2011 as a project to disseminate new writing by artists, and has commissioned works by Dora García, Holly Pester, Katrina Palmer, Hannah Rickards, and Camilla Wills. She co-ran Publish and be Damned from 2011–2013, and in 2014 set up Three Letter Words, an arts commissioning agency and charity. In 2015 she curated an exhibition reflecting upon Todd Haynes' 1995 film 'Safe' at HOME, Manchester (with Sarah Perks). O'Hare has worked as an editor at Afterall (2013–2016) and a lecturer at Central Saint Martins (2011–2017). She received her Masters in Curating Contemporary Art from the Royal College of Art (2010), and is currently completing a practice-based Fine Art PhD at Northumbria University titled *Centrefold (1974) — A Memoir*. Her research interests include gossip, feminist art histories, self-publishing, the politics of care, and pornography.

Muriel Swijghuisen Reigersberg is a research affiliate at The University of Sydney's Conservatorium of Music, PARADESIC archives. Her research interests include Australian Aboriginal Choral singing, the anthropology of religion and the relationship between music, health and wellbeing from an ethnomusicological perspective. She is currently an ambassador on the EU Horizon 2020 FREYA project, exploring the uses of persistent identifiers in digital scholarship for arts and humanities. Muriel is also a Researcher Development Manager (strategy) at the University of Sydney. ORCID: http://orcid.org/0000-0003-2337-7962

Sophie Rochester is the founder of The Literary Platform, a specialist digital publishing organisation. She was also founder of the Fiction Uncovered Prize, co-founder of The Writing Platform and co-author of *The Publishing Landscape in China*. She has been a speaker on digital publishing at TOC New York, the Frankfurt Book Fair, Bologna Book Fair, Editech Milan, British Council Crossing the River conferences in Beijing, Shanghai and Hong Kong. She is also a visiting lecturer at the London College of Communications MA in Publishing and UEA's MA in Creative Writing.

Joseph Turcotte holds a PhD from the York & Ryerson Joint Graduate Program in Communication & Culture. His research and policy analysis focusses on the political economy and social impacts of intellectual property (IP), innovation, and the knowledge-based economy. He researches and publishes extensively on how IP, knowledge/ information and data are developed, managed, and commercialized in the knowledge-based, digital economy. He is currently the Innovation Clinic Coordinator at IP Osgoode, Osgoode Hall Law School's Intellectual Property & Technology Law Program.

Eva Weinmayr is an artist, educator, researcher and writer based in London and Gothenburg. She investigates in her work the border crossings between contemporary art, radical education and institutional analysis by experimenting with modes of knowledge formation. In 2009 she co-founded AND Publishing, a feminist publishing platform and collaborative practice based in London. Recent projects include 'Boxing and Unboxing' at Marabouparken Konsthall Stockholm (with Rosalie Schweiker), 'The Piracy Project' an exploration of the philosophical, legal and social implications of book piracy (with Andrea Francke) and 'Let's Mobilize: What is Feminist Pedagogy?', an ongoing collective experiment with queer and feminist pedagogies (Valand Academy working group). Books include (*Pause*) *21 Scenes Concerning the Silence of Art in Ruins* (2010) and *Downing Street — Help! David Cameron Likes My Art* (2015). She is currently conducting a practice-based PhD on the micro-politics of publishing at Valand Academy in Gothenburg, Sweden.

Introduction: Whose Book is it Anyway? A View from Elsewhere on Publishing, Copyright and Creativity

Janis Jefferies and Sarah Kember

This anthology offers an approach to publishing that does more than ask if current copyright frameworks are fit for purpose in a digital age. It opens out the copyright debate, first to questions of open access, ethics and creativity and second to views from elsewhere — artist's perspectives, writer's perspectives, feminist, and international perspectives that are too often marginalized or elided altogether. The book investigates the future of publishing in the digital age, in particular the role of access, ethics and creativity and their relation to copyright within or from the perspective of creative practice. Contributions were commissioned as part of our role in CREATe (Centre for Copyright, Regulation, Enterprise and Technology)[1] and include publishers (such as Michael Bhaskar, co-founder of Canelo), industry experts (such as Sophie Rochester, founder of The Literary Platform and Yodomo), academics (including legal scholars Ronan Deazley and Smita Kheria as well as arts and humanities scholars such as Janneke Adema and Eva Weinmayr), writers (such as the poet John Cayley) and artists (including J. R. Carpenter).

---

[1] http://www.create.ac.uk/research-programme/theme-4/wp4d-whose-book-is-it-anyway-ip-collaborative-business-models-and-questions-of-ethics-and-creativity-in-digital-publishing/

Whose Book is it Anyway? follows the trajectory of a four-year research project conducted through a series of workshops held at venues ranging from Nesta, the London Book Fair and the British Library to *The Guardian* and the V&A. The research was predicated on what is colloquially termed the 'copyfight', brought into focus by UK reforms in intellectual property (IP) and open access[2] and producing something of an impasse or standoff between those in the publishing industry who are concerned to retain, or even strengthen copyright in a digital context and, on the other hand, the technology industry and its advocates in government who regard intellectual property rights as more of an impediment than an incentive to innovation and economic growth.

We began by examining a range of hopes and fears concerning the extent to which the UK copyright framework (prior to the implementation of the proposed reforms)[3] was considered fit for purpose in relation to writing and publishing in the digital age. Our concern was to frame these hopes and fears through what Raymond Williams terms a 'structure of feeling' about technology.[4] In other words, there seemed to be a degree of consensus that digital technology is a game changer in publishing, whether those changes were positive or negative with respect to copyright. The question concerning technology, and particularly technology as an agent of change, is almost as fraught as the question concerning intellectual property as an agent of creativity. The concept of technological determinism encompasses the possibility that technology causes, or conversely, is the effect of wider social and economic changes. As a causal agent, technology

---

2 The context for this research project, which ran from 2012–2016 was provided by proposed reforms by Professor Ian Hargreaves (May 2011) and Dame Janet Finch (June 2012), 'Digital Opportunity. A Review of Intellectual Property and Growth' https://assets.publishing.service.gov.uk/government/uploads/system/uploads/attachment_data/file/32563/ipreview-finalreport.pdf; 'Accessibility, Sustainability, excellence: How to Expand Access to Research Publications' (Report of the Working Group on Expanding Access to Published Research Findings), https://www.acu.ac.uk/research-information-network/finch-report-final

3 See 'Exceptions to Copyright: an Overview', Intellectual Property Office report, October 2014. This report summarises what has changed with respect to caricature, parody or pastiche; quotation; research and private study; text and data mining; education and teaching; archiving and preservation; public administration; accessible formats for disabled people, https://assets.publishing.service.gov.uk/government/uploads/system/uploads/attachment_data/file/448274/Exceptions_to_copyright_-_Guidance_for_creators_and_copyright_owners.pdf

4 Raymond Williams, *The Long Revolution* (London: Chatto & Windus, 1961).

sits in the middle of the copyfight, both maintaining, and effectively negating opposing viewpoints. We might point to a consensual technological determinism that both undermines and structures the opposition between a culture that is free (and freely shared) and one that is, necessarily, proprietorial. The consensus sounds something like this: in the digital era, copyright is broken and must therefore be fixed. Either copyright is broken and it must be reformed and reinforced or it is broken and must be rendered redundant or reduced through a number of exceptions. What maintains the consensus is an ontology of the digital *as* copying, sharing, openness and re-use — the idea that the Internet particularly is all about, or just *is* sharing, whether that takes place person to person or from many to many. Either we go with the very nature and being of technology or we take tougher steps to guard against it. However, it might be more useful to think less about the essence of technology and more about its affordances — the types of activity and behaviour that it, along with other forms of agency, both enables and constrains. The affordances of digital technology are less monolithic than its alleged essence. They might, for example, be about both owning and sharing cultural content and they are certainly not reducible to economic growth.

The technological consensus concerning the need for copyright reform dilutes the apparent conflict of the copyfight and, more importantly, depoliticizes the current debate about publishing. Taken together with the related agenda for open access reform, the question of copyright in a digital age delimits what can be said and done with respect to academic publishing, at least. In a closed workshop that took place at Goldsmiths, University of London in 2014, a small group of academic publishers, together with artists involved in publishing experiments, examined some of the issues that might, but at the time did not impinge on UK policy. These included questions about ethics and responsibility in publishing as well as issues about creative invention, experimentation and intervention that cut across, or combine with a neoliberal agenda solely focused on innovation. The workshop also considered the conditions of possibility or the social and political context surrounding publishing activity and underlying issues of scholarly practice, such as peer review, citation and free labour that are political in the sense that they adhere to existing divisions in gender, race, class and career stage.

It is interesting to note that the College Art Association (CAA) in the US commissioned a report on Fair Use, which was then published as a Code of Best Practice in Fair Use for the Visual Arts in 2015. The Associate Acquisitions Editor at MIT Press, Victoria Hindley, was sufficiently motivated to work with her colleagues to pursue a fair use initiative of their own. With support from the Executive Editor, Press Director and legal counsel Hindley helped to define a progressive position in support of responsible fair use. MIT Press has developed proposed new contract language in support of a position that no longer requires authors to indemnify the press when they have made a reasonable good faith determination of fair use; and, to further empower artists, the press has crafted permissions guidelines that take advantage of the CAA Code and refers authors to it. Martha Rosler, whose 'Bringing the War Home: House Beautiful 1967–72' is in the TATE's collection, has for many years incorporated into her work images circulating in what she has called the public sphere of mass media, including newspapers, magazines, and television, without considering copyright. Since Rosler is a leading contemporary critical voice within feminist discourse, processes like hers, as for many artists, constitute an essential form of critique and a means of inviting the reader/viewer to rethink the boundaries between the public and the private, the social and political.

In his contribution to this volume, Ronan Deazley draws our attention to commercial journal publishers that profit enormously from academic free labour (writing, editing, peer reviewing) and then refuse to implement copyright exceptions, for example, concerning the use of comic art within a piece of comic scholarship. The same publishers, we might add, may also be levying article processing charges for the privilege of publishing open access. As Deazley suggests, one option available to authors is to withdraw their labour. That labour might then be redirected towards more ethical, responsible and inventive publishers, including, among the workshop discussants, *Ada. A Journal of Gender, New Media and Technology*, Mattering Press, Mute Publishing and Goldsmiths Press.

Based on this and other workshops, our research suggested that the reform agenda in the UK limited publishing praxis and, while creating polarized, ideological stances, effectively neutered any meaningful political engagement — for example, about whether culture and knowledge should be publicly or privately owned — by means of a technological consensus. Where copyright reform required critique, critique tended to be subsumed within pro- and anti-reform stances. The value of critique lies in its ability to indicate a way through such dialectical structures. In our case, it was brought to bear on the impasse, the somewhat asymmetrical standoff in the relation between publishers and, specifically the Publishers Association (anti-reform) on the one hand, and the technology industries, specifically Google on the other. Publishing is represented at government level by the Department of Culture, Media and Sport (DCMS). The technology industries are represented by Business, Innovation and Skills (BIS). A 2013 DCMS report entitled 'Supporting the Creative Economy' rejected the proposal for reforms set out by Professor Ian Hargreaves, and not only lamented the UK government's favourable response to the proposal, but accused it of letting the tech industry, Google in particular, in through the back door:

> Following all the evidence we have received, we think Hargreaves is wrong in the benefits his report claims for his recommended changes to UK copyright law. We regret that the Hargreaves report adopts a significantly low standard in relation to the need for objective evidence in determining copyright policy. We do not consider Professor Hargreaves has adequately assessed the dangers of putting the established system of copyright at risk for no obvious benefit. We are deeply concerned that there is an underlying agenda driven at least partly by technology companies (Google foremost among them) which, if pursued uncritically, could cause irreversible damage to the creative sector on which the United Kingdom's future prosperity will significantly depend.[5]

Rather than aligning our CREATe project with either BIS or DCMS, pro- or anti-reform agendas, we sought to develop a critical framework based on the testimony of artists, writers and academics as well as publishers, agents and technology developers. Our aim was not to balance the debate as much as to open out the reform agenda and signal the possibility of moving beyond technologically deterministic hopes and fears as well as simplistic ideological divisions between a notion of free culture or knowledge and one that is proprietorial.

---

5   House of Commons Culture, Media and Sport Committee, *Supporting the Creative Economy: Third Report of Session 2013–2014*, Vol. I (London: The Stationery Office Limited, 2013), pp. 4–5, https://www.publications.parliament.uk/pa/cm201314/cmselect/cmcumeds/674/674.pdf

The problem with our initial question — about whether the UK copyright system was fit for purpose in a digital age — was that it had the capacity to reinforce rather than challenge existing ideological divisions. It could produce arguments in favour of change and also some defensive, 'no change needed' reactions. We commissioned a series of position papers (see appendix) that demonstrate that this polarization did not always occur, but by reframing the initial question, posing it more in terms of how writers and artists may eat, we strove to avoid false dichotomies and the worst pitfalls of a technological imaginary. We also wanted to question the alignment between creativity and economic growth that had been so clearly signalled in the first phase of the research, avoiding, as much as possible, the opposition between a neoliberal and romantic reading of creativity and instead asking artists, writers and publishers to reflect on the always antagonistic but never purely oppositional relation between writing for love and writing for money.

Financial incentive is one of the key assumptions underpinning intellectual property laws. That remains the case even as those laws become subject to reform. Hargreaves recognizes that rights that 'support growth by promoting innovation through the offer of a temporary monopoly to creators and inventors' might also 'stifle growth where transaction costs are high or rights are fragmented in a way that makes them hard to access'. If the problem with IP is that it fosters a closed market dominated by established players in technology and content, the solution, he suggests, is to redesign IP in order to facilitate a fairer, more transparent, more open and competitive market that encourages new entrants and enables rather than constrains further innovation. The solution to piracy in a digital world 'where copying and distribution are more or less free', is not, for Hargreaves, copyright enforcement as much as a modernization of copyright law that encourages 'open and competitive markets in licensed digital content'.[6] It is clear that Hargreaves' reforms are oriented towards the technology industries, but he applies the same principles to publishing and the so-called 'creative industries' because he recognizes their economic value.[7]

---

6   Hargreaves, 'Digital Opportunity', p. 10.
7   Ibid., p. 3.

The assumption that creators are predominantly if not exclusively motivated by economic rights and financial reward continues to be held at policy level despite a number of academic studies that have subjected it to critical examination.[8] Where Ruth Towse underlines the importance of moral rights, Schlesinger and Waelde, starting from the observation that 'both policy and law have relatively little engagement with most cultural work and what makes it tick', examine the relevance of the rights regime for how dancers and musicians make a living.[9] Focusing on portfolio work undertaken in conditions of relative economic precarity, they emphasize 'the trade-offs made between making money through commercial activities and making little or none through the pursuit of creative and aesthetic goals'.[10] On the basis that this trade-off applies to writers as much as dancers and musicians, and bearing in mind the fall in author's earnings — a drop of 19% in the decade from 2005 to 2015 — we might expect the balance to be increasingly skewed in favour of non-financial incentives.[11]

However, as Smita Kheria shows in her contribution to this book, it is as erroneous to dismiss the idea as to assume that economic reward is what drives writers to write. As a means of securing economic remuneration, of any scale, copyright has a more complex, less 'all or nothing' role to play in creative practice. From the point of view of the writers Kheria interviewed, copyright might contribute to earnings but, just as importantly, have a symbolic role in bestowing value and recognition on writing as a way of life. The role of copyright is seen by some writers to be more important in a digital environment that simultaneously threatens and validates their rights over an original work by deeming it worthy of being shared and reused. Here, the economic rights and moral interests of individual authors are reappraised — by the authors themselves — in relation to a wider online community of

---

8 Ruth Towes, 'Copyright and Artists: A View from Cultural Economics', *Journal of Economic Surveys* 20.4 (2006), 569–85; Philip Schlesinger and Charlotte Waelde, 'Copyright and Cultural Work: An Exploration', *Innovation. The European Journal of Social Science Research* 25.1 (2012), 11–18.
9 Schlesinger and Waelde, 'Copyright and Cultural Work', p. 6.
10 Ibid., p. 16.
11 Johanna Gibson, Phillip Johnson and Gaetano Dimita, *The Business of Being an Author: A Survey of Author's Earnings and Contracts* (Queen Mary: University of London, 2015), https://orca.cf.ac.uk/72431/1/Final Report - For Web Publication.pdf

users, including users who might become the authors of secondary or derivative works such as, for example, fan fiction.

If the role of copyright in creative practice is complex in as far as it is both economic and social, pertaining to individuals and communities, to what extent is that complexity reflected in copyright reforms? UK copyright reforms subsequent to Hargreaves' review are more limited than the scope of the review would indicate.[12] Centred on parody, quotation, research, text and data mining, education and teaching, archiving and preservation, public administration and the generation of accessible formats for people with disabilities, the reforms amount to a set of minimal copyright exceptions that are contained within the remit of fair dealing. Fair dealing is colloquially understood as 'fair stealing' and it is a means of preserving the principles of copyright by ensuring that the amount taken or borrowed from a work is reasonable and appropriate and the market value is not adversely affected. Fair dealing is the wiggle room within the existing UK (and Canadian) copyright system. At most, this has been extended slightly, while the system stays in place. Where copyright reforms in the UK are in themselves surprisingly conservative, the major challenge to copyright comes through related reforms in open access, which apply principally to academic publishing.

We will address the question of open access shortly, but it seems that complexity, derived from the experience of creative practitioners, along with criticality, is something of an anathema to copyright law and to the factions invested in it. Set up in order to analyse and critically investigate the case for IP reform, CREATe itself (both a research centre and a consortium of Scottish and English universities) was initially caught up in the copyright wars. In a blog published in *The Bookseller* (a UK trade publishing magazine) in 2013, CREATe director Martin Kretschmer was forced to deny an accusation by Richard Mollet, then Chief Executive of the Publishers Association, that the project was biased in favour of copyright reform.[13] Kretschmer also defended the role of academic research as a way of breaking the deadlock between what he called the 'incumbents' and the 'insurgents':

---

12   See 'Exceptions to Copyright'.
13   Martin Kretschmer, 'Copyright Control', *The Bookseller*, 28 March 2013, http://www.thebookseller.com/blogs/copyright-control

They speak with different voices, and face different challenges. Mollet's instincts are with the incumbents, and there is nothing wrong with that. Still, incumbents need happy customers as much as anyone, and insurgents are usually much better at sensing new needs or disaffection. Where there are large swathes of unhappy customers — for example in relation to research publications (witness the data mining debate) — the reflex to reach for stronger rights and enforcement may have similar results as it did in the music industry. We don't know but we can find out. This is what research is about.

The division between incumbents and insurgents, the copyright wars themselves, are a distraction, if not from the realities of technological change and the associated shifts in consumer demand,[14] then from the underlying politics of communication. This, as Sarah Kember has previously argued,[15] has to do with the privatization, marketization and standardization of scholarly and creative practice; the neoliberal framing of the so-called knowledge and creative industries and the transformation of the scholar, writer and artist into the entrepreneur or the knowledge and creative professional.

Kember's position is that copyright and open access reforms mask the politics of communication in a narrative of crisis centred on technology. It is also that open access effectively delivers the 'real' copyright reforms by obliging the public sector, universities in particular, to make published works freely available for commercial use in the private sector. As the sociologist John Holmwood notes, a key problem with open access, which on one level is simply about removing price barriers to published research and widening readership, is precisely this asymmetric obligation to be open.[16]

The Finch report on open access, published in 2012 (the year after Hargreaves' review of IP), maintains that barriers to access, especially when research is publicly funded 'are increasingly unacceptable in an online world'. That is, they 'restrict the innovation, growth and other

---

14 See Google's Senior Copyright Counsel William Paltry, whose sense of these realities is very much the case for the insurgents: 'We Need to Redefine What "Copy" Means', *The Guardian*, 13 March 2012, https://www.theguardian.com/law/2012/mar/13/how-to-fix-copyright-extract

15 'Why Write? Feminism, Publishing and the Politics of Communication', *New Formations* 83 (2014), 99–117 and 'Why Publish?' *Learned Publishing*, special issue The University Press Redux 29:S1 (2016), 348–53, https://doi.org/10.1002/leap.1042

16 John Holmwood, 'Commercial Enclosure: Whatever Happened to Open Access?', *Radical Philosophy* 181 (2013), 2–5.

benefits' that might otherwise accrue.[17] A concern here with public access to publicly funded research by means of 'enhanced transparency, openness and accountability' leads to an emphasis on 'closer linkages between research and innovation, with *benefits* for public policy and services, and for economic growth' [my emphasis]. Access here means access to research for industry and enterprises. The Finch recommendations in favour of gold open access publishing[18] funded by author or article processing charges (APCs) plus minimal restrictions on the rights of use and re-use are now incorporated into the UK Higher Education sector.[19] The changes are controversial, not least since the Creative Commons license (CC BY) mandated by Research Councils UK (RCUK) — which is now renamed as Research England/UKRI — allows for commercial reuse of research material with attribution rather than the author's permission. An alternative would be a non-commercial share-alike license (CC BY-NC-SA) or one that simply allows non-commercial users to download and share work as long as the author is credited (CC BY-NC-ND).

Reforms of open access are ongoing in the UK and across mainland Europe. At the time of writing, the UK is a signatory to Plan S, an initiative by the European Commission to accelerate the transition to full and immediate open access.[20] What makes the UK unique is that it ties a mandate (rather than a recommendation) to the national research audit, the Research Excellence Framework (REF), making open access article (REF 2021) and monograph (REF 2027) publishing a condition of entry *without* any commitment to additional public funding. This has raised concerns for the future of Arts, Humanities and Social Sciences in the UK, which receive significantly less funding than STEM (Science, Technology, Engineering and Maths) fields and will face the higher costs of monograph publishing. The British Academy's position paper on open access monograph publishing raises further questions, notably about the extent to which UK academics will be disadvantaged

---

17 Finch, 'Digital Opportunity', p. 5.
18 The difference between gold and green open access is explained here: https://www.jisc.ac.uk/guides/an-introduction-to-open-access
19 The National Research Excellence Framework (REF) 2021 mandates open access publishing for articles and conference proceedings. At the time of writing, there is very likely to be a mandate for open access monograph publishing for REF 2027.
20 https://www.scienceeurope.org/coalition-s/

by having restrictions placed on where they can publish, whether they or their institution can afford to and whether it will be feasible to collaborate with colleagues outside of the UK.[21]

Martin Paul Eve, an advocate of open access, or more specifically, of a re-politicized open access, still recognizes it as an instrument of neoliberalism understood as 'the practice of using the free market as the assignation of value.'[22] Key traits of neoliberalism include, for Eve, a concern with quantification and measurement, the 'belief that all aspects of society are best handled on a for-profit basis through competition' and an emphasis on openness, transparency and accountability in order to facilitate quantification. The UK's open access mandate certainly highlights neoliberal values, but beyond a top-down government agenda, the values of open access remain contested by various stakeholders, with a range of library and scholar-led publishing initiatives (such as new university presses) as well as funder initiatives driving the agenda forwards.

Dissent does exist within academia. Meera Sabaratnam and Paul Kirby, for example, refer to open access as a threat to academic freedom.[23] They argue that it places pressure on institutions to distribute inadequate funding (which they cannot do fairly, openly or transparently) and increases academic inequality — within and between institutions — 'by linking prestige in research and publishing to the capacity to pay APCs, rather than to academic qualities.' There is a question mark then, not only over who publishes and where, but over what is considered publishable — the kind of work produced. Academic research may very well be judged by standards other than peer review. David Berry correctly observes that open access is a disruption strategy within the UK's university sector, one that 'will have dire implications for

---

21 'Open Access and Monographs: Where Are we Now?', May 2018, https://www.thebritishacademy.ac.uk/publications/open-access-monographs-where-are-we-now
22 Martin Eve, 'Open Access, "Neoliberalism", "Impact", and the Privatisation of Knowledge', 10 March 2013, www.martineve.com/2013/03/10/open-access-neoliberalism-impact-and-the-privatisation-of-knowledge/
It might be argued that Eve's OLH (Open Library of the Humanities), a library subscription programme promoting open access work, is actually itself contributing to a free market in open access publishing.
23 Meera Sabaratnam and Paul Kirby, 'Open Access: HEFCE, REF2020 and the Threat to Academic Freedom', 4 December 2012, https://thedisorderofthings.com/2012/12/04/open-access-hefce-ref2020-and-the-threat-to-academic-freedom/

academic labour, thought and freedom if it is not contested.'[24] For him too, it is about obtaining 'greater public subsidy for the private sector's use of university research outputs' without any reciprocal contribution. For this reason, Kember has argued that academics concerned with the politics of communication should 'open out from open access'[25] and turn their attention from copyright per se[26] towards the incursion of venture capital into higher education and the profiteering by, for example, academia.edu, that is already taking place in the name of openness.

Whether or not it is possible to re-politicize open access itself — and a range of scholars and publishers, many associated with the Radical Open Access Movement[27] maintain that it is — or indeed whether it is possible to reverse neoliberal policies within higher education, it is possible and necessary to politicize the role of copyright and open access reform in publishing and to explore various modes and practices of critical intervention. Contributors to this volume engage these tasks in diverse ways and with very different voices and opinions. Some speak purely as creative practitioners while others, from within or outside of the academy, discuss the role of creative practice. Some contributors touch lightly on the question of copyright, extending it in relation to open access, ethics or creativity. There is not a singular argument or viewpoint here, but there is a shared sense of the value of creative practice and the importance of critical intervention in publishing. Danuta Kean, writing here, reminds us that publishing is an industry that is still somewhat self-defeating in its lack of racial diversity. Mindful of the legacy of artist and feminist publishing initiatives in the UK and internationally, we have sought the viewpoints and the investments of

---

24 David Berry, 'The Uses of Open Access', *STUNLAW: Philosophy and Critique for a Digital Age*, 16 February 2017, http://stunlaw.blogspot.com/2017/02/the-uses-of-open-access.html

25 Sarah Kember, 'Opening Out from Open Access: Writing and Publishing in Response to Neoliberalism', *Ada: A Journal of Gender, New Media, and Technology* 4 (2014), https://doi.org/10.7264/N31C1V51
See also Sarah Kember, 'Why Publish?', *Learned Publishing* 29:S1 (2016), 348–53, https://doi.org/10.1002/leap.1042

26 Noting that copyright and pricing mean different things to different publishers, protecting the vested interests of large commercial publishers like Elsevier while being necessary to the sustainability of small or independent publishers like Goldsmiths Press.

27 https://radicaloa.disruptivemedia.org.uk/about/

a range of different constituents in the future of academic and trade publishing.

We have organised the book into two sections. The first section extends questions of copyright to those of open access, ethics and creativity in publishing; the second looks at views from elsewhere. In Part I, John Cayley and Daniel C. Howe offer a statement (originally commissioned as one of our position papers — see appendix) by *The Readers Project*, a collective of poetic readers that emerge in relation to various texts. The text discussed and illustrated here is a poetic reading of Samuel Beckett's late novella *How It Is*. Cayley and Howe contrast their creative appropriation of Beckett's text — which runs 'counter to the customs and laws of intellectual property and defies conventions of authorship' while remaining respectful to the original work, oriented to the 'commons of language' and responsive to the evolving technologies of literary practice — with further developments in aggressive data mining, big tech and AI that no longer support those values. If the law was an ass prior to these developments, they ask, what is it now? Also in Part I, Louise O'Hare looks askew at copyright in Cuba through the prism of an anti-copyright art magazine. O'Hare foregrounds publishing itself as a creative practice that attends to form as well as content. Janneke Adema decouples the practice of writing from economic rights and remuneration and argues that we should think about publishing less in terms of creative autonomies — author and work — and more in terms of creative communities and relationalities in which authors and works intersect with each other in ways that are dynamic and co-constitutive. Adema's contribution resonates with that of Joseph Turcotte in Part II of the book. Turcotte maintains that IP law simply does not align with creative practice in as far as creativity is inherently relational and copyright is predicated on autonomies. Turcotte draws on a feminist critique of copyright law which argues that 'copyright is built around certain conceptions of the self, society and worth, which translate, through law, into norms about who can speak, who can listen, what can be said and with what force of authority'.[28] In as far as copyright

---

28 Carys J. Craig, Joseph F. Turcotte and Rosemary J. Coombe, 'What's Feminist about Open Access? A Relational Approach to Copyright in the Academy', *feminists@law* 1.1 (2011), http://journals.kent.ac.uk/kent/index.php/feministsatlaw/article/view/7/54

entrenches liberal assumptions and social norms, feminist legal studies has looked favourably on the open access movement that appears to supersede it and has foregrounded a key intervention that replaces a copyright system based on the autonomy of author and work, with one based on relationalities between authors and works within and across specific social situations.

Whose Book is it Anyway? combines these more speculative perspectives on the future of copyright and the future of publishing with those that look at current practice in a historical context. Michael Bhaskar, in Part I, argues that in a digital environment in which anyone can publish and so much content is freely shared, the traditional roles performed by publishers — filtering and amplification — become more, not less important. Sophie Rochester, also in Part I, returns to the question of what motivates writers when rights-related income is falling while J. R. Carpenter, in Part II, locates writing as a creative practice within traditions such as textual appropriation or borrowing that constitute a challenge to copyright. Eva Weinmayr, along with Carpenter, offers an artist's view on copyright as a system that strives to protect rather than proliferate ideas. Weinmayr offers a review of case law in an art context while Muriel Swijghuisen Reigersberg, echoing Adema and Turcotte, questions copyright's ability to recognize cross-cultural co-created works in a music context. Swijghuisen Reigersberg's main contribution to this volume is to highlight the challenge that co-authorship, along with indigenous cultural and moral rights, pose to open access as well as to copyright policy.

Taken together, these perspectives on creative practice provide a historical and critical framework for understanding and intervening in the current copyright dialectic. They demonstrate, sometimes by sharing examples of that practice (Cayley and Howe, Carpenter), sometimes from an international perspective (O'Hare, Swijghuisen Reigersberg, Turcotte and Groth) how the law has been, and is being lived with. Based on processes of appropriation, remix, 'reinterpretation, recombination and transformation', creative practices have always adapted to, worked around, and in a key sense flouted copyright law.[29] This of course raises a question about whether copyright, in its current, digital context,

---

29 Carys J. Craig, 'Introduction — Copyright, Communication & Culture: Towards a Relational Theory of Copyright Law', *Comparative Research in Law & Political Economy. Research Paper No. 23/2011*, 2011, https://digitalcommons.osgoode.yorku.ca/cgi/clpe/61

needs to be either strengthened or loosened. If copyright has, in effect, always been messy, the final question addressed in this book is not only whether copyright ever needed to be reformed along the lines originally determined by Hargreaves and Finch, but whether it even needs to be made relational or remixed, according to the perspectives foregrounded here. Simon Groth, in our final chapter, suggests that a remixed copyright system would not be based on rights protection for the individual, presumed to be autonomous author and his or her work, but rather on a combination of mutual, author to author, author to reader rights and responsibilities for the always already remixed work. Rather than regarding remix or relationality programmatically, as the next stage in the reformation of copyright, it might be better to see it as an intervention and as antagonist: a means of re-politicizing copyright and publishing in the face of a reformist technological consensus.

Works Cited

Berry, D. (2017) 'The Uses of Open Access', *STUNLAW: Philosophy and Critique for a Digital Age*, 16 February, http://stunlaw.blogspot.com/2017/02/the-uses-of-open-access.html

Craig, C. Turcotte, J. F. and Coombe, J. (2011) 'What's Feminist about Open Access? A Relational Approach to Copyright in the Academy', *feminists@law* 1.1, http://journals.kent.ac.uk/kent/index.php/feministsatlaw/article/view/7/54

Craig, C. J. (2011) 'Introduction — Copyright, Communication & Culture: Towards a Relational Theory of Copyright Law', *Comparative Research in Law & Political Economy. Research Paper No. 23/2011*, https://digitalcommons.osgoode.yorku.ca/cgi/clpe/61

Eve, M. P. (10 March 2013) 'Open Access, "Neoliberalism", "Impact" and the Privatisation of Knowledge', http://www.martineve.com/2013/03/10/open-access-neoliberalism-impact-and-the-privatisation-of-knowledge/

Finch, J. (2012) 'Accessibility, Sustainability, Excellence: How to Expand Access to Research Publications' (Report of the Working Group on Expanding Access to Published Research Findings), https://www.ncbi.nlm.nih.gov/pubmed/24400530

Gibson, J. Johnson, P. and Dimita, G. (2015) *The Business of Being an Author: A Survey of Author's Earnings and Contracts* (Queen Mary: University of London), https://orca.cf.ac.uk/72431/1/FinalReport-ForWebPublication.pdf

Hargreaves, I. (2011) 'Digital Opportunity. A Review of Intellectual Property and Growth', https://assets.publishing.service.gov.uk/government/uploads/system/uploads/attachment_data/file/32563/ipreview-finalreport.pdf

Holmwood, J. (2013) 'Commercial Enclosure: Whatever Happened to Open Access?' *Radical Philosophy* 181 (2013), 2–5.

House of Commons Culture, Media and Sport Committee. (2013) *Supporting the Creative Economy: Third Report of Session 2013–2014*, Vol. I (London: The Stationery Office Limited), pp. 4–5, https://www.publications.parliament.uk/pa/cm201314/cmselect/cmcumeds/674/674.pdf

IPO (2014) 'Exceptions to Copyright: An Overview', Intellectual Property Office report, https://assets.publishing.service.gov.uk/government/uploads/system/uploads/attachment_data/file/448274/Exceptions_to_copyright_-_Guidance_for_creators_and_copyright_owners.pdf

Kember, S. (2014) 'Opening Out from Open Access: Writing and Publishing in Response to Neoliberalism', *Ada: A Journal of Gender, New Media, and Technology* 4, https://doi.org/10.7264/N31C1V51

— (2014) 'Why Write? Feminism, Publishing and the Politics of Communication', *New Formations* 83, 99–117.

— (2016) 'Why Publish?' *Learned Publishing*, special issue The University Press Redux 29:S1, 348–53, https://doi.org/10.1002/leap.1042

Kretschmer, M. (28 March 2013) 'Copyright Control', *The Bookseller*, http://www.thebookseller.com/blogs/copyright-control

Paltry, W. (13 March 2012) 'We Need to Redefine what "Copy" Means', *The Guardian*, https://www.theguardian.com/law/2012/mar/13/how-to-fix-copyright-extract

Sabaratnam, M. and Kirby, P. (4 December 2012) 'Open Access: HEFCE, REF2020 and the Threat to Academic Freedom', *The Disorder of Things*, https://thedisorderofthings.com/2012/12/04/open-access-hefce-ref2020-and-the-threat-to-academic-freedom/

Schlesinger, P. and Waelde, C. (2012) 'Copyright and Cultural Work: An Exploration' *Innovation. The European Journal of Social Science Research* 25.1, 11–18.

The British Academy (2018) 'Open Access Monographs: Where Are We Now?', https://www.thebritishacademy.ac.uk/publications/open-access-monographs-where-are-we-now

Towes, R. (2006) 'Copyright and Artists: A View from Cultural Economics' *Journal of Economic Surveys* 20.4, 569–85.

Williams, R. (1961) *The Long Revolution* (London: Chatto & Windus).

PART I

OPENING OUT THE COPYRIGHT DEBATE: OPEN ACCESS, ETHICS AND CREATIVITY

1. A Statement by *The Readers Project*[1] Concerning Contemporary Literary Practice, Digital Mediation, Intellectual Property, and Associated Moral Rights

John Cayley and Daniel C. Howe

During an era already defined as digital, in the second decade of the twenty-first century, we have arrived at a historical moment when processes designated as artificially intelligent are engineered to work with vast quantities of aggregated 'data' in order to generate new artefacts, statements, visualizations, and even decisions derived from patterns 'discovered' in this data. The data in question may well be linguistic and, occasionally, the AI-processed outcomes may be aesthetically motivated. Thus, our brave new world contains experiments in virtual literary art, linguistic artefacts 'created' by artificial intelligence. Or, a little more accurately, we are able to read, if we want to, works of language art that have been generated by rebranded, connectionist-based machine 'learning,' by recurrent or convolutional neural networks. Who or what is the 'author' of such outcomes if we are to consider them as works of language art? The 'death of the author' or, at least, the problematic *question* of authorship was raised well before electronic literary practice appeared to

---

1 *The Readers Project* is a collection of distributed, performative, quasi-autonomous poetic 'readers' — active, procedural entities with distinct reading behaviors and strategies that explore the culture of reading, http://thereadersproject.org/

actualize postmodern theories in the late 1990s. Even then, works were authored by what N. Katherine Hayles now characterizes as 'cognitive assemblages' — human, medial, and computational. For these earlier works, however, their coding and its operations could be accounted for and anticipated by human author-engineers, still able to identify with their software and claim some moral rights with respect to the aesthetics of these processes.

Neural networks are not at all new. Yet with huge increases in raw computing power, and the spectacular accumulation of vast data sets, they are back in fashion and, likely, here to stay. One of a number of valid critiques of such algorithms is that they derive their patterns from the data in a manner that is highly abstract and largely inaccessible to human scrutiny, in the sense that we cannot, exhaustively, or in any detail, account for the specificities of what they produce. Thus, we might ask — in similar but differing circumstances as compared with earlier digital language art: is the language generated in this way *original*? Are we to consider an AI to be the *author* of such language?

But we must also ask: who owns the data? Who controls and benefits from its use? Answers to these questions will have momentous, potentially catastrophic consequences for cultural practice and production. The feverish enthusiasm surrounding AI seems likely to distort not only jurisprudence, but also socio- and political economic regulation with respect, for example, to the custom and law of intellectual property. If data sets and corpora are publicly available and these contain, for example, linguistic artefacts that are protected by copyright, AI processes operating on these corpora may appeal to the concept of 'non-expressive fair use.' It is presumed that the AI processes do not understand, appreciate, or care about — we might say they cannot 'read' — the expressive content of the protected artefacts in the corpora that they process. Thus the copyright holders of this content may have no claim, based on infringement, concerning whatever it is that the AI processes produce, whether or not this generates commercial or other benefits for the AI and its owners. That legal conceptions of this kind are being debated and, less often, established in court should not, in our opinion, cause us concern for the erosion of authors' rights (as subject to non-expressive fair use). Instead we should see this as a kind of retrospective justification — perhaps calculated on behalf of the beneficiaries — for land-grab, enclosure-style *theft* from and of the cultural commons, all within legislative regimes that are propping up an inequitable, non-mutual, and unworkable framework for the generative creativity that copyright is supposed to encourage. The conventional custom and law of intellectual property, we say, does not and cannot encourage such creativity once culture is subject to digitalization. Arguably, copyright law has been 'an ass' since at least the age of mechanical reproduction. These days, calling it a dinosaur is too polite; it is a transnational swarm of Jurassic-Park raptors in the service of vectoralist superpowers.[2]

The raptors need retrospective justification because, in the guise of the robots and spiders that scurry over the Web, for example, they undertake their activities regardless of copyright, finding whatever they find with no sense of moral rights concerning association or integrity, and effectively proceeding on the basis of something like a presumption of 'non-expressive fair use.' They, the robots, don't know what they're doing, so we all consider what they are doing to be 'OK' — copying, appropriating, and processing whatever they find, regardless of who may 'own' it in terms of copyright. And there is a lot of stuff that these robots process that is clearly and absolutely 'protected' in terms of current legislation. All blogs, for instance, whether or not copyright is explicitly claimed for them. The robots' owners may not, at first, historically, have known what their robots were doing (any more than the robots do), but this hasn't prevented them from translating such 'non-expressive fair use' into privately owned wealth, value, and power to an unprecedented extent and at historically breakneck velocities.

Compare the situation with respect to one of *The Readers Project*'s prominent outcomes. *The Project* is still squarely, for the moment, within the 'earlier' field of practice that I characterized, following Hayles, as a matter of cognitive assemblage: algorithmic cognisors working *with*

---

2 'Vectoralist' is the name that McKenzie Wark gave, persuasively, to a new exploitative ruling class which controls and profits from vectors of political and economic attention in a world where information is treated as a natural resource, extending earlier capitalist models and critiques. McKenzie Wark, *A Hacker Manifesto* (Cambridge, MA: Harvard University Press, 2004), https://archive.org/stream/pdfy-RtCf3CYEbjKrXgFe/A Hacker Manifesto - McKenzie Wark_djvu.txt

human cognisors, the latter more or less self-conscious concerning the aesthetics, innovation, and originality of *The Project* as a whole. The installation *Common Tongues* and the artists' book *How It Is in Common Tongues* both make transgressive use of networked search services in order to produce aesthetic works of conceptual and computational literature.[3] These works read and reframe Samuel Beckett's late novella, *How It Is* (1961). *The Project*'s software entities read through the work, seeking out and resolving its text into a sequence of phrases with particular characteristics. We call these Longest Common Phrases (or LCPs). Each LCP is the longest sequence of words, beginning from any specific point in the text, that can be found on the Internet, *not* written by or attributed to its author (as far as we can tell). We use Internet searches to find these phrases in other contexts, proving their continued circulation in the commons of language (an essential part of the cultural commons referred to above), unfettered by any liens of association or integrity. We then cite the web occurrences of these LCPs in *How It Is in Common Tongues*, a book released by *The Project*'s artists. In fact, we resolve the *entire* text of *How It Is* into common phrases as inscribed by thousands of other English language users. By doing so, we produce both an elegant aesthetic object and a text that reads quite differently from the original.

---

3 Please refer to *The Project*'s website http://thereadersproject.org, and, for further linked documentation of these works, to the ELMCIP Knowledge Base at http://elmcip.net/node/4677 (*Common Tongues*) and http://elmcip.net/node/5194 (*How it Is in Common Tongues*). For conceptual literature see, inter alia: Kenneth Goldsmith, *Uncreative Writing: Managing Language in the Digital Age* (New York: Columbia University Press, 2011) https://doi.org/10.1353/jjq.2012.0020; Craig Douglas Dworkin and Kenneth Goldsmith (eds.), *Against Expression: An Anthology of Conceptual Writing* (Evanston, IL: Northwestern University Press, 2011); and Vanessa Place and Robert Fitterman, *Notes on Conceptualisms* (Brooklyn, NY: Ugly Duckling Presse, 2009). Computational literature does not yet have so readily identifiable apologia. However Nick Montfort, http://nickm.com, is a major exponent and the work of Noah Wardrip-Fruin, both aesthetic and theoretical, is highly relevant and significant.

how it was I quote[1] before Pim with[2] Pim after Pim[3] how it is three parts I[4] say it as I hear it[5]

voice once without[6] quaqua on all sides[7] then in me when[8] the panting stops[9] tell me again finish telling me[a] invocation

past[b] moments old dreams[c] back again or fresh like those[d] that pass or[e] things things always and[f] memories I say them as I[10] hear them murmur[11] them in the mud

in[12] me that were without[13] when the panting stops[14] scraps of an ancient voice in[15] me not mine

my[16] life last state last version[17] ill-said ill-heard ill-recaptured[18] ill-murmured in the[19] mud brief[1a] movements of the lower face losses[1b] everywhere

recorded[1c] none the less it's[1d] preferable somehow[1e] somewhere

[1]www.nytimes.com/books/first/w/wiesel-sea.html (Aug 14, 2012. 1)
[2]www.cameracellularphone.org/tag/device (id. 1)
[3]www.kwarmmeud.com/darknesslakorns/?p=1501 (id. 4)
[4]www.youtube.lu/watch?v=MAsddbn_2LM (id. 2) [5]cucurbite.wordpress.com/ (id. 2620000)
[6]gorwathawarband.guildlaunch.com/forums/viewtopic.php?t=8563276 (id. 2)
[7]pplsorce.com/people/Jim_Quaqua/ (id. 3) [8]celebrityzap.com/AJ_Langer.html (id. 5)
[9]www.parrothouse.com/hlthcare.html (id. 4290)
[a]kindle.amazon.com/work/sample?asin=B002HHLW4M&pr=1&publisher=A3SWXVW6XL4CG8 (id. 1) [b]sonicliving.com/artist/182670/past (id. 3200) [c]www.blurb.ca/tags/design (id. 25) [d]www.iraised.it/s/web/index.php?page=7&q=come-back-quotes (id. 3)
[e]www.sqlsaturday.com/158/privacypolicy.aspx (id. 7070)
[f]www.ilovephilosophy.com/viewtopic.php?f=5&ct=142604&start=75 (id. 1)
[10]pulsitemeter.com/military/Past-of-Hear.html (id. 2) [11]www.bartleby.com/84/31.html (id. 29900) [12]www.facebook.com/dcctowing (id. 7860) [13]lfpoa.com/headlines/resignation.htm (id. 68300) [14]www.cioran63.com/archief76.html (id. 9)
[15]circle.ubc.ca/bitstream/handle/2429/22333/UBC_1980_A1 M37.pdf?sequence=1 (id. 1)
[16]twicsy.com/i/XVig9 (id. 8) [17]garagepunk.ning.com/profile/deuceloosely (id. 1)
[18]avevilonaso.comyr.com/life-in-forsyth-finnegans-wake.php (id. 1) [19]krex.k-state.edu/dspace/bitstream/2097/9824/1/LD2668R41985B72.pdf (id. 1)
[1a]www.highbeam.com/doc/1G1-63262234.html (id. 4430)
[1b]www.goodreads.com/trivia/submitted/1057191-jason (id. 1)
[1c]www.ustream.tv/recorded/24228375 (id. 843) [1d]www.xula.edu/cpsc/cs/megang/ (id. 19600)
[1e]socrates.berkeley.edu/~plab/Palmer_Chap-08.pdf (id. 5710)

[7]

Fig. 1.1. *How It Is In Common Tongues*. Image provided by the authors, CC BY 4.0.

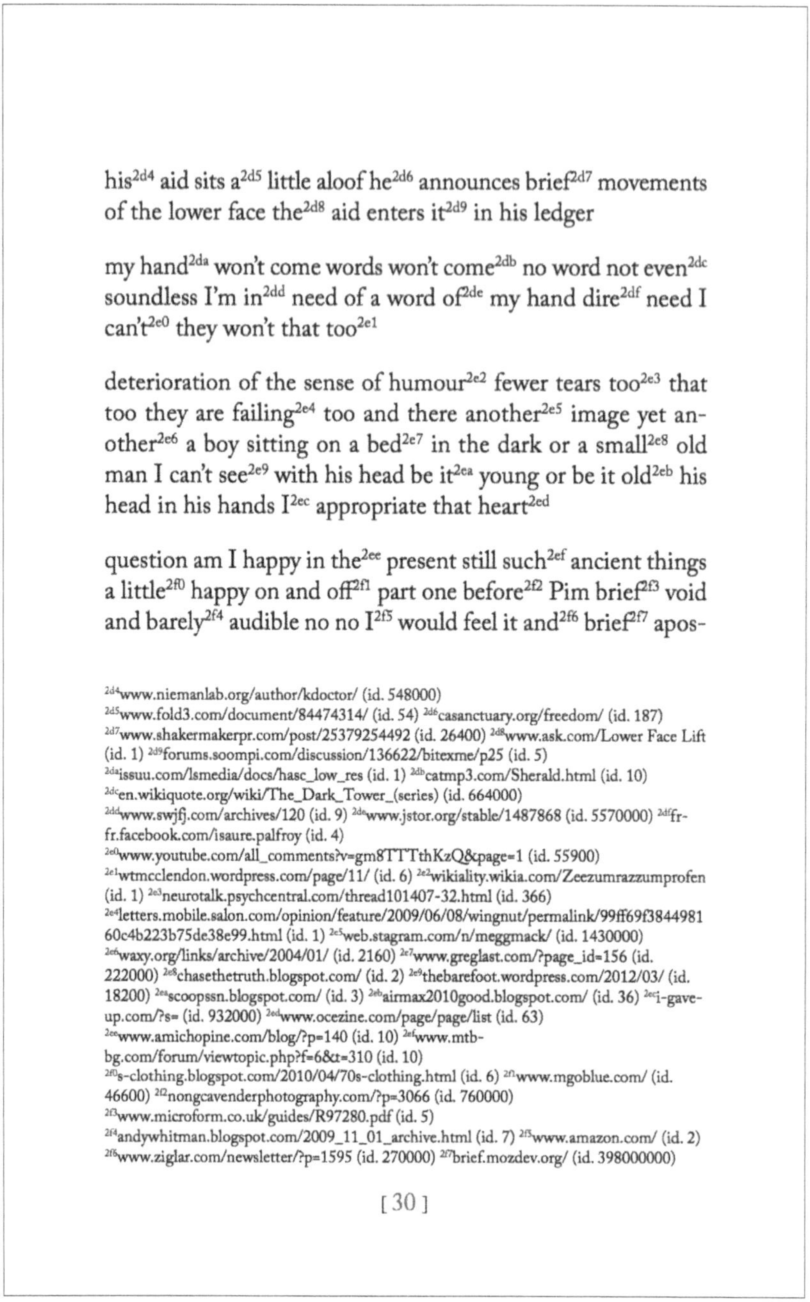

his[2d4] aid sits a[2d5] little aloof he[2d6] announces brief[2d7] movements of the lower face the[2d8] aid enters it[2d9] in his ledger

my hand[2da] won't come words won't come[2db] no word not even[2dc] soundless I'm in[2dd] need of a word of[2de] my hand dire[2df] need I can't[2e0] they won't that too[2e1]

deterioration of the sense of humour[2e2] fewer tears too[2e3] that too they are failing[2e4] too and there another[2e5] image yet another[2e6] a boy sitting on a bed[2e7] in the dark or a small[2e8] old man I can't see[2e9] with his head be it[2ea] young or be it old[2eb] his head in his hands I[2ec] appropriate that heart[2ed]

question am I happy in the[2ee] present still such[2ef] ancient things a little[2f0] happy on and off[2f1] part one before[2f2] Pim brief[2f3] void and barely[2f4] audible no no I[2f5] would feel it and[2f6] brief[2f7] apos-

[2d4]www.niemanlab.org/author/kdoctor/ (id. 548000)
[2d5]www.fold3.com/document/84474314/ (id. 54) [2d6]casanctuary.org/freedom/ (id. 187)
[2d7]www.shakermakerpr.com/post/25379254492 (id. 26400) [2d8]www.ask.com/Lower Face Lift (id. 1) [2d9]forums.soompi.com/discussion/136622/bitexme/p25 (id. 5)
[2da]issuu.com/lsmedia/docs/hasc_low_res (id. 1) [2db]catmp3.com/Sherald.html (id. 10)
[2dc]en.wikiquote.org/wiki/The_Dark_Tower_(series) (id. 664000)
[2dd]www.swjfj.com/archives/120 (id. 9) [2de]www.jstor.org/stable/1487868 (id. 5570000) [2df]fr-fr.facebook.com/isaure.palfroy (id. 4)
[2e0]www.youtube.com/all_comments?v=gm8TTTthKzQ&page=1 (id. 55900)
[2e1]wtmcclendon.wordpress.com/page/11/ (id. 6) [2e2]wikiality.wikia.com/Zeezumrazzumprofen (id. 1) [2e3]neurotalk.psychcentral.com/thread101407-32.html (id. 366)
[2e4]letters.mobile.salon.com/opinion/feature/2009/06/08/wingnut/permalink/99ff69f3844981 60c4b223b75de38e99.html (id. 1) [2e5]web.stagram.com/n/meggmack/ (id. 1430000)
[2e6]waxy.org/links/archive/2004/01/ (id. 2160) [2e7]www.greglast.com/?page_id=156 (id. 222000) [2e8]chasethetruth.blogspot.com/ (id. 2) [2e9]thebarefoot.wordpress.com/2012/03/ (id. 18200) [2ea]scoopssn.blogspot.com/ (id. 3) [2eb]airmax2010good.blogspot.com/ (id. 36) [2ec]i-gave-up.com/?s= (id. 932000) [2ed]www.ocezine.com/page/page/list (id. 63)
[2ee]www.amichopine.com/blog/?p=140 (id. 10) [2ef]www.mtb-bg.com/forum/viewtopic.php?f=6&t=310 (id. 10)
[2f0]s-clothing.blogspot.com/2010/04/70s-clothing.html (id. 6) [2f1]www.mgoblue.com/ (id. 46600) [2f2]nongcavenderphotography.com/?p=3066 (id. 760000)
[2f3]www.microform.co.uk/guides/R97280.pdf (id. 5)
[2f4]andywhitman.blogspot.com/2009_11_01_archive.html (id. 7) [2f5]www.amazon.com/ (id. 2)
[2f6]www.ziglar.com/newsletter/?p=1595 (id. 270000) [2f7]brief.mozdev.org/ (id. 398000000)

[30]

Fig. 1.2. *How It Is In Common Tongues*. Image provided by the authors, CC BY 4.0.

This new text is constantly interrupted by reference — by distracting invitations to turn to other networked writings. As such its paratext and punctuation is entirely novel and calls attention to alternate phrasings that generate strange, new, and differently engaging prose rhythms. It is a conceptual work: a new, distinct instance of digital language art. Nonetheless, it is also exhaustively associated with the Beckett's novella. Its punctuation and annotation have been produced by algorithmic processes that transact with Internet search services in deliberate contravention of these services' terms of use. Services providers, typically and non-mutually, regulate or deny robots — programmatic or algorithmic clients — access to their hoards. We claim that the transgressive — and controversial — practices by which we have created this work are significant additions to the existing repertoire of literary aesthetic practices. The work fully acknowledges and is highly respectful of its sources. It is undoubtedly non- if not anti-commercial. It is practice-based research that has already achieved considerable pedagogical traction with scholars and students internationally. Nonetheless, it is difficult to conceive that it would be read as an entirely original work, with little in the way of a 'regular' or 'mechanical' relation to its sources. *The Project's* position, however, is that it *is* an original work, taking phrases from the commons of language, composing and punctuating them in manner that produces an incisive work of critical language art. In any immediate or longer-term future, if the kind of algorithmic and human compositional processes that underlie this piece were denied or contradicted — either by inadequate custom and law, or by vectoralist superpowers unilaterally and arbitrarily enforcing the *force majeure* of their terms of service — this would be part, we believe, of nothing less than a more general cultural and artistic catastrophe.

Moreover, in installations of *Common Tongues*, LCPs from a section of *How It Is* are used to discover and present, as textual collage, *additional* human-selected contexts for these LCP phrases, additional aesthetic language composed neither by Beckett, nor by *The Project's* artists. These selections are quasi-algorithmically hand-stitched together (human authors editing generated text), maintaining syntactic regularity such that a new text is formed: one for which algorithmic processes guarantee that *none* of the constituent language is authored by the text's makers.

This text has its own significance and affect, though generated in regular relation with Beckett, and with hundreds of other writers. It could not have been made without the digital, without algorithms. It could not have been made without the writing of many others. As a creative work, it runs counter to the customs and laws of intellectual property and defies traditional conventions of authorship, yet it is clearly a critical and aesthetic response to the evolving circumstances of linguistic and literary practice. This is, we believe, another way of saying that it has value. But how should we recognize and preserve this value? How will we protect it from traditional literary estates and the aggressive cultural vectors that threaten? In the current historical moment, *The Readers Project* believes, we must allow interventions such as *How It Is in Common Tongues* to exist in the world of language art alongside conventional forms from the world of letters, and also in relation to commensurate works embraced and lauded by the visual and conceptual art worlds. Christian Marclay's *The Clock* comes immediately to mind, recently proclaimed as a 'masterpiece' and newly on show in Tate Modern as of autumn 2018.[4]

We argue that the existing custom and law of intellectual property is unable to comprehend or regulate a significant proportion, if not the majority, of contemporary literary aesthetic practices; not only the productions of conceptual and uncreative writing but also, for example, compositional practices of collage, which writers have always deployed, but which have been fundamentally reconfigured by instant networked access to material — much of it 'protected' — amenable to 'cut and paste.' In circumstances like these, the custom and law of intellectual property reveals itself to be irremediably flawed. We claim that the types of processes and procedures implemented in *The Project* show how literary practices have been so altered by digital affordances and mediation that the fundamental expectations of human writers and readers — regarding their roles, their relationships to one another and to the text that travels between them, and the associated commercial relationships — are changed beyond easy recognition, and beyond the scope of existing custom and law. *All* practices of reading and writing are now inextricably intertwined with their network mediation — the Internet and its services — and so the questions and conflicts surrounding

---

4   https://en.wikipedia.org/wiki/The_Clock_(2010_film)

copyright and intellectual property have shifted from *who creates and owns what*, to *who controls the most privileged and profitable tools for creation and dissemination*. The Readers Project works to address this new situation and highlight its inconsistencies and inequities.

Network services have arisen that allow practices of reading and writing to be automatically and algorithmically captured, processed, indexed, and otherwise co-opted for the commercially-motivated creation and maintenance of vectors of attention (advertising) and transaction (actual commerce). These vectors are themselves, as the results of indexing, processing, and analysis, fed back to human readers and writers, profoundly affecting, in turn, their subsequent practices of reading and writing. In cyclical fashion, reading and writing is fed back into the continually refined black boxes of proprietary, corporate-controlled, algorithmic process: the 'big software' of capture, analysis, index and so on. This is the grand feedback loop of 'big data,' encompassing and enclosing the commonwealth of linguistic practice. As a function of proprietary control and the predominance of neoliberal ideology amongst its supermanagers, this system is regulated by little more than calculations of the marginal profit that the vectoralist service providers derive. And now, as noted above, the 'black boxes' are filled with inscrutable, energy-consuming, waste-generating, expensive AI.

In the perhaps naïve belief that we might all benefit, human readers and writers have willingly thrown themselves into this artefactual cultural vortex. Is it too late now to reconsider, to endeavour to radically change both the new and traditional institutions that allowed us to enter this maelstrom? Or have inequalities in the distribution of power over the vectors of transaction and attention — commercial but especially cultural — simply become too great? This power was acquired far too quickly by naive and untried corporate entities that still remain largely untried and unregulated, though they are, perhaps, far less naïve than they once were.[5] Huge marginal profits allow the new corporations to acquire, on a grand scale, the estates of conventionally licensed intellectual property along with the interest and means to conserve them, via both legal and technical mechanisms. In a particularly

---

5   See John Cayley, 'Terms of Reference & Vectoralist Transgressions: Situating Certain Literary Transactions over Networked Services', *Amodern* 2 (2013), [n.p.], http://amodern.net/article/terms-of-reference-vectoralist-transgressions/, https://doi.org/10.5040/9781501335792.ch-012

vicious aspect of this cycle of wealth-and-power aggregation, these same mechanisms remain wholly inadequate to the task of regulating the culture and commerce of networks, clouds, and big data: the very culture and commerce that grant big software their profits. The raptors are out of the park.

Works Cited

Cayley, John (2013) 'Terms of Reference & Vectoralist Transgressions: Situating Certain Literary Transactions over Networked Services', *Amodern* 2, [n.p.], http://amodern.net/article/terms-of-reference-vectoralist-transgressions/, https://doi.org/10.5040/9781501335792.ch-012

Dworkin, Craig Douglas and Kenneth Goldsmith (eds.) (2011) *Against Expression: An Anthology of Conceptual Writing* (Evanston, IL: Northwestern University Press).

Goldsmith, Kenneth (2011) *Uncreative Writing: Managing Language in the Digital Age* (New York: Columbia University Press), https://doi.org/10.1353/jjq.2012.0020

Place, Vanessa and Robert Fitterman (2009) *Notes on Conceptualisms* (Brooklyn, NY: Ugly Duckling Presse).

Wark, McKenzie (2004) *A Hacker Manifesto* (Cambridge, MA: Harvard University Press), https://archive.org/stream/pdfy-RtCf3CYEbjKrXgFe/A Hacker Manifesto - McKenzie Wark_djvu.txt

2. London-Havana Diary: Art Publishing, Sustainability, Free Speech and Free Papers[1]

Louise O'Hare

May 2018, London

I've been prompted to sign off the essay about art publishing in Havana that I wrote for this anthology over two years ago, but I can't bear to do it. In part because the world seems so changed, and changing, in part because I am. I read in the essay a false confidence. Not that my report was proved incorrect, but that in attempting an overview, the writing failed to address its own relationship to the issues — of self-censorship, institutional power, and control of access to knowledge — that it purported to discuss. London on Havana. Had I forgotten that the exchange was supposed to go both ways?

I come across something written in 1994 by Coco Fusco, and wonder if her approach might offer a formal solution — a way to acknowledge the limits of my perspective and unpick some of the bias of much Anglophone reporting on Cuba. Fusco describes herself as a Cuban-American artist and writer, 'the daughter of a Cuban who emigrated to the US in 1954, and was deported in 1959 shortly after the triumph of

---

1 This chapter is an excerpt from an ongoing research and writing project titled *Centrefold 1974: A Memoir*, a practice-based Fine Art PhD at BxNU Institute of Contemporary Art, BALTIC 39, Northumbria University, 2014–2018.

the revolution.'[2] Titled 'El Diario de Miranda / Miranda's Diary', Fusco's text describes her experiences travelling, and writing about Cuba, and how these have inflected her understanding of herself as 'a child of the diaspora'.[3] It is a story of menacing uncertainty, gathering unverifiable reports of delays, threats, and surveillance. It's a story of letters received, refused visas refused, and quiet conversations, and covers dates just prior to and during the 'special period' — the euphemism for the economic crisis in Cuba that was precipitated by the continuing US trade embargo, the dissolution of the Soviet Union and the Comecon. Fusco explains that she gathered recollections and put them in a non-linear form to 'find the logic that links disparate events'. Of course that logic is entirely her own.

I visited Havana in May 2015 when the first flights from New York were arriving, which provoked in me a tourist's wistfulness for idiosyncrasies — the imagined authenticity of Cuba's isolation; alongside perhaps less patronizing fears of the growing impact of tourism and deregulation of the economy on the island, and excitement about what new connections and collaborations might be possible now that an end to the US embargo looked to be in sight. I was there to discuss the idea of setting up of an artist's magazine, a project that would require us to consider limits to free speech, as well as the models available for sustaining such a venture, alongside questions of what a magazine as a discursive platform or space might be — something further complicated by the fact that this would be a post-internet project operating in a place with limited broadband coverage.

Shifting between London and Havana, this diary will touch on intellectual property as part of a broader reflection upon limits to free speech and access to information. I'll touch on the impact neoliberal approaches to education, and arts funding, have on freedom of speech

---

2   Coco Fusco, 'El Diario de Miranda/Miranda's Diary', in Carol Becker (ed.), *The Subversive Imagination: The Artist, Society and Social Responsibility* (Oxford and New York: Routledge, 1994), p. 96, https://doi.org/10.4324/9781315021317. The diary details the period 1986–1993. Coco Fusco describes the children of her generation as those who 'didn't choose to leave or stay' and 'are traitors to the exile community's extremists', and 'ungrateful' to their parents, 'who saved us from the Caribbean "gulag"' (p. 97). The final diary entry (dated 'August 1992') reads: 'I receive word from *Third Text* that they cannot publish this piece as I have written it [...] all the names must be removed, and that all personal information about my experiences in Cuba must also be excised' (p. 110).

3   Ibid., p. 97.

and access to information in London, and I'll consider some attempts to cope with this reduced ability to share knowledge — two small scale projects (initially set up in the US) that use online platforms to gather supportive communities to enable new research and writing. These tactics — proposed by the digital library aaarg.org and the Publication Studio network — are placed alongside *El Paquete Semanal* (*The Weekly Package*) a cross-country file-sharing operation sometimes described as the 'Cuban internet'; discussions of the way the Cuban state tolerates piracy; and my experiences as an art worker and activist in the UK. In this I refuse to implement a boundary between political, and artistic work, gathering observations about the potential of Web 2.0 for community-making, creative practice and grassroots democratic change.

June 2015, Gatwick

No one stops me at the gate.

I was born in Bristol and am returning home from three weeks working with Cuban artists and writers discussing the potential for setting up a Havana-London magazine, featuring works by artists based in both cities, and translated into Spanish and English. Meetings and discussions around the idea were part of 'Hors Pistes: La Primavera del Amor', an events, residency and exchange programme organised by French-Canadian curator Catherine Sicot, and taking place in Havana around the 12th Havana Biennial.[4] The Havana Biennial takes place every three years, not two — organised by curators at the public gallery Centro de Arte Contemporáneo Wifredo Lam and funded by the state, it either doesn't have the resources or the inclination to chase the same pace as the rest of the sponsored, patronised, industry of the international art world.[5]

---

4   Curated by Catherine Sicot, 'La Primavera del Amor' (Spring-Summer 2015) was 'a platform for artistic development and production, international and local networking, and community outreach in Havana and suburbs.' The programme reflected upon 'identity, gender and sexuality and its relationship to media and technology', through publishing projects, film premieres, performances, workshops and panel discussions. For more information see: https://elegoa.com/en/content/la-primavera-del-amor

5   The biennial is funded by the state, while contributions from foreign governments cover the inclusion of artists from their countries.

It seems important to start with my white tourist body — the limits of my experience in relation to state bureaucracy. I'm officially returning from a holiday: Catherine advised that she was not able to arrange an artist's visa, as the programme itself was not officially recognized.

May 2013, London

We have finally published an interview between Catherine, Aurélie Sampeur and Candelario, discussing LASA, their social enterprise and arts commissioning project in San Agustín, a suburb on the outskirts of Havana. I work as an associate editor for Afterall and commissioned it months ago, but there were many delays as Catherine, who is usually based in Toronto, waited for confirmation of certain details from her colleagues in Cuba.[6]

Six days later I receive a worried response:

> Please remove the term 'post-revolution' or I will never be able to cross the Cuban border again. We are currently in year 56 of the Revolution here. It is a major faux-pas, and turns the article into anti-Castro propaganda [...]. Then it is also a mistake re: the content. What I was talking about was negotiating within the structures for artistic production established by the Revolution.

I immediately log in and quickly change the text online, kicking myself for not double-checking and — probably unfairly, I can't remember who changed it — write back blaming my American managing editor for the final edit.

May 2015, Havana

My plane lands at José Martí International and I am greeted by Catherine, and Reynier Guerra Capote; a student of literature at Havana University and her assistant on the project. Catherine and I have only met in person once before, but after emailing and Skyping I feel like we are old friends.

---

6   Catherine Sicot, Aurélie Sampeur, and Candelario, 'Artists at Work: Laboratorio Artístico de San Agustín', in Louise O'Hare (ed.), *Afterall Online*, 23 May 2014, https://www.afterall.org/online/artists-at-work_laboratorio-art_stico-de-san-agust_n_cuba

Later I meet Reynier for drinks in old Havana, the UNESCO heritage part of the old town where I am staying a couple of nights in an official hotel, the address a prerequisite for my tourist visa, before I'll head to rent a room with a family in Vedado, the leafy suburbs. Reynier is excited about the magazine idea, says there is nothing like it in the city, and doesn't seem very concerned about us getting into trouble. When telling friends and colleagues back home about my plans most had responded with concern: 'but there is no free press in Cuba!' Catherine too has been nervous, 'it could be considered activist', implying that the magazine could be subject to state censure and our Cuban collaborators put in a difficult situation, investigated, even arrested. However, my understanding of the constraints are that if you are not doing something counter-revolutionary, you will not be stopped. I recall Fidel's slogan: 'Within the Revolution, everything; against the Revolution, nothing.'[7] Are we being wilfully naïve?

December 2014, Havana

The artist Tania Bruguera attempts to restage *Tatlin's Whisper #6* (2009) — her open-mic performance offering invited speakers 'one minute free of censorship' — at the Plaza de la Revolución in Havana. She first attempts to gain permission, is refused and then does it anyway. She is arrested and detained overnight, then released but ordered to remain in Cuba while the police decide whether to press charges.

---

7   'Unlike previous socialist societies, freedom of form was guaranteed; only freedom of content remained at issue, the parameters for which were succinctly encapsulated in Fidel's maxim "Within the Revolution, everything; against the Revolution, nothing". In other words, all artwork that was not explicitly counterrevolutionary would be welcome.' Rebecca Gordon-Nesbitt, 'Whose Side are You On?: A Response to Coco Fusco', *Mute*, 29 January 2015, http://www.metamute.org/community/your-posts/whose-side-are-you-response-to-coco-fusco-'-state-detention-performance-politics-and-cuban-public'-e-flux-3
'Cuba always stood out among bureaucratic socialist countries for its rich and diverse visual arts. Though Cuban artists have never been put in a stylistic "straitjacket of socialist realism", there are however certain limitations to their freedom: "There is freedom of artistic creation as long as its content is not contrary to the revolution," states the constitution of the Republic of Cuba in chapter 5: "Education and culture".' Maciej Zurowski, 'More Glasnost, Less Perestroika: Interview with *Havana Times* Editor Circles Robinson', *Weekly Worker* 848, 13 January 2011, http://weeklyworker.co.uk/worker/848/more-glasnost-less-perestroika/

January 2015, New York

e-flux, a free digital art journal based in Lower Manhattan and funded by pumping out thrice-daily press releases to its coveted art world mailing list — selling its critically engaged kudos and the use of its contacts to 'public art centers and museums' internationally[8] — publishes an article by Coco Fusco from which the summary in the post above was paraphrased.

In the article Fusco points out that the Plaza de la Revolución in Havana is a restricted government space and can be considered 'the Cuban equivalent of the White House lawn'.[9] The article explains that *Tatlin's Whisper* had previously been staged at the Wifredo Lam gallery as part of the 10th Havana Biennial (2009), and that the new version for the Plaza de la Revolución was given the title *#YoTambienExijo* (*#IAlsoDemand*). The use of a hashtag is strange for a project in Cuba as most people do not have access to the Internet, and suggests it was aimed at an audience not on the island. Fusco notes: 'Bruguera's reliance on the Internet to convene the Cuban public has provoked a certain degree of skepticism from critics about her intentions', considering that Cuba 'is the country with the lowest level of connectivity in the hemisphere [...] The vast majority of Cubans lack access to the Internet, cell phones, and home-based landlines.'[10]

July 2015, London

An email from Reynier arrives — he is wondering if I might be able to help arrange visas for a trip to the UK during his summer holidays. He was expecting to visit Catherine in Toronto but despite numerous references, including recommendations from a professor at the University of Toronto, established artists and various arts professionals, Reynier's

---

8 'Who uses *e-flux*? Nearly all the leading art museums, biennials, cultural centers, magazines, publishers, art fairs, and independent curators worldwide [...] *e-flux* is read by 90,000+ visual arts professionals: 47% in Europe, 42% in North America, and 11% Other (South America, Australia, Japan, etc.) [...]' The promotional emails are 'made free for its 90,000+ readers', http://www.e-flux.com/about

9 Coco Fusco, 'The State of Detention: Performance, Politics, and the Cuban Public', *e-flux* 60, December 2014, https://www.e-flux.com/journal/60/61067/the-state-of-detention-performance-politics-and-the-cuban-public/

10 Ibid.

application has been rejected by Canada. His trip is suddenly cancelled, not because of Cuban restrictions, but because of unfathomable Canadian bureaucracy. I begin to look up the process on the UK customs site and reply back that I think it might be hard to organise at short notice.

July 2014, London

Caroline Woodley, Joyce Cronin and me are sitting at the outside tables of Caravan, the expensive restaurant that leases the entrance of Central Saint Martins (CSM), and eking out our coffees while we wait for an email to come through on Caroline's phone. Our office is on the top floor of the university and one of a number of rooms in the recently built art school that, rather oddly, have no natural light, and this morning we can't yet face going in. The Granary Building used to 'store Lincolnshire wheat for London's bakers', but the architects have left it difficult to differentiate from a mall: a panopticon-esque conversion with four floors of glass-walled studios overlooking a downstairs 'street' accessible past a barrier of swipe-card turnstiles.[11] Wide walkways look out over a large atrium, and feature areas for students to hang out and hot-desk in — a necessity for those students the courses not allocated studios — which are valued real estate. Located in a new development area behind Kings Cross station, it is hard not to see the art school as the vanguard of north London gentrification: Google is coming; Eurostar runs out of the station; the canals are suddenly accessible; and more shops arrive each week. Once, for a freshers' fair, University of the Arts London (UAL, of which CSM is now a part) produced a series of tote-bags that said 'Lifestyle not education'. The canvas bags continue to circulate around the building, faded by washing but still appalling.

The email we are waiting for is from the Arts Council England (ACE) with news as to whether we will lose our regular funding.[12]

---

11 '[...] The Granary Building is now the stunning new home of the world famous arts college — Central Saint Martins, part of the University of the Arts London. The building has been transformed by architects Stanton Williams. While the Western Transit Shed has been converted into unique office space with shops and restaurants at street level.' — 'Historic Buildings: The Granary Building', anonymous, undated, King's Cross Development website, https://www.kingscross.co.uk/granary

12 Every three years, arts organisations that are regularly supported by Arts Council England (ACE) must reapply for National Portfolio Organisation (NPO) status.

Afterall (which produces various books series, online content, and an eponymous journal) is financed by various streams that Caroline, as publishing director, oversees, endlessly strategizes over and worries about. The bones of the organisation are covered by UAL — editors and assistants are employed as administrative staff and have contracts with the university. With the basics covered our different publishing series are paid for in different ways: *Afterall* journal for example raises enough money from advertising to just about cover its print production costs, receives a fairly negligible amount from sales (through its distributor University of Chicago press), and then covers the rest (for example writers' fees, design work, and image rights) using money from its partnerships with public art institutions internationally (curators from these benefactor institutions then joining the editorial board). We know that this mix of funding means we are seen as more 'sustainable' by ACE, less reliant on them, and paradoxically less likely to be cut.[13] But still we are nervous. Solidarity disappears and I begin to envy our successful contemporaries — the other small contemporary arts organizations who have already received their news and started tweeting in relief: 'Thank you Arts Council #ACEfunding #artsfunding #npo'.

Why haven't we heard yet? The email is in Caroline's spam! We haven't been culled, but neither have we received the uplift we applied for, so we are at what ACE euphemistically calls 'standstill'. Like everyone else who has been 'successful', when inflation is taken into account over the next three years we will see our funding from ACE cut by 7.1%.[14] The relief that we don't have to organize another obsequious

---

13   The first chapter of Rebecca Gordon-Nesbitt's recent book on the cultural policy of the Cuban Revolution quotes Maria Miller's April 2013 speech stating that 'funding distributed by the Arts Council [England] should effectively act as seed funding [...] giving confidence of others to invest.' (p. 7). The quote is included as part of a summary of 'Cultural Policy under Capitalism', which describes the 'detrimental effect on the cultural field' of the 'withdrawal of the state in favour of market forces' (p. 1), explaining how recent US and European policy focuses on culture's 'perceived contribution to economic recovery' while excluding art from these 'creative industries' that have 'potential for wealth and job creation through the generation and exploitation of intellectual property' (pp. 6–7). See Rebecca Gordon-Nesbitt, *To Defend the Revolution Is to Defend Culture: The Cultural Policy of the Cuban Revolution* (Oakland: PM Press, 2015).

14   This is in comparison to the previous three-year period. 'The majority of organisations in the new portfolio (75 percent) have received *standstill* funding.' [my italics], 'Arts Council Announces Investment Plans for 2015 to 2018' (press release), Arts Council England, 1 July 2014; the press release has been reposted here

benefit auction, for a while at least, is palpable. We stay at the table watching the fountains, which burst out in synchronized squirts across the public-private square. Some say the water feature is designed to stop any potential student protest or gathering, but still it's fun to sit here on a sunny day and see it populated in number by screaming laughing toddlers from the estates up the road.

May 2015, Havana

Catherine films me talking about the magazine idea for one of the videos she is making about the residency program. The videos will be disseminated through *El Paquete Semanal* (*The Weekly Package*) a file sharing system that is sometimes described as the 'Cuban Internet', but could perhaps also be considered a kind of multimedia magazine. The anonymous organisers gather 2TB of material including documentaries, soap operas, e-magazines, art programmes and music videos with adverts — and then distribute them across Cuba through representatives carrying hard drives. User-subscribers then pay 2CUC (Cuban Convertible Peso) and select particular items or download the whole package for that week onto their computer or hard drive. I guess it's called the Cuban Internet because of the way it claims to be an ungoverned, un-edited space — anyone can submit content — and constitutes an archive of shared digital material. Catherine is paying 30CUC for 7 weeks' inclusion and has organized it through a friend of a friend. I gather that due to the lack of anti-government content and pornography, *El Paquete* is considered to be either self-censored or infiltrated and controlled by the government. It is not known who edits the content, but the advertising side of the operation is run by a Cuban firm called Etres, making use of changes to property law in 2011.[15] The

---

with an incorrect date: https://www.artscouncil.org.uk/arts-council-announces-investment-plans-2015–2018

15 The restrictions on the sale of computers were relaxed in 2008, and since then transmission of ebooks via manual USB stick transfer has become more and more commonplace. Wikipedia states that *El Paquete* started around 2008 and Etres has taken care of its advertising since 2011, when legal property reform of private enterprise allowed Etres to charge local businesses a small fee to advertise in *El Paquete*. An article in *frieze* describes how people have claimed to be the organisers of *El Paquete* and then been discredited, suggesting it is more of a phenomenon than a singular entity, with different versions distributed in different places and run by

government has also set up its own version as an alternative — *Mi Mochila* (*The Knapsack*) — you can download content and access this Cuban Intranet at *Joven Clubs* (*Joven Club de Computación y Electrónica*) — kids computer clubs — in cities and towns across the country.¹⁶

There is something wonderfully incongruous about the idea of a team of editors travelling the country sharing digital files — the Internet! — on foot. I don't wish to romanticise something that comes from a lack, but I wonder if this hand-held relay of information has benefits. Does it change the relationship between the users and the editors? Is it simply like the Internet before Web 2.0 or is there an opportunity for a publication to create a community of readers in a different way? If our magazine was circulated via *El Paquete*, how would we know the extent of its readership?

Later I'll be asked if the question of government infiltration affected what I said on camera, and I'll shrug: Why would it be any different from anything I ever write online, and doesn't London have the most CCTV cameras per person in the world?

December 2015, London

I have been contracted to run a module on art publishing for Central Saint Martins, and I decide to use some of the allocated teaching hours to pay speakers for events open to the public. Sean Dockray, the programmer of aaarg.org, is in London from Melbourne, and agrees to

---

different organisations. See 'Data Roaming', Orit Gat, *frieze*, 30 July 2016, https://frieze.com/article/data-roaming

16   'According to the government, there are some 600 Joven Clubs, approximately one for every 18,000 Cubans. But the Joven Clubs' online access is restricted to the Cuban "intranet," which accesses only Cuban email addresses, websites and resources. The centers also offer classes in Microsoft Word and Excel, and host visits by domestic bloggers. But the emphasis is solidly on [the] "domestic." When Fidel Castro announced the creation of the centers in 1987, he envisioned them as supports for the domestic pillars of collective society: "The Joven Club of the factory, of the institutions, and the Joven Clubs of the masses, because these are the neighborhood institutions; this is the family doctor, the Cuban family computer."' — Annie Nelson, 'The View from inside Cuba's not-so-Worldwide Web', *Tech President*, 5 April 2013, http://techpresident.com/news/wegov/23702/cuba-highly-restricted-internet-access-leaves-population-hungry-more. See also: Jason Koebler, 'Cuba's Communist Computer Clubs for Children: Photos from Beyond', *Vice Motherboard*, 28 August 2015, https://motherboard.vice.com/en_us/article/78xg8z/the-communist-computer-club-for-kids

a conversation event with my students at Housmans, a left-wing radical bookshop down the road from the university.[17] Sean is generous with his time and ends up talking with us for hours about his intentions for the website, his surprise at how quickly it started working, and how much it relies on those who use it.

Aaarg largely consists of critical theory texts shared by hundreds of users who have started collections, suggested themes, or added to existing selections, by scanning and uploading PDFs of articles in their possession. The website functions as a private library that evolves with new areas of interest added by its members in response to their scholarship, current issues and concerns. Dockray explains to us his irritation with users who simply start uploading everything they have onto the site — such misguided generosity turns it into a pointless archive, a file-sharing dump.[18] Discussing the site we start to apply models of pre-internet printed matter to this post-internet platform: talking about it as a kind of mutating anthology, or a magazine of republished materials, with an editorial-*ship* that is its readership. Understanding it as a magazine or a library seems to acknowledge the creative and caring maintenance work of the users, and of Dockray; the particular knowledge of the community of participant-librarians is crucial to the useful functioning of the site.

Aaarg.org changes its number of 'a's whenever the website address gets too well known.[19] I've read that the name is the acronym of 'Artists, Architects, and Activists Reading Group',[20] and notice that Dockray doesn't seem at all interested in an anti-copyright or IP stance — instead

---

17 'More aaaaaa: Sean Dockray in Conversation', Tuesday 8 December, Housmans Bookshop, London, event organised by Three Letter Words in collaboration with Housmans Bookshop and the 'Publishing/Writing' module, MRes Art: Theory and Philosophy, Central Saint Martins, University of the Arts London, http://threeletterwords.org/more-as-sean-dockray-in-conversation-housmans-london-tuesday-8-december-10-30-a-m-1-00-p-m/

18 Dockray does his best to discourage the sharing of whole ebooks; he takes down material immediately if a publisher or writer complains, and emphasises that he wants the site to be used as a place to share material that is hard to find and not otherwise available.

19 'More a's?' was Dockray's response to a question about the future for aaarg from Morgan Currie, 'Small Is Beautiful: A Discussion with AAAARG Architect Sean Dockray', *Masters of Media*, University of Amsterdam, 5 January 2010, https://mastersofmedia.hum.uva.nl/blog/2010/01/05/small-is-beautiful-a-discussion-with-aaaarg-architect-sean-dockray/

20 See the description here: https://monoskop.org/Aaaaarg

he is utterly focused on what aaarg provides as a collaboratively curated collection of materials, and as a way to think about the potential of pedagogy and collaboration outside expensive institutional frameworks.[21] I'm performing the same function here; in this text I am advocating for the potential for aaarg to be tolerated and understood as a small library.

If you are employed as an academic, or you are a student, you can easily access university libraries and catalogues of digitised scholarly articles. However for those who have finished their formal education it is difficult to access any of this kind of material, or to find ways to connect and collaborate. For these people aaarg isn't about free access to something that might have fallen behind a paywall on JSTOR, but is rather a place to discuss ideas, to find people with the same or similar speciality interests. I've found aaarg to be particularly useful when people share items that are now out-of-print and would otherwise be completely unavailable. Visiting lecturers and artists, critics, curators, writers, poets — those in precarious creative work on the edges of academia and those who work outside it — number those who make use aaarg, contributing to it as a forum and discovering idiosyncratic selections of research.

January 2016, London

I'm writing the first version of this text and I email Reynier to ask him about his experience of IP restrictions. He replies more quickly than I expect — as a student at Havana University he has better access to the Internet than most Cubans. As well as his free education he currently receives 150MB data/month for free (an amount that has increased considerably, last year they received just 30MB).[22] He and his friends

---

21   Later with Fiona Whitton, Dockray established the online platform the Public School (2007). A description on its website (currently unavailable but due to be updated with an archive) described the Public School as 'a framework that supports autodidactic activities.' The platform was developed as part of their work as the Telic Arts Exchange (2005–2012). See http://thepublicschool.org/

22   'But the most important vehicle for popular participation in the arts is the national system of art education that operates free of charge through primary and secondary schools, specialized art schools and high schools, university-level art education, and the Casa de la Cultura, which is an art institution present in

use Facebook on their smart phones whilst at university because the app is conveniently designed to work well with slower connections.

Reynier explains how the US blockade stops artistic exchange between Cubans and Americans — linking to an article in *Art Law Journal*, which tells the story of an American writer unable to clear copyright for a film adaptation of a popular children's book written by his Cuban friend, because to make a formal contract with the friend amounts to a transaction and is therefore illegal.[23] Reynier summarises the situation:

> In the early days of the Revolution the state ignored intellectual property, establishing public libraries across the country and reproducing everything they wanted for them. In the 1990s, this changed and Cuba started to conform to international law regarding copyright.[24] Not that this more recent official stance has necessarily meant a strict approach in practice. For example, due to the embargo it is not possible for Cubans to buy US goods, including movies, software, or music legally. The government cannot therefore commercialise these products themselves, so they have allowed the private sector to illegally reproduce the material, tolerating piracy.

I go on to read a couple of articles that claim that both *El Paquete* and the government version, *Mi Mochila*, contain pirated American series

---

every municipality. The Casa de la Cultura offers free and low-cost art lessons for children and adults and provides space for exhibitions and performances. Cuba has a strong movement of aficionados that promotes and organizes artistic expression from all sectors of population, but especially youth.' Miren Uriarte, 'The Right Priorities: Health, Education and Literacy', in her *CUBA: Social Policy at the Crossroads: Maintaining Priorities, Transforming Practice. An Oxfam America Report*, 2002, https://www.oxfamamerica.org/publications/cuba-social-policy-at-the-crossroads/, pp. 6–18 (p. 12).

23 Nicole Martinez, 'How Does Relaxing the Cuba Trade Embargo Affect Artists?', *Art Law Journal* (online), 11 May 2015 (the article is no longer available on their website).

24 In 1967 Fidel proclaimed the abolition of copyright. In October of the same year, at a preparatory seminar for the Cultural Congress of Havana, artists and writers willingly renounced the commercial rights to their work in return for social recognition and the value inherent in the creative act. Paraphrased from Rebecca Gordon-Nesbitt, 'The Emancipatory Potential of Culture under Socialism', in her *To Defend the Revolution Is to Defend Culture: The Cultural Policy of the Cuban Revolution* (Oakland: PM Press, 2015), pp. 103–04. Cuba has been a member of the World Trade Organisation since 20 April 1995, https://www.wto.org/english/thewto_e/countries_e/cuba_e.htm and acceded to the Berne Convention soon after (with some exceptions in November 1996, http://www.wipo.int/treaties/en/notifications/berne/treaty_berne_176.html).

and films, and seem to complain about the visibility of pirated DVDs for sale in Cuba. I start to imagine the badly printed covers of American blockbusters lined up on a wall, and realise I am actually recalling a scene from central London, not Centro Havana.

June 2017, London

I guess I will be back writing this when I know the result. After polling closes on Thursday we are gathering in the 1Love pop-up community centre in Canary Wharf and watching the results together. We need a place we can be all night, with a prayer room for those observing Ramadan, and so this venue will be perfect. We are going to bring the baby and are hoping she sleeps in the pram, amongst other cautious, bigger hopes. We plan to be out all day, knocking on doors in Thurrock, our nearest marginal, doing the work of 'getting the vote out' — leaving reminders and encouraging those who said they would vote for us to actually go and cast it. I didn't know this was what happened on polling day until a few weeks ago, but apparently it's crucial.

I keep fantasising about it. I see us crying in red t-shirts like we are watching the final of a big game. Are we happy or sad? I remember last year, waking at 3am and watching the results of the EU referendum coming through from the light of our phones. The baby asleep, the BBC website, checking in on Facebook to see comments of dismay as the Leave vote got clearer.

It will be strange to be physically with our Tower Hamlets Momentum friends, reacting in the moment. When other important news reports have arrived we've been apart, but sending messages in our WhatsApp group. The 'chat' has got more and more frequent these weeks since the snap election was called. Two hundred or so messages a day: witty responses, declarations of support and love, secret irritations and theories shared. The chat gives a focus, something to engage with when confronted with the helpless inevitability of watching the news unfold, out of your hands but there in your bed. I write a wry comment, Gavin smiles at it sitting across the room from me. I worry that we won't all be as witty in person, but I can't imagine not being there in the flesh, I can't imagine missing it: missing watching it collectively, in solidarity, whatever it is.

May 2015, Havana

Catherine has gathered a group of artists and writers and we've been meeting every few days, in each other's flats, perched with laptops in lounges, sitting at kitchen tables. Today we are discussing what is already available in terms of arts magazines — Reynier has brought along *Upsalón*, which is stapled and monotone, focused on contemporary literature and published by the Faculty of Arts at the University of Havana. As well as university-run publications that cover art criticism there are two official arts magazines: *Artecubano*, which focuses on fine art in a fairly academic art historical way, and *Revolución y Cultura* which is multidisciplinary. Both are perfect-bound with coated covers and colour illustrations, but the design feels dated and they appear drab and heavy. Yanelys Nuñez Leyva describes her frustration that there is no print publication that has regular listings of upcoming shows, or reviews of current exhibitions. She writes on art for the *Havana Times*, an online magazine founded in 2008 that was initially approved by the Cuban Journalists' Association (UPEC) before its permission was withdrawn, apparently because some of its writers were publishing blogs critical of the government (it is now run out of Nicaragua).[25]

---

25 *Havana Times* (HT) features both 'journalist and non-journalist writing' in Spanish and English, and was set up in 2008 by Circles Robinson while he was working in Cuba (for 'a Cuban government agency that assisted the Cuban media with translations'). Robinson says it set out to 'distance our publication from the polarized and conservative Cuban government media as well as from the mostly foreign-based anti-Castro media', and describes the funding of the site as 'self-financed', 'an after-work "labor of love" [...] with a little help from my friends', declaring that '*HT* has refused to apply for any grants from direct or indirect US government funding sources.' The website was initially supported by the Cuban Journalists' Association (UPEC), but six months later this support was withdrawn: 'The sharp criticism of government policies by several of our bloggers was too much for an organization [UPEC] that is totally dependent economically and ideologically on the government/party line.' Circles Robinson, 'About Us: Havana Times Reaches 8th Birthday', *Havana Times*, 17 October 2016, https://havanatimes.org/?p=121610
In an interview with the *Weekly Worker* (The Communist Party of Great Britain's online/print publication) Robinson describes his aim 'to promote a combination of conventional and new-style reporting, as well as commentary that reflects critical support for the Cuban revolution, which is not necessarily synonymous with its leaders.' He also explains that he is a US citizen and had been living in Nicaragua before he came to work in Cuba, having returned there with his family after his contract working for the Cuban government came to an end. 'I had a major conflict at work resulting from some of my co-workers and myself openly questioning the unethical conduct of our immediate boss. To get me to support his behaviour he

Llópiz (Julio César Llópiz) is graphic designer and an artist; he shows us some artists' books he's made — digital printed booklets, hand-folded and of limited print run, that are clearly benign from an activist perspective: there's no reason they would be considered publishing in any kind of illegal — counter-revolutionary — way. He then shows us a newsprint project that looks unofficial, but it turns out it isn't — *Noticias Artecubano* — a monthly newspaper edited by the same team as *Artecubano*. He has been running a column for the paper called 'La Fracción por Llópiz' where he invites other artists to make work for the page. Printed cheaply in black and red *Noticias Artecubano* looks like the kind of mass-produced paper you might pick up at a protest — its cheap form immediately suggests wide distribution. I imagine if we were to produce our 'magazine' in a format like this, it would look mass-produced and be likely to raise concerns from the authorities due to its apparent potential reach.

May 2015, Bermuda Triangle

Looking out the airplane window I imagine I am gazing at the edge of the earth: flying into a curve of bright white glinting light. I feel so far away, so physically distant from home, yet my conversations with Catherine — communicating over three thousand miles — have compounded my idealism about the potentials of the internet for enabling ongoing discourse, and my enthusiasm that we might be able to set up ways of working between Havana and London. The hope is that editors in both localities could feed in remotely, creating a platform for Cuban artists in the UK and vice versa, that would be sustainable on a small scale without the need for massive travel grants.

Yesterday I met with Louisa Bailey and got her go-ahead (in theory) to publish the Havana-London magazine with her branch

---

threatened to make a case against me using *Havana Times* and the fact that I had started it "without permission", though this was done in my free time. In the end, they simply refused to renew my yearly work contract. While no reason was given, I never felt that *HT* was the main issue in this. Since my residency in Cuba was dependent on the job, I was given a month's notice to leave the country. My family is from Nicaragua and I had lived there for many years before coming to Cuba, so we decided to return there.' Circles Robinson in Zurowski, 'More Glasnost, Less Perestroika'.

of Publication Studio, which she launched in London in February. She's been flat out since then, printing, cutting, gluing and packing copies of her first publication, and all UK orders for books made by similarly tiny 'studios' across the globe.[26] Publication Studio (PS) is an interesting model for small-scale publishing — each of its 'nonfranchise franchise'[27] of thirteen studios internationally (from Sao Paulo to Malmö) works locally with artists and writers to produce books which are then printed on demand using the same affordable machinery — perfect binder, guillotine and digital printer — that each studio owns (or borrows).[28] As with all print-on-demand models this means that by printing and binding books 'one-at-a-time, by hand and on request' they avoid the upfront costs and potential waste of bulk printing.[29] But the interesting thing about Publication Studio is the way its network works across territories — because each studio follows similar design formats, shares files online and uses similar equipment, it means publications commissioned and edited by one studio can be easily produced and sold by a studio on the other side of the world. So, if you lived in Malmö, you could order a copy of our magazine from the studio there, and have a copy quickly and easily made — no need for shipping from Havana or London.

The description, 'nonfranchise franchise' pithily acknowledges that new studios benefit from the brand and ability to print and sell a whole back catalogue of PS titles, but it also indicates that PS avoids the homogenisation normally associated with franchises by also being a site for production — creating an international network of local editors, writers, artists… and publics. It's a two-way thing — new studios bring new readerships to existing publications, and PS provides an existing context and readership for new ones. Publication Studio is often described as a really great model for sustainable, small-scale publishing practice,

---

26   Publication Studio Glasgow was launched in November 2016.
27   'Nonfranchise franchise' was Bridget Kinsella's way of describing Publication Studio in an article for *Publishers Weekly*. Bridget Kinsella, 'Publication Studio: A Nonfranchise Franchise', *Publishers Weekly*, 23 May 2011, http://publishersweekly.com/pw/by-topic/industry-news/publisher-news/article/47387-publication-studio-a-nonfranchise-franchise.html
28   There were thirteen studios during the editing process of this text. For an up-to-date list of Publication Studios visit https://publicationstudio.biz/about/
29   Louisa Bailey, 'Sustainable Publishing', in *Plastic Words* (London: Publication Studio, 2015), p. 63.

and the sustainability might be true in environmental terms — there is little wasted paper — every book printed has been ordered, and there is no need to fly books across the globe. However, although 'the retail price of the book covers the cost of materials and labour and a small profit that is split between the studio and the author(s)', its economic viability is flawed: it relies on free labour and risking time on fundraising attempts.[30] The small profit is negligible and Louisa, who works two other jobs to pay her London rent, spends the 'spare' time she doesn't spend making the books on applying for grants.

May 2015, Havana

We are at 'Sometimes Art Space', the living room of Solveig Font, in Vedado where she and her partner Llópiz (Julio César Llópiz) intermittently organise art exhibitions, inviting an extended network of friends and colleagues. The space is not official but also not illegal — it's listed as part of the biennial satellite programme. Our conversation is again circling around how the magazine might be tolerated. We talk about the term *permissive / permisivo*, its vernacular association with tolerance of sexuality, and in relation to the testing of other freedoms — the careful dance around what is allowed and what is pushing too far — and despite our reluctance to give her any more airtime we find ourselves talking again about Tania Bruguera.

Solveig describes the meeting between Raul and Obama as an important delicate moment — most Cubans have family in America; fragile international policy is not an abstraction. However she does have some sympathy with the first iteration of *El Susurro de Tatlin #6* (*Tatlin's Whisper #6*) for the way it negotiated the system, and used the art context to create a 'state of exception.'[31] *El Susurro de Tatlin #6* was part of a

---

30 Bailey, 'Sustainable Publishing', p. 63.
31 'Estado de Excepción' ('State of Exception') was the title of a series of group exhibitions curated by Tania Bruguera and Marilyn Machado as part of the Havana Biennial 2009, and to commemorate the end of her project *Cátedra Arte de Conducta* (*Behaviour Art School*, 2002–2009).
    On *El Susurro de Tatlin #6* (2009), Coco Fusco, in a letter she wrote in response to the article by Claire Bishop, 'Tania Bruguera at the 10th Havana Biennial', *Artforum*, Summer 2009, noted that 'An important question about the usefulness of the piece is whether this performative spectacle effectively diverted attention away from ongoing activism on behalf of civil rights in Cuba, focusing the Western gaze

number of exhibitions and events that took place at the 2009 biennial to commemorate the end of Bruguera's project *Cátedra Arte de Conducta* (*Behaviour Art School*, 2002–2009), and we discuss how she refused to let this art school become official, a situation Solveig finds questionable: why not test its potential?[32]

Reynier is the most critical of the artist: if the work was an intentional provocation, the duration of the performance 'expanded' by the responses it received from the Cuban police and the international press, then the provocation encompasses the way an American press utilised her critique for their ends, any delay to the end of the embargo, and the negative impact on the freedoms that Cuban artists have and the steps being made towards enlarging these.[33] Bruguera has suggested

---

instead on the theatrical props that frame official Revolutionary discourse and the emotive charge that those props impart.' See 'Public Address', *Artforum*, October 2009, pp. 38–40, http://www.taniabruguera.com/cms/260-0-Public+Address.htm

32 Contrary to my understanding presented here of what happened, Claire Bishop has said that *Cátedra Arte de Conducta* closed due to government pressure: 'In a similar fashion, her art school, the Catedra Arte de Conducta, proceeded on the premise that more can be achieved by negotiating with the Instituto Superior de Arte, which enabled international teachers to be invited legally to Cuba, than by remaining militantly outside it. (When the state cannot recognize Arte de Conducta as desirable and expedient, Bruguera closed it down.)' 'Public Address', 'Claire Bishop responds', in ibid.

Although we are talking about a magazine, we don't discuss Bruguera's first 'alternative institution', the newspaper *Memoria de la Postguerra* (*Postwar Memory*, 1993–1994), perhaps because we are specifically talking about a magazine as exhibition space, not as a vehicle for news or activism. *Memoria* has been called 'positive institutional critique' and Bruguera has noted that, as with the *Cátedra Arte de Conducta* (Behavior Art School, 2002–2009, http://www.taniabruguera.com/cms/492-0-Ctedra+Arte+de+Conducta+Behavior+Art+School.htm), she was creating an 'alternative institution' — challenging the government-controlled press, and the official national newspaper (*Granma*), by producing her own. W. J. T. Mitchell, 'How to Make Art with a Jackhammer: A Conversation with Tania Bruguera', *Afterall* 42, Autumn/Winter 2016, p. 55, https://doi.org/10.1086/689803

The first issue of *Memoria* featured a list of 'Internacionales' — artists who had left Cuba — printed like a list of war dead, and her website describes the paper as for 'debate of non-authorized topics, criticism generally silenced by the state.' The paper seems to have been as much about a Cuban-American voice, as a Cuban one, and was eventually censored. See http://www.taniabruguera.com/cms/564-0-Postwar+Memory+II.htm

33 In this phrasing I have adapted 'duration is expanded' from a description by Daniel R. Quiles. 'The work's duration was followed — and effectively expanded — by the appearance of state power, effectively transforming the privileged moment (the "you had to be there" school of performance) into a narrative of provocation or resistance whose importance supersedes that of the original.' D. R. Quiles, 'The Vicissitudes of Conduct,' *Third Text*, September 2016, http://thirdtext.org/vicissitudes-of-conduct

she works alone to stop other artists getting into trouble,[34] but Reynier suggests that her lone authorship, far from being sacrificial, only serves herself, pointing out that *Tatlin's Whisper #6* (2009) was bought *by the Guggenheim* — the emphasis upon the name of the American millionaire dynasty.

Back home I check and confirm: *Tatlin's Whisper #6 (Havana Version)* was purchased via the UBS MAP Purchase Fund and it acceded to the Solomon R. Guggenheim Museum collection in November 2014, a month before Bruguera's attempted restaging.[35] Further searching shows me that Bruguera's place in American academia was pretty much secured on her return to the US — she received a Yale Greenberg Fellowship, a six-month residency at the university starting in August 2015.[36] According to Wikipedia, Maurice Raymond 'Hank' Greenberg is a Republican and an American business executive, former chairman and CEO of American International Group (AIG), which was the world's eighteenth largest public company and the largest insurance and financial services corporation in history.

April 2015, London

'Please join us at 10am, Rolls Building, Royal Courts of Justice, London.' We send an email to all our subscribers calling for support for the students who have been taken to court by University of the Arts London. Since March around 80 graduate students (who I figure will each be paying around £9,000 a year in fees) have been sleeping in the reception area of Central Saint Martins to oppose the cuts to foundation degree courses across UAL.

Foundation courses are one of the last free courses the university runs, and help bring more diverse groups into the arts, but it seems that, with ongoing government cuts to further and higher education, they have stopped being cost-effective for the university.

---

34 Tania comments that the experience of collectively making the newspaper *Memoria de la Postguerra* and inadvertently getting others into trouble had caused her to want to work alone and in performance, although she later 'regretted having answered to political pressure in such a way, using my own body instead of pursuing the social body'. Mitchell, 'How to Make Art with a Jackhammer', p. 53.

35 See Guggenheim collection online: https://www.guggenheim.org/artwork/33083.

36 The title of the work is listed in English (without any Spanish version) on the Guggenheim website. See https://worldfellows.yale.edu/tania-bruguera

Having failed to shift the students from their occupation, UAL has decided to get them out by cherry-picking a few students, some of them student union reps, and taking them individually to court over costs.

January 2016, London

I tweet, post and share a crowdfunder for the legal defence of 'Sean Dockray (the initiator of the online library aaarg.org) and Marcell Mars (who registered the latest domain, aaaaarg.fail).'[37] The fundraiser reaches $10,000 over its initial $5,000 goal in a matter of days, but they are being sued for $500,000 by a publisher in Quebec, and the site explains they have no idea what the eventual legal costs will be.

I don't know how their lawyers are running the case, but perhaps they will argue, as Dockray has in the past, that digital property — ebook ownership — contradicts the First Sale Doctrine, which was established in America in 1908 and gave the owner the right the sell, lease or rent their copy of a book — making it possible that second-hand bookshops and public libraries could be legal.[38]

Dockray has also written eloquently about the care behind the act of scanning, and the feeling of intimacy when reading someone's scanned PDF, seeing the marks of previous readings, pencilled notes and spillages. The use of scans on the site also indicates that the papers are from printed books in people's possession — property they have the right to share with those they choose. Perhaps by emphasising that this is *someone's* book, dwelling on a smudged fingerprinted scan serves to indicate that aaarg is not a place designed for illegal file-sharing but rather a semi-private digital library.[39]

The current network of thousands of aaarg users grew from just one email Dockray sent to a list of friends, collaborators and colleagues, inviting them to share and make use of what he had built.[40] It feels depressingly

---

37 See https://uk.gofundme.com/aaaaarg
38 Ebooks actually only provide a license for use and access and this contradicts the First Sale Doctrine. See Sean Dockray, 'Interface, Access, Loss', in Marysia Lewandowska and Laurel Ptak (eds.), *Undoing Property?* (Stockholm and Berlin: Sternberg Press & Tensta konsthall, 2013), p. 189.
39 When aaarg first started it only contained scanned documents because the PDF files of the time were too big to share in this way (it now also holds PDFs).
40 The site is semi private: in order to access aaarg.org you need to be invited or to be told the website address (which migrates, changing its number of 'a's to avoid legal

apt that Dockray might be saved by an online crowdfunder — one of an industry of businesses that position themselves as benevolent community-builders in order to collect their cut, and that first emerged around the same time Dockray was coding away, making his 'scaffold'. 'Scaffold' is Dockray's word for what aaarg.org is, which I understand to mean that it is not the architecture — it is not part of the academic institution — but it is attached to it and supports it.

January 2015, London

Mute, a magazine that lost its regular Arts Council funding in 2012 and yet somehow continues intermittently posting well-researched writing online, publishes an article by Rebecca Gordon Nesbitt, which takes further Coco Fusco's criticism of Tania Bruguera and *#YoTambienExijo* by elaborating upon the 'blatant hypocrisy' employed when Cuba is discussed in Anglophone press. 'It is no surprise that freedom of expression is the first resort of those seeking to discredit alternatives to capitalism.' Gordon Nesbitt suggests that 'in commissioning Fusco', 'a full-time faculty member at Parsons The New School for Design', 'the editors of *e-flux* exposed the prejudices of their location'. She quotes Howard S. Becker, on 'hierarchies of credibility,' and describes how tenured academics, 'with the most power and access to information' are assumed to be neutral, yet of course take sides to help 'maintain the existing order.'[41]

September 2015, London

I am talking at the symposium that instigated this anthology, organised by Goldsmiths and funded by the 'Centre for Copyright and New Business Models in the Creative Economy'.[42] I'm expected to discuss

---

threats). There is an 'invite' button on the site that warns: 'Any registered user can invite anyone else, but please don't invite the wrong people.'

41 Rebecca Gordon-Nesbitt, 'Whose Side Are You On?: A Response to Coco Fusco', *Mute*, 29 January 2015, http://www.metamute.org/community/your-posts/whose-side-are-you-response-to-coco-fusco-'-state-detention-performance-politics-and-cuban-public'-e-flux-3

42 'Friction and Fiction: IP, Copyright and Digital Futures', Goldsmiths University symposium, Victoria & Albert Museum, London, 26 September 2015.

ideas for a copyright system that is 'not based on normativity and national copyrights.'[43] It seems like a good opportunity to promote *Sonrisa* (*Smile*), our magazine project, but I'm four months pregnant and acutely aware of how unlikely it is that the magazine will ever actually happen, now I'm having a baby.[44] I end up talking about the unsustainability of my work in London running independent print projects, and, in response to the comments that Cuba has no free press, I talk about the problematics of American descriptions of artists' books as a 'democratic' form:

> Since the 1970s a largely US-based discourse on art publishing has defined 'artists' books' (over more rarefied book arts) by their gesture towards seeking a mass audience — their presentation as "cheaply produced democratic multiples."[45] These books are celebrated for their potential — entirely unrealised — to be a cheap way to get art to the masses.[46] This well-meaning, inclusive, ethos, is oppositional in many

---

43   'If we were starting from scratch, we might devise a copyright system which is global and diverse rather than based on territoriality, normativity and national copyrights.' — Description for the panel 'A View from Elsewhere' (Chair: Casey Brienza), 'Friction and Fiction: IP, Copyright and Digital Futures', ibid., https://www.gold.ac.uk/calendar/?id=8946

44   *Sonrisa* refers to Stewart Home's declaration that anyone could make an issue of *SMILE*, the magazine he founded in 1984. The resulting magazines, produced by numerous editors yet understood as part of a series, represent a refusal of homogenised branding and editorial authorship, and a desire for collective cumulative magazine-making. 'Countless issues have been produced by others, making it impossible to know how many issues have actually been published.' Gwen Allen, 'A compendium of Artists' Magazines from 1945 to 1989', *Artists' Magazines: An Alternative Space for Art* (Cambridge, MA: MIT Press, 2011), p. 297.

45   Writing in 1995, US-based art historian Johanna Drucker described how 'the idea of the book as democratic multiple' (p. 69) had become 'a definitive paradigm for artists' books' (p. 72), suggesting that the availability of inexpensive printing technologies post-1945 'combined with major changes in the mainstream art world of the late 1950s and early 1960s' (p. 69) to define the artists' book as something mass produced and un-editioned (p. 69).
This dream was encapsulated in Lucy Lippard's much repeated comment of 1974: 'One day I'd like to see artists' books ensconced in supermarkets, drugstores, and airports and not incidentally, to see artists able to profit economically from broad communication rather than the lack of it' (p. 80), and evidenced by the buying strategies of bookshops and library acquisition policies — the stipulations that emerged in the early 1970s that publications must be in editions over 100 to qualify as an 'artists' book' (p. 81). J. Drucker, in 'The Artist's Book as Democratic Multiple', in *The Century of Artists' Books* (New York: Granary Books, 1995), pp. 69–91.

46   Something accepted by Lippard: 'Yet even then, I think we knew accessibility was pie in the sky. Very little contemporary art is truly accessible [...]. The fact remains that while the democratic impulse has engendered many artists' books, distribution has foiled most of us.' L. Lippard, 'Double Spread', in Maria Fusco and Ian Hunt

ways to the overwhelmingly market-led, patron focused and elite, state of the UK and US 'art world'-cum-market. However I can't help but feel cynical about a discourse on publishing that leaves us with the production of limited edition art works as enfranchisement (however 'affordable'). A celebration of Fordism as democracy — bravo Ed Ruscha — genius self-promoting entrepreneur![47]

May 2015, Havana

There is an opening tonight and the bar at La Fábrica de Arte Cubano (FAC) is heaving. The FAC is an ex-factory building in the outer edges of Vedado and contains film screening rooms, concessions selling silk-screened t-shirts, vast dance and music spaces, and quieter exhibition areas where paintings are displayed on temporary partition walls. FAC describes itself as a 'space'. In Havana a 'gallery' is always run by the government, whereas 'space' and 'independent' always indicate something unofficial by various degrees — side-projects by artists, like Solveig and Llópiz's 'Sometimes Art Space' and larger tourist businesses like this one. The centre feels a bit like the ICA in London with its similarly multidisciplinary program: cinema, performances, exhibitions, and café bar. It's certainly got a very different feeling to the quiet

---

(eds.), *Put About: A Critical Anthology on Independent Publishing* (London: Book Works, 2004), pp. 86–87.

Drucker also points to 'some paradoxes' with the use of the term 'democracy' — questioning the idea that democracy resides in a publication's affordability rather than the accessibility of its content, and pointing out the 'terrific confusion' 'between the idea of what is affordable for an artist to make and what is affordable to buy' (bulk production requiring capital up front). Drucker, 'The Artist's Book as Democratic Multiple', p. 72.

47 This is a reference to the US canon, which positions the first artists' book as Ed Ruscha's *Twentysix Gasoline Stations* (1962). *Twentysix Gasoline Stations* features a series of black and white photographs of 'exactly that' (J. Drucker, 'The Artist's Book', p. 76) and has become a 'cliché in critical works trying to establish a history of artists' books', a kind of 'founding father' tendency, which overlooks the 'numerous mini-genealogies' in the field. (Drucker, 'The Artist's Book as Idea and Form', p. 11). The claims of a democracy in the mass-produced artists' book form, and Ruscha's later statement 'I want to be the Henry Ford of book making', chime with the content of *Twentysix Gasoline Stations* (the gas station — the journey along Route 66 — the car, albeit unseen). See 'I want to be the Henry Ford of book making', *National Observer*, 28 July 1969, referenced by Gagosian in the press release for their gallery exhibition 'Ed Ruscha: Books & Co', Gagosian, Madison Avenue, New York, March–April 2013, https://gagosian.com/media/exhibitions/2013/ed-ruscha-books-co/Gagosian_Ed_Ruscha_Books_Co_2013_Press_Release.pdf

government-run Wifredo Lam over in old Havana. The closest parallel to the Wifredo Lam in the UK (in funding terms) would have to be the Tate Britain — Tate is an executive non-departmental public body, directly funded by and accountable to the state (the Department for Culture, Media and Sport).[48] However the DCMS is only one of Tate's many sponsors; it receives funding from a mass of other enterprises and subsidiaries, including BP, and its various patron schemes — Young, Silver, Gold and Platinum — each provide different levels of access.

Luis Manuel Otero Alcantâra (Luis Manuel) arrives. Catherine describes him best: 'dressed up as a female dancer from the famous Havana-based cabaret Tropicana — fuchsia frou-frou, fishnet stockings, and gold heels way too small [...]'.[49] He is here as part of his performance *Miss Bienal* (2015) for which he has been to every single opening and art event over the course of the biennial month, greeting visitors, handing out business cards, and posing for selfies, accompanied always by Yanelys, who has been helping him with makeup, staging photos, and moral support. The commissioned performance is a result of Catherine's mentoring programme with Luis Manuel, a setup that was potentially problematic for them both because Luis Manuel is not an 'official' artist. He was not educated as an artist (he was originally a professional athlete), so he cannot

---

48 I double-check this on the Tate website and I am amused to see the image used on the page describing their governance is a photograph of Tania Bruguera, *Tatlin's Whisper #5*, 2008 © Tania Bruguera. The performance involved two uniformed mounted policemen on horseback herding visitors within the Turbine Hall, and provides a British representation of the mechanisms of state power, just as menacing as the image of the dove and podium, flanked by a male and female uniformed guard, used on the Guggenheim website for *Tatlin's Whisper #6 (Havana version)*, 2009. I enjoy the coincidence and wonder if this was posted with a sense of irony. 'Tate is an executive non-departmental public body sponsored by the Department for Digital, Culture, Media and Sport (DCMS) and an exempt charity defined by Schedule 3 to the Charities Act 2011. It is exempt from registration with, and oversight by, the Charity Commission and is regulated by DCMS in accordance with a management agreement agreed by the Secretary of State for Digital, Culture, Media and Sport for charity law purposes.' http://www.tate.org.uk/about-us/governance
When I was at FAC the department was called the 'Department for Culture, Media and Sport'; it added 'Digital' on 3 July 2017. BP announced plans to end its twenty-six-year sponsorship of Tate in March 2016.
49 Catherine Sicot, 'Miss Bienal Inaugurates La Primavera del Amor: Genesis of a Platform for Research and Intercultural Artistic Production in Cuba', June 2014–2015', *Public* 26.52 (2015), 58–67 (p. 63), https://doi.org/10.1386/public.26.52.59_1

be a member of the artists' union and participate in exhibitions in government-run galleries, and he cannot travel abroad as easily as official artists.[50]

Luis Manuel's business card looks pretty official though, it reads 'Welcome to the 12th Havana Bienal' and features — like a funding credit — the official logo of the very official biennial, appropriating the brand and placing it without permission alongside the 'La Primavera del Amor' one. Luis Manuel hands it out, accepts photographs, and then moves on evading any further interaction.[51]

Leaving the FAC we walk past the entrance to *El Cocinero* — a bar and restaurant with views across the city from the top of an old smoke stack. It is owned by the same person who owns FAC. A bouncer in a suit is officious over the wait list, barring the downstairs entrance.

June 2015, London

I'm scrolling down, catching up with what has happened since I've been away and I see that a number of friends have shared an article by an online magazine based in Brooklyn, lamenting the second arrest of Tania Bruguera. This is the first I have heard of it, despite being in Havana at the time.

---

50 'The state doesn't recognize me as an artist because I didn't go to art school. [...] Cuba is a paternalist country that generates a political, economic, and social structure for those who follow its educational path. You graduate from a school and they give you a card that identifies you as an artist, and gives you benefits according to that. Artists in Cuba are privileged: they belong to a different social class; they can travel abroad easily.' Luis Manuel Otero Alcántara, 'Luis Manuel Otero Alcántara photo-documentary', *Wondereur* [online sales platform], Toronto, undated (ca.2015), https://www.wondereur.com/artists/luis-manuel-otero-alcantara

51 Catherine writes that the Tropicana cabaret was stigmatised but not banned by the Revolution, so it was ready to be re-exploited in 1990s with the opening up of tourism on the island. She describes Luis Manuel's performance as 'passive and passive-aggressive' in the experience of Western audiences: it frustrates, because it 'generates expectations but nothing "else" ever happens.' She points out that it can be read as an implementation of 'typical capitalist (*yuma* [foreigner]) strategies: networking, marketing, advertising, branding and especially self-promotion' and she notes that 'homophobia still widely dominates in Cuba. All the pictures of Miss Bienal posing in the company of visitors and circulated on Facebook actually give a rather false measure of the reception of the work.' Luis Manuel 'felt a lot of rejection, especially from Cubans who avoided eye contact, laughed to hide their discomfort'. Was this performance a joke on the realities of Cuban progressiveness? Was it a satire of the exploitation of the Cuban 'outsider artist' by the art tourists and industry? See Sicot, 'Miss Bienal Inaugurates La Primavera del Amor'.

Hyperallergic tells me that Bruguera was taken into custody for a few hours, after attempting a 100-hour long reading of Hannah Arendt's *The Origins of Totalitarianism* in her home.[52] A picture shows her smiling outside her home earlier in May, alongside two men the caption describes as 'Guggenheim curator Pablo Leon Dela Barra, and Cuban-American curator Gean Moreno'. The image is taken from Leon Dela Barra's Facebook page and he is making a 'V' with his fingers. More posts from other friends and colleagues — re-performances of *Tatlin's Whisper #6* in Creative Time, New York, the Hammer, LA, and Tate Britain, described as acts of solidarity.

April 2015, London

The protest is busy and the art students have of course made very good banners. Sofia Landström, a student we have taught and one of those who has been unfairly singled out, is dressed smarter than I've seen her, ready for court; she speaks passionately to the crowd.

Suddenly Caroline gathers us into a group and tells us we are *not there as* Afterall *but as individuals.*

May 2015, Havana

Catherine is confused and upset. FAC have suddenly, no warning, pulled our participation from its program. The owner is angry that Luis Manuel attended the opening night, and so we can't run the further planned screenings for 'La Primavera del Amor' in his space. He states it is nothing to do with homophobia but is about the performance happening without his permission.

May 2015, Havana

We are in Catherine's flat discussing distribution, and Reynier suggests we focus the Cuban distribution on a free ebook version of the magazine, like *VISTAR*, which describes itself as 'Cuba's first music magazine' and

---

52   Ari Akkermans, 'Artist Tania Bruguera Temporarily Detained During the Havana Biennial', *Hyperallergic*, 25 May 2015, https://hyperallergic.com/209591/artist-tania-bruguera-temporarily-detained-during-the-havana-biennial/

is distributed purely through *El Paquete*. Clicking its pages I'm surprised to see a Havana address and advert for what looks like an iPhone — has Apple arrived on the island already? On closer inspection it is for a tech repair shop.

I've seen various dog-eared copies of Condé Nast publications, things like American *Vogue*, knocking around some cafes and ask 'Are there any more gossip-like mags?'

Luis Manuel replies sharply: 'we don't have *People*'.

'I know *that*.'

The economics that influence the form and content of mass-market print magazines obviously wouldn't work in Cuba. Glossies are normally largely funded by advertising — daydream fodder: they rely on disposable incomes and luxury markets. Magazines like these celebrate decadence — their focus on the new and upcoming means they are quickly out-of-date, expensive throwaways. In London the textures of art magazines seem to have diversified since *Frieze* became better known as an art fair: think of *CURA*, *Mousse*, *Kaleidoscope*, the Italian magazines that probably aren't that cheaply produced but yet seem to gesture towards the low-fi and counter cultural — perfect bound with matt finishes.[53] The art market needs to be news, it invests in this constant commentary, and this increase in art publishing might mean more voices, and levels of irreverence, but I'm not sure what this paper-thin trickle-down offers in terms of criticality. Sometimes it's entertaining, sometimes it just feels like drowning in a heavy bulk of marketing material.

Maybe the idea of setting up a 'magazine' was always fundamentally insensitive, especially when I was arriving so empty-handed — without a funding plan. *VISTAR* is funded by advertising; it operates from the Dominican Republic, has only ever been digital, and after Cuba its widest readership — its greatest number of hits — comes from Miami.[54] I'm

---

53 The first Frieze Art Fair took place in Regents Park, London, in 2003. *CURA* was founded in Rome (2009), *Mousse* was founded in Milan (2006), as was *Kaleidoscope* (2009), which was originally free.

54 Judy Cantor-Navas, 'Cuba's First Music Magazine *Vistar* Speaks to a New Generation: Interview with Robin Pedraja', *Billboard.com*, 5 November 2015, http://www.billboard.com/articles/columns/latin/6753751/cuba-music-magazine-vistar-new-generation There is a glossy magazine called *ART OnCuba* published in Spanish and English, but this is a Miami-based publication. It started in 2013 and describes itself as the 'first Cuba-focused monthly and quarterly bilingual magazine publication with national distribution in the U.S.' It is owned by Fuego Enterprises, Inc., Miami, a 'diversified holdings company focused on business opportunities in Cuba and the

nervous about seeming to parachute in content in a similar way. I don't want to help produce another example of the neo-liberalism creeping into the island. My interest in Cuba was inspired by an nostalgic idea of different models for working together that I might find here, but — 'We don't have *People*' — Luis Manuel's irritation with me somehow seems to nail the problem with that — different perspectives and desires, completely different feelings about the proximity and distance of US culture and hegemony.

Reading back over this text I cut most of my other descriptions of Reynier and Luis Manuel. Dear London-London diary, how am I to avoid flattening my friends, making them into example of a Cuban millennial demographic? Talking about her experience with exchange projects Catherine warns 'We are always in danger of cultural colonialism'.

June 2017, London

No sign of the US trade embargo against Cuba being lifted. I receive an email from *Cuba Counterpoints* announcing their 'Open Letter to Donald Trump'. Trump is due to announce his US-Cuba policy agenda in Miami on Friday. The letter demands that he does not reverse the course set by the Obama administration and limit travel to Cuba as well as educational and scholarly exchanges.

May 2017, Melbourne

Sean Dockray comments on Facebook: 'Working on my defence is like the biggest, most consuming grant application ever'.

In some ways it feels wrong to end with this quip, a moment of semi-private speech, a wry comment to friends and colleagues with whom Sean shares the experience of arts funding bureaucracies. I'm conscious that there is little humour in the difficult situation he is now confronted with, day in day out, as he attempts to negotiate this ongoing legal battle. Yet it seems the best way to end: the situation still evolving and the act of sharing the post suggesting some remaining hopes for the potential of online connections and international solidarity.

US with operations in Media and Entertainment, Telecommunications, Travel, Real Estate and other industries.' See https://oncubanews.com/en/about-us/

Works Cited

Akkermans, Ari (25 May 2015) 'Artist Tania Bruguera Temporarily Detained during the Havana Biennial', *Hyperallergic*, https://hyperallergic.com/209591/artist-tania-bruguera-temporarily-detained-during-the-havana-biennial/

Alcántara, Luis Manuel Otero ([n.d.], ca. 2015) 'Luis Manuel Otero Alcántara Photo-documentary', *Wondereur*, Toronto, https://www.wondereur.com/artists/luis-manuel-otero-alcantara

— (2015) *Miss Bienal*.

Allen, Gwen (2011) *Artists' Magazines: An Alternative Space for Art* (Cambridge, MA: MIT Press).

Bailey, Louisa (2015) 'Sustainable Publishing', *Plastic Words* (London: Publication Studio).

Bishop, Claire (Summer 2009) 'Tania Bruguera at the 10th Havana Biennial', *Artforum*.

Bruguera, Tania (1993–1994) *Memoria de la Postguerra* (Postwar Memory).

— (2002–2009) *Cátedra Arte de Conducta* (Behaviour Art School).

— (2008) *Tatlin's Whisper* #5.

— (2009) El Susurro de Tatlin #6 [*Tatlin's Whisper* #6 (Havana Version)].

— (2014–2015) *#YoTambienExijo* (*#IAlsoDemand*).

Currie, Morgan (5 January 2010) 'Small Is Beautiful: A Discussion with AAAARG Architect Sean Dockray', *Masters of Media*, University of Amsterdam, https://mastersofmedia.hum.uva.nl/blog/2010/01/05/small-is-beautiful-a-discussion-with-aaaarg-architect-sean-dockray/

Dockray, Sean, Marysia Lewandowska and Laurel Ptak (eds.) (2013) 'Interface, Access, Loss', in *Undoing Property*? (Stockholm and Berlin: Sternberg Press & Tensta konsthall), pp. 183–94.

Drucker, Johanna (1995) *The Century of Artists' Books* (New York: Granary Books).

Fusco, Coco (1994) 'El Diario de Miranda/ Miranda's Diary', in Carol Becker (ed.), *The Subversive Imagination: The Artist, Society and Social Responsibility* (Oxford and New York: Routledge), pp. 119–34, https://doi.org/10.4324/9781315021317

— (October 2009) 'Public Address' (letters), *Artforum*, 38–40, http://www.taniabruguera.com/cms/260-0-Public+Address.htm

— (December 2014) 'The State of Detention: Performance, Politics, and the Cuban Public', *e-flux* 60, https://www.e-flux.com/journal/60/61067/the-state-of-detention-performance-politics-and-the-cuban-public

Fusco, Maria and Ian Hunt (ed.) (2004) *Put About: A Critical Anthology on Independent Publishing* (London: Book Works).

Gat, Orit (30 July 2016) 'Data Roaming', *Frieze*, https://frieze.com/article/data-roaming

Gordon-Nesbitt, Rebecca (29 January, 2015) 'Whose Side are You On?: A Response to Coco Fusco', *Mute*, http://www.metamute.org/community/your-posts/whose-side-are-you-response-to-coco-fusco-'-state-detention-performance-politics-and-cuban-public'-e-flux-3

— (2015) *To Defend the Revolution Is to Defend Culture*: *The Cultural Policy of the Cuban Revolution* (Oakland: PM Press).

Kinsella, Bridget (23 May 2011) 'Publication Studio: A Non-franchise Franchise', *Publishers Weekly*, http://publishersweekly.com/pw/by-topic/industry-news/publisher-news/article/47387-publication-studio-a-nonfranchise-franchise.html

Koebler, Jason (28 August 2015) 'Cuba's Communist Computer Clubs for Children: Photos from Beyond', *Vice Motherboard*, https://motherboard.vice.com/en_us/article/78xg8z/the-communist-computer-club-for-kids

Martinez, Nicole (11 May 2015) 'How Does Relaxing the Cuba Trade Embargo Affect Artists?', *Art Law Journal* [online journal: the article is no longer available at their website].

Mitchell, W. J. T. (Autumn/Winter 2016) 'How to Make Art with a Jackhammer: A Conversation with Tania Bruguera', *Afterall* 42, https://doi.org/10.1086/689803

Nelson, Annie (5 April 2013) 'The View from Inside Cuba's not-so-worldwide Web', *Tech President*, http://techpresident.com/news/wegov/23702/cuba-highly-restricted-internet-access-leaves-population-hungry-more

Quiles, D. R. (September 2016) 'The Vicissitudes of Conduct,' *Third Text*, http://thirdtext.org/vicissitudes-of-conduct

Ruscha, Ed (1962) *Twentysix Gasoline Stations*.

Sicot, Catherine, Aurélie Sampeur, and Candelario (23 May 2014) 'Artists at Work: Laboratorio Artístico de San Agustín', in Louise O'Hare (ed.), *Afterall Online*, https://www.afterall.org/online/artists-at-work_laboratorio-art_stico-de-san-agust_n_cuba

— (2015) 'Miss Bienal Inaugurates La Primavera del Amor: Genesis of a platform for research and intercultural artistic production in Cuba', June 2014–2015', *Public* 26.52, 59–67, https://doi.org/10.1386/public.26.52.59_1

Uriarte, Miren (2002) 'The Right Priorities: Health, Education and Literacy', in her *CUBA*: *Social Policy at the Crossroads*: *Maintaining Priorities, Transforming Practice. An Oxfam America Report*, https://www.oxfamamerica.org/publications/cuba-social-policy-at-the-crossroads/

Zurowski, Maciej (13 January 2011) 'More Glasnost, Less Perestroika: Interview with *Havana Times* Editor Circles Robinson', *Weekly Worker* 848, http://weeklyworker.co.uk/worker/848/more-glasnost-less-perestroika/

3. The Ethics of Emergent Creativity: Can We Move Beyond Writing as Human Enterprise, Commodity and Innovation?

Janneke Adema

In 2013, the Authors' Licensing & Collecting Society (ALCS)[1] commissioned a survey of its members to explore writers' earnings and contractual issues in the UK. The survey, the results of which were published in the summary booklet 'What Are Words Worth Now?', was carried out by Queen Mary, University of London. Almost 2,500 writers — from literary authors to academics and screenwriters — responded. 'What Are Words Worth Now?' summarises the findings of a larger study titled 'The Business Of Being An Author: A Survey Of Authors' Earnings And Contracts', carried out by Johanna Gibson, Phillip Johnson and Gaetano Dimita and published in April 2015 by Queen Mary University of London.[2] The ALCS press release that accompanies the study states that this 'shocking' new research into authors' earnings finds a 'dramatic fall, both in incomes, and the number of those working full-time as writers'.[3] Indeed, two of the main findings

---

1. The Authors' Licensing and Collecting Society is a British membership organisation for writers, established in 1977 with over 87,000 members, focused on protecting and promoting authors' rights. ALCS collects and pays out money due to members for secondary uses of their work (copying, broadcasting, recording etc.).
2. This survey was an update of an earlier survey conducted in 2006 by the Centre of Intellectual Property Policy and Management (CIPPM) at Bournemouth University.
3. 'New Research into Authors' Earnings Released', *Authors' Licensing and Collecting Society*, 2014, https://web.archive.org/web/20160504001652/http://www.alcs.co.uk/About-Us/News/News/What-are-words-worth-now-not-much.aspx

of the study are that, first of all, the income of a professional author (which the research defines as those who dedicate the majority of their time to writing) has dropped 29% between 2005 and 2013, from £12,330 (£15,450 in real terms) to just £11,000. Furthermore, the research found that in 2005 40% of professional authors earned their incomes solely from writing, where in 2013 this figure had dropped to just 11.5%.[4]

It seems that one of the primary reasons for the ALCS to conduct this survey was to collect 'accurate, independent data' on writers' earnings and contractual issues, in order for the ALCS to 'make the case for authors' rights' — at least, that is what the ALCS Chief Executive Owen Atkinson writes in the introduction accompanying the survey, which was sent out to all ALCS members.[5] Yet although this research was conducted independently and the researchers did not draw conclusions based on the data collected — in the form of policy recommendations for example — the ALCS did frame the data and findings in a very specific way, as I will outline in what follows; this framing includes both the introduction to the survey and the press release that accompanies the survey's findings. Yet to some extent this framing, as I will argue, is already apparent in the methodology used to produce the data underlying the research report.

First of all, let me provide an example of how the research findings have been framed in a specific way. Chief Executive Atkinson mentions in his introduction to the survey that the ALCS 'exists to ensure that writers are treated fairly and remunerated appropriately'. He continues that the ALCS commissioned the survey to collect 'accurate, independent data,' in order to 'make the case for writers' rights'.[6] Now this focus on rights in combination with remuneration is all the more noteworthy if we look at an earlier ALCS funded report from 2007, 'Authors' Earnings from Copyright and Non-Copyright Sources: a Survey of 25,000 British and German Writers'. This report is based on the findings of a 2006 writers' survey, which the 2013 survey updates. The 2007 report argues conclusively that current copyright law has empirically failed

---

4   Johanna Gibson, Phillip Johnson, and Gaetano Dimita, *The Business of Being an Author: A Survey of Author's Earnings and Contracts* (London: Queen Mary University of London, 2015), p. 9, https://orca.cf.ac.uk/72431/1/Final Report - For Web Publication.pdf

5   ALCS, *Press Release. What Are Words Worth Now? Not Enough*, 8 July 2014, https://www.alcs.co.uk/news/what-are-words-worth-now-not-enough

6   Gibson, Johnson, and Dimita, *The Business of Being an Author*, p. 35.

to ensure that authors receive appropriate reward or remuneration for the use of their work.⁷ The data from the subsequent 2013 survey show an even bleaker picture as regards the earnings of writers. Yet Atkinson argues in the press release accompanying the findings of the 2013 survey that 'if writers are to continue making their irreplaceable contribution to the UK economy, they need to be paid fairly for their work. This means ensuring clear, fair contracts with equitable terms and a copyright regime that support creators and their ability to earn a living from their creations'.⁸ Atkinson does not outline what this copyright regime should be, nor does he draw attention to how this model could be improved. More importantly, the fact that *a copyright model is needed* to ensure fair pay stands uncontested for Atkinson and the ALCS — not surprising perhaps, as protecting and promoting the rights of authors is the primary mission of this member society. If there is any culprit to be held responsible for the study's 'shocking' findings, it is the elusive and further undefined notion of 'the digital'. According to Atkinson, digital technology is increasingly challenging the mission of the ALCS to ensure fair remuneration for writers, since it is 'driving new markets and leading the copyright debate'.⁹ The 2013 study is therefore, as Atkinson states 'the first to capture the impact of the digital revolution on writers' working lives'.¹⁰ This statement is all the more striking if we take into consideration that none of the questions in the 2013 survey focus specifically on digital publishing.¹¹ It therefore seems

---

7   M. Kretschmer and P. Hardwick, *Authors' Earnings from Copyright and Non-Copyright Sources: A Survey of 25,000 British and German Writers* (Poole: CIPPM/ALCS Bournemouth University, 2007), p. 3, https://microsites.bournemouth.ac.uk/cippm/files/2007/07/ALCS-Full-report.pdf

8   ALCS, *Press Release*, 8 July 2014, https://www.alcs.co.uk/news/what-are-words-worth-now-not-enough

9   Gibson, Johnson, and Dimita, *The Business of Being an Author*, p. 35.

10 Ibid.

11 In the survey, three questions that focus on various sources of remuneration do list digital publishing and/or online uses as an option (questions 8, 11, and 15). Yet the data tables provided in the appendix to the report do not provide the findings for questions 11 and 15 nor do they differentiate according to type of media for other tables related to remuneration. The only data table we find in the report related to digital publishing is table 3.3, which lists 'Earnings ranked (1 to 7) in relation to categories of work', where digital publishing ranks third after books and magazines/periodicals, but before newspapers, audio/audio-visual productions and theatre. This lack of focus on the effect of digital publishing on writers' incomes, for a survey that is 'the first to capture the impact of the digital revolution on writers' working lives', is quite remarkable. Gibson, Johnson, and Dimita, *The Business of Being an Author*, Appendix 2.

that — despite earlier findings — the ALCS has already decided in advance what 'the digital' is and that a copyright regime is the only way to ensure fair remuneration for writers in a digital context.

Creative Industries

This strong uncontested link between copyright and remuneration can be traced back to various other aspects of the 2015 report and its release. For example, the press release draws a strong connection between the findings of the report and the development of the creative industries in the UK. Again, Atkinson states in the press release:

> These are concerning times for writers. This rapid decline in both author incomes and in the numbers of those writing full-time could have serious implications for the economic success of the creative industries in the UK.[12]

This connection to the creative industries — 'which are now worth £71.4 billion per year to the UK economy',[13] Atkinson points out — is not surprising where the discourse around creative industries maintains a clear bond between intellectual property rights and creative labour. As Geert Lovink and Ned Rossiter state in their *MyCreativity Reader*, the creative industries consist of 'the generation and exploitation of intellectual property'.[14] Here they refer to a definition created as part of the UK Government's Creative Industries Mapping Document,[15] which states that the creative industries are 'those industries which have their origin in individual creativity, skill and talent and which have a potential for wealth and job creation through the generation and exploitation of intellectual property'. Lovink and Rossiter point out that the relationship between IP and creative labour lies at the basis of the definition of the creative industries where, as they argue, this model of creativity assumes people only create to produce economic value. This is part of a larger

---

12　Ibid., p. 35.
13　Ibid.
14　Geert Lovink and Ned Rossiter (eds.), *MyCreativity Reader: A Critique of Creative Industries* (Amsterdam: Institute of Network Cultures, 2007), p. 14, http://www.networkcultures.org/_uploads/32.pdf
15　See: https://www.gov.uk/government/publications/creative-industries-economic-estimates-january-2015/creative-industries-economic-estimates-january-2015-key-findings

trend Wendy Brown has described as being quintessentially neoliberal, where 'neoliberal rationality disseminates the model of the market to all domains and activities' — and this includes the realm of politics and rights.[16] In this sense the economization of culture and the concept of creativity is something that has become increasingly embedded and naturalised. The exploitation of intellectual property stands at the basis of the creative industries model, in which cultural value — which can be seen as intricate, complex and manifold — becomes subordinated to the model of the market; it becomes economic value.[17]

This direct association of cultural value and creativity with economic value is apparent in various other facets of the ALCS commissioned research and report. Obviously, the title of the initial summary booklet, as a form of wordplay, asks 'What are words worth?'. It becomes clear from the context of the survey that the 'worth' of words will only be measured in a monetary sense, i.e. as economic value. Perhaps even more important to understand in this context, however, is how this economic worth of words is measured and determined by focusing on two fixed and predetermined entities in advance. First of all, the study focuses on individual human agents of creativity (i.e. creators contributing economic value): the value of writing is established by collecting data and making measurements at the level of individual authorship, addressing authors/writers as singular individuals throughout the survey. Secondly, economic worth is further determined by focusing on the fixed and stable creative objects authors produce, in other words the study establishes from the outset a clear link between the worth and value of writing and economic remuneration based on individual works of writing.[18] Therefore in this process of determining the economic worth of words, 'writers' and/or 'authors' are described and positioned in a certain way in this study (i.e. as the central agents and originators of creative objects), as is the form their creativity takes in the shape of quantifiable outputs or commodities. The value of both these units of measurement (the creator

---

16   Wendy Brown, *Undoing the Demos: Neoliberalism's Stealth Revolution* (Cambridge, MA: MIT Press, 2015), p. 31.
17   Therefore Lovink and Rossiter make a plea to, 'redefine creative industries outside of IP generation'. Lovink and Rossiter, *MyCreativity Reader*, p. 14.
18   Next to earnings made from writing more in general, the survey on various occasions asks questions about earnings arising from specific categories of works and related to the amount of works exploited (published/broadcast) during certain periods. Gibson, Johnson, and Dimita, *The Business of Being an Author*, Appendix 2.

and the creative objects) are then set off against the growth of the creative industries in the press release.

The ALCS commissioned survey provides some important insights into how authorship, cultural works and remuneration — and ultimately, creativity — is currently valued, specifically in the context of the creative industries discourse in the UK. What I have tried to point out — without wanting to downplay the importance either of writers receiving fair remuneration for their work or of issues related to the sustainability of creative processes — is that the findings from this survey have both been extracted and subsequently framed based on a very specific economic model of creativity (and authorship). According to this model, writing and creativity are sustained most clearly by an individual original creator (an author) who extracts value from the work s/he creates and distributes, aided by an intellectual property rights regime. As I will outline more in depth in what follows, the enduring liberal and humanist presumptions that underlie this survey continuously reinforce the links between the value of writing and established IP and remuneration regimes, and support a vision in which authorship and creativity are dependent on economic incentives and ownership of works. By working within this framework and with these predetermined concepts of authorship and creativity (and 'the digital') the ALCS is strongly committed to the upkeep of a specific model and discourse of creativity connected to the creative industries. The ALCS does not attempt to complicate this model, nor does it search for alternatives even when, as the 2007 report already implies, the existing IP model has empirically failed to support the remuneration of writers appropriately.

I want to use this ALCS survey as a reference point to start problematising existing constructions of creativity, authorship, ownership, and sustainability in relation to the ethics of publishing. To explore what 'words are worth' and to challenge the hegemonic liberal humanist model of creativity — to which the ALCS adheres — I will examine a selection of theoretical and practical publishing and writing alternatives, from relational and posthuman authorship to radical open access and uncreative writing. These alternatives do not deny the importance of fair remuneration and sustainability for the creative process; however, they want to foreground and explore creative relationalities that move beyond the individual author and her ownership of creative objects as the only model to support creativity and cultural exchange. By looking at alternatives while at the same time complicating the values and assumptions underlying the dominant narrative for IP expansion, I want to start imagining what more ethical, fair and emergent forms of creativity might entail. Forms that take into consideration the various distributed and entangled agencies involved in the creation of cultural content — which are presently not being included in the ALCS survey on fair remuneration, for example. As I will argue, a reconsideration of the liberal and humanist model of creativity might actually create new possibilities to consider the value of words, and with that perhaps new solutions to the problems pointed out in the ALCS study.

Relational and Distributed Authorship

One of the main critiques of the liberal humanist model of authorship concerns how it privileges the author as the sole source and origin of creativity. Yet the argument has been made, both from a historical perspective and in relation to today's networked digital environment, that authorship and creativity, and with that the value and worth of that creativity, are heavily distributed.[19] Should we therefore think about how we can distribute notions of authorship and creativity more ethically when defining the worth and value of words too? Would this perhaps mean a more thorough investigation of what and who the specific agencies involved in creative production are? This seems all the more important given that, today, 'the value of words' is arguably connected not to (distributed) authors or creative agencies, but to rights holders (or their intermediaries such as agents).[20] From this perspective, the problem

---

19 Roger Chartier, *The Order of Books: Readers, Authors, and Libraries in Europe Between the 14th and 18th Centuries*, 1st ed. (Stanford: Stanford University Press, 1994); Lisa Ede and Andrea A. Lunsford, 'Collaboration and Concepts of Authorship', *PMLA* 116.2 (2001), 354–69; Adrian Johns, *The Nature of the Book: Print and Knowledge in the Making* (Chicago, IL: University of Chicago Press, 1998); Jerome J. McGann, *A Critique of Modern Textual Criticism* (Charlottesville, VA, University of Virginia Press, 1992); Sarah Robbins, 'Distributed Authorship: A Feminist Case-Study Framework for Studying Intellectual Property', *College English* 66.2 (2003), 155–71, https://doi.org/10.2307/3594264

20 The ALCS survey addresses this problem, of course, and tries to lobby on behalf of its authors for fair contracts with publishers and intermediaries. That said,

with the copyright model as it currently functions is that the creators of copyright don't necessarily end up benefiting from it — a point that was also implied by the authors of the 2007 ALCS commissioned report. Copyright benefits rights holders, and rights holders are not necessarily, and often not at all, involved in the production of creative work.

Yet copyright and the work as object are knit tightly to the authorship construct. In this respect, the above criticism notwithstanding, in a liberal vision of creativity and ownership the typical unit remains either the author or the work. This 'solid and fundamental unit of the author and the work' as Foucault has qualified it, albeit challenged, still retains a privileged position.[21] As Mark Rose argues, authorship — as a relatively recent cultural formation — can be directly connected to the commodification of writing and to proprietorship. Even more it developed in tandem with the societal principle of *possessive individualism*, in which individual property rights are protected by the social order.[22]

Some of the more interesting recent critiques of these constructs of authorship and proprietorship have come from critical and feminist legal studies, where scholars such as Carys Craig have started to question these connections further. As Craig, Turcotte and Coombe argue, IP and copyright are premised on liberal and neoliberal assumptions and constructs, such as ownership, private rights, self-interest and individualism.[23] In this sense copyright, authorship, the work as object, and related discourses around creativity continuously re-establish and strengthen each other as part of a self-sustaining system. We have seen this with the discourse around creative industries, as part of which economic value comes to stand in for the creative process itself, which, according to this narrative, can only be sustained through an IP regime. Furthermore, from a feminist new materialist position, the current discourse on creativity is very much a

---

the survey findings show that only 42% of writers always retain their copyright. Gibson, Johnson, and Dimita, *The Business of Being an Author*, p. 12.

21   Michel Foucault, 'What Is an Author?', in James D. Faubion (ed.), *Essential Works of Foucault, 1954–1984, Volume Two: Aesthetics, Method, and Epistemology* (New York: The New Press, 1998), p. 205.

22   Mark Rose, *Authors and Owners: The Invention of Copyright* (Cambridge, MA: Harvard University Press, 1993).

23   Carys J. Craig, Joseph F. Turcotte, and Rosemary J. Coombe, 'What's Feminist About Open Access? A Relational Approach to Copyright in the Academy', *Feminists@law* 1.1 (2011), http://journals.kent.ac.uk/index.php/feministsatlaw/article/view/7

material expression of creativity rather than merely its representation, where this discourse has been classifying, constructing, and situating creativity (and with that, authorship) within a neoliberal framework of creative industries.

Moving away from an individual construct of creativity therefore immediately affects the question of the value of words. In our current copyright model emphasis lies on the individual original author, but in a more distributed vision the value of words and of creative production can be connected to a broader context of creative agencies. Historically there has been a great discursive shift from a valuing of imitation or derivation to a valuing of originality in determining what counts as creativity or creative output. Similar to Rose, Craig, Turcotte and Coombe argue that the individuality and originality of authorship in its modern form established a simple route towards individual ownership and the propertisation of creative achievement: the original work is the author's ownership whereas the imitator or pirate is a trespasser of thief. In this sense original authorship is 'disproportionately valued against other forms of cultural expression and creative play', where copyright upholds, maintains and strengthens the binary between imitator and creator — defined by Craig, Turcotte and Coombe as a 'moral divide'.[24] This also presupposes a notion of creativity that sees individuals as autonomous, living in isolation from each other, ignoring their relationality. Yet as Craig, Turcotte and Coombe argue, 'the act of writing involves not origination, but rather the adaptation, derivation, translation and recombination of "raw material" taken from previously existing texts'.[25] This position has also been explored extensively from within remix studies and fan culture, where the adaptation and remixing of cultural content stands at the basis of creativity (what Lawrence Lessig has called Read/Write culture, opposed to Read/Only culture).[26] From the perspective of access to culture — instead of ownership of cultural goods or objects — one could also argue that its value would

---

24   Ibid., p. 8.
25   Ibid., p. 9.
26   Lawrence Lessig, *Remix: Making Art and Commerce Thrive in the Hybrid Economy* (New York: Penguin Press, 2008); Eduardo Navas, *Remix Theory: The Aesthetics of Sampling* (Vienna and New York: Springer, 2012); Henry Jenkins and Owen Gallagher, '"What Is Remix Culture?": An Interview with Total Recut's Owen Gallagher', *Confessions of an Aca-Fan*, 2008, http://henryjenkins.org/2008/06/interview_with_total_remixs_ow.html

increase when we are able to freely distribute it and with that to adapt and remix it to create new cultural content and with that cultural and social value — this within a context in which, as Craig, Turcotte and Coombe point out, 'the continuous expansion of intellectual property rights has produced legal regimes that restrict access and downstream use of information resources far beyond what is required to encourage their creation'.[27]

To move beyond Enlightenment ideals of individuation, detachment and unity of author and work, which determine the author-owner in the copyright model, Craig puts forward a post-structuralist vision of *relational* authorship. This sees the individual as socially situated and constituted — based also on feminist scholarship into the socially situated self — where authorship in this vision is situated within the communities in which it exists, but also in relation to the texts and discourses that constitute it. Here creativity takes place from within a network of social relations and the social dimensions of authorship are recognised, as connectivity goes hand in hand with individual autonomy. Craig argues that copyright should not be defined out of clashing rights and interests but should instead focus on the kinds of relationships this right would structure; it should be understood in relational terms: 'it structures relationships between authors and users, allocating powers and responsibilities amongst members of cultural communities, and establishing the rules of communication and exchange'.[28] Cultural value is then defined within these relationships.

Open Access and the Ethics of Care

Craig, Turcotte and Coombe draw a clear connection between relational authorship, feminism and (the ideals of) the open access movement, where as they state, 'rather than adhering to the individuated form of authorship that intellectual property laws presuppose, open access initiatives take into account varying forms of collaboration, creativity and development'.[29] Yet as I and others have argued elsewhere,[30] open

---

27 Craig, Turcotte, and Coombe, 'What's Feminist About Open Access?, p. 27.
28 Ibid., p. 14.
29 Ibid., p. 26.
30 Janneke Adema, 'Open Access', in *Critical Keywords for the Digital Humanities* (Lueneburg: Centre for Digital Cultures (CDC), 2014), https://meson.press/keywords/; Janneke Adema, 'Embracing Messiness', *LSE Impact of Social Sciences*, 2014,

access or open access publishing is not a solid ideological block or model; it is made up of disparate groups, visions and ethics. In this sense there is nothing intrinsically political or democratic about open access, practitioners of open access can just as well be seen to support and encourage open access in connection with the neoliberal knowledge economy, with possessive individualism — even with CC licenses, which can be seen as strengthening individualism —[31] and with the unity of author and work.[32]

Nevertheless, there are those within the loosely defined and connected 'radical open access community', that do envision their publishing outlook and relationship towards copyright, openness and authorship within and as part of a relational ethics of care.[33] For example Mattering Press, a scholar-led open access book publishing initiative

---

http://blogs.lse.ac.uk/impactofsocialsciences/2014/11/18/embracing-messiness-adema-pdsc14/; Gary Hall, *Digitize This Book!: The Politics of New Media, or Why We Need Open Access Now* (Minneapolis, MN: University of Minnesota Press, 2008), p. 197; Sarah Kember, 'Why Write?: Feminism, Publishing and the Politics of Communication', *New Formations: A Journal of Culture/Theory/Politics* 83.1 (2014), 99–116; Samuel A. Moore, 'A Genealogy of Open Access: Negotiations between Openness and Access to Research', *Revue Française des Sciences de l'information et de la Communication*, 2017, https://doi.org/10.4000/rfsic.3220

31 Florian Cramer, *Anti-Media: Ephemera on Speculative Arts* (Rotterdam and New York: nai010 publishers, 2013).

32 Especially within humanities publishing there is a reluctance to allow derivative uses of one's work in an open access setting.

33 In 2015 the *Radical Open Access Conference* took place at Coventry University, which brought together a large array of presses and publishing initiatives (often academic-led) in support of an 'alternative' vision of open access and scholarly communication. Participants in this conference subsequently formed the loosely allied Radical Open Access Collective: radicaloa.co.uk. As the conference concept outlines, radical open access entails 'a vision of open access that is characterised by a spirit of on-going creative experimentation, and a willingness to subject some of our most established scholarly communication and publishing practices, together with the institutions that sustain them (the library, publishing house etc.), to rigorous critique. Included in the latter will be the asking of important questions about our notions of authorship, authority, originality, quality, credibility, sustainability, intellectual property, fixity and the book — questions that lie at the heart of what scholarship is and what the university can be in the 21st century'. Janneke Adema and Gary Hall, 'The Political Nature of the Book: On Artists' Books and Radical Open Access', *New Formations* 78.1 (2013), 138–56, https://doi.org/10.3898/NewF.78.07.2013; Janneke Adema and Samuel Moore, 'Collectivity and Collaboration: Imagining New Forms of Communality to Create Resilience In Scholar-Led Publishing', *Insights* 31.3 (2018), https://doi.org/10.1629/uksg.399; Gary Hall, 'Radical Open Access in the Humanities' (presented at the Research Without Borders, Columbia University, 2010), http://scholcomm.columbia.edu/2011/01/18/radical-open-access-in-the-humanities/; Janneke Adema, 'Knowledge Production Beyond The Book? Performing the Scholarly Monograph in Contemporary Digital

founded in 2012 and launched in 2016, publishes in the field of Science and Technology Studies (STS) and works with a production model based on cooperation and shared scholarship. As part of its publishing politics, ethos and ideology, Mattering Press is therefore keen to include various agencies involved in the production of scholarship, including 'authors, reviewers, editors, copy editors, proof readers, typesetters, distributors, designers, web developers and readers'.[34] They work with two interrelated feminist (new materialist) and STS concepts to structure and perform this ethos: *mattering*[35] and *care*.[36] Where it concerns *mattering*, Mattering Press is conscious of how their experiment in knowledge production, being inherently situated, puts new relationships and configurations into the world. What therefore *matters* for them are not so much the 'author' or the 'outcome' (the object), but the process and the relationships that make up publishing:

> [...] the way academic texts are produced <u>matters</u> — both analytically and politically. Dominant publishing practices work with assumptions about the conditions of academic knowledge production that rarely reflect what goes on in laboratories, field sites, university offices, libraries, and various workshops and conferences. They tend to deal with almost complete manuscripts and a small number of authors, who are greatly dependent on the politics of the publishing industry.[37]

For Mattering Press *care* is something that extends not only to authors but to the many other actants involved in knowledge production, who often provide free volunteer labour within a gift economy context. As Mattering Press emphasises, the ethics of care 'mark vital relations and practices whose value cannot be calculated and thus often goes unacknowledged where logics of calculation are dominant'.[38] For

---

Culture' (PhD dissertation, Coventry University, 2015), https://curve.coventry.ac.uk/open/file/8222ccb2-f6b0-4e5f-90de-f4c62c77ac86/1/ademacomb.pdf

34 Julien McHardy, 'Why Books Matter: There Is Value in What Cannot Be Evaluated', *Impact of Social Sciences*, 2014, n.p., http://blogs.lse.ac.uk/impactofsocialsciences/2014/09/30/why-books-matter/

35 Karen Barad, *Meeting the Universe Halfway: Quantum Physics and the Entanglement of Matter and Meaning* (Durham, N.C. and London: Duke University Press, 2007).

36 Annemarie Mol, *The Logic of Care: Health and the Problem of Patient Choice*, 1st ed. (London and New York: Routledge, 2008).

37 Sebastian Abrahamsson and others, 'Mattering Press: New Forms of Care for STS Books', *The EASST Review* 32.4 (2013), http://easst.net/easst-review-volume-32-4-december-2013/mattering-press-new-forms-of-care-for-sts-books/

38 McHardy, 'Why Books Matter'.

Mattering Press, care can help offset and engage with the calculative logic that permeates academic publishing:

> […] the concept of care can help to engage with calculative logics, such as those of costs, without granting them dominance. How do we calculate so that calculations do not dominate our considerations? What would it be to care for rather than to calculate the cost of a book? This is but one and arguably a relatively conservative strategy for allowing other logics than those of calculation to take centre stage in publishing.[39]

This logic of care refers, in part, to making visible the 'unseen others' as Joe Deville (one of Mattering Press's editors) calls them, who exemplify the plethora of hidden labour that goes unnoticed within this object and author-focused (academic) publishing model. As Endre Danyi, another Mattering Press editor, remarks, quoting Susan Leigh Star: 'This is, in the end, a profoundly political process, since so many forms of social control rely on the erasure or silencing of various workers, on deleting their work from representations of the work'.[40]

Posthuman Authorship

Authorship is also being reconsidered as a polyvocal and collaborative endeavour by reflecting on the agentic role of technology in authoring

---

39 Ibid.
40 Susan Leigh Star, 'The Sociology of the Invisible: The Primacy of Work in the Writings of Anselm Strauss', in Anselm Leonard Strauss and David R. Maines (eds.), *Social Organization and Social Process: Essays in Honor of Anselm Strauss* (New York: A. de Gruyter, 1991). Mattering Press is not alone in exploring an ethics of care in relation to (academic) publishing. Sarah Kember, director of Goldsmiths Press is also adamant in her desire to make the underlying processes of publishing (i.e. peer review, citation practices) more transparent and accountable Sarah Kember, 'Why Publish?', *Learned Publishing* 29 (2016), 348–53, https://doi.org/10.1002/leap.1042. Mercedes Bunz, one of the editors running Meson Press, argues that a sociology of the invisible would incorporate 'infrastructure work', the work of accounting for, and literally crediting everybody involved in producing a book: 'A book isn't just a product that starts a dialogue between author and reader. It is accompanied by lots of other academic conversations — peer review, co-authors, copy editors — and these conversations deserve to be taken more serious'. Jussi Parikka and Mercedes Bunz, 'A Mini-Interview: Mercedes Bunz Explains Meson Press', *Machinology*, 2014, https://jussiparikka.net/2014/07/11/a-mini-interview-mercedes-bunz-explains-meson-press/. For Open Humanities Press authorship is collaborative and even often anonymous: for example, they are experimenting with research published in wikis to further complicate the focus on single authorship and a static marketable book object within academia (see their living and liquid books series).

content. Within digital literature, hypertext and computer-generated poetry, media studies scholars have explored the role played by technology and the materiality of text in the creation process, where in many ways writing can be seen as a shared act between reader, writer and computer. Lori Emerson emphasises that machines, media or technology are not neutral in this respect, which complicates the idea of human subjectivity. Emerson explores this through the notion of 'cyborg authorship', which examines the relation between machine and human with a focus on the potentiality of in-betweenness.[41] Dani Spinosa talks about 'collaboration with an external force (the computer, MacProse, technology in general)'.[42] Extending from the author, the text itself, and the reader as meaning-writer (and hence playing a part in the author function), technology, she states, is a fourth term in this collaborative meaning-making. As Spinosa argues, in computer-generated texts the computer is more than a technological tool and becomes a co-producer, where it can occur that 'the poet herself merges with the machine in order to place her own subjectivity in flux'.[43] Emerson calls this a 'break from the model of the poet/writer as divinely inspired human exemplar', which is exemplified for her in hypertext, computer-generated poetry, and digital poetry.[44]

Yet in many ways, as Emerson and Spinosa also note, these forms of posthuman authorship should be seen as part of a larger trend, what Rolf Hughes calls an 'anti-authorship' tradition focused on auto-poesis (self-making), generative systems and automatic writing. As Hughes argues, we see this tradition in print forms such as Oulipo and in Dada experiments and surrealist games too.[45] But there are connections here with broader theories that focus on distributed agency too, especially where it concerns the influence of the materiality of the text. Media theorists such as N. Katherine Hayles and Johanna Drucker have

---

41 Lori Emerson, 'Digital Poetry as Reflexive Embodiment', in Markku Eskelinen, Raine Koskimaa, Loss Pequeño Glazier and John Cayley (eds.), *CyberText Yearbook 2002–2003*, 2003, 88–106, http://cybertext.hum.jyu.fi/index.php?browsebook=2
42 Dani Spinosa, '"My Line (Article) Has Sighed": Authorial Subjectivity and Technology', *Generic Pronoun*, 2014, https://genericpronoun.com/2014/05/14/my-line-article-has-sighed/
43 Spinosa, 'My Line (Article) Has Sighed'.
44 Emerson, 'Digital Poetry as Reflexive Embodiment', p. 89.
45 Rolf Hughes, 'Orderly Disorder: Post-Human Creativity', in *Proceedings of the Linköping Electronic Conference* (Linköpings universitet: University Electronic Press, 2005).

extensively argued that the materiality of the page is entangled with the intentionality of the author as a further agency; Drucker conceptualises this through a focus on 'conditional texts' and 'performative materiality' with respect to the agency of the material medium (be it the printed page or the digital screen).[46]

Where, however, does the redistribution of value creation end in these narratives? As Nick Montfort states with respect to the agency of technology, 'should other important and inspirational mechanisms — my CD player, for instance, and my bookshelves — get cut in on the action as well?'[47] These distributed forms of authorship do not solve issues related to authorship or remuneration but further complicate them. Nevertheless Montfort is interested in describing the processes involved in these types of (posthuman) co-authorship, to explore the (previously unexplored) relationships and processes involved in the authoring of texts more clearly. As he states, this 'can help us understand the role of the different participants more fully'.[48] In this respect a focus on posthuman authorship and on the various distributed agencies that play a part in creative processes is not only a means to disrupt the hegemonic focus on a romantic single and original authorship model, but it is also about a sensibility to (machinic) co-authorship, to the different agencies involved in the creation of art, and playing a role in creativity itself. As Emerson remarks in this respect: 'we must be wary of granting a (romantic) specialness to human intentionality — after all, the point of dividing the responsibility for the creation of the poems between human and machine is to disrupt the singularity of human identity, to force human identity to intermingle with machine identity'.[49]

---

46 N. Katherine Hayles, 'Print Is Flat, Code Is Deep: The Importance of Media-Specific Analysis', *Poetics Today* 25.1 (2004), 67–90, https://doi.org/10.1215/03335372-25-1-67; Johanna Drucker, 'Performative Materiality and Theoretical Approaches to Interface', *Digital Humanities Quarterly* 7.1 (2013), http://www.digitalhumanities.org/dhq/vol/7/1/000143/000143.html; Johanna Drucker, 'Distributed and Conditional Documents: Conceptualizing Bibliographical Alterities', *MATLIT: Revista do Programa de Doutoramento em Materialidades da Literatura* 2.1 (2014), 11–29.

47 Nick Montfort, 'The Coding and Execution of the Author', in Markku Eskelinen, Raine Kosimaa, Loss Pequeño Glazier and John Cayley (eds.), *CyberText Yearbook 2002–2003*, 2003, 201–17 (p. 201), http://cybertext.hum.jyu.fi/index.php?browsebook=2

48 Montfort, 'The Coding and Execution of the Author', p. 202.

49 Lori Emerson, 'Materiality, Intentionality, and the Computer-Generated Poem: Reading Walter Benn Michaels with Erin Moureacute's Pillage Land', *ESC: English*

Emergent Creativity

This more relational notion of rights and the wider appreciation of the various (posthuman) agencies involved in creative processes based on an ethics of care, challenges the vision of the single individualised and original author/owner who stands at the basis of our copyright and IP regime — a vision that, it is worth emphasising, can be seen as a historical (and Western) anomaly, where collaborative, anonymous, and more polyvocal models of authorship have historically prevailed.[50] The other side of the Foucauldian double bind, i.e. the fixed cultural object that functions as a commodity, has however been similarly critiqued from several angles. As stated before, and as also apparent from the way the ALCS report has been framed, currently our copyright and remuneration regime is based on ownership of cultural objects. Yet as many have already made clear, this regime and discourse is very much based on physical objects and on a print-based context.[51] As such the idea of 'text' (be it print or digital) has not been sufficiently problematised as versioned, processual and materially changing within an IP context. In other words, text and works are mostly perceived as fixed and stable objects and commodities instead of material and creative processes and entangled relationalities. As Craig et al. state, 'the copyright system is unfortunately employed to reinforce the norms of the analog world'.[52] In contrast to a more relational perspective, the current copyright regime views culture through a proprietary lens. And it is very much this discursive positioning, or as Craig et al. argue 'the language of "ownership," "property," and "commodity"', which 'obfuscates the nature of copyright's subject matter, and cloaks the social and cultural conditions of its production and the implications of its protection'.[53] How can we approach creativity in context, as socially and culturally situated, and not as the free-standing, stable product of a transcendent

---

  Studies in Canada 34 (2008), 66.
50 Marcus Boon, *In Praise of Copying* (Cambridge, MA: Harvard University Press, 2010); Johanna Drucker, 'Humanist Computing at the End of the Individual Voice and the Authoritative Text', in Patrik Svensson and David Theo Goldberg (eds.), *Between Humanities and the Digital* (Cambridge, MA: MIT Press, 2015), pp. 83–94.
51 We have to take into consideration here that print-based cultural products were never fixed or static; the dominant discourses constructed around them just perceive them to be so.
52 Craig, Turcotte, and Coombe, 'What's Feminist About Open Access?', p. 2.
53 Ibid.

author, which is very much how it is being positioned within an economic and copyright framework? This hegemonic conception of creativity as property fails to acknowledge or take into consideration the manifold, distributed, derivative and messy realities of culture and creativity.

It is therefore important to put forward and promote another more *emergent* vision of creativity, where creativity is seen as both processual and only ever temporarily fixed, and where the work itself is seen as being the product of a variety of (posthuman) agencies. Interestingly, someone who has written very elaborately about a different form of creativity relevant to this context is one of the authors of the ALCS commissioned report, Johanna Gibson. Similar to Craig, who focuses on the relationality of copyright, Gibson wants to pay more attention to the networking of creativity, moving it beyond a focus on traditional models of producers and consumers in exchange for a 'many-to-many' model of creativity. For Gibson, IP as a system aligns with a corporate model of creativity, one which oversimplifies what it means to be creative and measures it against economic parameters alone.[54] In many ways in policy driven visions, IP has come to stand in for the creative process itself, Gibson argues, and is assimilated within corporate models of innovation. It has thus become a synonym for creativity, as we have seen in the creative industries discourse. As Gibson explains, this simplified model of creativity is very much a 'discursive strategy' in which the creator is mythologised and output comes in the form of commodified objects.[55] In this sense we need to re-appropriate creativity as an inherently fluid and uncertain concept and practice.

Yet this mimicry of creativity by IP and innovation at the same time means that any re-appropriation of creativity from the stance of access and reuse is targeted as anti-IP and thus as standing outside of formal creativity. Other, more emergent forms of creativity have trouble existing within this self-defining and sustaining hegemonic system. This is similar to what Craig remarked with respect to remixed, counterfeit and pirated, and un-original works, which are seen as standing outside the system. Gibson uses actor network theory (ANT)

---

54 Johanna Gibson, *Creating Selves: Intellectual Property and the Narration of Culture* (Aldershot, UK, and Burlington: Routledge, 2007), p. 7.
55 Gibson, *Creating Selves*, p. 7.

as a framework to construct her network-based model of creativity, where for her ANT allows for a vision that does not fix creativity *within* a product, but focuses more on the material relationships and interactions between users and producers. In this sense, she argues, a network model allows for plural agencies to be attributed to creativity, including those of users.[56]

An interesting example of how the hegemonic object-based discourse of creativity can be re-appropriated comes from the conceptual poet Kenneth Goldsmith, who, in what could be seen as a direct response to this dominant narrative, tries to emphasise that exactly what this discourse classifies as 'uncreative', should be seen as *valuable in itself*. Goldsmith points out that appropriating is creative and that he uses it as a pedagogical method in his classes on 'Uncreative Writing' (which he defines as 'the art of managing information and representing it as writing'[57]). Here 'uncreative writing' is something to strive for and stealing, copying, and patchwriting are elevated as important and valuable tools for writing. For Goldsmith the digital environment has fostered new skills and notions of writing beyond the print-based concepts of originality and authorship: next to copying, editing, reusing and remixing texts, the management and manipulation of information becomes an essential aspect of creativity.[58] Uncreative writing involves a repurposing and appropriation of existing texts and works, which then become materials or building blocks for further works. In this sense Goldsmith critiques the idea of texts or works as being fixed when asking, 'if artefacts are always in flux, when is a historical work determined to be "finished"?'[59] At the same time, he argues, our identities are also in flux and ever shifting, turning creative writing into a post-identity literature.[60] Machines play important roles in uncreative writing, as active agents in the 'managing of information', which is then again represented as writing, and is seen by Goldsmith as a bridge between human-centred writing and full-blown 'robopoetics' (literature written by machines, for machines). Yet Goldsmith is keen

---

56   Ibid.
57   Kenneth Goldsmith, *Uncreative Writing: Managing Language in the Digital Age* (New York: Columbia University Press, 2011), p. 227.
58   Ibid., p. 15.
59   Goldsmith, *Uncreative Writing*, p. 81.
60   Ibid.

to emphasise that these forms of uncreative writing are not beholden to the digital medium, and that pre-digital examples are plentiful in conceptual literature and poetry. He points out — again by a discursive re-appropriation of what creativity is or can be — that sampling, remixing and appropriation have been the norm in other artistic and creative media for decades. The literary world is lagging behind in this respect, where, despite the experiments by modernist writers, it continues neatly to delineate avant-garde from more general forms of writing. Yet as Goldsmith argues the digital has started to disrupt this distinction again, moving beyond 'analogue' notions of writing, and has fuelled with it the idea that there might be alternative notions of writing: those currently perceived as uncreative.[61]

Conclusion

There are two addendums to the argument I have outlined above that I would like to include here. First of all, I would like to complicate and further critique some of the preconceptions still inherent in the relational and networked copyright models as put forward by Craig et al. and Gibson. Both are in many ways reformist and 'responsive' models. Gibson, for example, does not want to do away with IP rights, she wants them to develop and adapt to mirror society more accurately according to a networked model of creativity. For her, the law is out of tune with its public, and she wants to promote a more inclusive networked (copy) rights model.[62] For Craig too, relationalities are established and structured by rights first and foremost. Yet from a posthuman perspective we need to be conscious of how the other actants involved in creativity would fall outside such a humanist and

---

61 It is worth emphasising that what Goldsmith perceives as 'uncreative' notions of writing (including appropriation, pastiche, and copying), have a prehistory that can be traced back to antiquity (thanks go out to this chapter's reviewer for pointing this out). One example of this, which uses the method of cutting and pasting — something I have outlined more in depth elsewhere — concerns the early modern commonplace book. Commonplacing as 'a method or approach to reading and writing involved the gathering and repurposing of meaningful quotes, passages or other clippings from published books by copying and/or pasting them into a blank book.' Janneke Adema, 'Cut-Up', in Eduardo Navas (ed.), *Keywords in Remix Studies* (New York and London: Routledge, 2017), pp. 104–14, https://hcommons.org/deposits/item/hc:16745/

62 Gibson, *Creating Selves*, p. 27.

subjective rights model.⁶³ From texts and technologies themselves to the wider environmental context and to other nonhuman entities and objects: in what sense will a copyright model be able to extend such a network beyond an individualised liberal humanist human subject? What do these models exclude in this respect and in what sense are they still limited by their adherence to a rights model that continues to rely on humanist nodes in a networked or relational model? As Anna Munster has argued in a talk about the case of the monkey selfie, copyright is based on a logic of exclusion that does not line up with the assemblages of agentic processes that make up creativity and creative expression.⁶⁴ How can we appreciate the relational and processual aspects of identity, which both Craig and Gibson seem to want to promote, if we hold on to an inherently humanist concept of subjectification, rights and creativity?

Secondly, I want to highlight that we need to remain cautious of a movement away from copyright and the copyright industries, to a context of free culture in which free content — and the often free labour it is based upon — ends up servicing the content industries (i.e. Facebook, Google, Amazon). We must be wary when access or the narrative around (open) access becomes dominated by access to or for big business, benefiting the creative industries and the knowledge economy. The danger of updating and adapting IP law to fit a changing digital context and to new technologies, of making it more inclusive in this sense — which is something both Craig and Gibson want to do as part of their reformative models — is that this tends to be based on a very simplified and deterministic vision of technology, as something requiring access and an open market to foster innovation. As Sarah Kember argues, this technocratic rationale, which is what unites pro-and anti-copyright activists in this sense, essentially de-politicises the debate around IP; it is still a question of determining the value of creativity

---

63 For example, animals cannot own copyright. See the case of Naruto, the macaque monkey that took a 'selfie' photograph of itself. Victoria Richards, 'Monkey Selfie: Judge Rules Macaque Who Took Grinning Photograph of Himself "Cannot Own Copyright"', *The Independent*, 7 January 2016, https://www.independent.co.uk/news/weird-news/monkey-selfie-judge-rules-macaque-who-took-grinning-photograph-of-himself-cannot-own-copyright-a6800471.html

64 Anna Munster, 'Techno-Animalities — the Case of the Monkey Selfie' (presented at the Goldsmiths University, London, 2016), https://www.gold.ac.uk/calendar/?id=9990

through an economic perspective, based on a calculative lobby.[65] The challenge here is to redefine the discourse in such a way that our focus moves away from a dominant market vision, and — as Gibson and Craig have also tried to do — to emphasise a non-calculative ethics of relations, processes and care instead.

I would like to return at this point to the ALCS report and the way its results have been framed within a creative industries discourse. Notwithstanding the fact that fair remuneration and incentives for literary production and creativity in general are of the utmost importance, what I have tried to argue here is that the 'solution' proposed by the ALCS does not do justice to the complexities of creativity. When discussing remuneration of authors, the ALCS seems to prefer a simple solution in which copyright is seen as a given, the digital is pointed out as a generalised scapegoat, and binaries between print and digital are maintained and strengthened. Furthermore, fair remuneration is encapsulated by the ALCS within an economic calculative logic and rhetoric, sustained by and connected to a creative industries discourse, which continuously recreates the idea that creativity and innovation are one. Instead I have tried to put forward various alternative visions and practices, from radical open access to posthuman authorship and uncreative writing, based on vital relationships and on an ethics of care and responsibility. These alternatives highlight distributed and relational authorship and/or showcase a sensibility that embraces posthuman agencies and processual publishing as part of a more complex, *emergent* vision of creativity, open to different ideas of what creativity is and can become. In this vision creativity is thus seen as relational, fluid and processual and only ever temporarily fixed as part of our ethical decision making: a decision-making process that is contingent on the contexts and relationships with which we find ourselves entangled. This involves asking questions about what writing is and does, and how creativity expands beyond our established, static, or given concepts, which include copyright and a focus on the author as a 'homo economicus', writing as inherently an enterprise, and culture as commodified. As I have argued, the value of words, indeed the economic

---

65 Sarah Kember, 'Why Write?: Feminism, Publishing and the Politics of Communication', *New Formations: A Journal of Culture/Theory/Politics* 83.1 (2014), 99–116.

worth and sustainability of words and of the 'creative industries', can and should be defined within a different narrative. Opening up from the hegemonic creative industries discourse and the way we perform it through our writing practices might therefore enable us to explore extended relationalities of emergent creativity, open-ended publishing processes, and a feminist ethics of care and responsibility.

This contribution has showcased examples of experimental, hybrid and posthuman writing and publishing practices that are intervening in this established discourse on creativity. How, through them, can we start to performatively explore a new discourse and reconfigure the relationships that underlie our writing processes? How can the worth of writing be reflected in different ways?

Works Cited

(2014) 'New Research into Authors' Earnings Released', *Authors' Licensing and Collecting Society*, https://web.archive.org/web/20160504001652/http://www.alcs.co.uk/About-Us/News/News/What-are-words-worth-now-not-much.aspx

Abrahamsson, Sebastian, Uli Beisel, Endre Danyi, Joe Deville, Julien McHardy, and Michaela Spencer (2013) 'Mattering Press: New Forms of Care for STS Books', *The EASST Review* 32.4, http://easst.net/easst-review-volume-32-4-december-2013/mattering-press-new-forms-of-care-for-sts-books/

Adema, Janneke (2017) 'Cut-Up', in Eduardo Navas (ed.), *Keywords in Remix Studies* (New York and London: Routledge), pp. 104–14, https://hcommons.org/deposits/item/hc:16745/

— (2014) 'Embracing Messiness', *LSE Impact of Social Sciences*, http://blogs.lse.ac.uk/impactofsocialsciences/2014/11/18/embracing-messiness-adema-pdsc14/

— (2015) 'Knowledge Production Beyond The Book? Performing the Scholarly Monograph in Contemporary Digital Culture' (PhD dissertation, Coventry University), https://curve.coventry.ac.uk/open/file/8222ccb2-f6b0-4e5f-90de-f4c62c77ac86/1/ademacomb.pdf

— (2014) 'Open Access', in *Critical Keywords for the Digital Humanities* (Lueneburg: Centre for Digital Cultures (CDC)), https://meson.press/keywords/

— and Gary Hall (2013) 'The Political Nature of the Book: On Artists' Books and Radical Open Access', *New Formations* 78.1, 138–56, https://doi.org/10.3898/NewF.78.07.2013

— and Samuel Moore (2018) 'Collectivity and Collaboration: Imagining New Forms of Communality to Create Resilience in Scholar-Led Publishing', *Insights* 31.3, https://doi.org/10.1629/uksg.399

ALCS, Press Release (8 July 2014) 'What Are Words Worth Now? Not Enough', https://www.alcs.co.uk/news/what-are-words-worth-now-not-enough

Barad, Karen (2007) *Meeting the Universe Halfway: Quantum Physics and the Entanglement of Matter and Meaning* (Durham, N.C., and London: Duke University Press).

Boon, Marcus (2010) *In Praise of Copying* (Cambridge, MA: Harvard University Press).

Brown, Wendy (2015) *Undoing the Demos: Neoliberalism's Stealth Revolution* (Cambridge, MA: MIT Press).

Chartier, Roger (1994) *The Order of Books: Readers, Authors, and Libraries in Europe Between the 14th and 18th Centuries*, 1st ed. (Stanford, CA: Stanford University Press).

Craig, Carys J. (2011) *Copyright, Communication and Culture: Towards a Relational Theory of Copyright Law* (Cheltenham, UK, and Northampton, MA: Edward Elgar Publishing).

— Joseph F. Turcotte, and Rosemary J. Coombe (2011) 'What's Feminist About Open Access? A Relational Approach to Copyright in the Academy', *Feminists@law* 1.1, http://journals.kent.ac.uk/index.php/feministsatlaw/article/view/7

Cramer, Florian (2013) *Anti-Media: Ephemera on Speculative Arts* (Rotterdam and New York, NY: nai010 publishers).

Drucker, Johanna (2015) 'Humanist Computing at the End of the Individual Voice and the Authoritative Text', in Patrik Svensson and David Theo Goldberg (eds.), *Between Humanities and the Digital* (Cambridge, MA: MIT Press), pp. 83–94.

— (2014) 'Distributed and Conditional Documents: Conceptualizing Bibliographical Alterities', *MATLIT: Revista do Programa de Doutoramento em Materialidades da Literatura* 2.1, 11–29.

— (2013) 'Performative Materiality and Theoretical Approaches to Interface', *Digital Humanities Quarterly* 7.1 [n.p.], http://www.digitalhumanities.org/dhq/vol/7/1/000143/000143.html

Ede, Lisa, and Andrea A. Lunsford (2001) 'Collaboration and Concepts of Authorship', *PMLA* 116.2, 354–69.

Emerson, Lori (2008) 'Materiality, Intentionality, and the Computer-Generated Poem: Reading Walter Benn Michaels with Erin Moureacute's Pillage Land', *ESC: English Studies in Canada* 34, 45–69.

— (2003) 'Digital Poetry as Reflexive Embodiment', in Markku Eskelinen, Raine Koskimaa, Loss Pequeño Glazier and John Cayley (eds.), *CyberText Yearbook 2002–2003*, 88–106, http://cybertext.hum.jyu.fi/index.php?browsebook=2

Foucault, Michel, 'What Is an Author?' (1998) in James D. Faubion (ed.), *Essential Works of Foucault, 1954–1984, Volume Two: Aesthetics, Method, and Epistemology* (New York: The New Press).

Gibson, Johanna (2007) *Creating Selves: Intellectual Property and the Narration of Culture* (Aldershot, England and Burlington, VT: Routledge).

— Phillip Johnson and Gaetano Dimita (2015) *The Business of Being an Author: A Survey of Author's Earnings and Contracts* (London: Queen Mary University of London), https://orca.cf.ac.uk/72431/1/Final Report - For Web Publication.pdf

Goldsmith, Kenneth (2011) *Uncreative Writing: Managing Language in the Digital Age* (New York: Columbia University Press).

Hall, Gary (2010) 'Radical Open Access in the Humanities' (presented at the Research Without Borders, Columbia University), http://scholcomm.columbia.edu/2011/01/18/radical-open-access-in-the-humanities/

— (2008) *Digitize This Book!*: *The Politics of New Media, or Why We Need Open Access Now* (Minneapolis, MN: University of Minnesota Press).

Hayles, N. Katherine (2004) 'Print Is Flat, Code Is Deep: The Importance of Media-Specific Analysis', *Poetics Today* 25.1, 67–90, https://doi.org/10.1215/03335372-25-1-67

Hughes, Rolf (2005) 'Orderly Disorder: Post-Human Creativity', in *Proceedings of the Linköping Electronic Conference* (Linköpings universitet: University Electronic Press).

Jenkins, Henry, and Owen Gallagher (2008) '"What Is Remix Culture?": An Interview with Total Recut's Owen Gallagher', *Confessions of an Aca-Fan*, http://henryjenkins.org/2008/06/interview_with_total_remixs_ow.html

Johns, Adrian (1998) *The Nature of the Book*: *Print and Knowledge in the Making* (Chicago, IL: University of Chicago Press).

Kember, Sarah (2016) 'Why Publish?', *Learned Publishing* 29, 348–53, https://doi.org/10.1002/leap.1042

— (2014) 'Why Write?: Feminism, Publishing and the Politics of Communication', *New Formations: A Journal of Culture/Theory/Politics* 83.1, 99–116.

Kretschmer, M., and P. Hardwick (2007) *Authors' Earnings from Copyright and Non-Copyright Sources* : *A Survey of 25,000 British and German Writers* (Poole, UK: CIPPM/ALCS Bournemouth University), https://microsites.bournemouth.ac.uk/cippm/files/2007/07/ALCS-Full-report.pdf

Lessig, Lawrence (2008) *Remix*: *Making Art and Commerce Thrive in the Hybrid Economy* (New York: Penguin Press).

Lovink, Geert, and Ned Rossiter (eds.) (2007) *MyCreativity Reader*: *A Critique of Creative Industries* (Amsterdam: Institute of Network Cultures), http://www.networkcultures.org/_uploads/32.pdf

McGann, Jerome J. (1992) *A Critique of Modern Textual Criticism* (Charlottesville, VA: University of Virginia Press).

McHardy, Julien (2014) 'Why Books Matter: There Is Value in What Cannot Be Evaluated.', *Impact of Social Sciences* [n.p.], http://blogs.lse.ac.uk/impactofsocialsciences/2014/09/30/why-books-matter/

Mol, Annemarie (2008) *The Logic of Care*: *Health and the Problem of Patient Choice*, 1st ed. (London and New York: Routledge).

Montfort, Nick (2003) 'The Coding and Execution of the Author', in Markku Eskelinen, Raine Kosimaa, Loss Pequeño Glazier and John Cayley (eds.), *CyberText Yearbook 2002–2003*, 2003, 201–17, http://cybertext.hum.jyu.fi/index.php?browsebook=2, pp. 201–17.

Moore, Samuel A. (2017) 'A Genealogy of Open Access: Negotiations between Openness and Access to Research', *Revue Française des Sciences de l'information et de la Communication* 11, https://doi.org/10.4000/rfsic.3220

Munster, Anna (2016) 'Techno-Animalities — the Case of the Monkey Selfie' (presented at the Goldsmiths University, London), https://www.gold.ac.uk/calendar/?id=9990

Navas, Eduardo (2012) *Remix Theory: The Aesthetics of Sampling* (Vienna and New York: Springer).

Parikka, Jussi, and Mercedes Bunz (11 July 2014) 'A Mini-Interview: Mercedes Bunz Explains Meson Press', *Machinology*, https://jussiparikka.net/2014/07/11/a-mini-interview-mercedes-bunz-explains-meson-press/

Richards, Victoria (7 January 2016) 'Monkey Selfie: Judge Rules Macaque Who Took Grinning Photograph of Himself "Cannot Own Copyright"', *The Independent*, https://www.independent.co.uk/news/weird-news/monkey-selfie-judge-rules-macaque-who-took-grinning-photograph-of-himself-cannot-own-copyright-a6800471.html

Robbins, Sarah (2003) 'Distributed Authorship: A Feminist Case-Study Framework for Studying Intellectual Property', *College English* 66.2, 155–71, https://doi.org/10.2307/3594264

Rose, Mark (1993) *Authors and Owners: The Invention of Copyright* (Cambridge, MA: Harvard University Press).

Spinosa, Dani (14 May 2014) '"My Line (Article) Has Sighed": Authorial Subjectivity and Technology', *Generic Pronoun*, https://genericpronoun.com/2014/05/14/my-line-article-has-sighed/

Star, Susan Leigh (1991) 'The Sociology of the Invisible: The Primacy of Work in the Writings of Anselm Strauss', in Anselm Leonard Strauss and David R. Maines (eds.), *Social Organization and Social Process: Essays in Honor of Anselm Strauss* (New York: A. de Grutyer).

4. Are Publishers Worth it? Filtering, Amplification and the Value of Publishing

Michael Bhaskar

Publishers in Peril…

Publishers often take it for granted that they are worth it. Authors are sometimes more sceptical.

While this has arguably been true for centuries, now an ensemble of technological, cultural and business innovations mean the monopoly control that professional publishers exerted on the activity of publishing is crumbling. The question 'are publishers worth it?' has accordingly transitioned from abstract concern to genuine worry. This is potentially a disaster in slow motion. No fewer than 23 publishers have revenues of over $1 billion.[1] But if publishers cannot prove they are worth it then, for perhaps the first time, there are other options. Forces beyond their control now threaten the business models that sustained them for generations. Publishers today need to justify their existence. Can they do this? If so, how? Are publishers worth it?

Self-publishing is hardly new. The shift is that the Internet and more specifically Internet-based platforms, of which Amazon is the most notable, now provide realistic outlets. Publishers used to be a critical component in the distribution of text — the crucial link between writers on the one hand, and bookshops or distribution centres on the other.

---

[1] 'The World's 57 Largest Book Publishers, 2015', *Publishers Weekly*, 26 June 2015, http://www.publishersweekly.com/pw/by-topic/international/international-book-news/article/67224-the-world-s-57-largest-book-publishers-2015.html

Without publishers, distributing work at scale and finding the right customers was always going to be tricky, even if you had somehow managed to print large amounts of your work and funded an extensive marketing campaign. The infrastructure of distribution remained in the hands of publishers. Platforms such as Kindle Publishing Direct, and at a deeper level the entire open publishing architecture of the Internet, threaten to upend this. Giant web platforms aggregate potential readerships in a way only previously possible through mass media, and mass media was better accessed via publishers than direct. Theoretically, distribution is no longer a complex series of tightly managed intermediaries. It is open to anyone with the nous and desire to see their work reach an audience.

Even if the reality is often more ambiguous than this picture, it still threatens the idea of professionalised institutions designed to do the work of distribution. It opens the market for publishing to non-publishers. Classical economics suggests this will have consequences: an increase in competition on this scale cannot leave markets unscathed. Furthermore, the mechanism by which publishing has managed its monetisation — intellectual property — is undergoing its own revolution. The roots are to some extent shared. The Internet's openness and the limitless capacity of digital technology to produce copies has spurred interest in new forms of intellectual property. These upend assumptions that until recently were baked into our conceptions of a publisher.

Open access (OA) is one such example. Open access can be defined as 'the removal of price and permission barriers to scholarly research. Open access means peer-reviewed academic research work that is free to read online and that anybody may redistribute and reuse, with some restrictions.'[2] The idea is that research created using public money and academic labour should not be sold back to the public or the academic community at exorbitant prices. Research is hampered, knowledge is stultified and money wasted on an economic model whose primary beneficiary is seen to be publishers. Moreover all the tertiary benefits stemming from possible research nixed by the cost barrier are lost — the projects never even started by those unable to access material outside the academy. Those price barriers keep rising: the amount academic

---

[2] Martin Eve, *Open Access and the Humanities: Contexts, Controversies and the Future* (Cambridge: Cambridge University Press, 2014).

libraries pay for journal subscriptions has increased 300% above inflation in the 30 years since 1986.

Open access advocates don't dispute that publishing is work, that it requires resources and those resources are not free. It simply suggests changing the funding model. This is reflected in the idea that researchers pay article processing costs (APCs) or book processing costs (BPCs) to cover the work done. These, in theory, reflect the overheads involved in administering and producing published matter — not only the cost of managing peer review, but the costs of typesetting complex formulas, the editing, printing and even marketing. APCs are usually in the region of £1500–2000 but can be much higher. The point is this inverts the business model of the publisher: it's hard to see how, in the long term, academic publishing conglomerates like RELX can sustain their more than comfortable 30% profit margins.

OA, like self-publishing, doesn't threaten *publishing*; it just threatens a certain instantiation of *publisher*. This of course doesn't make it less significant, as whatever happens complex civilisations require publishing of some kind to operate. But it asks difficult questions of what the aims of publishing are and how the activities of a publisher should be funded. It suggests a different way is possible and that publishers may be worth it: worth the time, the profits, worth the dedication to a career, worth existing at all. Just as we are seeing a new generation of self-published authors dominate the ebook charts, so we are seeing exotic new forms of publishing organisation: the Public Library of Science, the Open Library of the Humanities, arXiv, Knowledge Unlatched…

All of this takes place within the wider context of a Free Culture movement first espoused by bands of Californian dreamers like Richard Stallman. He proposed the GNU, a new kind of licence defying old prescripts of copyright, allowing reuse as part of its proposition. From here, from copyleft, Creative Commons and even, in some incarnations, blockchain, and through advocates from Larry Lessig to Cory Doctorow to millions of everyday pirates, new forms of IP have been proposed and adopted with varying degrees of success. Publishers are not too worried as there is no chance copyright will suddenly disappear. But the atmosphere is now one in which it is possible to imagine publishing without the key plank of publishers' monetisation. That should prompt some reflection, again, about why publishers should get paid as much they do.

If writers felt they benefitted from the system there would be less for publishers to worry about. Unfortunately it's doubtful writers feel that way. Again the wider context is shaped by the technological-cultural vortex of the Internet. In 2006 the writer Nicholas Carr and the legal and Internet theorist Yochai Benkler had a wager. Benkler argued that by 2011 most content on the Internet would be peer-produced and lie outside market mechanisms of payment. It would, in other words, be produced for free. Carr felt that in 2011 most writing on the Internet would be paid for by publishers. Given the rise of social media in the intervening years it seems incontestable that most 'content' broadly defined was submitted freely; people, by and large, were not getting paid. Even if some still were, and even if the great web platforms can hardly be said to exist beyond 'market mechanisms' (indeed, they embody them), most content produced in most places around the world is produced for free. Some years on from the start of the debate, this can only be more true: as of 2017 Facebook has over two billion users, against well under one billion in 2011. Free and unpaid content dominates the Internet to a greater degree than ever: much of it produced for publication by traditionally professional publishers.

Economics suggests the price of content will fall across the board; premiums for producing material must fall in the context of many other people producing free content. Such big picture tectonic shifts can feel imperceptible. Yet recent research I conducted at Canelo suggests this feeds through into collapsing author incomes, falling book prices and an ever widening spread between a small number of 'winners' and a great morass of 'losers' in the world of letters.[3]

Professional authors are struggling — even more than professional publishers. While profits are up at major groups like Penguin Random House and Simon & Schuster most authors cannot live off their writing alone. In 2005 an ACLS commissioned survey found that 40% of authors earned their money from writing. By 2013 this had dropped to just 11.5%. In 2013, 17% of writers earned no money at all from their writing. Between 2007 and 2013 author earnings fell by 28% in real terms.[4]

---

3   Unless otherwise stated all information is from Canelo/Arts Council England, 'Literature in the 21st Century: Understanding Models of Support for Literary Fiction', Arts Council Report, 15 December 2017, https://www.artscouncil.org.uk/publication/literature-21st-century-understanding-models-support-literary-fiction

4   Sarah Shaffi, '"Huge Inequality" in Writer Earnings', *The Bookseller*, 20 April 2015, http://www.thebookseller.com/news/huge-inequality-writer-earnings

Much of this is predicated on a fall in book sales and book prices (it is worth saying that I am talking here about trade publishing). Data from Nielsen Bookscan shows book sales are still down from their highs of 2007 for hardbacks and 2008 for paperbacks. Although the Total Consumer Market (TCM) has shown signs of buoyancy since 2015, the years 2008–2014 saw year-on-year declines for both hardbacks and paperbacks only slightly mitigated by the rise of digital formats. For example, £10m was wiped off the market for hardbacks in the years 2007 to 2011. The picture is even worse in the US: bookstore sales went from $17bn in 2007 to just $10.9bn in 2014.

Compounding the issue of sales is the falling price of books, a less frequently discussed but no less powerful phenomenon for the long-term viability of both paid-for publishing and full-time writers. Again Nielsen Bookscan data shows us that the average selling price for hardback fiction is down 33.7% in real terms since 2001. The average selling price of a paperback is down 33.5% in real terms over the same period. Sales would have had to increase by a third since 2001 to maintain income levels, but of course they have not. Falling sales and the falling price of books both have to be seen in the wider context of the digital revolution, where plentiful text and entertainment is available for free or at very low cost.

Some writers are doing well out of the current system. In 2015 the top 1% of authors accounted for 32.8% of all sales. Beyond this, the top 0.1% accounted for 13% of sales. That year the amount earned by top 0.1% increased 21% against 2014. Mega-brands are doing fine. Go down into what used to be termed the midlist, a once respectable place now rightly feared by writers, and the picture worsens considerably. The 10,000th best-selling book per year in the UK sells between 94 and 99 units. The 1000th bestselling book sells between 3000 and 4000 units a year. Not too bad; but when you factor in all the costs of production and publishing, hardly enough to sustain a career. Few writers can survive on their work alone.

The reality of self-publishing; the radical new forms of IP; the disruption engendered by the web; the continued crisis in sales. Putting all these together, authors of many shades have reason to feel disenchanted with publishing. In the old world there wasn't a lot to be done. Authors had to lump it. But, as suggested earlier, we live amidst a revolution, opening new possibilities that could, if deployed imaginatively, create a whole new publishing ecosystem — and in some cases has already done so. The threat ultimately is a multifaceted, but it amounts to the possibility of disintermediation in the value chain for the first time coupled with a sense, rightly or wrongly, that publishers are not doing their job.

In *The Content Machine* I outlined a theory of publishing, suggesting its value lies in filtering and amplification.[5] That is, that the primary value-adding function of publishing is firstly to select from the great range of possible texts according to a set of professional criteria, and secondly, take these to a wider audience than would have been the case without the publisher's intervention. Amplification is, in other words, disseminating a text beyond what would otherwise be possible, whether this is through printing or marketing or file creation or any combination of activities. The question becomes, given all this, given the position of authors, are publishers the best people to filter and amplify? Or have they instead become redundant organisations co-opting value? As sketched out above, this is a live question.

Case Study: Meet Jacob Tonson, 'Prince of Publishers'; a Model for Publishing

In order to explore why publishers are worth paying for, I want to look at someone who really did get paid: the seventeenth- and eighteenth-century publisher Jacob Tonson. As much as any publisher in history perhaps, Tonson became fabulously wealthy. A pioneer of intellectual property, he can be seen as the classic rentier, the model of publisher as parasite; the kind of publisher that can safely be consigned to history. Was he just a clever manipulator of IP? From another perspective, this would be too simple. Tonson wasn't just riding on the back of his authors but making them. He is an extreme example in either direction, but because of this he illustrates the cases against and for publishers in spectacular fashion — and despite the different historical context, his career hints at their continued but changing role.

Tonson was one of the greatest men of letters of his day. He knew, and worked with, everyone. Rotund, epicurean, bibulous, garrulous, he

---

5   Michael Bhaskar, *The Content Machine: Towards a Theory of Publishing from the Printing Press to the Digital Network* (London: Anthem Press, 2013).

was an instantly recognisable, be-turbaned figure on the London literary scene — the 'prince of publishers'. He is more than anyone the 'father of modern publishing', not a printer, not a 'stationer', not a bookseller but something else, something new: a professional publisher.

The Great Fire of 1666 wrought havoc on the London book trade, destroying thousands of books and the premises of their creation. Demand for books, as for so many other things, spiked. It was in this context that Jacob Tonson started his apprenticeship in the trade. Becoming a freeman of the Company of Stationers in 1677, he was then in a position to strike out on his own and capitalise. By the 1690s Tonson was well on the way to being a grand figure, rich enough from his publishing to employ servants, and inheriting his brother's business. He managed to ride the wave that resulted from the lapsing of the Licencing Acts in 1695, a major blow to publishers.[6]

All of this was built on an empire of copyright. As his biographer notes, 'Many commentators have noticed that it was Tonson and not Milton who made a fortune from *Paradise Lost*'.[7] Piracy was, especially after the end of the Licencing Act, a constant problem. While the Act was a restrictive measure that gave considerable control to the government, it also protected those publishers granted licences to print a work. Printing was restricted to just a few cities. Arch-Royalist Sir Roger L'Estrange, Surveyor of the Imprimery (printing presses) had a team looking for unlicensed printers and the number of printers in London was reduced to twenty, down from sixty. Yet L'Estrange was much more concerned with sedition than piracy, although all he really cared about was that the publishing industry lay under his orbit and the multitude of booksellers clustered on streets like Little Britain or Paternoster Row groaned under the weight of the pirated works they sold (at least until the Great Fire).

Tonson jealously guarded his copyrights, and used his influence within the Stationers and in London society at large to force the Copyright Act of 1709 through the House of Lords on its third reading. This was vindication for publishers, and, as the most prolific publisher of his day, for Tonson in particular. It spurred him on to launch his huge

---

6   The lapsing of the Licencing Acts removed the monopoly-granting powers of the Company of Stationers, temporarily challenging publishers' exclusivity over given works.

7   Harry M. Geduld, *Prince of Publishers: A Study of the Work and Career of Jacob Tonson* (Bloomington, IN: Indiana University Press, 1969), p. 11.

Shakespeare project. He bought *The Spectator*, the great organ of Addison and Steele that typified journalism. In the 1710s Tonson presided over a cultural and political institution at his workplace, the Shakespeare's Head, sited just off the Strand.

With the accession of George I in 1714 and his favouring of the Whigs, Tonson won a large number of government contracts, further solidifying his wealth. Tonson even managed to make the astronomical sum of £40,000 gambling on the French Mississippi scheme which, like the South Sea Bubble, was later to crash in spectacular style. On his deathbed he had a fortune of at least £80,000, a vast sum today. With the timing of the serially lucky, Tonson had bowed out at his zenith. He was rich, a friend and confidant of aristocrats and the most powerful men of his day.

Here is a picture of a publisher who grew obscenely wealthy and influential on the back of luck and copyright. But it doesn't tell the whole story. Tonson's contribution to literature and English culture more widely is enormous. He worked with the great writers of his day: Dryden, Swift, Pope, Congreve and Addison for example. He published more books than his peers, both vast folios in small upscale print runs, and much cheaper larger print run books for populist consumption. He founded the literary reputations of giants like Shakespeare and Milton.

He had a knack for building writers and making them work critically and commercially. He had an insatiable appetite for reading, an eye for what would be critically and commercially successful and he worked in detail with writers to perfect their texts. Tonson's textual scholarship was first rate. He also had a sharp business mind — unsold copies of Dryden, whose reputation is due to Tonson more than anyone else, would be rebound as *Miscellanies* allowing for a second bite of the cherry and the clearing of valuable unsold stock. On acquiring Dryden's rights, which he did assiduously, Tonson improved the quality of the printing. He released Dryden's prologues and epilogues in new, distinct editions. This was all part of a campaign from Tonson that kept Dryden in print and kept new editions and works coming every year; the public would not be allowed to forget him. This wasn't just copyright ownership; this was brand building.

There were famously differences between Dryden and Tonson, but this was a new kind of relationship. Tonson's influence was enormous — he steered Dryden's writing towards public taste, which he made it his business to understand. As Dryden himself acknowledged, his translation of Virgil was thanks to encouragement from Tonson. Tonson once again employed his nous to publish it — this would be a subscription book, allowing him to cover costs in advance, guarantee an audience, build buzz and pay for a sumptuous printing. Tonson worked closely with his writers to find the audience for these subscriptions. For this Dryden was paid £50 for every two books of both *The Aeneid* and *The Georgics*, and received 60% of the subscriptions from the first edition. There were 101 names on the five-guinea subscription list and 252 on the two-guinea subscription list (which includes one Sam. Pepys Esq.). The total profit for Dryden is placed at around £700–800, a very handsome return for the time. This was fair, leaving only a tiny margin. Nonetheless a furious row broke out about the quality of the coinage, a major economic issue. The book is an extraordinary edition, beautifully printed, cleverly and well typeset and designed in a way few other English books of the period are. It displays care, attention to detail and craft throughout, with intricate engravings. Even after Dryden's death Tonson fiercely guarded his author, fending off assaults from rival writers like Addison who were keen to promote themselves.

Most authors were in a perilous situation. Once they had sold their 'copy', it was out of their control. Printers would maximise their profits regardless of an author's wellbeing or reputation. This partly explains why writers so favoured the theatre. Until Tonson, the relationship between writers and publishers was fractious; most publishers weren't willing to invest in, develop and take risks on writers. Nor was it just modern writers who benefitted. Without Tonson's critical interventions Milton and Shakespeare may never have been recognised as the pillars of English letters they became. Tonson was tireless in boosting their literary reputation and invested large sums in the publication and republication of their work. In addition to publishing many of the major names of the time, Tonson was secretary of the influential Kit-Cat Club, comprised of the intellectuals, magnates, artists and Whiggish aristocracy of the time, a roll-call of the great, good and celebrated of early eighteenth century Britain. He was a regular figure at book markets in the UK and Europe, introducing new and better quality Dutch type to his printing. In the words of his biographer: 'Tonson's association with the Kit-Cat Club sets him apart from the generations of bookseller-stationers who preceded him; for he was the earliest publisher to understand and exploit the delicate art of public relations, and this, no less than his achievements as a populariser of Dryden, Milton, and Shakespeare, distinguishes him as *the earliest professional publisher*.'[8]

So it's clear that Tonson made a lot of money. But it's also clear that he was fair to writers in the process. More than that we consistently see him filter and amplify: expertly choosing works for focus, finding the writers that mattered, and then working hard taking them to wide audiences, certainly much wider than would have been the case without his intervention. He did this consistently and with demonstrable success. Inasmuch as Tonson was an IP owner he extracted value, but really IP is here the mechanism by which filtering and amplifying can take place. Tonson almost went out of business thanks to widespread piracy. Had he done so the canon would be a poorer place.

This in turn tells us two things. Firstly that, in theory, the model for the for-profit professional publisher can work well. The most extreme forms of value co-option can be coincident with the most extreme forms of value creation. The model of publishing most of us used to accept as normal has this ideal at its heart. Secondly that just as the problems for publishers lies in today's technical, economic and artistic context, so the solution must lie in that context, as it did for Tonson

Too Much to Read

Jacob Tonson was worth paying for. That's cold comfort to publishers today, facing falling sales, a grim retail environment and a tougher publicity climate, all in ferocious competition with one another, all against the backdrop of the wider existential challenge of disintermediation and transformed business models. However if we focus on one further feature of this environment we can appreciate how a renewed focus on filtering and amplification can create a new model — one in which publishers can justify their intervention in an age of disruption.

What Tonson did was new. He was part of a series of publishers in the seventeenth and eighteenth century who delimited publishing from printing or bookselling and created a new role that was neither. Printers

---

8   Ibid., p. 171.

and booksellers had also been involved with filtering and amplifying, but publishers from Henry Herringman to John Murray adapted to changes in society, the shift in institutions around printing, innovations like IP, the swelling economic climate and so on, to produce a new forms of filtering and amplification. The model of publisher currently under peril has had a good run: what we need is an evolution, something that responds to our own time — something that, like Tonson in his day, is worth paying for.

It would be wrong to suggest this isn't happening. Earlier I listed new OA initiatives like the Public Library of Science, arXiv and Open Library of the Humanities. These are new forms of publisher, reacting to problems with the prevalent models. What's different about these organisations is not just their commitment to OA but their complete redesign of the institution of a publisher, structurally speaking, to achieve it. They may not, for example, be for-profit businesses, or have traditional premises and full time staff, or ever deal with printing. They may bypass structural roles like overseeing traditional peer review. Or they may resemble a technology start-up or platform more than a publishing house. To face disintermediation and its attendant threats, professional publishers must re-gear their core operations, the heart of their value propositions, their filtering and amplification, around the new context. At the same time many academic publishers like Springer Nature, in addition to continuing their existing activities, are experimenting with OA, even if this could be seen as a way of buttressing their existing models.

The salient thing to note is the extraordinary superabundance of content springing from the same techno-cultural matrix as disintermediation and the collapse of paid writing.

We have grown numb to the barrage of statistics illustrating this, so I will confine myself to a few observations. One million books were published in the English language last year. These are books with ISBNs. This is a vast quantity of books and a statistic that is not referenced by publishers nearly enough. Alone it changes the equation of what it means to be a publisher — few other sectors have such a diversity and weight of new product entering the market every year. Alone it transforms the economics of the publishing business; yet business models have not caught up. It also doesn't factor in the rapid growth of self-publishing in recent years. And of course, it doesn't factor in anything non-book.

For years information production increased. The ever-industrialising media machine was capable of manufacturing more content every year. Yet digital technology supercharged this trend, from the explosion in size of traditional news operations like the *New York Times* or *The Guardian* to blogs and social media. Data, in general, has been increasing at a rate of something like 60% per annum in the 2010s. This is not only remarkable in itself but comes with significant externalities: according to the neuroscientist Daniel Levitin the average American is exposed to 175 newspapers-worth of information every day.[9] For most of our history information was incredibly scarce; now the opposite is true.

When written content exists in such excess, the gatekeeping role of the publisher, far from becoming less important, is massively enhanced. We need all the filters we can get to manage the surplus of text that is in large part enabled by the productive capacities of the digital network. In such saturated environments, value shifts to secondary selection from primary production. This is difficult for publishers inasmuch as they are producers of books, but good if we see publishers as arbiters and selectors. The truth is they are always both, but thinking in terms of an overloaded market — a market where the marginal value of adding another book is decidedly limited — allows publishers, and everyone in the book world, to have a clear sense of where their value lies. The choices an imprint makes define everything else in the publishing process. Perhaps the most important thing any publisher does is say no. When there are so many books, if a publisher's choices aren't meaningful, they are nothing.

Lastly, content abundance puts greater emphasis on the wider network of curation. It explains why Amazon invented the category of personalisation: the first algorithms for recommending products online were created by an Amazon engineer called Greg Linden. What a publisher does, in the context of excess, is absolutely critical as it is an un-ignorable marker around a work that says: 'this matters'. Expert curation of books isn't as easy as it looks. Peer review, in-depth knowledge, extraordinary taste are all things that take time, and while algorithms can help here they cannot replace this process. There is no shortcut to becoming a trusted intermediary.

---

9   Daniel J. Levitin, *The Organized Mind: Thinking Straight in the Age of Information Overload* (London: Penguin Viking, 2014).

This surplus also impacts the amplification side. We should acknowledge the limits of disintermediation in the present. Over the long term, disintermediation could be total. Today it's not. *Fifty Shades of Grey* was a major self-published bestseller, with six-figure ebook sales. Yet without the power and reach of Random House, one of the world's largest trade publishers, it is unlikely in the extreme it would have gone on to sell over 100 million copies around the world. Only the amplificatory powers of a major institution could have achieved that in today's landscape.

As I have described elsewhere, amplification mutates in a time of excess — it changes from distribution to audience building.[10] It pushes us back to the old chestnut of market-making — sales, marketing and publicity. It's hardly a secret that books don't sell themselves, but when the competition is so extreme that fact is underlined. What other industry faces so many comparable product launches in any given year? Without serious amplification, no book stands a chance.

Two Challenges

In a world in which everyone is a content producer, the value of content falls. Paradoxically however, the value of the best content, or perhaps the right context, rises. This is why, even as the number of journal articles has mushroomed, growing at between 9% and 13% every year for the past half century, the value — pecuniary and otherwise — of the top journals like Nature and Science has only increased. It's why publishers *are* worth paying for, now as much as in the age of Tonson. Publishers will not do this alone. Instead we will need, and are building, vast and intricate ecosystems of curation that govern and stabilise the metastasizing universe of words. Benkler may have won his wager. That however only harms one conception of a publisher; it necessitates the need for another.

The challenge is twofold. How on the one hand to rebuild publishing so that it takes into account all of those peril factors? How to make publishing, in other words, feel like it's worth paying for to all the stakeholders — authors and readers being by far the most important? This involves, as suggested above, a rebuilding of the conception of the

---

10 Bhaskar, *The Content Machine*.

institution of the publisher in a way analogous to that of Tonson (and a great deal of other pioneering publishers throughout history). This is happening, but in piecemeal fashion. Academic and journal publishing as we have seen has made strides towards the change. News media is undergoing a bout of Schumpeterian creative destruction, with new organisations from Buzzfeed to Vice to Vox Media redefining the nature of a news publisher. Trade publishing has in this most fundamental respect been more conservative but we are seeing a new generation of digital publishers and an explosion, in the UK at least, of new indies including names like Tilted Axis, CB Editions, Fitzcarraldo Editions, Salt Books, Galley Beggar Press, Influx Press, Penned in the Margins, Tramp Press, Bluemoose Books, Jacaranda Books, Myriad Press, Gallic Books, And Other Stories, Bitter Lemon Press, Peirene Press and UK arms of American independents like Europa Editions and Melville House.

But.

It's probably not quite enough. No 'new' publisher, in trade publishing at least, has made a Tonsonian contribution to date, although perhaps, in the moment, it will be hard to identify. We need publishers as above all else as curators and amplifiers — and seen to be such, with a business model that is felt to be fair by all parties. That is a primary challenge and make no mistake, it is a real and live challenge.

Behind that lurks something even larger. Every publisher, of any kind, faces a collective problem: that same superabundance applies to all forms of media — entertainment, data and information — and publishing thus faces competition from anything from Candy Crush to *House of Cards*. We have less free time than ever before. And beyond that, the nature of digital media, with its thousands of bleeps, each capable of delivering a small dopamine hit, is restructuring our brains. Our attention spans are quite literally being whittled away. The dominant form is rapidly becoming the image, both static and moving. People would rather share video on Snapchat or browse Instagram feeds than experience the evanescent sugar rush of a tweet. It's still reading. Even as we publish more books than ever, and there are suggestions those books are getting longer, our capacity to absorb them is reduced.

It will be the responsibility of publishers to find a way through this. If they can do both these challenges, well, I for one think that would be worth paying for — but maybe I would. After all, I'm a publisher.

5. Who Takes Legal Responsibility for Published Work? Why Both an Understanding and Lived Experience of Copyright Are Becoming Increasingly Important to Writers

Alison Baverstock

Three years on the Board of Management of the Society of Authors (2012–2015) offered me opportunities to appreciate what writers worry about, issues of which they ought to be aware — and their comprehension levels for both. Copyright hovered between, and we discussed whether we should campaign to have its basic principles added to the primary school curriculum. The principle that an author should possess the rights for work they have created is neither hard to explain nor, once broadly understood, hard to deny — and a classroom demonstration is easy to organise. After the weekly story or news-writing session, take the written contribution of one child and announce you are going to photocopy and sell it at the school gate, with the entire proceeds going to the person making the copies. The resulting outrage will likely be long remembered — and have lasting implications for everyone's future willingness to credit a creator. While the principle of copyright is relatively easy to grasp, authors often struggle to understand how it functions in contracts, and routinely find that getting published can mean being asked to sign their copyright over to the publisher for minimal returns. Encouraging authors to understand copyright, and other legalities arising from writers' desire to share their work, raises many issues from individual responsibilities and organisational ethics to business and financial interests. The UK Publishers Association's Code of Practice on Contracts lays early emphasis on the importance of publishers ensuring their authors are clear about their legal responsibilities and future commitments:

> (4) The publisher should be willing and take any opportunity to explain the terms of the contract and the reasons for each provision, particularly to an author who is not professionally represented.[1]

In 2016, Clé, their Irish counterparts, for the first time organised a seminar for Irish authors on how to understand contracts.[2] The literary agent Carole Blake was a strong believer in authors understanding what they were committing to when they decided to publish their work, and her bestselling book offered a substantial chapter — sixty-five pages with a supporting bibliography — on contracts and how to interpret the seemingly archaic wording of what was being proposed or agreed.[3]

Until relatively recent times, copyright has been just one of many aspects of publishing little understood by authors. Writers were similarly ignorant about how to influence their cover designs — frustrated to find themselves collectively cover-badged within genres to which they did not feel they belonged in order for the publisher to make a consistent and visible appearance within a specific market — and their marketing, but while they routinely grumbled at Society of Authors meetings they largely left it to the publishing professionals to do what they thought best. If they spotted trends within the industry, and tried to produce something similar for a publisher, they were generally late and jostling within a very crowded market — hence the much over-announced 'next Harry Potter'. Publishing rights consultant Lynette Owen confirmed her belief that 'I do think there is still a lack of understanding by some published authors — and I have often been surprised by authors who

---

1 The Publishers Association, *PA Code of Practice on Author Contracts*, 2010, https://www.publishers.org.uk/resources/rights-and-contracts/
2 Lynette Owen, 'Author-Publisher Contracts: A Workshop for Authors', Dublin, Ireland, 10 March 2016.
3 Carole Blake, *From Pitch to Publication* (London: Macmillan, 1999). A second edition was long-promised but remained undelivered when Blake died in 2017.

make assumptions without going back to check the terms of their contract.'[4]

Traditional publishers however routinely filled the gap on their behalf. Although officially the contracts given out by traditional publishers require authors to indemnify them against associated legal risk, in practice publishers employed lawyers to the check content received, and the industry has a long-standing track record of choosing to support authors. Examples include Penguin's extremely expensive and sustained backing for Salman Rushdie after publication of *Satanic Verses* and, as I experienced during my first job in the industry, Heinemann Educational Books assuming temporary responsibility in 1983 for housing and maintaining Ngugi wa Thiong'o, when he was forced to live in exile from his native Kenya. Those who have a literary agent benefit from additional handholding. Literary agent Lizzy Kremer of David Higham Associates commented:

> Our ability to offer contractual guidance based on the law and on industry precedent and on our insight into the commercial realities of the Industry today features high on the list of reasons why authors appoint agents, although it is our negotiating power and experience as much as our legal insight that enables us to be as effective as we are in these matters.[5]

Literary agent Gordon Wise of Curtis Brown, also the immediate past President of the Association of Authors' Agents (AAA)[6] commented along similar lines:

> I wouldn't say that clients come to us seeking formal legal advice in isolation, but they certainly come expecting a package that includes experienced advice and negotiating power in relation to contracts, and assistance and someone to help lead the charge when things go wrong. Few agents are formally legally trained and would not claim to be, but good and established and reputable agents are experienced in the vast array of customs and practices under which publishing agreements operate and why they are drafted in the way they are, and look to see how to evolve them intelligently as technology and market practices change — without the Author losing ground. Some large agencies, like

---

4   Interview by the author with Lynette Owen, 2017.
5   Interview with author.
6   http://agentsassoc.co.uk/

ours, have access to in-house legal counsel but that is not a resource that can be offered in a bespoke hands-on way to every client as the lawyers are working across the needs of the company as a whole, but they are available for troubleshooting and advice, for strategic work on major deals, and for general overseeing of contracts processes and monitoring publisher requests for changes to boilerplate. Should a major legal situation arise we would discuss with the client what need there might be for third party advice. But we have a team of contracts managers who vet every contract and are in regular contact with the publishers' contracts teams.[7]

Other agents I spoke to took a similar line; Heather Holden-Brown of the HHB Agency commented that authors regularly need to have explained the difference between licensing publishing rights as opposed to copyright, and the meaning of specific clauses such as 'reversion of rights'.[8] Several agents said they recommended that authors who want specific legal advice should join the Society of Authors: although a range of services are offered by the Society, the benefit of legal guidance over contracts that comes with a subscription remains the most common reason for joining, as well as the most frequent source of member enquiries. The Society vets over 1,000 contracts a year, and staff who undertake this work make up about a quarter of the workforce. The Society also lobbies collectively on behalf of members (e.g. with the BBC and the Publishers Association) and informs members about wider legal changes that are intended to protect authors such as the so-called 'transparency triangle' in the European Union digital single market proposals. Published sources (e.g. Society of Audiovisual Authors, 2016[9]) suggest that authors earn more when such safeguards exist — although the position will become more complicated after Brexit. They also collaborate with the Association of Authors' Agents, as Wise confirmed:

> We do of course recommend to authors that they join the Society of Authors, which has excellent legal services for members and a body of specialist knowledge in relation to publishing IP, and the AAA often

---

7   Interview with author.
8   Ibid.
9   Society of Audiovisual Authors, 'Audiovisual Authors' Remuneration — From Remuneration to Transparency?', 12 September 2016, http://www.saa-authors.eu/en/blog/150-audiovisual-authors-remuneration---from-remuneration-to-transparency

works in tandem with The Society of Authors to ensure that authors' contracts are legally sound and respect authors' rights.[10]

Times are however changing, and authors are having to become more aware of their legal responsibilities themselves. For some, this increased awareness has come from their experience of making work freely available in order to build a market presence, being less concerned about piracy and more concerned about visibility. Based on his research at Kingston, Masters student Philip Dyson commented:

> From the consumer point of view, readers and creative consumers in general sample, or 'stream' lots of creative content, either through cheap subscriptions like Netflix or Spotify, or do it for free. But when they find an artist that they do really like, they will go out of their way to pay for this content, e.g. by buying the CD, book, or whatever other format the artist works in) and in the case of some authors they will pay through the roof for related paraphernalia. The point being that consumers do not want to pay for content in general, but rather for specific content that they want. A good example is Justin Bieber, who is famous not because of a record label but because he could post his music videos on YouTube for free, which enabled him to build up his fan base. When looking at copyright issues with digital technology, the music industry has played a big part in my research, and it's interesting how publishers in this sector are adapting. For example, independent music publisher Kobalt[11] have completely streamlined their business model, while offering rigorously transparent information for their musicians — they even have a financial tracking app that enables artists to see how much money they are making, where they are making it and how much the publisher is making, all from their phone.[12]

How publishing companies manage the situation has also prompted authors to take more responsibility themselves. While large publishing companies continue maintain in house legal expertise, an industry-wide need to reduce costs and hence preserve margins has prompted a discernible shift in some companies away from employing in-house contracts staff, with the process increasingly managed through the issuing of standard contracts wherever possible, and these being passed on to authors by their commissioning editors. While this cuts down the

---

10   Ibid.
11   www.kobaltmusic.com
12   Interview with author.

number of people with whom the author has to deal, it arguably has the side effect of making it more difficult for authors to raise issues that concern them since to do so they would have to negotiate with the editor who agreed to publish their work, and to whom they might therefore feel indebted.

Literary agents too are finding that the costs of offering legal support are rising all the time. Literary agent Andrew Lownie commented:

> Authors do appreciate legal expertise. I've a little experience having gone to law school but I use experts. I'm finding my bills for legal and contractual advice are becoming very large — £600 today for just one author (whose commission earnings are not much more) to sort out incorrect royalties and sloppy contracts. We are cutting back on publishing controversial books in the agency's publishing imprint. This is because of the costs — even though we sometimes share them — and the time involved.[13]

This was confirmed by Heather Holden-Brown:

> We do have one or two go-to legal advisers who sometimes we would use to advise an author. That said, sometimes we would put them in direct touch as we are not lawyers and it may be appropriate that the legal adviser works with the author and the author pays for their services.[14]

While trade authors are thus moving towards greater awareness of their contractual obligations, academic authors have had to take responsibility for their output for much longer. Academics imbued with the principle of 'publish or perish' and seeking publication in peer-reviewed journals are routinely offered a set of editorial instructions according to which their material must be organised before submission. Each journal has different requirements; many now offer pre-submission editorial intervention for which the author must pay (e.g. editorial support and copyediting). The growth of open access (OA) within journals publishing has arguably had the unexpected side-effect of making academic authors aware of the costs of reviewing submissions and editorial preparation for publication, reinforcing their personal responsibility for what they submit (e.g. being required to negotiate with their institution or funding council to pay for the OA that will enable immediate dissemination).

---

13 Ibid.
14 Ibid.

Once they have formatted it appropriately, and decided they are ready to offer their work for consideration, academics are required formally to assume responsibility for despatch; having pressed the 'Submit' button themselves, they now regularly receive an 'Are you sure?'. In the process they assume responsibility for what is despatched, including the (lead) author's responsibility for managing content on behalf of others. Prosecutions for misrepresentation of ownership or falsification of data fall upon the individual (not the institution), well publicised and generally career-ending.

The question of who takes responsibility for securing and managing the legal ownership of writing, as well as the wider issue of whether the content is appropriate, is particularly interesting in the context of self-publishing. This article is predicated on my growing understanding, fuelled by a programme of research into the processes and practice of self-publishing over the past eight years, that the decision to self-publish often sparks the author's interest in, and understanding of, the legal responsibilities and associated opportunities created by sharing content. Nowhere is this more evident than in the attitudes of the self-publishing community (a word not lightly used) towards copyright.

Background: An Assumption of Ignorance on the Part of the Self-Published

As self-publishing grew in the early twenty-first century, it was treated with disdain.[15] At industry conferences (e.g. *Writing in a Digital Age*, a series of conferences organised by The Literary Consultancy, 2012–2014 at the Free Word Centre) there was an ongoing assumption that authors were either of the published or self-published variety, and the publisher's role was to distinguish between the two, rather like the child's fishing game in which players with magnetised rods tried to locate all the similarly equipped fish.

The range of those who dismissed self-publishing was broad: traditional publishers; the traditionally published; those aspiring to traditional publication; retailers; the literary press; academia — who in

---

15 Alison Baverstock, 'Big Audio-Visual Dynamite: The Publishing Revolution', *Mslexia* 38 (July/August/September 2008), 8–12.

my case considered a research interest in self-publishing a remarkably poor use of time.¹⁶ But their collective disdain ignored two significant associated human truths:

- Firstly, that finishing a piece of writing that has long burned inside you feels good, even if it goes no further. Writing prompts reflection, consideration, reordering and crafting — all of which tend to deliver a positive experience, even if the associated work remains unpublished.

- Secondly that in the process of self-publishing, authors learn about publishing in general; they gain feedback and metrics related to those who read their material (e.g. how long they read for, which points they linger over, where they stop) — and they are empowered by this information.

The resistance to self-publishing was not total, although arguably only because the literary mainstream failed to exclude self-published authors, rather than because they offered such authors opportunities for participation. While most literary prizes did not allow self-published submissions, the literary press declined to review self-published titles and the professional press (largely paid for by publishers' advertising) mostly avoided discussing the potential impact of these developments, more mainstream journalists (and particularly those working for local presses) found that stories of those who had successfully self-published appealed to their readers and gave them more stories to tell (author gets published; this is what they wrote about; here's who's reading it; plucky author beat the traditional system; these people said it was impossible/encouraged them; here's how they did it; now you can do it too — and here are ten top tips).¹⁷ The first self-published book to win a major prize (Siobhan Curham's *Dear Dylan*, which won MIND Book of the Year in 2010) got much more publicity than previous winners for just these reasons: there was more story to tell. With technology and publishing services increasingly available to support the process,

---

16 Alison Baverstock, 'Why Self-Publishing Needs to be Taken Seriously', *Logos, Journal of the World Publishing Community* 23.4 (2013), 41–46.

17 See for example Rachel Abbott, '14 Hour Days, Marketing and Dealing with Snobbery: My Life as a Self-Published Bestseller', *The Guardian*, 30 March 2016, https://www.theguardian.com/books/2016/mar/30/self-publish-and-be-damned-rachel-abbott-kindle

publishing services companies started establishing themselves to serve the market (e.g. White Fox and Reedsy), and high profile self-published authors were in plentiful supply to interview.[18]

My investigation into self-publishing began in 2007. I began by looking at the trends in general[19] and then progressed to qualitative interviews with fifty-seven self-published authors, mostly of print books although sometimes with an accompanying ebook; this was published by a traditional publisher as *The Naked Author*.[20] A quantitative survey of self-published authors followed, with options for additional comments.[21] Three traditional assumptions were quickly challenged:

1. **Self-publishers are poorly educated, too untalented to get published and are mostly retired hobbyists**. Rather they emerged as educated, busy and affluent. My cohort was twice as likely to be in full-time employment as retired. They were also generally educated (76% had a degree; 44% of them at either Masters or PhD level) and from a professional background, hence with resources to spend on their projects.

2. **Self-publishing delivers no satisfaction**. My questionnaire checked for this repeatedly and found that whatever issue posed (What is your overall satisfaction level with self-publishing? Would you do it again? Would you recommend self-publishing?), the associated responses were very positive; supporting comments noted profound satisfaction levels whatever the final format achieved. Publishers have tended to sniff at poorly produced books and assume that only publication that matched their own professional standards would deliver satisfaction. What rather emerged was that the completion itself mattered, not wider production standards

---

18   Danuta Kean, 'Buying Houses in Cash and Selling Millions: Meet Self-Publishing's "Hidden" Authors', *The Guardian*, 8 June 2017, https://www.theguardian.com/books/2017/jun/08/buying-houses-in-cash-and-selling-millions-meet-self-publishings-hidden-authors

19   Baverstock, 'Big Audio-Visual Dynamite'.

20   Alison Baverstock, *The Naked Author: A Guide to Self-Publishing* (London: Bloomsbury, 2011).

21   A. Baverstock and J. Steinitz, 'Who Are the Self-Publishers?' *Learned Publishing* 26.3 (2013), 211–23; A. Baverstock and J. Steinitz, 'What Satisfactions Do Self-Publishing Authors Gain from the Process?' *Learned Publishing* 26.4 (2013), 272–82.

or significant dissemination; even stories of manuscripts lost or compromised in production were not accompanied by dissatisfaction with the associated process.

3. **Self-publishing means 'going it alone'**. Assuming that vanity lay at the root of all self-publishing, its detractors were confident that self-aggrandisement would pre-empt legal awareness among those insufficiently talented to secure the support of a traditional investor; 'going it alone' would mean just that — and hence careful attention would not be paid to the legal obligations associated with publishing. Perhaps unsurprisingly, given that those involved were busy and affluent, they also tended to have the resources to complete what they had begun, and I found they regularly commissioned services from industry suppliers: editorial, marketing and increasingly legal advice (19% of my cohort had sought professional legal advice).

Meanwhile, new services were emerging to cater for the needs of those who wanted to develop their writing (with or without the goal of publication) and the digital economy offered many new ways of sharing and encouraging wider involvement in literary composition. Writing development agencies such as Rebecca Swift's The Literary Agency[22] (founded 1996) and Cornerstones Literary Agency[23] (founded 1998) provided support for writers with a story to tell and the freedom to develop their work without a prescribed goal. The market was extended through writing holidays, writing conferences, strands for writers within literary festivals (pioneered by Catherine Lockerbie, Director of the Edinburgh Book Festival), and even publishers and agents joined in, offering paid services to writers (e.g. The Faber Academy[24] and the writing courses run by some literary agencies such as Curtis Brown Creative).[25]

Meanwhile independent editors have found they like working for self-publishing authors, particularly those who have done it before, and who tend to appreciate their services, pay their going rate punctually,

---

22 https://literaryconsultancy.co.uk/
23 http://www.cornerstones.co.uk/
24 https://www.faberacademy.co.uk/
25 http://www.curtisbrowncreative.co.uk/

and not try to negotiate 'fixed contracts' as is the increasingly common and much resented practice within the wider industry.[26] All these trends have significant long-term implications for the availability of the publishing services economy on which the traditional industry has long relied. Publishers may in future find that services on which they previously depended are being accessed and used by others (notably self-publishing authors), and are therefore no longer available to publishers as and when they need them. If, as has been widely understood, the difference between a published and a self-published title is the involvement of an editor, the irony may be that publishers have a reduced supply of editorial services available to them, and hence their ability to present effectively edited manuscripts as a unique identifier of their involvement is threatened.

The Growth of Contract Checking and Legal Services for Independent Authors

Taking responsibility for publishing your own work can present difficulties. Gordon Wise again:

> At Curtis Brown, we probably see more authors come to us who have self-published via KDP rather than third parties having been involved, and we're familiar with the KDP terms (although famously, of course, these can change!). But it's certainly true in the world of self-publishing, where the 'vanity publishers' of old seem to have migrated, that there seem to be the most liberties taken with authors' rights in terms of contracts served on unwitting authors, and this area is worryingly unregulated. The Society of Authors sees a number of very unreliable contracts from this quarter. And from 'publishers' who are probably offering little more than an author could get for themselves through using KDP and a reputable freelance services bureau or other provider.[27]

In this uncertain environment, there is a notable emergence of self-publishing agencies offering a supportive and expert service. For

---

26 A. Baverstock, R. Blackburn, and M. Iskandarova, 'Who Are the Independent Editors, How Did They Reach Their Role and What Are Their Associated Job Satisfactions?' *Learned Publishing* 28.1 (2015), 43–53; A. Baverstock, R. Blackburn, and M. Iskandarova, 'How Is the Role of the Independent Editor Changing in Relation to Traditional and Self-Publishing Models of Publication?' *Learned Publishing* 28.2 (2015), 123–31.

27 Interview with author.

example, SilverWood Books (founded 2007) highlighted the need for authors to be aware of the legal responsibilities that accompany publishing. Helen Hart, MD comments:

> At SilverWood, we try to help authors recognise their responsibility to protect themselves. Ignoring legal issues, especially those related to seeking adequate copyright permission, can have expensive long-term consequences. We have always included a brief article about copyright on the SilverWood website (in our 'Learning Zone') and regularly draw attention to it by sharing the link on social media, and also during individual conversations with authors.
>
> However, we're seeing an increasing number of manuscripts flagged by an editorial assistant or copy editor with comments about permissions and copyright, so last year we took more formal steps.
>
> Now, whenever the SilverWood team identifies that an author has included quotations or images that they haven't generated themselves, we send the author a one-page factsheet containing general information and links to formal resources. We also send a copyright permissions form that the author must complete. This specifically focuses the author's attention on the issues surrounding copyright and the need to seek and record formal permission for the use of copyrighted material.
>
> All authors who've received our form have completed it, and most have expressed gratitude for having their attention drawn to a matter they might otherwise have overlooked.
>
> Although it is the self-publishing author's responsibility to ensure they have gained permission, many do not realise it is necessary. There is still a common misconception that if material is on the internet, it's fine to use it. Authors who choose to work with a company like SilverWood have the advantage of being able to access experts who can offer guidance, and help the author make informed decisions.[28]

Particularly noteworthy has been the emergence of a market among authors for paid-for advice on legal issues, for example Kevin Stewart, until 2008 Director of Group Contracts at Hodder Headline, moved to an external contracts consultancy and now works for Contracts People.[29] Similarly, Clare Hodder, Rights Director of Macmillan, established her own consultancy practice in 2014 (Clare Hodder Consulting).[30] Contract checking has long been The Society of Authors' most accessed member service, and in 2012 the society formalised what they meant

---

28   Ibid.
29   www.contractspeople.co.uk
30   www.clarehodderconsulting.org.uk

by self-published authors (who are qualified to join if they have self-published and sold 300 or more copies of a single title in print form or 500 or more copies of a single title in ebook/digital form within a 12 month period; those who have sold fewer are able to apply for Associate membership). The Alliance of Independent Authors[31] (founded in 2011) sees legal advice as one of the main services it provides. Its director, Orna Ross comments:

> In the past, income for authors rested on the existence of strong copyright legislation and adherence. As we take digital reading into a future of Blockchain[32] and Cryptocurrency,[33] it is likely to rest elsewhere. For now, it is undoubtedly true that the pressing problem for most authors, self-published or trade-published, is not piracy but obscurity.
>
> We recommend our members not to choose DRM.[34] If a book is being pirated, the majority of those downloading it wouldn't have bought it anyway. And any self-respecting pirate can remove it and have a DRM-free version of your ebook file in no time. One thing we do recommend to those troubled by piracy is benefitting from the US Digital Millennium Copyright Act, which criminalises technology/services designed to get around Digital Rights Management (commonly known as DRM) controlling access to copyrighted works, for example, www.DMCA.com offers take-down notices when authors find that their sites are offering their books.[35]
>
> We publish a guide: 'How authors sell publishing rights',[36] to present our members with information and leave them to make up their own minds. *Each indie author is the expert in his or her own publishing life.*[37]

---

31 http://allianceindependentauthors.org/
32 www.blockchain.com is a leading software platform for digital assets.
33 'A cryptocurrency is a digital or virtual currency that uses cryptography for security. A cryptocurrency is difficult to counterfeit because of this security feature. […] A defining feature of a cryptocurrency, and arguably its biggest allure, is its organic nature; it is not issued by any central authority, rendering it theoretically immune to government interference or manipulation', Jake Frankenfield, 'Cryptocurrency', *Investopedia*, 10 December 2018, https://www.investopedia.com/terms/c/cryptocurrency.asp
34 Digital rights management (DRM) offers a variety of technologies that can be used to restrict access to, and hence usage of, proprietary hardware and work that is copyrighted. DRM seeks to control how such copyrighted work is used and modified, but therefore also restricts it being read, recommended and more widely disseminated.
35 A commercial service 'providing website owners with a secure system that protects their valuable content from theft or copyright infringement', https://www.dmca.com/
36 H. Sedwick and O. Ross, 'How Authors Sell Publishing Rights', 2016, https://www.ornaross.com/my-book/how-authors-sell-publishing-rights/
37 Interview with the author, 2017.

The last sentence is particularly significant. Self-publishing authors can become particularly well informed if they read all the information available on new possibilities for sharing material and building an audience. Ross comments further:

> There are new players in the giveaway frame, such as BookFunnel[38] and Instafreebie[39] and they have added a new way of distributing free books, and a new purpose: to enable authors to build their database of followers by effectively trading email addresses for free books. While the jury's still out on the long-term benefits of the latter approach, as we discover how many of these subscribers will unsubscribe — as is their legal right — or not bother to read their freebies, we are airing a debate about the pros and cons of giving away work.

The response of their members has been varied. Alli member Jan Ruth sees sharing material as an opportunity:

> I chose to promote my latest title in this way partly as an experiment, because this time I wanted to split the performance between my own efforts through Twitter and my Facebook Author Page, and Book Blast. I did it this way because I wanted to achieve something long-term; I wanted to attract readers who would hopefully stay engaged and add to my slowly growing audience, my personal readership.[40]

Another Alli member, Michael Jason Brandt, however uses the same platform to make the case against making work available freely:

> The vast (vast, vast) majority of free downloads never get read, so giveaways don't actually accomplish what they're intended to do: spread the word, get reviews. On top of that, many authors pay money to advertise these giveaways, and spring for shipping in the case of hard copies, so they're actually paying people to get a free copy and not read it.[41]

Of course author experimentation with formats and free samples is nothing new. In 2000 Stephen King experimented with publishing

---

38   https://bookfunnel.com/
39   https://www.instafreebie.com/
40   Jan Ruth, 'Opinion: The Value of Free Books', Self-Publishing Advice Blog, Alliance of Independent Authors, 10 March 2014, http://selfpublishingadvice.org/opinion-the-value-of-free-books-by-jan-ruth/
41   Michael Jason Brandt, 'Opinion: Why Indie Authors Shouldn't Give Away Free Books', Self-Publishing Advice Blog, Alliance of Independent Authors, 27 February 2017, https://selfpublishingadvice.org/opinion-why-indie-authors-shouldnt-give-away-free-books/

The Plant in online instalments, with the proviso that he would stop writing if the level of readers paying their $1 per instalment fell below 75%.[42] The trust element failed, and the finished version, if it indeed exists, remains uncirculated. Along similar lines, Alison Flood reported in *The Guardian* that best-selling author Paolo Coelho 'has long been a supporter of illegal downloads of his writing, ever since a pirated Russian edition of *The Alchemist* was posted online in 1999 and, far from damaging sales in the country, sent them soaring to a million copies by 2002 and more than twelve million today.' Flood quotes Coelho:

> 'The good old days, when each idea had an owner, are gone forever. First, because all anyone ever does is recycle the same four themes: a love story between two people, a love triangle, the struggle for power, and the story of a journey. Second, because all writers want what they write to be read, whether in a newspaper, blog, pamphlet, or on a wall,' he said. 'The more often we hear a song on the radio, the keener we are to buy the CD. It's the same with literature. The more people 'pirate' a book, the better. If they like the beginning, they'll buy the whole book the next day, because there's nothing more tiring than reading long screeds of text on a computer screen.'

In 2012 he announced he was launching a new programme on The Pirate Bay,[43] and 'exhorting readers to download all his work for free.'[44]

But Coelho was *already* a best-selling traditionally published author when he began experimenting with flexing his rights. A much wider range of self-publishing authors are becoming much better informed in the process of experimentation in the publishing of their own work, and given that the self-publishing community habitually circulates information about routes to success, this increased awareness is surely likely to spread.

---

42 Knowledge@Wharton, 'Stephen King's Novel Idea: Will It Change the Publishing Industry?', 16 August 2000, http://knowledge.wharton.upenn.edu/article/stephen-kings-novel-idea-will-it-change-the-publishing-industry/
43 http://www.thepiratebay.se.net/
44 Alison Flood, 'Paulo Coelho Calls on Readers to Pirate Books', *The Guardian*, 1 February 2012, https://www.theguardian.com/books/2012/feb/01/paulo-coelho-readers-pirate-books

Academic Publishing

Within academic publishing the picture is more complex, but self-publishing can still create additional opportunities.

Some form of open access is now routinely demanded by most universities and funding bodies. But open access is not just one thing; providing unhindered access to content (which is what OA means) can come in many forms — which could include self-publishing. It therefore behoves academic authors to establish the official requirements of their organisation and funding body (most have developed their own specific institutional guidelines) and to consider what is in their best interests. Kate Pool, Deputy Chief Executive of the Society of Authors comments:

> As part of their OA requirements, some funding bodies and universities now seem to favour a Creative Commons licence, although in The Society's view they are never a good option and a standard, limited, non-exclusive licence would generally be far more appropriate in every way. The Society's concerns about Creative Commons licences are summed up in a recent edition of *The Author*[45] but centre on the licence being granted to everyone worldwide, and CC being irrevocable and impossible to terminate, with further complications in that if a work includes quotations or images from other sources, it is very likely that the right holders of such items will not give consent for Creative Commons use.[46]

Summarising, she stresses the need for authors to assess their intentions:

> If they want high academic penetration and/or access to REF or other funding, or are using material generated during the course of their academic work, as students or teachers, they will need to be mindful of existing institutional restraints/conditions and will in any case want to go with a highly regarded publisher in their field, if they are given assurances about rigorous peer review, even when the publishing terms are (as they will be) dire. If a specialist author simply wants to get their work 'out there' and to keep as much control as possible over it into the bargain, then self-publishing may be the preferable option. If you self-publish you can of course choose how widely/narrowly you make the work available.[47]

---

45 Society of Authors, 'Creative Commons Licences', *The Author*, 2016, 78–79.
46 Interview with the author.
47 Ibid.

Implications for the Wider Creative Economy

The increasing numbers of informed authors has significant implications for the wider creative economy.

As self-publishing grew in the early twenty-first century, those involved became increasingly confident; much less constrained by publishing traditions, they could write what they liked rather than what they were asked to provide — and were regularly sustained by direct, unmediated feedback from their readers with whom they felt a real connection. Given the acknowledged difficulty in establishing a new author's profile within an already overcrowded market, advice from traditional investors has often been for authors to stick to a single genre — often to the frustration of those who felt they had more than one kind of material within them. Now self-publishing authors increasingly experiment across platforms and new genres have begun to emerge, such as the generic, and often redemptive, memoir tacking an area of interest to many but without a celebrity author (e.g. Lisa Genova's *Still Alice*) or characters developed from established titles (e.g. E. L. James's *Fifty Shades of Grey*, which was first self-published online before its success led to its being re-released by Vintage Books in 2012). What is more, the desire of these authors for self-determination mirrored developments within other creative areas, as this quote by pop star Ed Sheeran demonstrates:

> I think the moment you start trying to please a fan base is when you start going downhill. I'm going to always, always write about what I want, even if it doesn't necessarily cater to most of them.[48]

---

48   Elizabeth Perle, 'Ed Sheeran on Writing His New Album in "A Couple Of Weeks" And Why No One Cares About His Personal Life', *Huffpost UK*, 21 May 2013, https://www.huffingtonpost.co.uk/entry/ed-sheeran-i-genuinely-do_n_3304554. Although Sheeran's principles are clearly stated, his options are arguably much more open as a highly successful pop star. It is also fairly clear that he actually has a sharp eye on commercial concerns e.g. from this 2017 GQ profile: 'It is the perfect demonstration of how his mind works: he admitted that Irish folk music "isn't the coolest thing", as his label feared, but told them it that it was going to be "f***ing massive" because there are 400 million people in the world who will say they are Irish even if they aren't. For Sheeran, there is no conflict between the demands of creativity and commerce.' (George Chesterton, 'How Ed Sheeran Became the Biggest Male Popstar on the Planet', *GQ*, 2 February 2017, https://www.gq-magazine.co.uk/article/ed-sheeran-new-album-divide) That song was also released on St Patrick's Day — in various ways it was very carefully tailored to a certain fan base.

The self-published did not necessarily always seek to market their work, either conventionally or at all. I found self-publishing authors might decide to finalise their work without immediate dissemination; to hold their story in a format that, while far from traditionally perfect, offered the chance for subsequent revisiting. Some authors wrote live (e.g. publishing daily instalments on a blog or live within a chat room), seeking immediate feedback; new methods of sharing emerged (countable downloads, charity-based projects, collective funding through seeking external investors, auctioning opportunities for a named individual to have their name or organisation incorporated within a work). The marketing and dissemination could come later, if the author so desired; the important thing for the short term was ensuring that the work existed. This prompted my definition of self-publishing49 as 'the process of assuming personal responsibility for the finalisation and production of content'.[50]

The existence of better informed and more confident self-publishing authors will likely have consequences for the creative economy.

1. Informed Authors

Authors who have self-published are changed; they are more aware of the processes and details involved in producing something special and more aware of the risks and opportunities of making work available. In the process they gain metrics about their market and information on how adjusting prices and changing jackets can impact on a customer's sensitivity to 'pricing points' and willingness to pay; they become aware that slight tweaks can cause a disproportionate response. So if, as now regularly happens, they subsequently find that publishing is vastly more complicated than they had previously realised, and that they would rather devote their energies to writing and so take up an offer of professional representation from a traditional agent or publisher — they still approach the negotiation empowered. Armed with statistics and a confidence that comes from understanding why their market appreciates their work, they are likely to be more effective and less grateful negotiators.

---

49 Alison Baverstock, 'Self-Publishing's Vices and Virtues', *The Guardian*, 20 November 2014, https://www.theguardian.com/books/booksblog/2014/nov/20/self-publishing-vices-virtues-alison-baverstock
50 Baverstock, *The Naked Author*, p. 32.

What is more, a confidence in their connections with readers may overtake their awareness of their legal responsibilities. The Group Contracts Director of a major publishing house commented that while she would hope authors with self-publishing experience would be more knowledgeable, rather than less, about the book publication process, in fact 'the only anecdotal evidence I can give was an author who self-published in the US but we took her on for ebook and print publication in the UK. We struggled to convince her about the importance of the editorial process (she wanted to release her book in the US without any editorial filter, even a copy-edit, as she "Didn't want to keep her fans waiting") and she didn't understand the necessity of having territorial restrictions in place so wasn't prepared to stop US copies getting into territories she had granted exclusively to us.'[51]

2. Competition for Reader Attention

Publishers and authors are now competing for reader loyalty. Selling through specialist retailers (bookshops) in the past distanced both publishers and authors from eyeball to eyeball contact with their customers; publishers have only recently been able to establish a direct relationship with their readers and purchasers, because of their new ability to get involved in online distribution.

But their access is not unique. Readers can also now approach authors directly, through their websites, social media presence and literary festivals, which have grown hugely in recent years. Against the background of a less deferential society, readers now regularly feel empowered to speak to, if not challenge, their favourite author — rather than write a respectful letter to their publishing house and hope it gets passed on. In the process the writers understand how their work is appreciated and what their readers want. A commonly quoted reason for self-publishing is a desire to provide the kind of books the author had themselves wanted, and equally common are expressions of responsibility towards both the craft of the writer and the preferences of their previously underserved readership.

---

51   Personal conversation with the author.

3. Self-Publishing Authors Display the Characteristics Needed by Publishers Today

This blend of proactivity and personal responsibility is precisely what publishers now need from their authors. The diversification of the media has led to an exponential expansion in the information and entertainment options available to the market, and a consequent lack of predictability about how people spend their leisure time. Amazon has disrupted the standard selling model and authors who not only understand their market, but know how to reach them, are extremely useful. Publishers have always appreciated the 'marketable author'; now the self-determination and resilience that enables writers to self-publish effectively are being sought by traditional investors. Publishers are actively seeking *author entrepreneurs*, who can not only write but are sufficiently proactive and motivated to work in partnership with their investors. As agent Heather Holden-Brown commented: 'Self-published authors are probably better at knowing opportunities and the commercially-minded ones learn how to take them. It's interesting that some authors, having discovered self-publishing, prefer it as they have control, potentially make more money and are not competing against other authors on a publisher's list.'

In conclusion, within the publishing industry, rights have emerged as *the* key area for future development; knowledge of rights is crucial if an author or publisher is to take proposed content and cross-sell it from one market to another, traversing boundaries and reaching out to new markets — and in the process establishing a wider and hence more sustainable platform for future delivery from which other content and associated products can be sold.

Self-publishing is having a significant impact on the traditional publishing industry; it's now routine for the weekly bestseller lists in US and UK to feature authors who began by self-publishing. Professional publishers are noting areas in which self-publishers have been successful — often previously overlooked or significantly under-estimated — and signing up those authors who, through a process of trial and error, have a measurable connection with their readers, possess significant business and legal understanding, and demonstrate resilience — and hence require less hand-holding. These are exactly the kind of invested partners the traditional industry needs in order to plan for the future, when to survive customers must be found beyond the comfortable cultural homelands of regular book-buyers that have been relied upon in the past. Those offering publishing services[52] are finding that self-publishing offers a much wider, and significantly more profitable, market for their professional capabilities than the traditional industry alone.

In short, rather than delegating responsibility to others, today it behoves all authors to understand their markets and know their legal responsibilities and their rights. Those who look after these things for you will probably look after themselves first. Or as Bertolt Brecht has Polly Peachum say in *The Threepenny Opera*: 'The law was made for one thing alone, for the exploitation of those who don't understand it.'[53]

---

52 Alison Baverstock, 'Ten Ways Self-Publishing Has Changed the Books World', *The Guardian*, 8 April 2013, https://www.theguardian.com/books/booksblog/2013/apr/08/self-publishing-changed-books-world
53 Bertholt Brecht, *The Beggar's Opera*, Act 3, scene 1, http://ota.ox.ac.uk/text/3257.html

Works Cited

Abbott, R. (30 March 2016) '14 Hour Days, Marketing and Dealing with Snobbery: My Life as a Self-Published Bestseller', *The Guardian*, https://www.theguardian.com/books/2016/mar/30/self-publish-and-be-damned-rachel-abbott-kindle

Baverstock, A. (2015) 'How Is the Role of the Independent Editor Changing in Relation to Traditional and Self-Publishing Models of Publication?' *Learned Publishing* 28.2, 123–31.

— (7 September 2015) 'Invisible no Longer! How Editors Are Well Placed to Benefit from Changes Within Publishing', Society of Editors and Proofreaders Conference.

— (8 September 2015) 'Crystal Ball Gazing', Plenary at Conference of Society of Editors and Proofreaders.

— (20 November 2014) 'Self-Publishing's Vices and Virtues', *The Guardian*, https://www.theguardian.com/books/booksblog/2014/nov/20/self-publishing-vices-virtues-alison-baverstock

— (2013) 'Why Self-Publishing Needs to be Taken Seriously', *Logos, Journal of the World Publishing Community* 23.4, 41–46.

— (May 2013) 'From Cinderella to Belle of the Ball', *Editing Matters, Journal of Society for Editors and Proofreaders*.

— (2013) 'Is Self-Publishing an Option?' *Lloyds Bank Shoreline Magazine*.

— (8 April 2013) 'Ten Ways Self-Publishing has Changed the Books World', *The Guardian* https://www.theguardian.com/books/booksblog/2013/apr/08/self-publishing-changed-books-world

— (December 2012) 'Now that Self-Publishing Offers Everyone a Potential Platform Through Which to Share Material, who (if Anyone) is Bearing an Associated Responsibility for Ensuring the Content Made Available is Fit for Dissemination?', *Proceedings of Annual International Conference of Journalism and Mass Communication*.

— (2011) *The Naked Author*: *A Guide to Self-Publishing* (London: Bloomsbury).

— (28 October 2011) 'In Depth — Self-Publishing', *The Bookseller*, http://www.thebookseller.com/feature/depth-self-publishing

— (7 October 2010) 'You're Not so Vain After all', *Times Higher Education*, https://www.timeshighereducation.com/news/kingston-university-youre-not-so-vain-after-all/413711.article

— (16 January 2008) 'Author Empowerment', *The Bookseller*, http://www.thebookseller.com/blogs/author-empowerment

— (July/August/September 2008) 'Big Audio-Visual Dynamite: The Publishing Revolution', *Mslexia* 38, 8–12.

— and Blackburn, R. and Iskandarova, M. (2015) 'Who Are the Independent Editors, How Did They Reach Their Role and What Are Their Associated Job Satisfactions?' *Learned Publishing* 28.1, 43–53.

— and Steinitz, J. (2013) 'Who Are the Self-Publishers?' *Learned Publishing* 26.3, 211–23.

— and Steinitz, J. (2013) 'What Satisfactions Do Self-Publishing Authors Gain from the Process?' *Learned Publishing* 26.4, 272–82.

Blake, C. (1999) *From Pitch to Publication* (London: Macmillan).

Brandt, M. J. (27 February 2017) 'Opinion: Why Indie Authors Shouldn't Give Away Free Books', Self-Publishing Advice Blog, Alliance of Independent Authors, https://selfpublishingadvice.org/opinion-why-indie-authors-shouldnt-give-away-free-books/

Brecht, B. (1928) *The Beggar's Opera*, http://ota.ox.ac.uk/text/3257.html

Chesterton, G. (2017) 'How Ed Sheeran Became the Biggest Male Popstar on the Planet', *GQ* 2 February, https://www.gq-magazine.co.uk/article/ed-sheeran-new-album-divide

Curham, S. (2010) *Dear Dylan* (Milton Keynes: Authorhouse).

Genova, L. (2007) *Still Alice* (New York: Gallery Books).

Flood, A. (1 February 2012) 'Paulo Coelho Calls on Readers to Pirate Books', *The Guardian* https://www.theguardian.com/books/2012/feb/01/paulo-coelho-readers-pirate-books

Frankenfield, J. (10 December 2018) 'Cryptocurrency', *Investopedia*, https://www.investopedia.com/terms/c/cryptocurrency.asp

Kean, D. (8 June 2017) 'Buying Houses in Cash and Selling Millions: Meet Self-Publishing's "Hidden" Authors', *The Guardian*, https://www.theguardian.com/books/2017/jun/08/buying-houses-in-cash-and-selling-millions-meet-self-publishings-hidden-authors

Knowledge@Wharton (16 August 2000) 'Stephen King's Novel Idea: Will it Change the Publishing Industry?', http://knowledge.wharton.upenn.edu/article/stephen-kings-novel-idea-will-it-change-the-publishing-industry/

Owen, L. (10 March 2016) 'Author-Publisher Contracts: A Workshop for Authors', Dublin, Ireland.

Perle, E. (21 May 2013) 'Ed Sheeran On Writing His New Album In "A Couple Of Weeks" And Why No One Cares About His Personal Life', *Huffpost UK*, https://www.huffingtonpost.co.uk/entry/ed-sheeran-i-genuinely-do_n_3304554

Publishers Association, The (2010) *PA Code of Practice on Author Contracts*, https://www.publishers.org.uk/resources/rights-and-contracts/

Ruth. J. (10 March 2014) 'Opinion: The Value of Free Books', Self-Publishing Advice Blog, Alliance of Independent Authors, http://selfpublishingadvice.org/opinion-the-value-of-free-books-by-jan-ruth/

Sedwick, H. and Ross, O. (2016) 'How Authors Sell Publishing Rights', https://www.ornaross.com/my-book/how-authors-sell-publishing-rights/

Society of Audiovisual Authors (12 September 2016) 'Audiovisual Authors' Remuneration — From Remuneration to Transparency?', http://www.saa-authors.eu/en/blog/150-audiovisual-authors-remuneration---from-remuneration-to-transparency

Society of Authors (2016) 'Creative Commons Licences', *The Author*, 78–79.

6. Telling Stories or Selling Stories: Writing for Pleasure, Writing for art or Writing to Get Paid?

Sophie Rochester

Digital Disruption of Traditional Publishing Models

A YouGov poll[1] in 2007 found that 'more Britons dreamt about becoming an author' than any other profession in the UK, followed by sports personality, pilot, astronaut and event organiser on the list of most coveted jobs.[2] The same poll showed that 10% of Britons aspired to be an author — 1 in 10 of the population in 2007. For some, these statistics might be surprising, especially given that in the same year it was reported that 80% of published authors were earning less than £10,000[3] per year and that the majority of published titles sold fewer

---

1 The YouGov poll questioned 2,461 people across Britain. YouGov conducts its public opinion surveys online using Active Sampling. Panel members are recruited from a host of different sources, including via standard advertising, and strategic partnerships with a broad range of websites. See: https://yougov.co.uk/about/panel-methodology/
2 Michelle Pauli, 'Writing Tops Poll of Ideal Jobs', *The Guardian*, 21 August 2017, https://www.theguardian.com/books/2007/aug/21/news.michellepauli
3 Hesmondhalgh highlights that in the emerging forms of digital distribution there are small numbers of big hits and, if anything, the reliance on hits is becoming more entrenched. See David Hesmondhalgh, *The Cultural Industries* (London: Sage Publications, 2013), p. 330.

than 1,000 copies.[4] It also demonstrates the many complex reasons why people choose to write — are they writing for pleasure, for art or to get paid?

The year these statistics were gathered, 2007, is significant in that this was the year before Amazon's Kindle Direct Publishing (KDP) platform launched in the UK, which effectively made it possible for anyone to become an author.[5] If 1 in 10 people wants to be a writer, and *can* be a writer, then this brings us to the thorny question: '*who should get paid?*'

While the traditional publishing industry had a long-established process to effectively filter through the sheer number of submissions, known as the slush pile, the emergence of popular self-publishing platforms has had a huge impact on the writing economy. The traditional process — an author is represented by a literary agent, who sells a title to a publisher, who edits this title and pushes it out to retailers, who in turn disseminate it to readers — has been increasingly disrupted. One of the key responsibilities of traditional publishers to their authors was, and still is, to maximize sales channels, yet here Amazon's Kindle was offering a publishing platform to anyone who wanted to publish, *and* a direct sales channel that in 2015 controlled 95% of the UK ebook market.[6]

Self-Published Marketplace Impacting on Traditional Publishing

One of the first things that self-published writers quickly realized was that to heavily price-promote would increase their chances of visibility in the Amazon store, putting pressure on traditional publishers to drive down the price of their own ebooks. As more and more people chose to

---

[4] John Crace, 'Don't Give Up the Day Job', *The Guardian*, 22 August 2007, https://www.theguardian.com/books/booksblog/2007/aug/22/dontgiveupthedayjob

[5] 'Since 2007, it has been possible for authors to create manuscripts, upload them to Amazon's Kindle Direct Publishing platform (or one of a number of others, such as Lulu) and then achieve multinational distribution without gatekeeping agents, editors, or publishers.' See Joel Waldfogel, 'How Digitization Has Created a Golden Age of Music, Movies, Books, and Television', *Journal of Economic Perspectives*, 31.3 (2017), 195–214 (p. 199).

[6] Michael Kozlowski, 'Amazon Controls 95% of the Ebook Market', *Good eReader*, 27 March 2015, http://goodereader.com/blog/electronic-readers/amazon-controls-95-of-the-ebook-market-in-the-uk

self-publish, however, the issues of discoverability became increasingly complex,[7] and understanding how to promote oneself as a self-published author fast became a new fixation. Companies responded to help meet this need, such as book discovery start-up, Jellybooks,[8] who in 2013 launched a new tool to help authors, publishers and agents to improve the online visibility of their books. A new writing economy began to emerge, designed to help self-published writers better understand how PR, marketing and social media might drive their book sales. All this was happening at a time of year-on-year growth of ebook sales, a collapse in high street bookselling (with Borders and BOOKS etc. closing) and a buy-out of Waterstones that created a major wobble for traditional publishers.

Despite this turbulence, the attraction of being published 'traditionally' showed no signs of waning. Major self-publishing stars, such as Amanda Hocking, chose to move their titles to traditional publishing houses, with an explanation that they just wanted to get on with writing, without having to think about the editing, marketing and selling of books.

> Just the editing process alone has been a source of deep frustration, because although [Amanda] has employed own freelance editors and invited her readers to alert her to spelling and grammatical errors, she thinks her eBooks are riddled with mistakes. 'It drove me nuts, because I tried really hard to get things right and I just couldn't. It's exhausting, and hard to do. And it starts to wear on you emotionally. I know that sounds weird and whiny, but it's true.'[9]

These moves represented an interesting shift for traditional publishers, perhaps putting them into the position of 'publishing services provider' as opposed to 'curator'.

These changes marked a new era for traditional publishing, with a focus on writers having to demonstrate the existence of an audience for their work in order to get published. An example of this was the

---

7 Georgina Atwell, 'Myths of Discoverability', *The Bookseller*, 8 October 2014, http://www.thebookseller.com/blogs/myths-discoverability

8 Jellybooks, 'About', 2017, https://www.jellybooks.com/about/about-jellybooks/introduction

9 Ed Pilkington, 'Amanda Hocking, the Writer who Made Millions by Self-Publishing Online', *The Guardian*, 12 January 2012, https://www.theguardian.com/books/2012/jan/12/amanda-hocking-self-publishing

publishing trend surrounding the commissioning of YouTube stars such as Zoella, to publish what are effectively 'books as merchandise' for their fans. It could be argued, however, that for the more commercial imprints within traditional publishing houses this model was long established, and that self-publishing and social media stars had merely added themselves to the mix of the well-established celebrity memoir and television tie-in.

The Squeeze of the Mid-List

The so-called 'democratisation' of publishing has created opportunities for new and emerging writers, but has simultaneously rocked traditional publishing's delicate ecosystem, with 'mid-list' writers reportedly suffering the most.[10]

Reading and writing have, without a doubt, changed significantly in the past decade; with new writing platforms and social media playing a big part in the way readers consume and share books, and even in the creative process of writing. Today, readers and writers are gathering in online communities and could be construed as being the new gatekeepers of fiction.

> Faced with a dizzying array of choices and receiving little by way of expert help in making selections, book buyers today are deciding to play it safe, opting to join either the ever-larger audiences for blockbusters or the minuscule readerships of a vast range of specialist titles. In this bifurcation, the mid-list, publishing's experimental laboratory, is being abandoned.[11]

---

10   Figures from Nielsen BookScan in 2015 revealed that the gap between publishing's rich and poor continues to widen and the top 1% of authors account for nearly a third of all UK book sales.
The Bookseller estimated that the UK print sales, reported by Nielsen, came from 55,000 authors, which means that the 50 writers who accounted for 13% of the £1.49bn in sales represent less than 0.1%. The top 500 — or top 1% — of authors clocked up 32.8% of sales, while the top 10% amassed 57%. The £199m netted by the top 50 authors represents a 21% increase on 2014, compared to a 6.6% rise for the UK print market as a whole. See Richard Lea, 'Earnings Soar for UK's Bestselling Authors as Wealth Gap Widens in Books Industry', *The Guardian*, 15 January 2016, https://www.theguardian.com/books/2016/jan/15/earnings-soar-for-uks-bestselling-authors-as-wealth-gap-widens-in-books-industry

11   Colin Robinson, 'The Loneliness of the Long Distance Reader', *New York Times*, 4 January 2014, www.nytimes.com/2014/01/05/opinion/sunday/the-loneliness-of-the-long-distance-reader.html

Some of the UK's best-known writers, including Julian Barnes and Hilary Mantel, wrote for many years before achieving bestseller status. Hilary Mantel wrote her first novel in 1985, but it was her thirteenth book *Wolf Hall* that went on to win The Man Booker Prize in 2009, some twenty-four years later.

Traditionally publishers would nurture a writer's career over this long period, before a 'break-out' work of fiction. However, according to some author organisations such as The Book Society, commercial pressures on publishers exacerbated by the struggles of high street retailers and the impact of digital have compromised this nurturing process. Nicola Solomon, chief executive at the Society of Authors, said:

> Publishers are not investing in authors in a way they would have once, to see if they will take off after their fourth or fifth book, if their first or second were steady, but didn't go through [to a huge readership].[12]

At the Edinburgh International Book Festival in 2011, writer Ewan Morrison predicted a bleak future for professional writers in light of the digital disruption of the publishing industry. In a summary of his speech for *The Guardian*, Morrison stated:

> The digital revolution will not emancipate writers or open up a new era of creativity, it will mean that writers offer up their work for next to nothing or for free. Writing, as a profession, will cease to exist.[13]

In 2012, to help us understand the digital needs of writers, The Writing Platform launched an online survey and invited writers to contribute. We had over 500 respondents: 67% female, 33% male; 45% between the ages of 35 and 55; 75% of respondents live in the UK, 9% in the US, 5% in Australia, 3% in Canada, and the rest spread around the world, including the Philippines, Lithuania and Venezuela. 35% of these were aspiring writers; 33% traditionally published writers; 15% both traditionally and self-published; and 9% self-published. Out of this number, only 20% agreed that the statement that most accurately described their

---

12 Jennifer Rankin, 'Publish and Be Branded: The New Threat to Literature's Laboratory', *The Guardian*, 13 January 2014, http://www.theguardian.com/books/2014/jan/13/publish-brand-literature-hilary-mantel-jk-rowling

13 Ewan Morrison, 'Are Books Dead, and Can Authors Survive?', *The Guardian*, 22 August 2011, https://www.theguardian.com/books/2011/aug/22/are-books-dead-ewan-morrison

aspirations as a writer was, 'I want to make money from my writing'. By far the greatest number of people agreed with the statement 'I want my work to be read by lots of people' (39%).[14]

'Quality' and Critical Acclaim

For some literary writers, critical acclaim can hold equal importance to making money from their writing. However, one of the other casualties of digital disruption has been the cutting back, and sometimes total elimination, of the books review pages by the national newspapers.

In 2010, national literary editors were already admitting that review space had become 'an established novelist monopoly',[15] and publicists learnt quickly that it was becoming increasingly difficult to promote fiction from emerging novelists. As review space began to shrink, so too did the opportunities to break out or develop the careers of new writers.

Like other content industries, the global book publishing industry started to focus its marketing efforts on online searches (using search engine optimisation or SEO) and in the fight for online discoverability, understanding the use of 'keywords' to link readers with writers became imperative. While this might work for the discovery of non-fiction titles or genre fiction, for the more mercurial literary fiction category this poses a problem.

So are we in the midst of a shift in power from the traditional gatekeepers of fiction to the mass of readers growing more verbal and powerful online every day? And are there any advantages to this shift?

China and Online Reader/Writer Communities

One significant change is a new kind of reader/writer 'prosumer'[16] emerging as a dominant creative force in publishing, most readily

---

14 The Writing Platform Team, 'The Writing Platform Survey Results', The Writing Platform, 8 February 2013, http://www.thewritingplatform.com/2013/02/the-writing-platform-survey-results/
15 Michael Prodger (previously Literary Editor of *The Telegraph*), personal interview/statement made in support of the Fiction Uncovered promotion, 2010.
16 Ritzer and Jurgenson highlight that on Web 2.0 there has been a dramatic explosion in prosumption — in which the consumer is also a producer — namely on the blogosphere and social networking communities. See George Ritzer and Nathan

demonstrated by platforms such as Wattpad, which now boasts a total monthly audience of over 45 million,[17] who regularly read, vote, and comment on new writing. The Wattpad community collectively spends 15 billion minutes each month using Wattpad.

While some might argue that this shift is having an impact on how 'quality' writing is defined in the digital age — with the power of popularity and monetisation of writing apparently usurping 'craft and quality'[18] — there are others who argue that traditional publishers are being forced to widen their nets for writers, taking notice of genres that have long been ignored or dismissed.

Wattpad's business model followed closely the successful 'online literature' sites of China. Online Literature emerged in China in 1990 and it has grown rapidly since then, with companies like Cloudary (sometimes called Shanda or Shengda) leading the way. Readers in China now regularly access Online Literature, predominantly long-form serialised fiction, on their smartphones and tablets.

In the past ten years, the Online Literature sites have grown substantially, and this publishing system operates independently of the state-run publishers. The China Internet Network Information Centre (CNNIC) reported that China had 293 million Online Literature readers in 2014, an increase of 7.1% year on year.[19] The fast development was attributed to the rise in mobile phone use in China, and the platforms being widely supported by mobile companies.[20]

Like traditional publishers in the West acquiring rights for the new YouTube superstars and bestselling self-published writers, Chinese publishers started to take notice of the writers establishing themselves through online literature platforms. While traditional Chinese publishers might dismiss the quality of fiction being published on online literature sites, the lines between the traditional Chinese publishing industry and its grassroots online literature counterpart appear to be blurring, and

---

Jurgenson, 'Production, Consumption, Prosumption: The Nature of Capitalism in the Age of the Digital "Prosumer"', *Journal of Consumer Culture*, 10.1 (2010), 13–36 (p. 19).
17 Wattpad, 'About', https://www.wattpad.com/about/
18 Richard Sennett, *The Craftsman* (London: Penguin Allen Lane, 2008).
19 N.A., 'Mo Yan: Network Literature Is a Part of Literature', *Culture & Influence*, 10 October 2013, http://en.gmw.cn/2013-10/10/content_9125756.htm
20 Chinese Network Literature Marketing Research Annual Report, 2013.

the ways in which 'quality' is judged is also in transition. Dr Xiang Ren explains:

> I don't agree that the quality of content, particularly online user-generated literature should be assessed by traditional criteria. They have value because millions of readers enjoy reading them.[21]

So who does define 'quality' of writing in the digital age — the traditional gatekeepers or the readers?

Diversity

One of the longstanding criticisms of traditional gatekeepers in publishing is that, for too long, they have failed to diversify the writers who are commissioned. The recent report, *Writing the Future: Black and Asian Writers and Publishers in the UK Market Place*, commissioned by Arts Council England and conducted by Spread the Word, established that an 'old mono-culture still prevails' in publishing, despite efforts to make the industry more diverse. In relation to digital, the report stated that,

> Certainly from a customer point of view, the digital revolution has made it easier for readers to find exactly what they're looking for; a boon for readers searching for the BAME penned titles they can't find elsewhere. Speaking in Beige magazine, Rebecca Idris, winner of the 2013 Polari First Book Prize for her self-published 'gaysian' novel *The Sitar*, said: 'For niche books like mine, about sub-cultures, it's perfect because anybody who's reading around your book's subject just needs to type in a few keywords and they'll get it immediately, so your audience is perfectly targeted'.[22]

---

21 Qtd. in Sophie Rochester and Xin Lin, *The Publishing Landscape in China: New and Emerging Opportunities for British Writers* (London: Nesta, 2015), p. 18, http://theliteraryplatform.com/wp-content/uploads/sites/2/2015/05/The_Publishing_Landscape_in_China_2015.pdf.

22 Danuta Kean, 'Digital or Be Damned?', in Danuta Kean and Mel Larson (eds.), *Writing the Future: Black and Asian Writers and Publishers in the UK Market Place* (London: Spread the Word, 2016), p. 17, https://www.spreadtheword.org.uk/wp-content/uploads/2016/11/Writing-the-Future-Black-and-Asian-Authors-and-Publishers-in-the-UK-Marketplace-May-2015.pdf

If digital is able to offer new routes to publication for a wider group of writers then this is a perhaps a welcome side effect of disruption to the ecosystem.

A new 'publisher' can look very different today — it could be a literary agent or a crowd-funded community such as Unbound. Literary agents are able to operate as publishers, publishers can reach readers directly and, crucially, writers are now able to publish directly to publishing platforms such as KDP.

The economics of being a writer have mostly been considered in the context of the ebook or print book market. The digital revolution, however, has created, and will continue to create new opportunities for writers. The emergence of content marketing as a new emphasis for brands is just one interesting example, with well-known and established literary writers such as William Boyd writing for Land Rover, Neil Gaiman writing for Blackberry and Faye Weldon writing for Bulgari. A new generation of storytelling platforms, from videogames to VR experiences, are creating writing commissions for traditionally published authors.

The most interesting twenty-first-century publishers will be those looking to embrace the best of new technology and see how it can grow its audiences for writing across all platforms. Similarly, the writers who will perhaps profit most from the digital revolution are those that quickly identify and exploit this range of new opportunities.

Works Cited

(10 October 2013) 'Mo Yan: Network Literature is a Part of Literature', *Culture & Influence*, http://en.gmw.cn/2013-10/10/content_9125756.htm

(2013) *Chinese Network Literature Marketing Research Annual Report*.

Atwell, Georgina (8 October 2014) 'Myths of discoverability', *The Bookseller*, http://www.thebookseller.com/blogs/myths-discoverability

Crace, Jim (22 August 2007) 'Don't Give Up the Day Job', *The Guardian*, https://www.theguardian.com/books/booksblog/2007/aug/22/dontgiveupthedayjob

Hesmondhalgh, David (2013) *The Cultural Industries* (London: Sage Publications).

Kean, Danuta (2016) 'Digital or Be Damned?', in Danuta Kean and Mel Larson (eds.), *Writing the Future: Black and Asian Writers and Publishers in the UK Market Place* (London: Spread the Word), p. 17, https://www.spreadtheword.org.uk/wp-content/uploads/2016/11/Writing-the-Future-Black-and-Asian-Authors-and-Publishers-in-the-UK-Marketplace-May-2015.pdf

Lea, Richard (15 January 2016) 'Earnings Soar for UK's Bestselling Authors as Wealth Gap Widens in Books Industry', *The Guardian*, https://www.theguardian.com/books/2016/jan/15/earnings-soar-for-uks-bestselling-authors-as-wealth-gap-widens-in-books-industry

Mantel, Hilary (2010) *Wolf Hall* (London: Fourth Estate).

Pauli, Michelle (21 August 2007) 'Writing Tops Poll of Ideal Jobs', *The Guardian*, https://www.theguardian.com/books/2007/aug/21/news.michellepauli

Pilkington, Ed (12 January 2012) 'Amanda Hocking, the Writer who Made Millions by Self-Publishing Online', *The Guardian*, https://www.theguardian.com/books/2012/jan/12/amanda-hocking-self-publishing

Prodger, Michael (2010) Personal interview/statement made in support of the Fiction Uncovered promotion.

Rankin, Jennifer (13 January 2014) 'Publish and Be Branded: The New Threat to Literature's Laboratory', *The Guardian*, http://www.theguardian.com/books/2014/jan/13/publish-brand-literature-hilary-mantel-jk-rowling

Ritzer, George and Nathan Jurgenson (2010) 'Production, Consumption, Prosumption: The Nature of Capitalism in the Age of the Digital "Prosumer"', *Journal of Consumer Culture* 10.1, 13–36.

Robinson, Colin (4 January 2014) 'The Loneliness of the Long Distance Reader', *New York Times*, www.nytimes.com/2014/01/05/opinion/sunday/the-loneliness-of-the-long-distance-reader.html

Rochester, Sophie and Xin Lin (2015) *The Publishing Landscape in China: New and Emerging Opportunities for British Writers* (London: Nesta), http://theliteraryplatform.com/wp-content/uploads/sites/2/2015/05/The_Publishing_Landscape_in_China_2015.pdf

Sennett, Richard (2008) *The Craftsman* (London: Penguin Allen Lane).

The Writing Platform Team (2013) 'The Writing Platform Survey Results', *The Writing Platform* 8 February, http://www.thewritingplatform.com/2013/02/the-writing-platform-survey-results/

Tivnan, Tom (15 January 2016) 'Review of 2015: Donaldson is Top Author, Extends Record Run', *The Bookseller*, http://www.thebookseller.com/news/review-2015-donaldson-is-top-author-extends-record-run-320324

Waldfogel, Joel (2017) 'How Digitization Has Created a Golden Age of Music, Movies, Books, and Television', *Journal of Economic Perspectives* 31.3, 195–214.

Wattpad (2016) 'About', https://www.wattpad.com/about/

YouGov ([n.d.]) 'Panel Methodology', https://yougov.co.uk/about/panel-methodology/

7. Copyright in the Everyday Practice of Writers

Smita Kheria

1. Introduction

> Copyright ensures that authors, composers, artists, film makers and other creators receive recognition, payment and protection for their works.[1]

The preceding statement, by the European Commission, typifies conventional wisdom about copyright in relation to creators. While the importance of copyright in creative practices, particularly economically in terms of providing financial rewards, continues to be presumed in current copyright policy, recent copyright scholarship has started to empirically query how creative practitioners relate to copyright law.

Of all creative practitioners, historically, writers have received copyright protection for the longest amount of time: the Statute of Anne 1710 gave protection to authors in their writings for the first time in the United Kingdom. Yet, we know little about how writers in the UK perceive the role of copyright in their practice today, especially in the context of a changing technological and socio-economic environment,

---

1 European Commission, 'Digital Single Market Policy: Copyright', 2018, https://ec.europa.eu/digital-single-market/en/policies/copyright

one in which writers' incomes are falling and the economic value of copyright to creators, as well as the legitimacy of copyright itself, is being questioned. Therefore, it would seem pertinent to ask: How do writers perceive copyright and relate to it? Is copyright seen as valuable by them? And if so, who by, and why? This chapter addresses these questions by drawing on new empirical research conducted as part of a project titled 'Individual Creators', and funded by Research Councils UK through the research programme of CREATe.[2] The research comprised a large qualitative study (the IC study) that examines the relationship between copyright and the everyday life of creative practitioners across different creative disciplines (writing, visual arts, and music).

This chapter focuses on the data collected in the IC study that is particular to the profession of writing and copyright, with an emphasis on writers' perceptions and understandings of copyright, to assess the legitimacy of copyright in their day-to-day practice. Section 2 provides an example of an incident (drawn from ethnographic data from the IC study) that evidences the importance of being aware of authors' perspectives on copyright, while also being cognisant both of how individual earnings are made and the degree of importance placed on copyright by individual writers. Section 3 briefly reviews two strands of recent empirical research that question copyright's legitimacy in individual creators' livelihoods. Using data from the IC study, the remainder of the chapter challenges the inference that copyright has little to no economic value in writers' everyday practice. Section 4 briefly describes the IC study and the research methods. Sections 5–7 draw upon original interview data to present some thematic findings on how writers perceive the role of copyright in their day-to-day practices.[3] These findings indicate that the writers in question strongly perceive copyright to underpin their creative practices economically, *and* as rights that matter to them personally. Section 8 provides a conclusion.

---

2   CREATe is a national research hub based in the United Kingdom and funded by Research councils UK. The centre's aim is to investigate the future of creative production in the digital age, and in particular the role of copyright. See www.create.ac.uk. Unless otherwise stated, all quoted interviews were undertaken as part of this study. The author would like to thank the interviewees and research informants for facilitating and contributing to the underlying research project.

3   The chapter focusses on economic rights under copyright and not moral rights.

2. Copyright, Creators, and the Green Party: A Public Spat

In April 2015, two weeks before a general election in the United Kingdom, copyright received unusual media scrutiny when a policy document by the Green Party,[4] containing its plans for intellectual property, came to the attention of certain artistically inclined members of the electorate. On the night of 22 April, illustrator and author Sarah McIntyre tweeted a screenshot of the Green Party's policy on 'Intellectual Property' highlighting their plan to *'introduce generally shorter copyright terms, with a usual maximum of 14 years.'*[5] The screenshot was accompanied by the following comment:

> WHAT? Green Party aim to cut down copyright to 14 years. How are we supposed to earn a living?[6]

The plan was not in the Green Party's Election manifesto for 2015 but was instead found in a 'policy document' that seemed to elaborate on the election manifesto. The manifesto itself, under 'Information and Digital Rights', stated that 'We need copyright laws that reward creators but that are consistent with digital technologies' and it claimed that the Green Party would 'make copyright shorter in length, fair and flexible', but did not offer any further details.[7] Nevertheless, McIntyre's tweet, and a similar post by her on Facebook, quickly led to a discussion on both platforms, as various concerned illustrators and writers noted their views on the proposal and discussed its implications.[8]

---

4   The Green Party is a left-wing political party, see https://www.greenparty.org.uk/we-stand-for/; see generally N. Carter, 'The Greens in the UK General Election of 7 May 2015', *Environmental Politics*, 24.6 (2015), 1055–60.
5   Green Party, 'Economy: Part of the Green Party Policies for a Sustainable Society', EC1011. Policy version as at April 2015 (on file with the author; no longer available online).
6   See Sarah McIntyre, 'WHAT? Green Party aim to cut down copyright to 14 years. How are we supposed to earn a living? http://policy.greenparty.org.uk/ec.html', Twitter, 22 April 2015, https://twitter.com/jabberworks/status/590978835979571201
7   Green Party, 'For the Common Good: General Election Manifesto 2015', p. 61, https://www.greenparty.org.uk/assets/files/manifesto/Green_Party_2015_General_Election_Manifesto_Searchable.pdf
8   For example, see tweets on 23 April 2015 by Linda Grant: https://twitter.com/lindasgrant/status/591119358988050432/photo/1; and by Philip Pullman: https://twitter.com/PhilipPullman/status/591167079493033984

On 23 April, several newspapers picked up on the social media debate and reported that authors were shocked and alarmed by the Green Party's policy, and noted that it would be seen as an 'appalling injustice' if this shorter copyright term were to come to effect.[9] McIntyre told *The Telegraph*:

> It took me a long time to get into publishing and I've only started earning royalties. It's very hard to make a living this job, hardly anyone gets rich at it. JK Rowling and Julia Donaldson are the exceptions, most writers and illustrators earn below minimum wage […]. It scares me when it looks like someone wants to take away yet another source of income. It sounds like the Greens want us to rely on the Arts Council for funding instead of earning money directly from our work, and that would involve writing endless complicated grant proposals. I'd rather let my readers decide whether my work is worth their money than a handful of people in a government office.[10]

Initially, there was some confusion as to what the Green Party meant by 'a maximum of 14 years':[11] a maximum term of fourteen years after publication of a work, or a maximum term of fourteen years after the death of the author? After some back and forth,[12] Caroline Lucas, the Green Party's only Member of Parliament, admitted that the party had 'got it wrong'[13] and agreed to review its policy on copyright.[14] By 27 April, traditional news media coverage, for the most part, had ended and the party's offer to review the policy was seen as a victory (or at least a resolution, of sorts) for the authors.[15]

---

9   See K. Brown, 'Authors Criticise Green Party Plan to Reduce Copyright to 14 Years', *Telegraph*, 23 April 2015, http://www.telegraph.co.uk/culture/books/booknews/11557810/Authors-criticise-Green-Party-plan-to-reduce-copyright-to-14-years.html; J. Elgot, 'Green Party Plan to Limit Copyright Attacked by Writers and Artists', *The Guardian*, 23 April 2015, https://www.theguardian.com/politics/2015/apr/23/green-party-plan-to-limit-copyright-attacked-by-writers-and-artists
10 K. Brown, 'Authors Criticise Green Party Plan', *Telegraph*, 23 April 2015, http://www.telegraph.co.uk/culture/books/booknews/11557810/Authors-criticise-Green-Party-plan-to-reduce-copyright-to-14-years.html
11 Ibid.
12 Ibid.
13 Caroline Lucas, 'Copyright — Standing up for Brighton's Creative Industries, Artists and Writers', 25 April 2015, https://www.carolinelucas.com/latest/copyright-standing-up-for-brightons-creative-industries-artists-and-writers
14 Green Party, 'Greens to Review Copyright Policy', 27 April 2015, https://www.greenparty.org.uk/news/2015/04/27/greens-to-review-copyright-policy/
15 K. Brown, 'Green Party to Review Controversial Copyright Plans', *Telegraph*, 27 April 2015, http://www.telegraph.co.uk/culture/books/booknews/11565548/Green-Party-to-review-controversial-copyright-plans.html

Even if the party hadn't agreed to a review, the policy was never likely to result in legal reform in relation to the duration of copyright:[16] not with just a single Green Party Member of Parliament,[17] and not with long-standing international and EU frameworks in place that provide for a minimum term of copyright protection.[18] In fact, in response to the 'Twitterstorm' about the policy, a Green Party spokesman had noted that they had 'no plans to implement this in the near future.'[19] The specific issue of setting a fair term of copyright protection was clearly more complex than the party's policy makers had envisaged. The Green Party has since changed its policy: in the last revision of the policy document, dated April 2016, the offending phrase, quoted earlier, is no longer present in EC1011.[20]

---

16 While legal reform may not have been plausible in this context, it is worth noting that the duration of copyright protection has proven to be a particularly controversial aspect of the copyright framework, and one that has received significant attention in academic scholarship in the last few decades. Not only is the current term of protection seen as too long because it restricts the public domain and creates the problem of orphan works, various pieces of legislation that have extended the duration of protection in both the EU and US have been strongly critiqued. For examples pertaining to the EU see K. Puri 'The Term of Copyright Protection — Is it Too Long in the Wake of New Technologies?', *European Intellectual Property Review*, 12.1 (1990), 12–20; N. Dawson, 'Copyright in the European Union — Plundering the Public Domain', *Northern Ireland Legal Quarterly*, 45 (1994), 193–209; P. Katzenberger et al., 'Comment by the Max-Planck Institute on the Commission's Proposal for a Directive to Amend Directive 2006/116 Concerning the Term of Protection for Copyright and Related Rights', *European Intellectual Property Review*, 31.2 (2009), 59–72; M. Kretschmer et al., 'Creativity Stifled? A Joint Academic Statement on the Proposed Copyright Term Extension for Sound Recordings', *European Intellectual Property Review*, 30.9 (2008), 341–47; For examples pertaining to the US, see R. Posner, 'The Constitutionality of the Copyright Term Extension Act: Economics, Politics, Law, and Judicial Technique in Eldred v Ashcroft', *The Supreme Court Review*, 2003 (2003), 143–62; L. Lessig, 'Does Copyright Have Limits: Eldred v. Ashcroft and Its Aftermath', *Queensland University of Technology Law and Justice Journal*, 5.2 (2005), 219–30; R. Brauneis, 'A Brief Illustrated Chronicle of Retroactive Copyright Term Extension', *Journal of the Copyright Society of the USA*, 62.4 (2015), 479–502.

17 It was only in 2010 that the Green Party returned its first Member of Parliament, Caroline Lucas, for the constituency of Brighton Pavilion; while Lucas was successfully re-elected in the 2015, the party did not gain further seats in that election. See: https://www.parliament.uk/biographies/commons/caroline-lucas/3930

18 See Art. 7, Berne Convention for the Protection of Literary and Artistic Works, https://wipolex.wipo.int/en/text/283698; Directive 2011/77/EU, http://data.europa.eu/eli/dir/2011/77/oj

19 K. Brown, 'Green Party to Review Controversial Copyright Plans', *Telegraph*, 27 April 2015, http://www.telegraph.co.uk/culture/books/booknews/11565548/Green-Party-to-review-controversial-copyright-plans.html

20 Green Party, 'Economy', 2016, https://policy.greenparty.org.uk/ec.html

With respect to the representation of authors' perspectives in understanding the role of copyright and the legitimacy of copyright itself, this public spat serves two broader purposes. First, it is a cautionary tale for the Green Party not to ignore the impact of its policies on creative practitioners — a sentiment summed up in a tweet by a writer, Tom Cox, in his response to the controversial policy:

> That collective 'Oh' you just heard was a fuckload of authors seeing this & changing their minds about voting Green.[21]

The optimal duration of copyright protection is by no means an easy issue on which to formulate a policy.[22] However, the Green Party's mistake stemmed from a lack of proper consultation with artists and creative practitioners and a failure to attempt to understand how duration of copyright plays a role in their livelihoods; and instead to rely, perhaps uncritically, on one academic view, derived from economic modelling, that proposes an optimal duration of copyright to be around fifteen years from publication.[23] The incident demonstrates what can happen if those formulating policy fail to consult creators, and what can happen when there is misapprehension with respect to understanding creators' livelihoods and how much importance they place on those aspects of the copyright framework that help them sustain professional creative practices.

Second, the incident also highlights the contested nature of copyright in the digital world. The contestations were reflected, in particular, in the social media discussions on the policy, which continued long after traditional news coverage had ended. Here, the specific issue of duration of copyright protection simply functioned as a springboard to challenge the legitimacy of copyright protection itself. Authors'

---

21 See Tom Cox, 23 April 2015, https://twitter.com/cox_tom/status/591130047882342400/photo/1

22 The extensive critique of the current term of protection, and recent extensions to it, indicates a clear trend in academic scholarship suggesting that the current duration of protection is too long. See footnote no. 16 above. However, there doesn't appear to be any academic consensus on the optimal duration of copyright protection i.e. how long protection *should* last.

23 K. Brown, 'Authors Criticise Green Party Plan to Reduce Copyright to 14 Years', *Telegraph*, 23 April 2015, http://www.telegraph.co.uk/culture/books/booknews/11557810/Authors-criticise-Green-Party-plan-to-reduce-copyright-to-14-years.html; see also, R. Pollock, 'Forever Minus a Day? Calculating Optimal Copyright Term', *Review of Economic Research on Copyright Issues*, 6.1 (2009), 35–60.

criticisms of the Green Party's policy were countered with attacks on the role of copyright for creators: one example being a claim that instead of protecting creators, copyright was the 'worst thing' to happen to creatives and was a 'clusterfuck'. The discussions left some authors bewildered and frustrated with what they saw as a general lack of understanding about the actual role played by copyright in creative practices and creators' livelihoods. McIntyre, whose posts had sparked the spat, responded by discussing the importance of copyright on her blog and by sharing other authors' views in defence of copyright.[24]

While we know little, in academic scholarship, about how writers in the UK perceive the role of copyright in their practice today, the relationship between copyright law and creative practices has received increasing empirical attention in recent years. The next section briefly outlines the potential role and value of copyright exploitation in the careers of writers and reviews two stands of recent empirical research on writers' earnings and the negative space of IP.[25]

3. Copyright and Writers' Livelihoods

Copyright, being a property right,[26] and a negative right, in common with other intellectual property rights, gives the right owner the ability to exclude others from the market.[27] However, it is not simply

---

24 See S. McIntyre, 'In Defense of Copyright', *Jabberworks*, 27 April 2017, http://jabberworks.livejournal.com/703055.html

25 A further strand of such empirical research has examined how copyright can be a hindrance to certain creative practices and creative communities but doesn't question the legitimacy of the framework. For example, for the impact on arts and humanities researchers, see S. Kheria, C. Waelde, and N. Levin, 'Digital Transformations in the Arts and Humanities: Negotiating the Copyright Landscape in the United Kingdom', in R. Hobbs (ed.), *The Routledge Companion to Media Education, Copyright and Fair Use* (Abingdon: Routledge, 2018), pp. 182–200; for the impact on documentary filmmakers, see P. Aufderheide and P. Jaszi, 'Untold Stories: Creative Consequences of the Rights Clearance Culture for Documentary Filmmakers', Center for Social Media, 2004, http://archive.cmsimpact.org/sites/default/files/UNTOLDSTORIES_Report.pdf; for the impact on online creative communities, see C. Fiesler, J. L. Feuston and A. S. Bruckman, 'Understanding Copyright Law in Online Creative Communities', in *Proceedings of the 18th ACM Conference on Computer Supported Cooperative Work & Social Computing* (CSCW '15), 2015, 116–29.

26 Section 1, Copyright Designs and Patents Act 1988 (CDPA) in the United Kingdom, https://www.legislation.gov.uk/ukpga/1988/48/contents

27 C. Waelde et al., *Contemporary Intellectual Property: Law and Policy* (Oxford: Oxford University Press, 2016), para 1.44; P. Torremans, 'Questioning the Principles of

a negative right. It has both an external and internal aspect in terms of being beneficial to the right owner.[28] The external aspect captures the 'negative' aspect of the right i.e. the ability to exclude infringers from undertaking uses of a protected work that are exclusively granted to the copyright owner.[29] In contrast, the internal aspect is the ability to exploit the uses of a protected work that are exclusively granted to the copyright owner, usually through contractual arrangements (e.g. an assignment or license)[30] in return for economic or other gain.

The internal aspect of copyright facilitates writing-related income streams for writers: a) sale and licensing of copyright in written works, usually individually negotiated through a copyright contract with a publisher, in return for advances, royalties, and other types of profit-sharing arrangements; b) statutorily prescribed and collectively negotiated income for secondary uses of written works, such as payments for photocopying or lending of books.[31] Economic literature has largely focussed on the internal aspect of copyright, and it both presumes and emphasises that this is what is crucial for creators: it is the internal aspect of copyright that enables copyright contracts to operate and allows creators to receive monetary returns.[32] Consequently, recent empirical research on copyright and writers in the UK, has largely focussed on examining the role of the internal aspect of copyright, through assessing how writers earn a living and how much of their earnings emanate from exploitation of copyright in their works. This next part briefly reviews such research, and identifies what lessons it may offer on the legitimacy of copyright.

Territoriality: The Determination of Territorial Mechanisms of Commercialisation', in P. Torremans (ed.), *Copyright Law: A Handbook of Contemporary Research* (Cheltenham: Edward Elgar, 2009), pp. 460–82 (p. 461); *Ashdown v Telegraph* [2001] E.M.L.R. 44 para 30.

28 A. Rahmatian, 'Dealing with Rights in Copyright-Protected Works: Assignments and Licences,' in E. Derclaye (ed.), *Research Handbook on the Future of EU Copyright* (Cheltenham: Edward Elgar, 2009), pp. 286–316 (p. 286–87).

29 s.16 CDPA.

30 ss.90 and 92 CDPA.

31 These two categories are classified as 'Statutory right: individually negotiated income' and 'Statutory right: collectively negotiated income', in M. Kretschmer, 'Copyright and Contract Law — Regulating Creator Contracts: The State of the Art and a Research Agenda' *Journal of Intellectual Property Law*, 18.1 (2010), 141–72.

32 Kretschmer, 'Copyright and Contract Law', p. 143; on the significance of royalty contracts between authors and intermediaries, see generally R. Watt, 'Copyright Law and Royalty Contracts', in R. Towse and C. Handke (eds.), *Handbook on the Digital Creative Economy* (Cheltenham: Edward Elgar, 2013), pp. 197–208.

A. Writers' Earnings

In July 2015, Creative Scotland published its 'Literature and Publishing Sector Review', an independent study it commissioned to provide an overview of, amongst others, the future challenges and opportunities in literature and publishing in Scotland. The review asked, 'Can one make a living out of writing?' and then noted that: 'The answer for most writers is — with great difficulty.'[33] This statement is not surprising. Writing, as a profession, along with other creative practice-based careers, has been found to be risky and poorly remunerated, with average income appearing to be continuously falling in real terms in the United Kingdom, and many writers relying on sources of income other than writing.

In the last two decades, several earnings' surveys have obtained authors' earnings data by being administered through organizations representing them in the UK (Authors' Licensing and Collecting Society and the Society of Authors) and they indicate a downward trend in earnings from writing. In 2000, Pool published the results of a questionnaire survey, administered to members of the Society of Authors (SoA), a body of professional writers, in SoA's quarterly journal *The Author*.[34] The survey asked the respondents to provide 'approximate total gross income arising directly from their freelance writing in the previous year'.[35] Out of the 6,600 members of the society, 1,711 responded, and the survey revealed that the average (mean) earnings of the authors was only £16,600 per annum.[36] It also found that: 75% respondents earned under £20,000, and 46% earned under £5,000; at the other end of the spectrum, 5% earned over 75,000, and 3% earned over £100,000; and, writing was the only source of income for a mere 230 writers, about 13.5% of the respondents.[37]

---

33 Nordicity, 'Literature and Publishing Sector Review', Creative Scotland, June 2015, p. 22.
34 K. Pool, 'Love, Not Money', *The Author* (Summer 2000), 58–66.
35 C. Squires, 'Novelistic Production and the Publishing Industry in Britain and Ireland', in B. W. Shaffer (ed.), *A Companion to the British and Irish Novel, 1945–2000* (Oxford: Wiley Blackwell, 2005), pp. 177–93 (p. 190), https://doi.org/10.1002/9780470757611.ch12
36 M. Kretschmer and P. Hardwick, *Authors' Earnings from Copyright and Non-copyright Sources: A Survey of 25,000 British and German Writers* (Bournemouth: Bournemouth University, 2007), https://microsites.bournemouth.ac.uk/cippm/files/2007/07/ACLS-Full-report.pdf, p. 60.
37 L. Michael, 'Making a Living as a Writer', in S. Earnshaw (ed.), *The Handbook of Creative Writing* (Edinburgh: Edinburgh University Press, 2014), pp. 510–17 (p. 512).

Another survey, published in 2007, was commissioned by the Authors' Licensing and Collecting Society (ALCS).[38] The UK part of this survey was posted to 19,500 ordinary members of ALCS in 2006, and 1,345 questionnaires were returned (hereafter, 2006 survey).[39] From the full sample of respondents, it was found that the mean (average) earnings of UK authors were £16,531 per year, whereas the median (typical) earnings were £ 4000;[40] and only 20.3% of all writers earned all their income from writing.[41] However, a considerable number of UK responses were from academics and teachers (for whom non-copyright sources of earnings are more important), and other professionals or retired.[42] These were excluded from the category of professional authors — those who spend more than 50% of their time on self-employed writing[43] — being the most relevant category for policy purposes.[44]

The smaller sub-set of responses from professional authors indicated that the mean (average) earnings from writing were £28,340 and median (typical) earnings were £12,330 from a total of 525 respondents.[45] 40% of the professional authors were found to earn all their income from writing, 59.6% earned more than 50% of their individual income from writing, and 60% required a second source of income.[46] The report also noted significant inequality in the distribution of income within the profession with the top 10% of professional authors earning more than 50% of the total income, and the bottom 50% earning about 8% of the total income.[47]

A follow-up survey on authors' earnings, and commissioned by ALCS to be an update of the study above, amongst other reasons, was published in 2015.[48] The online survey was administered to a total of 35,000 members of 2 organisations, ALCS and SoA, in 2014, and 1,477

---

38 Kretschmer and Hardwick, 'Authors' Earnings from Copyright and Non-copyright Sources'.
39 Out of the total, 1,334 contained useful information although the number of valid responses on some of the survey questions is below this figure. Ibid., pp. 73–74.
40 Ibid., pp. 10 and 86.
41 Ibid., p. 24.
42 Ibid., pp. 8 and 78.
43 Ibid., p. 97.
44 Ibid., p. 22.
45 Ibid., pp. 5 and 99.
46 Ibid., p. 24.
47 Ibid., p. 23.
48 J. Gibson, P. Johnson and G. Dimita, *The Business of Being an Author: A Survey of Authors' Earnings and Contracts* (London: Queen Mary, University of London, 2015), https://orca.cf.ac.uk/72431/1/Final Report - For Web Publication.pdf

respondents completed the survey (hereafter, 2014 survey).[49] It found a decline in the income of professional authors, those who spend more than 50% of their time on self-employed writing: from a total of 630 respondents, the mean (average) earnings from writing were £28,577, a figure not far from the 2006 survey, but representing a decline in real terms; and, the median (typical) earnings were £11,000, less than minimum wage.[50]

Only 11.5% of the professional authors were found to earn all their individual income from self-employed writing, while 62% earned more than 50% of their individual income from such writing; nearly 90% needed to earn money from sources other than writing; and even writers who are better paid were found to earn from other sources.[51] Similar to the 2006 survey, it reported inequality in the distribution of income with the top 10% of professional authors earning 58% of the total income and the bottom 50% earning only 7% of the total income.[52] The 2014 survey also made some attempt to find out how the income from self-employed writing was split and found that the most significant contribution to such income came from royalty payments, followed by payments by ALCS, and from the Public Lending Right.[53]

The most recent earnings' survey was commissioned by the ALCS in 2017, as a follow up to the two surveys above.[54] A very brief overview of the survey results was made available in June 2018, and indicates that over 5,500 writers responded to the survey (hereafter, 2017 survey).[55] The median (typical) earnings of professional authors have continued to fall and were £10,437, again, less than minimum wage;[56] and, only 13.7% of the professional authors were found to earn all their income from writing.[57] Although full results are due to be published later in 2018, these figures suggest that writers' earnings are continuing to decline.

---

49 Although the number of responses to some of the survey questions is below this number. Ibid., p. 6.
50 Ibid., pp. 9, 10, and Table 2.4.
51 Ibid., p. 9 and Table 2.3.
52 Ibid., p. 8.
53 Ibid., p. 10 and Table 2.6.
54 ALCS, 'Authors' Earnings: A Survey of UK Writers', June 2018, https://wp.alcs.co.uk/app/uploads/2018/06/ALCS-Authors-earnings-2018.pdf
55 Ibid., p. 2.
56 Ibid., p. 4.
57 Ibid., p. 3.

The trend emerging from the earnings' data in these four surveys, which span the last two decades in the UK, seems to be clear: writing is a risky profession, marked by low earnings, and populated by a large number of authors who earn less than minimum wage from self-employed writing. With income inequality quite pronounced, many writers have portfolio careers as they seek additional sources of income to supplement that generated by their writing. But what does all of this imply, with respect to the legitimacy of copyright? Would it be fair to assume that copyright doesn't matter to writers in their everyday practice, at least not in terms of financial return? If this is true, would it be then correct to suggest that copyright protection is ultimately unnecessary for writers?

If one takes a reductive approach that focuses solely on the earnings data found in these surveys, one could easily conclude that copyright has little or no economic value in writers' everyday practice. The inference is that having a high percentage of writers who do not earn all, or even most, of their income from the exploitation of their writing, and who instead earn it from non-copyright sources, indicates a situation where copyright is no longer economically important to writers.[58] However, this chapter challenges this inference. In Sections 5–7 below, interview data from the IC study will be used to demonstrate that writers perceive copyright to be economically important to them, and the reality of writers' everyday practice and their perceptions of copyright is more complex and multi-faceted than what earnings data alone might suggest.

B. The Negative Space of IP

It is worth briefly addressing another strand of recent research that hasn't evaluated the profession of writing but that seems to raise questions about the legitimacy of copyright law in the context of benefits accruing to individual creative practitioners. This research has examined several areas of creative production where, arguably, copyright protection is either unavailable, not sufficiently available, or simply fails to work

---

58 An early review of several earnings surveys from a range of creative sectors (writing, music, and visual arts) questions whether copyright law matters to creators to economically because it 'empirically fails to secure the financial independence of creators'. M. Kretschmer, 'Does Copyright Law Matter? An Empirical Analysis of Creators Earnings', 21 May 2012, p. 1.

efficiently in protecting specific types of creative practitioners and their outputs; this includes stand-up comedians, tattoo artists, and haute-cuisine chefs.[59] This research demonstrates that social norms can come to the aid of creative practitioners where copyright protection is either absent or not frequently relied upon, and such norms often negate the need for legal protection. This growing body of scholarship, partly consisting of empirical research, has been categorised by some as the 'negative space of intellectual property'.[60]

While this research seems to question the necessity of copyright protection, it is not without limitations. Legitimate concerns over whether industries such as the fashion industry can be classified under the 'negative space' have been raised.[61] This negative space scholarship has also been noted to be scant,[62] and to represent a very small size of economic activity in terms of the creative sectors that fall in the negative space. Consequently, its implications for the legitimacy of copyright, and its relevance for other creative practices (e.g. writing) are arguably very limited i.e. while this research shows that legal protection may not be necessary for every type of creative endeavour and creative practitioner, and that some creative activities can flourish without

---

59 D. Oliar and C. Sprigman, 'There's No Free Laugh (Anymore): The Emergence of Intellectual Property Norms and the Transformation of Stand-Up Comedy', *Virginia Law Review*, 94.8 (2008), 1787–1867, http://www.virginialawreview.org/sites/virginialawreview.org/files/1787.pdf; E. Fauchart and E. Von Hippel, 'Norms-based Intellectual Property Systems: The Case of French Chefs', *Organization Science* 19.2 (2008), 187–201; A. K. Perzanowski, 'Tattoos & IP Norms', *Minnesota Law Review* 98 (2013), 511–91.

60 E. L. Rosenblatt, 'A Theory of IP's Negative Space', *Columbia Journal of Law & the Arts*, 34.3 (2011), 317–65; K. Raustiala and C. J. Sprigman, 'When Are IP Rights Necessary? Evidence from Innovation in IP's Negative Space', 13 September 2016, UCLA School of Law, Law and Economics Research Paper Series No. 16–15.

61 K. Raustiala and C. Sprigman, 'The Piracy Paradox: Innovation and Intellectual Property in Fashion Design', *Virginia Law Review*, 92.8 (2006), 1687–777; cf. Robert P. Merges, 'Philosophical Foundations of IP Law: The Law and Economics Paradigm', 1 January 2016, UC Berkeley Public Law Research Paper No. 2920713; see also, C. S. Hemphill and J. Suk, 'The Law, Culture and Economics of Fashion', *Stanford Law Review* 61 (2009), 1147–200; S. Scafidi, 'Intellectual Property and Fashion Design', in Peter K. Yu (ed.), *Intellectual Property and Information Wealth: Copyright and Related Rights*, Vol. 1 (Santa Barbara, CA: Praeger Publishers Inc., 2006), p. 115–32; S. Scafidi, 'Fashion Designers Deserve The Same Protection as Other Creatives', *The Business of Fashion*, 15 March 2016, https://www.businessoffashion.com/community/voices/discussions/what-is-the-real-cost-of-copycats/op-ed-fashion-designers-deserve-the-same-protection-as-other-creatives

62 Raustiala and Sprigman, 'When are IP rights Necessary?', p. 6.

copyright, it does not negate the necessity for copyright protection in all other creative sectors and for all other creative practitioners. In fact, this chapter presents a contrast to this research, by demonstrating a *positive* space of copyright, and the potential for a continuing positive role for copyright in the context of professional writing.

4. The Role of Copyright in the Everyday Practice of Writers: IC Study

The key aim of the IC study was to understand, through socio-legal research, how copyright law trickles down and is played out in day-to-day creative practice, in a changing digital, technological, and economic environment. Choosing creators as its main informants, and treating them as key copyright policy stakeholders, distinct from the intermediaries or other right owners that may claim to represent them, the study focussed on creators' own practices and understandings, in relation to the relevance or irrelevance of copyright. The need for more evidence and evidence-based policy in copyright has been recognised,[63] and the study is a contribution to such a call for evidence by capturing and reflecting the perspectives of individual creators on copyright.[64]

At the time of writing, the dataset for the IC study comprised semi-structured interviews with 130 individual creative practitioners working across different creative disciplines (writing, visual arts, and music). This chapter draws on a part of this dataset, specifically original first-hand accounts of the perspectives and practices of 25 writers based in the UK. To obtain, examine, and analyse the interviews, a socio-legal approach was adopted, and a grounded theory methodology was employed.[65] Random and snowball sampling was used to select

---

63   See I. Hargreaves, 'Digital Opportunity: A Review of Intellectual Property and Growth', 18 May 2011, https://www.gov.uk/government/publications/digital-opportunity-review-of-intellectual-property-and-growth

64   A pre-launch consultation for the CREATe centre had highlighted 'the importance of reflecting the interests of the individual creator in debates about copyright', see: www.create.ac.uk/launch/

65   Grounded theory originated in the works of Barney Glaser and Anselm Strauss and involves an inductive process in which theory is 'derived from data, systematically gathered and analyzed through the research process' and 'in this method, data collection, analysis, and eventual theory stand in close relationship to one

interviewees. Random sampling was used to select, and engage with, primary creators who were participating in selected literary and arts events and festivals, and attending venues and hubs that showcase creative works.[66] Snowball sampling was used to follow up on any referrals that interviewees provided. The interview data was obtained in conjunction with the collection of ethnographic data such as observations at festivals and events, and secondary data from online ethnography of social media sites such as Facebook and Twitter.[67]

In terms of the perceived relevance of copyright to the day-to-day practice of the writers who were interviewed, a relatively consistent pattern emerged.[68] On the whole the writers believed that the existence of copyright protection in their works (irrespective of whether or not they always availed themselves of their rights, either in terms of exploiting the rights, or excluding others by enforcing the rights) was of importance to them personally, and of benefit to their professional writing practice. The next three sections will elaborate on this by presenting some thematic findings pertaining to writers in the IC study.

---

another.' A. L. Strauss and J. M. Corbin, *Basics of Qualitative Research: Techniques and Procedures for Developing Grounded Theory* (Thousand Oaks: Sage Publications, 1998), p. 12. See also, B. G. Glaser and A. L. Strauss, *The Discovery of Grounded Theory: Strategies for Qualitative Research* (London: Aldine Publishing, 1967); B. G. Glaser, *Theoretical Sensitivity: Advances in the Methodology of Grounded Theory* (Mill Valley: Sociology Press, 1978). 'Sociolegal studies are a branch of legal studies that are distinguished from doctrinal research through the deployment of one or more research methodologies drawn largely but not exclusively from the social sciences.' M. Salter and J. Mason, *Writing Law Dissertations: An Introduction and Guide to the Conduct of Legal Research* (Harlow: Pearson Education, 2007), p. 132. See also, S. Wheeler and P. Thomas, 'Socio-Legal Studies', in D. Hayton (ed.), *Law's Future(s)* (Oxford: Hart Publishing, 2000), pp. 267–80.

66 Key arts events and festivals, taking place within the duration of the research project, 2013–2017, were identified and creators participating in such events were randomly sampled from the festival guides; venues and hubs that showcase creative works and were industry partner associates of the CREATe centre were contacted to facilitate engagement with creators at their upcoming events, or to suggest other venues or hubs that could be contacted. Notable events, spaces, and organisations, that enabled observations and interviews with writers included GoNorth, the Edinburgh International Book Festival, and a three-week visiting scholar position at Master-Artist-in-Residence program no. 155 at Atlantic Center for the Arts.

67 The incident outlined in Section 2 is drawn from such ethnography.

68 Being qualitative in nature, the study is not statistical and the findings are not designed to be used to draw general inferences about the writing practices of all writers. Indeed, as will be demonstrated, even the writers whose practices are discussed here are different in nature, and they are informed by a range of factors in their meaning-making and decision-making around copyright.

5. Internal Aspect of Copyright: Writers' Perspectives on Financial Return from Copyright

The majority of writer interviewees valued the internal aspect of copyright in their practices i.e. the ability to exploit their rights and earn a monetary return. First, income derived from the exploitation of rights was perceived to be an important component of the 'portfolio of earnings' of the interviewees. This applied both to writers who were primarily making a living from exploiting their self-employed writing but also to those writers who were not sustaining themselves primarily through writing, and were instead juggling writing with other activities. Second, the financial reward derived from exploiting copyright in self-employed writing was found to be relevant in two primary ways: the monetary return played a practical role in earning a livelihood and sustaining creative practices; and the monetary return also played, for many but not all, a more personal role in allowing them to feel recognised and rewarded for their writing. This section elaborates on these findings and argues that these narratives challenge the notion that copyright is no longer economically important to writers.

A. Writers' Careers and Sources of Earnings

A large majority of the interviewees pointed to the precariousness of trying to maintain a career as a writer and the profession was generally characterised as one marred with uncertainty, such that yearly earnings are often impossible to predict. Despite the various challenges present in the writing profession today, the interviews indicated that copyright is still perceived to be economically important to writers.

Like much previous survey-based research, outlined above, interviewees' earnings were also found to be largely *portfolio based*. However, within this portfolio, the economic rights provided by copyright were seen as a key asset, and one that nearly all the writer interviewees were exploiting for monetary return, either through a publisher or other intermediaries, or on their own. Some sources of earnings that were pointed out in the interviews as being important were as follows:

- Book advances (advance on royalties) from the publisher.
- Royalties from the publisher in relation to sale of physical books, ebooks, audio books, apps, and other forms of exploitation.
- Income from the exploitation of foreign rights, translation rights, and dramatization for film, television and theatre; sometimes separately negotiated with intermediaries other than the book publisher.
- Income from self-publication in relation to direct sale of physical books, ebooks, audio books, apps, and other forms of exploitation.
- Income from self-publication after rights reversion.
- Income from ad-hoc commissioned writing e.g. ghost writing.
- Public lending rights (PLR) payments.

The actual 'portfolio of earnings' of each interviewee was different, and there was variation in the importance of different sources of earnings within individual portfolios. In addition to this, some interviewees undertook certain ancillary but related activities which provided additional revenue that helped sustain their writing careers. They emphasised how the economic benefits from these activities were related directly to successful ownership and exploitation of rights in their writing. These activities included, but are not restricted to, the following:

- Grants: for example to undertake research towards a new work.
- Book festival bookings: where a writer is booked to make a personal appearance and which will most likely include a book reading or participation in a panel discussion.
- School bookings: where a writer, particularly writers of children's books, are invited to make personal appearances at schools. This will include book readings and meet-and-greet events with children and parents.

Although revenue from exploitation of copyright was clearly important to the 'portfolio of earnings' of the interviewees, as detailed below, the size and nature of such revenue changed from practice to practice, and also fluctuated from year to year within any specific creator's practice.

B. Copyright Mattered, in Terms of Financial Return, to Those who Were Primarily Making a Living from Writing

For several interviewees, their income entirely, or largely, stemmed from the exploitation of their writing and, consequently, the internal aspect of copyright was seen to be vital for the sustenance of their creative practice. Keay, a writer and historian, emphasised that his livelihood was largely dependent on income from his writing, something he also likes to state on his website:

> Though hailed as one of our most outstanding historians (*Yorkshire Post*), John Keay is not attached to any academic faculty and survives on the royalty receipts from his books.[69]

While emphasising the importance of royalties in his practice, he also pointed to the Royal Literary Fund (of which he is a fellow) as an example of a charitable organisation that provides assistance to writers using funds derived largely from other authors' writing:

> I mean most of my income consists of royalties and so it's crucial from that point of view. It's also very important to me because [...] Royal Literary Fund Fellows are paid out of a Royal Literary Fund which is basically royalties, I mean it's royalties on works of authors who are long deceased in most cases.[70]

For several other interviewees e.g. Brookmyre, Mina, Sheridan, Wagner, and Mills, the exploitation of their writing had been their primary source of income for many years. Brookmyre, having built a successful career spanning twenty years, indicated that while writing had been his main source of income in this period, prior to landing his first publishing deal, he had juggled writing with part-time work, not unlike many other writers:

---

69 See https://www.johnkeay.com/biography
70 For the Royal Literary Fund, see https://www.rlf.org.uk/home/about-the-rlf/

> I would take two months of the year off to write a novel because I knew I could afford those two months off, it helped that, I mean I was doing lots of shifts to make sure that I could afford that break […] once I got a publishing deal that was me able to fund myself full-time after that.

Similarly, Haughton, who had been an illustrator for several years before he started writing children's books, was very clear about the degree to which he depended on rights exploitation for generating income:

> Yeah, all of my money basically comes from selling my rights […] yes, 100%.

C. Copyright Also Mattered, in Terms of Financial Return, to Those who did not Primarily Make a Living from Writing

While many interviewees were earning a living entirely or primarily from writing, there were also several interviewees who were not sustaining themselves primarily through writing, and were instead juggling writing with other activities. These interviewees had to rely on non-copyright sources of income for making a living (e.g. a combination of second jobs and ancillary activities mentioned above). However, what was striking was that they also perceived the copyright-related income to be important in terms of financial return and a valuable part of their portfolio of earnings. Despite supplementing their income from a range of activities other than writing, they saw the internal aspect of copyright as vital for the sustenance of their creative practice in the short and the long term.

Moffat, a writer and historian, who has juggled several roles while writing many books, indicated that he couldn't survive on what he earned from his writing alone. For a period in the past, he had benefitted from simultaneously publishing certain books and also producing them as a TV series where each use fed off on the other, and he was able to make a living from exploitation of his writing alone:

> It was also a very good source of income. When I did the books and the TV together that was a living, that worked […]. So, yeah, that was, and so that was my version of journalism as it were, that was how I did it. But yeah, because we are in a long recession here in Britain these things are going to shrink, they are going to disappear sadly.

While emphasising that surviving as an author had become tougher than before, for various reasons, and that he wasn't writing full-time due to having other unrelated jobs, he acknowledged that exploitation of copyright benefitted him materially and contributed to his portfolio of earnings in many ways, including advances and royalties, public-lending-right income (he indicated he was in the top quartile for public-lending-right returns), and self-publication.

Similarly, Duffy, a playwright and co-director of a theatre company, outlined a diverse portfolio of earnings that included teaching, holding workshops, and relying on public funding for creative activities, within which writing for television and theatre (whether it was exploitation of her rights through being commissioned for a play, or in writing shorter works for television) were an important part of her portfolio.

Strachan also emphasised the importance of royalties in sustaining her writing career. Additionally she pointed to the precariousness that comes with being unable to predict the size of the next royalty cheque and having to juggle multiple strands of a 'portfolio career'; a portfolio in which two such strands were book advances and income derived from the sale of previous publications. In this context she considered copyright protection to be a 'huge thing'.

Murdoch had dabbled in music when he was quite young, and then worked in the pharmaceutical industry for twenty-five years, but had started writing entirely by accident, and was first published in 2008. At the time of interview, he wrote and played music full-time, but felt that his writing practice was at the cusp of change. Although his portfolio of earnings had been particularly mixed and continuously changing, copyright had a monetary role in it because returns from retaining and exploiting his rights in both writing and music contributed to 'him ticking away'.

D. Rights Matter in Sustaining Practices in the Digital Environment

Many interviewees, while indicating that copyright was important to their ability to make a living from writing, underlined the importance of rights in the digital environment, and suggested that their ability to sustain professional careers would be diminished in absence of rights. Morgan, an author of educational books and teenage fiction, amongst other things, was forthright in expressing the view that rights were perhaps more important than ever. In particular, and primarily because of changes in the marketplace brought about by digital culture, she articulated very clearly how intimately tied to the economic benefit she believed copyright to be:

> I think it is even more important than it ever was, because it's even harder than it ever was to earn a living. I think it goes to the core of it that when you have written, or drawn or you know whatever, obviously it's just words, but if you created something, if no one can earn any money out of it fine, but if anyone's going to make any money out of it, it should be the person who created it, and the people who are then with their permission going to take it to the market. And because that ability is undermined so often now, and because it's so easy for people to illegally — either because they don't know it's illegal, or just because they do and don't care — make money from it themselves, I think it becomes even more important. So, with advances and royalties going down and ebook income or sales going up, then I think it becomes even more important.

Smart, while appreciating the value of copyright, felt that balancing acceptance of 'free culture' with the necessity to 'get paid' was a difficult task. For him, giving content away was necessary in building an online following, and this served as a conduit to generating sales from a growing fan base. At the same time he was critical of people's sense of entitlement because exploitation of rights remained important to generate an income and sustain a practice:

> I think with any art form the internet has made people feel very self-entitled, it has made them feel like 'now I should have everything for free, I should have music for free, and movies for free, and books,' not necessarily thinking that the people behind them might want rewarding, I might need funding to keep going.

In articulating her views on the economic value of copyright to her writing practice, Czerkawska explicitly tied in the notion of copyright as an incentive, as something without which she could not function as a writer:

> Because there is an awful lot that you do as a writer that I think if you weren't being paid in some way, and you didn't have the rights, you simply wouldn't do it [...]. I can imagine that I would dabble a bit here and there, but if you didn't have the incentive of the rights in what you

had, you wouldn't, [...] because people have said it to me all the time, 'well you would do it anyway,' but you wouldn't do it in quite the same way... no, you wouldn't do it over a period of time... yes, if it became unsustainable you just wouldn't do it. Because there is a lot of what you do that is sheer hard slog, it's not all fun and games, some of it is, but in a big project there is lots of times when you do find yourself thinking, 'why on earth am I doing it, you know, why am I putting myself through this?' And, if you didn't have that incentive, that there was copyright, there was the potential to keep going with this, for it to have a life beyond you, you simply wouldn't do it, you know? You might dabble a bit, you know, write the odd little poem, or the odd little story. Again I think that does sow a seed of misunderstanding of the way a professional writer works.

Other writers also similarly indicated that while they wrote 'for the love of' writing, ultimately, if the monetary benefits were not there in the end, they wouldn't be able to continue to dedicate most of their time, or as much time, to writing, or be able to remain a professional writer.

It is important to note here that while the internal aspect of copyright clearly mattered to the interviewees in terms of financial return, said return was not simply associated with sustaining creative practices but also with notions of reward and recognition. For instance, Arbuthnott, who continued to teach full-time while also having published several books for children, stated that while her writing income was not plenteous enough to pay all her bills, it was important to her both monetarily, and personally:

> I have a nice life because of the writing money [...] it's definitely important. And it's important in terms of how the world values you, that you are paid.

Murdoch, also explained how he valued the rights personally:

> I think there is an intrinsic notion that you should have, you should own what you have done, I think that's a kind of, it feels right inside you. I'm not talking about money here, I'm talking about a feeling thing. I think it feels right to feel as if, you know, [...] you've created that from nothing, or, bits of things, and like, at the end of the day it's unique to you, and that should be recognised as yours.

E. Concluding Remarks

It was clear that writer interviewees perceived financial return from copyright to matter to their writing practices and to them personally. Writer interviewees who earned their living primarily from writing, as well as those who did not earn all their income from writing, both indicated that they perceived the internal aspect of copyright to have a continued role in their practice, despite the changing technological and market conditions. This challenges the notion that copyright has little or no economic value in writers' everyday practice — an inference that can result from a reductive approach that focuses solely on earnings data derived from the surveys (reviewed in Section 3 above).

The surveys on writers' earnings provide a valuable measurement of the direct monetary reward received by authors from exploitation of copyright. However, they do not provide a full picture of either the role or the importance of copyright in writers' livelihoods and practices. It can be concluded from the findings above that earnings data alone offers little when it comes to understanding the role of the internal aspect of copyright in writers' practices. This is because the earnings surveys in the UK, so far, have not captured writers' own beliefs and understandings of the economic importance of copyright, i.e. while the surveys capture what writers earn, they do not capture how writers 'value' those earnings personally or in relation to their writing careers. Future research in this area, particularly earnings surveys, might benefit from assessing if writers perceive the role of copyright-related income in their portfolio of earnings to be significant for career sustenance, and whether or not said careers could be properly maintained if copyright-related earnings were removed.

6. Internal Aspect of Copyright: Writers' Perspectives on Ownership and Control of Economic Rights

While the legitimacy of the economic role of copyright in writers' practices was positively affirmed by the interview data, it did not, by any means, indicate that the 'copyright framework' was perfect in its operation. However, several writers indicated that copyright could function as an *even more* important and efficient component of building a successful professional practice, when opportunities arise for authors to own and retain rights, or have more control over their exploitation. Several interviews highlighted initiatives they had taken in directly exploiting some of their economic rights themselves. In this context, the resulting monetary benefits were a contributing factor in emphasising the importance of copyright to their lives as writing professionals.

A. Hard-Fought Rights

Mills and Wagner, two figures central to the success of the British comic *2000AD*, spoke candidly about their struggles to own rights over their creations in an industry that, in the early years, typically claimed ownership over all IP created by comic artists (writers and illustrators) by treating it as 'work for hire'.[71] They identified the financial benefits for their practices when they had initial ownership of their work, as well as when they retained some control over their rights. They both recollected how they had to fight for deals that would both benefit them in the long term and offer much better rewards than the fixed payment they were receiving for creating some of the most successful and iconic British comics. Mills recalled:

> […] why they decided to give me the copyright I don't know. It was probably because I had been really relentlessly banging on about it […] You know, just working dawn to dusk you get a good fixed income but it's not enough. So somewhere down the line I think they must have relented […] they said 'yeah, if you want copyright on your stories you can' and so I immediately wrote a whole batch of stories which I still own the copyright on, and I have actually been able to use in other ways, you know? It's not like they have just been collecting dust.

Wagner, who was the original writer of the *2000AD* story 'Judge Dredd', and at the time working in an industry that he describes as 'just using people, creaming everything off for themselves', stated that for years

---

71   The term 'work for hire' refers to US law on ownership of copyright in a work made for hire, see s.101 US Copyright Act 1976, https://www.copyright.gov/title17/. Under US law, the authorship and first ownership of copyright vests with the employer or commissioning client, and not the artist, see s.201 Copyright Act 1976. The interviewees often used the US terminology, as a short hand, to simply indicate situations where they did not have first ownership of copyright in their work.

he sat by and watched the huge amounts of money his character was generating yet shared none of the rewards. He eventually decided to fight for a share of the royalties that various Judge Dredd licensing deals had earned and was successful; an experience that led him to view writers holding on to their rights as something that is vitally important:

> because I got rights, because I fought for my rights in Judge Dredd, I was able to buy a house. Right. Now that, before that I was living on the breadline [...] Earning very little. And then, you know, when we eventually fought for our rights and got some sort of rights deal we started earning decent money.

The benefits of self-employed writing, derived from seeking better returns from copyright exploitation, were noted particularly by writers who worked in the comics industry. For instance, Davis noted that one of the reasons he sought to switch from doing 'work for hire' writing, to publishing his own work was to invest in his career and work towards a time 'later in life' when royalties might provide a source of income. Consequently, for many interviewees, there was also an aspirational aspect with regard to how they perceived copyright in terms of economic benefits i.e. they wished to own copyright in their works as an investment in the *potential for reward* from owning and exploiting rights.

B. Rights Reversion

The examples provided by the interviewees were not restricted to situations in which they felt they weren't able to own the rights in the first place, or control the rights in their self-employed writing. A number of the interviewees also raised the matter of reversion of rights and highlighted that there are economic gains from having a reversion clause inserted in a publishing contract. In the context of the shift from physical to digital sales it had proved to be a useful means of generating additional revenue from delisted books that a publisher had no intention of reprinting. Once rights were returned, the author was free to self-publish titles electronically so that new value could be extracted from back catalogue items. Arbuthnott for instance felt reversion rights had become important, that the aspect of ownership, and of attaining control, allowed writers to be entrepreneurial, even if the financial rewards were not always significant:

> [T]he number of copies sold, though you may not think is worthwhile, but it's, you know, it's all adding up in my pocket thank you, and I would like it.

This pointed to a disjunction between the business interests of the publisher and those of writers. Publishers' sales figures expectations would have to be met for them to continue publishing a book, or indeed keep it in their catalogue, but self-directed writers would not face the same business pressures when dealing with an electronic format. One author offered another example in which reversion had provided a level of control that suited their objectives while contextualising the role of the publisher:

> I've had a publisher come to me and say, 'I would really like to take this book of yours and I could do a hardback in a digital version,' and I was like, 'get out of town, what the fuck do I need you for?' […] I can do that, so the difficult thing is the mass-market paperback and the kind of mass-market distribution to really make those sales, and so they are not doing that job they can just sit there on an ebook and scratch their arses which is, you know they would love to do that, but I personally would not be happy with them doing that.

Sheridan gave a good example of the importance of reversion rights in terms of how useful they are for elderly authors who may not have made enough money from writing to have been able to plan financially for their retirement. For this group any extra money made from royalties is critical so the reissuing of older out-of-print works as ebooks could prove to be a boon for them:

> I mean I know quite a few older authors who have discovered the digital world with vim, you know because they have got this backlist [chuckling] of thirty-five books that literally just sit in libraries because those are the people that read them, they suddenly think, 'oh I could put these up' and they do put them up and they get a certain kind of readership online and suddenly there is this kind of extra, extra income, and you know they can keep it up online and pass those kinds of properties onto their kids which is a nice thing to be able to think of doing.

Anderson was keen to stress the importance of back-catalogue items for writers and talked about having helped others to get their work reissued digitally. In particular, she provided the example of a Scottish writer in her nineties with a substantial body of work built up over years of professional writing:

> For instance Alanna Knight […] an historical crime fiction writer, in her nineties now, had this fantastic back catalogue of this Victorian detective set in Edinburgh […] it continues to be published, I mean she does one, one of him every eighteen months, but I helped her get at least half a dozen of her back catalogue online […] that has been fantastic for her because she has a big American readership […] there's lots of complaints we can make about Amazon, but the truth is the money drops into your bank account once a month.

However, Arbuthnott noted that, going forward, possible growth in the use of print on demand (POD) by publishers could influence how they approach reversion clauses in future:

> I think it has become important, I think it has become more contentious as well because you now have print on demand […] publishers I think may begin to just get a little bit slidy [sic] about what they regard as out of print. And I think that it needs to be quite tight wording, I think, reversion clauses, so that the writer is not being taken advantage of.

This interview data about the benefits of rights reversion are very much in line with results from the 2014 survey (referred to in Section 3 above), in which a good attempt had been made to understand aspects of copyright contracts that writers enter into. The 2014 survey had found that 57% of respondents' contracts had reversion clauses, and where there was a reversion clause, 38% of respondents exercised their right under the clause.[72] Interestingly, where the right was exercised, the survey found that '70% of writers went on to make more money from the work, including by self-publication.'[73]

The direct connection between holding onto or reclaiming rights, and their potential to generate earnings in the future was raised by many other interviewees. However, significantly, the interviewees seemed to be quite pragmatic in pointing out that they can never predict what direction their careers might take when they decide to keep their rights, or how much economic return they might see from their rights; however this didn't, in itself, make their rights unimportant to them. They perceived that not having rights or giving the rights up along the way simply meant that any latent potentiality to benefit financially would disappear; while keeping the rights gave them an opportunity to benefit financially.

---

72 Gibson, Johnson and Dimita, 'The Business of Being an Author', p. 16.
73 Ibid.

C. Awareness of Rights and how to Exploit Them

Several interviewees emphasised that there was a strong correlation between the economic value of copyright (and the financial benefits they could derive from its protections), and their actual knowledge and awareness (or lack thereof) of the machinations of the publishing industry and the legal frameworks governing it, and their access to professional advice and representation through agents. A number of interviewees remarked that those new to the sector were often unprepared when it came to dealing with matters that were understood to be integral to succeeding as a professional writer: for example, how to read contracts, negotiate percentages, request reversion clauses, pursue foreign rights deals, and avail themselves of licensing opportunities.

It was clear that writers who had a better awareness of the tangible benefits associated with holding copyright, or had good professional representation, were better positioned to exploit protected works and consequentially succeeded at earning a living exclusively from writing. Mina was quite explicit about this fact and indicated that failure to comprehend the intricacies of the profession, and in particular to properly understand one's rights, could ultimately determine if a writer will succeed or fail:

> I think awareness of the law, awareness of different types of copyright, awareness of the importance of it being a living… of people protecting their work… I think new writers coming up are really unaware of how they can protect their rights, they have no clue, and they learn by trial and error or by making mistakes… if your first few books don't sell, because the market is so, well, it's so carefully assessed now… it used to be you could have a good career as a mid-list author and take off at book ten. You can't do that anymore because they [the publishers] have got all the numbers and they know what's selling and what's not… so I think lots of people are losing their books, early doors, and then you just don't hear from them anymore, we are losing fantastic writers, it's a real shame.

Mina gave the example of foreign rights to underline why good knowledge of rights and how they should be exploited was crucial. She pointed out that it was possible to increase income by selling foreign rights to foreign rights agents rather than selling world rights to a British publisher for an advance. She explained:

> […] if you are a crime writer and you sell the foreign rights to a foreign rights agent you can make seven or ten times as much as you do in the British market. Whereas if you sell the world rights in the British market they might not have publishers abroad… So, you know, things like making sure that you sell your rights in the right packages to people is quite important for how much you can make… whenever I meet someone, I always say to them, 'listen, don't sell the world rights, only sell the UK rights,' because otherwise it's just lost.

In the earnings' surveys (referred to in Section 3 above), there has also been some attempt to measure the extent to which writers have professional representation or seek professional advice. For instance, the 2006 survey found only 65% respondents took professional advice before entering into contracts and 43.5% had agents.[74] The 2014 survey found that, consistent with the 2006 survey, 42% of professional authors had agents, but only 53% took professional advice before entering into contracts.[75] The interview data in the IC study demonstrates that experienced writers clearly associate the benefits derived from copyright exploitation with both good professional representation and good personal knowledge and awareness of rights and how to utilise them effectively.

7. External Aspect of Copyright

Although the primary focus of this paper is the legitimacy of the internal aspect of copyright as per the perceptions of writers, it is worth briefly noting some of the interview findings with respect to the external aspect of copyright (the ability to exclude others), an issue that has rarely been focussed on in the economic literature. A large majority of interviewees considered the writer's ability to exclude others on the basis of copyright, and its potential deterrent effect, as quite important, especially when it came to preventing unauthorised copying and modification by others

---

74 Kretschmer and Hardwick, 'Authors' Earnings from Copyright and Non-copyright Sources', pp. 30 and 174.
75 Gibson, Johnson and Dimita, 'The Business of Being an Author', pp. 12 and 17.

for commercial gain, and also more generally when unauthorised acts might not be in line with the artist's political or ideological beliefs. In fact, when asked about the role of copyright in their practice several interviewees associated the question, first and foremost, with the external aspect of copyright; and offered to explain whether or not prevention of infringement was important in their opinion, and if so, when and why.

Having the ability to exclude others by enforcing copyright (either themselves or through intermediaries such as publishers) was perceived by the interviewees to be economically valuable to their practice, but it was also important to them on a personal level. However, such notions of perceived value were quite variable and markedly contextual; it was the writer's (or their representative's) ability to *choose* whether or not to enforce their rights that was perceived to be important.

While nearly all the interviewees valued the external aspect of copyright, they were clear that they did not perceive strong or strict enforcement of rights as a necessity in every situation. It was important for some to be able to gauge whether the enforcement was required, dependent upon the context of infringement; crucially this was seen as an expression of the *choice* afforded by having copyright protection. Having the right to choose and control how others use one's work is something Czerkawska believed to be valuable:

> you should have the right to say no, you, nobody else should be able to come along and take that away from you, and say well you know, I'm going to do something […] Intellectual property, the central creation of what you have made, I do believe very strongly that you should be able to do what you want with that.

As to when the external aspect of copyright might come into play in interviewees' practices, online infringement was often provided as an example. However, on this matter, the interviewees differed widely in their views on when enforcement was necessary. Although a number of interviewees thought that some form of rights infringement was inevitable, especially in the digital domain, a variety of responses were offered. For instance, Brookmyre, in the context of file sharing, seemed to accept that with the advent of ebooks it was simply unavoidable that some people would share his work freely:

> I am aware that on the internet now people will be passing on links to download like 10,000 books at a time, obviously it's a concern on one level, yet on another level you think well often it's a bit like someone lending a book or a bit like when we used to tape records that yes, that was an infringement of copyright but it was also a very effective way of sharing and introducing people to new work.

While Brookmyre indicated that online enforcement is a matter that is handled by his publishers, he personally viewed some infringement as inevitable, in that there will always be a segment of his readership that will illegally download his work. He did not necessarily see it as something negative:

> I think for the most part, maybe I'm being just optimistic, but often it's people who weren't going to go and buy your book anyway, and if they end up reading one of your books, that way then there is maybe a chance they will go and buy another one, but maybe they'll illegally download another one, I don't know.

Similarly, Murdoch contextualised things in terms of online music sharing, and expressed the opinion that it this is not necessarily a bad thing, that it can increase an artist's overall exposure, although he admitted sharing would be problematic if it ever meant that the potential for lost revenue was significant:

> I've always thought about rights. And I'm probably more relaxed now than I was in the past… [but] if I had a million-selling book tomorrow, and everybody started ripping it off I'd probably be a bit annoyed, I'm a human being.

In contrast to those who demonstrated a certain amount of contextually bound flexibility in their views on online infringement, a number of other writers were much less forgiving. Clarke, like Brookmyre, understood the challenges presented by so-called 'free culture,' but took the opposite view with respect to the online sharing of her works. She was of the opinion that sharing would not necessarily provide the benefits claimed by others and that not everyone would see a general upturn in readership. According to Clarke, a direct relationship exists between the loss of book sales and the potential for this to damage a writer's chances of finding new book deals or renewing existing contracts: which, in turn, could serve to undermine one's ability to continue earning a living from writing. Her perception was that infringement amounted to theft:

> [W]ell, it feels like it's stealing from me basically. And it's, the more it happens, for some authors, if it is taking away that many sales, that can damage their chances of getting another contract. So that can stop them writing books. But people don't see it as stealing and I do.

Clarke was also eager to highlight that the majority of writers do not earn significant amounts for their activities (a point that was raised by many interviewees) so percentages received for book sales were squeezed when readers did not pay for titles. For her, and several other interviewees, there was an overarching sense that rights generate income and therefore are an essential component of sustaining a writing career, so the external aspect of copyright mattered economically:

> well, it's the revenue source, it's my life, and my livelihood, and if I don't get paid properly for that, you know, which is a small amount anyway then I would have to stop writing books… it's intellectual property. It's not because I put a piece of myself into it, it's just, it's lost income.

The perspectives on the necessity of rights enforcement were heterogeneous. This also applied to contexts other than online infringement. However, variables such as the nature and context of infringement, its potential economic or reputational impact on an individual practice, and personal or ideological beliefs, were some of the factors that interviewees mentioned in assessing whether or not rights should be enforced. For example, some considered fanfiction to be paying homage to an author, and as the kind of activity that they would deem acceptable, but infringements that are attempts by others to profit from their works are unacceptable.

Overall, it was clear that, despite the existence of differing views regarding the point at which the external aspect of copyright became relevant, and for which reason (economic sustenance of their creative practice or more personal reasons), the interviewees were unanimous in seeing the external aspect of copyright as crucial in protecting their creative interests, and as something that afforded them the ability to choose how it is contextually applied. Recent empirical research on copyright and writers in the UK has largely focussed on the internal aspect of copyright (exploitation of rights and earnings), but the findings in this section suggest that the external aspect (ability to exclude others) also has an important value in writers' everyday practice and cannot be ignored in assessing the legitimacy of copyright. Future research in this area would benefit from acknowledgement and assessment of the potential economic value of the external aspect of copyright.

8. Conclusion

This chapter focussed on writers and copyright with an emphasis on writers' relationship with copyright in their everyday practice. After reviewing two recent strands of empirical research that question the legitimacy of copyright law in the context of benefits accruing to creative practitioners (in Section 3), the chapter drew on the IC study (in Sections 5–7) to provide original accounts of how writers relate to copyright law. The thematic findings demonstrate that writers value both the internal and external aspects of copyright in terms of their careers and more personally.

As to the internal aspect of copyright, the interview data indicates that writers place significant value on the direct monetary benefits afforded by the exploitation of the copyright in their writing. Irrespective of the amount and type of associated earnings, it emerged that the authors perceived clear monetary benefits, as well as personal benefits in some cases, from holding and exploiting the economic rights afforded by copyright. This applied to those whose income largely stemmed from writing, as well as those who were not yet earning (or indeed may never earn) enough to depend solely on writing as a livelihood. It appeared that all earnings from copyright exploitation counted, and that such income was vital for the sustenance of any long-term creative practice — and even more so when the extant uncertainties connected with the success or failure of a publication, or indeed the size of future royalty yields, are considered. The financial rewards were perceived to be a crucial part of the 'earnings portfolio' that enabled them to sustain writing careers, but also acted as recognition and reward.

Additionally, as to the internal aspect of copyright, the interview data also showed that writers do not only associate economic rights with the actual financial return they receive, but also believe that owning and controlling such rights as writers carries *a potential for* better earnings, but not *a guarantee*. Finally, the interview data also demonstrated that the external aspect of copyright, although often ignored in economic literature, is also seen as valuable by writers and is perceived to be crucial in protecting their creative interests. The value associated with the writer's ability to choose whether or not to enforce their rights, and the relevance of the context of the infringement to this choice, demonstrated that writers' relationship with copyright is complex and cannot be studied only in terms of monetary returns and earnings surveys alone.

What do these findings imply with respect to the legitimacy of copyright? A focus on earnings data alone may suggest that copyright has little or no value in writers' careers. However, richer, complementary, socio-legal work examining the overall role of copyright (both internal and external aspects) in the everyday practice of writers, and captured by the research presented in this chapter, strongly challenges this suggestion. Original first-hand accounts from writers indicate that copyright plays a positive role in their practices, albeit not a perfect role. Further, the legitimacy of copyright cannot be judged by whether it can ensure sufficient earnings for all writers to make a living, or whether it can 'secure the financial independence of creators'. Copyright provides a mechanism for writers to enter the market and receive monetary reward for their work; but it does not guarantee success in said market. It appears that the writer interviewees are aware of the role that copyright plays in supporting their practices, in that it provides them both with an opportunity and potential to earn, yet they do not expect copyright itself to guarantee market success.

The scholarship on the negative space of IP generally seeks to challenge the assumptions of copyright policy. In contrast, this chapter affirms that some of the policy assumptions — copyright provides recognition, payment, and protection (set out at the start of the chapter) — hold true so far as writers' own beliefs and perspectives are concerned, albeit heterogeneously, and in a complex manner. While said scholarship questions the legitimacy of copyright law in some areas of creative production (e.g. stand-up comedians, tattoo artists, and haute-cuisine chefs), this chapter demonstrates that copyright law continues to play a role in the long standing, albeit changing, profession of writing.

Is copyright relevant to the everyday lives of writers and seen as valuable by writers in the context of professional writing? The answer from the IC study is a resounding yes. However, at a broader level, this answer also poses critical questions for copyright policy: could copyright serve writers' interests more effectively? Clearly, these are difficult times for writers. In an environment in which writing incomes are falling and writing careers are markedly precarious, could rules strengthening authorial ownership and control of economic rights, and their exploitation, be a possible way forward?

Works Cited

ALCS (June 2018) 'Authors' Earnings: A Survey of UK Writers', https://wp.alcs.co.uk/app/uploads/2018/06/ALCS-Authors-earnings-2018.pdf

Aufderheide, P. and P. Jaszi (2004) 'Untold Stories: Creative Consequences of the Rights Clearance Culture for Documentary Filmmakers', Center for Social Media, http://archive.cmsimpact.org/sites/default/files/UNTOLDSTORIES_Report.pdf

Brauneis, R. (2015) 'A Brief Illustrated Chronicle of Retroactive Copyright Term Extension', *Journal of the Copyright Society of the USA* 62.4, 479–502.

Brown, K. (27 April 2015) 'Green Party to Review Controversial Copyright Plans', *Telegraph*, http://www.telegraph.co.uk/culture/books/booknews/11565548/Green-Party-to-review-controversial-copyright-plans.html

Brown, K. (23 April 2015) 'Authors Criticise Green Party Plan to Reduce Copyright to 14 Years', *Telegraph*, http://www.telegraph.co.uk/culture/books/booknews/11557810/Authors-criticise-Green-Party-plan-to-reduce-copyright-to-14-years.html

Carter, N. (2015) 'The Greens in the UK General Election of 7 May 2015', *Environmental Politics* 24.6, 1055–60, https://doi.org/10.1080/09644016.2015.1063750

Dawson, N. (1994) 'Copyright in the European Union — Plundering the Public Domain', *Northern Ireland Legal Quarterly* 45, 193–209.

Elgot, J. (23 April 2015) 'Green Party Plan to Limit Copyright Attacked by Writers and Artists', *The Guardian*, https://www.theguardian.com/politics/2015/apr/23/green-party-plan-to-limit-copyright-attacked-by-writers-and-artists

European Commission (2018) 'Digital Single Market Policy: Copyright', https://ec.europa.eu/digital-single-market/en/policies/copyright

Fauchart, E. and E. Von Hippel (2006) 'Norms-based Intellectual Property Systems: The Case of French Chefs', *Organization Science* 19.2 (2008), 187–201.

Fiesler, C., J. L. Feuston and A. S. Bruckman (2015) 'Understanding Copyright Law in Online Creative Communities', in *Proceedings of the 18th ACM Conference on Computer Supported Cooperative Work & Social Computing* (CSCW '15), 116–29.

Green Party (2016) 'Economy', https://policy.greenparty.org.uk/ec.html

— (27 April 2015) 'Greens to Review Copyright Policy', https://www.greenparty.org.uk/news/2015/04/27/greens-to-review-copyright-policy/

— (2015) 'Economy: Part of the Green Party Policies for a Sustainable Society', https://policy.greenparty.org.uk/assets/images/policy/pdfs/Economy.pdf

— (2015) 'For the Common Good: General Election Manifesto 2015', https://www.greenparty.org.uk/assets/files/manifesto/Green_Party_2015_General_Election_Manifesto_Searchable.pdf

Gibson, J., P. Johnson and G. Dimita (2015) *The Business of Being an Author: A Survey of Authors' Earnings and Contracts* (London: Queen Mary, University of London), https://orca.cf.ac.uk/72431/1/Final Report - For Web Publication.pdf

Glaser, B. G. (1978) *Theoretical Sensitivity: Advances in the Methodology of Grounded Theory* (Mill Valley: Sociology Press).

— and A. L. Strauss (1967) *The Discovery of Grounded Theory: Strategies for Qualitative Research* (London: Aldine Publishing).

Hargreaves, I. (18 May 2011) 'Digital Opportunity: A Review of Intellectual Property and Growth', https://www.gov.uk/government/publications/digital-opportunity-review-of-intellectual-property-and-growth

Hemphill, C. S. and J. Suk (2009) 'The Law, Culture and Economics of Fashion', *Stanford Law Review* 61, 1147–200.

Katzenberger, P. et al. (2009) 'Comment by the Max-Planck Institute on the Commission's Proposal for a Directive to Amend Directive 2006/116 Concerning the Term of Protection for Copyright and Related Rights', *European Intellectual Property Review* 31.2, 59–72.

Kheria, S., C. Waelde, and N. Levin (2018) 'Digital Transformations in the Arts and Humanities: Negotiating the Copyright Landscape in the United Kingdom', in R. Hobbs (ed.), *The Routledge Companion to Media Education, Copyright and Fair Use* (Abingdon: Routledge), pp. 182–200.

Kretschmer, M. (21 May 2012) 'Does Copyright Law Matter? An Empirical Analysis of Creators Earnings', *SSRN Electronic Journal* [n.p.].

Kretschmer, M. (2010) 'Copyright and Contract Law — Regulating Creator Contracts: The State of the Art and a Research Agenda' *Journal of Intellectual Property Law* 18.1, 141–72.

Kretschmer, M. et al. (2008) 'Creativity Stifled? A Joint Academic Statement on the Proposed Copyright Term Extension for Sound Recordings', *European Intellectual Property Review* 30.9, 341–47.

— and P. Hardwick (2007) *Authors' Earnings from Copyright and Non-copyright Sources: A Survey of 25,000 British and German Writers* (Bournemouth: Bournemouth University), https://microsites.bournemouth.ac.uk/cippm/files/2007/07/ACLS-Full-report.pdf

Lessig, L. (2005) 'Does Copyright Have Limits: Eldred v. Ashcroft and Its Aftermath', *Queensland University of Technology Law and Justice Journal* 5.2, 219–30.

Lucas, C. (25 April 2015) 'Copyright — Standing up for Brighton's Creative Industries, Artists and Writers', https://www.carolinelucas.com/latest/copyright-standing-up-for-brightons-creative-industries-artists-and-writers

McIntyre, S. (27 April 2017) 'In Defense of Copyright', *Jabberworks*, http://jabberworks.livejournal.com/703055.html

Merges, R. P. (1 January 2016) 'Philosophical Foundations of IP Law: The Law and Economics Paradigm', UC Berkeley Public Law Research Paper No. 2920713, [n.p.].

Michael, L. (2014) 'Making a Living as a Writer', in Steven Earnshaw (ed.), *The Handbook of Creative Writing* (Edinburgh: Edinburgh University Press), 510–17.

Nordicity (June 2015) 'Literature and Publishing Sector Review', *Creative Scotland*.

Oliar, D. and C. Sprigman (2008) 'There's No Free Laugh (Anymore): The Emergence of Intellectual Property Norms and the Transformation of Stand-Up Comedy', *Virginia Law Review* 94.8, 1787–867, http://www.virginialawreview.org/sites/virginialawreview.org/files/1787.pdf

Perzanowski, A. K. (2013) 'Tattoos & IP Norms', *Minnesota Law Review* 98 (2013), 511–91.

Pollock, R. (2009) 'Forever Minus a Day? Calculating Optimal Copyright Term', *Review of Economic Research on Copyright Issues* 6.1, 35–60.

Pool, K. (2000) 'Love, Not Money', *The Author*, 58–66.

Posner, R. (2003) 'The Constitutionality of the Copyright Term Extension Act: Economics, Politics, Law, and Judicial Technique in Eldred v Ashcroft', *The Supreme Court Review 2003*, 143–62.

Puri, K. (1990) 'The Term of Copyright Protection — Is it Too Long in the Wake of New Technologies?', *European Intellectual Property Review* 12.1, 12–20.

Rahmatian, A. (2009) 'Dealing with Rights in Copyright-Protected Works: Assignments and Licences,' in E. Derclaye (ed.), *Research Handbook on the Future of EU Copyright* (Cheltenham: Edward Elgar), pp. 286–316.

Raustiala, K. and C. J. Sprigman (13 September 2016) 'When Are IP Rights Necessary? Evidence from Innovation in IP's Negative Space', UCLA School of Law, Law and Economics Research Paper Series No. 16–15 [n.p.].

— and C. J. Sprigman (2006) 'The Piracy Paradox: Innovation and Intellectual Property in Fashion Design, *Virginia Law Review* 92.8, 1687–777.

Rosenblatt, E. L. (2011) 'A Theory of IP's Negative Space', *Columbia Journal of Law & the Arts* 34.3, 317–65.

Salter, M. and J. Mason (2007) *Writing Law Dissertations: An Introduction and Guide to the Conduct of Legal Research* (Harlow: Pearson Education).

Scafidi, S. (15 March 2016) 'Fashion Designers Deserve The Same Protection as Other Creatives', *The Business of Fashion*, https://www.businessoffashion.com/community/voices/discussions/what-is-the-real-cost-of-copycats/op-ed-fashion-designers-deserve-the-same-protection-as-other-creatives

— (2006) 'Intellectual Property and Fashion Design', in P. K. Yu (ed.), *Intellectual Property and Information Wealth: Copyright and Related Rights*, Vol. 1 (Santa Barbara, CA: Praeger Publishers Inc.), 115–32.

Squires, C. (2005) 'Novelistic Production and the Publishing Industry in Britain and Ireland', in B. W. Shaffer (ed.), *A Companion to the British and Irish Novel, 1945–2000* (Oxford: Wiley Blackwell), pp. 177–93, https://doi.org/10.1002/9780470757611.ch12

Strauss, A. L. and J. M. Corbin (1998) *Basics of Qualitative Research: Techniques and Procedures for Developing Grounded Theory* (Thousand Oaks: Sage Publications).

Torremans, P. (2009) 'Questioning the Principles of Territoriality: The Determination of Territorial Mechanisms of Commercialisation', in P. Torremans (ed.), *Copyright Law: A Handbook of Contemporary Research* (Cheltenham: Edward Elgar), pp. 460–82.

Waelde, C. et al. (2016) *Contemporary Intellectual Property: Law and Policy* (Oxford: Oxford University Press).

Watt, R. (2013) 'Copyright Law and Royalty Contracts', in R. Towse and C. Handke (eds.), *Handbook on the Digital Creative Economy* (Cheltenham: Edward Elgar), pp. 197–208.

Wheeler, S. and P. Thomas (2000) 'Socio-Legal Studies', in D. Hayton (ed.), *Law's Future(s)* (Oxford: Hart Publishing), pp. 267–80.

8. Comics, Copyright and Academic Publishing: The Deluxe Edition

Ronan Deazley and Jason Mathis

Foreword

Versions. And more versions. The comics industry is adept at selling its fan base the same content, again and again, differently packaged and presented. We buy individual comics, and then trade paperback collections, hardback editions, deluxe hardbacks, omnibus collections, slipcase editions and more. Often, we buy simply because we want the best possible version of the work available. But also, these subsequent versions typically include additional material, making the new version an almost essential acquisition for the dedicated collector and fan. This material can take many forms: an insight into the author's writing process, or excerpts from his or her original pitch to the publisher; early development ideas and drawings reproduced from the artist's sketchbook; sample pages of artwork reproduced in pencil, then inked, then coloured, offering a window into the highly collaborative process that delivers the finished story in whatever version we care to read. In any event, we buy multiple versions; we are fans, collectors, addicts.

This essay is also a version of an earlier work. Indeed, different versions of it have been made available online twice before. The first time was in December 2013 as a work in progress, released as part of the working paper series managed by CREATe, RCUK's Centre for Copyright and New Business Models in the Creative Economy. This version was in turn based on my inaugural lecture delivered in October 2013 at the

University of Glasgow. For that lecture, I had decided to speak to some of the tensions that bind copyright and academic publishing, explored through the prism of the emerging discipline of comics scholarship. My reason for choosing the field of comics scholarship was simple enough: I love comics. They have been a part of my life for over three decades. As a teenager and through my student years at university, I worked in the first comic shop to open in Belfast: Dark Horizons. Sadly, Dark Horizons no longer exists, but the friendships I forged there remain true today. And, in many respects, but for Dark Horizons you would not be reading what you are currently reading.

The first version, made available online in late 2013, featured quotations and extracts from the work of numerous comic artists and authors such as Mark Millar, Chris Ware, Dave Sim and Chester Brown. I didn't seek any copyright permission to make use of their work; I didn't need to. That was the point. But the first version was also illustrated in part by Jason Mathis, a comic artist and friend. If I was going to deliver a lecture about copyright and comics I wanted to produce a version of that lecture that was, in part, a comic. The resulting collaboration was enjoyable and educational in equal measure. My initial idea was simply to produce an illustrated afterword to a more traditional piece of academic writing: a two-page 'manifesto' to sign off the work in an atypical but hopefully engaging way. Working with Jason, I learned much about writing for and creating comics; about structure, flow and narrative; about the interplay between text and the visual. In turn, we decided to create a written account of my inaugural lecture that was more ambitious and more playful than I had originally envisaged. Our joint labour produced the first version of this work.

The second version was a bona fide publication, made available in May 2014 through *The Comics Grid*, an online, open access journal dedicated to comics scholarship. That version was a more traditional academic piece, more fitting for a scholarly journal. It was published with the same illustrative material that had been included in the CREATe version but without any of the illustrations specifically created by Jason, and without the 'manifesto'. This was an article, not a comic. But, the *Comics Grid* version also included additional material outlining a more technically complex argument about the scope of the copyright exception for non-commercial research. This was material

8. Comics, Copyright and Academic Publishing 183

I had decided not to present as part of my inaugural lecture, in part because of time restraints but also because I was mindful of writing for and speaking to a public and largely non-expert audience. And so, producing a second version of the work as an article in *The Comics Grid* offered an opportunity for presenting important additional arguments about copyright and scholarship before the very community I hoped to engage: comics scholars. What the *Comics Grid* version lacked in visual appeal (Jason's wonderful illustrations), it made up for in additional, rigorous academic commentary.

This version that you are reading now — whether in analogue or digital form — represents a coming together of the CREATe version and the *Comics Grid* version. Essentially, after a period of three years, I have taken both previous incarnations and created a new, enhanced, all-singing, all-dancing version of an argument that, in my opinion, still has currency, still has value within the current climate of scholarly publication. Almost all of Jason's illustrations from the original working paper have been re-introduced to the *Comics Grid* version. In addition, new illustrated material has been added, specially commissioned for this new 'deluxe' version. This is probably the definitive version of this work, but who knows what the future may hold.

The law, of course, has moved on. When both earlier versions were first made available, I speculated on the possible impact of forthcoming changes to the copyright regime in the guise of a new exception for quotation. That exception was subsequently introduced in October 2014. I have chosen not to amend the structure of the original argument to reflect or accommodate this and other changes to the law. Rather, I have introduced clarifications and additional information within new footnotes to signal when and how the law has changed (see for example footnotes 10, 21, 30 and 31). I have also introduced new information concerning other documents, publications and websites that have been amended since first publication (again, within footnotes). For example, the Publishers' Association's *Permissions Guidelines* are discussed throughout the piece; they too have been updated by the Publishers' Association to reflect the changes to copyright implemented in October 2014. Only very occasionally have I made alterations to the main body of the text itself, and often those changes are simply to smooth the transitions between text and image in this new 'deluxe' edition.

In the two previous versions, I suggested that the impact of the new quotation exception for academics was likely to be marginal 'if not entirely bargained away as part of the publication process'. In short, if proprietary academic publishers choose not to take advantage of the new exception, there would be little scope for the academic community to do so either. And certainly, little appears to have changed regarding the publishers discussed in this essay. For example, *European Comic Art* still requires contributing authors 'to submit copyright agreements and all necessary permission letters for reprinting or modifying copyrighted materials, both textual and graphic'. There is no need for them to do so. There is no need for publishers to insist that authors secure copyright permissions whenever their use of third-party content falls within the scope of one or more of the copyright exceptions. But, publishers are risk averse. And in any event, they are dealing with authors that are intellectually entrapped: scholars who want or feel compelled to publish in proprietary journals for a myriad of reasons, whether personal, professional, institutional, or otherwise; so, why not rely on the scholar to mitigate and manage the risk? In the complex ecology of academic publishing, this is just one of the ways that academic publishers extract value from the academic community at large. As a community, we produce and then peer review content for publishers for free, and the economic value of that subsidy to publishers is staggering. Requiring academics to manage (and often pay for) copyright compliance is just another form of subsidy. But, the research-monitoring apparatchiks tell us that these are the journals we should publish in; so, for the most part, we do it.

And in recent years, a new revenue stream has opened up for academic publishers, driven by the UK government's commitment to ensuring open access to publicly funded research. As you read this, it is worth reflecting on the fact that almost all journal articles currently published by UK academics are made publicly accessible in some shape or form under various open access routes. This has been driven by research council mandates, by the emergence of a network of institutional repositories at universities, and by HEFCE's announcement in March 2014 that almost all publications must be made open access to be eligible for submission to the next REF exercise. Much of this is managed through Green open access: placing pre-publication versions of published articles in institutional repositories, often to be released after a publisher-imposed embargo period. Just like the comics industry, academia too now deals in multiple versions of the same work. The impact, relevance and benefits offered by this recent proliferation of versions is a matter of some conjecture.

But in any event, this is not the government's preferred mechanism for ensuring open access to research: that lies with Gold open access and involves paying an Article Processing Charge (an APC) to the relevant publisher in return for making the work immediately available to anyone in the world without restriction. So, in addition to the cost of producing and peer reviewing content for academic publishers, in addition to the cost of undertaking unnecessary copyright compliance activities to ensure publication, and in addition to the cost of journal subscriptions that UK universities pay to the publishers already benefitting from these subsidies, we now provide an additional subsidy in the form of APCs. In 2015, the spend by UK universities on APCs was estimated at £33M; and this could rise to £83M by 2020 (Tickell, 2016). Moreover, this new revenue stream does not appear to have been offset by a commensurate drop in journal subscription charges, or at least not yet. Proprietary academic publishing has many virtues. But it's also a con, a cheat, and a fix. You know it. I know it. They know it.

But, this is not a piece of work about the current state of the art regarding open access publishing. It is about comics, copyright and academia. It is about missed opportunities, about how we ignore or are required to overlook the opportunities the copyright regime offers for making use of other people's work without the need for permission. In that respect, it's also about autonomy and freedom of expression. And it's about resistance. But above all else, it is a love letter. We hope you enjoy it.

Ronan Deazley
March 2017

Introduction

8. Comics, Copyright and Academic Publishing 187

Fig. 8.1 Millar and McCrea, *Crisis* #31 (1989), pp. 17/5–6.

Comics Scholarship and Clearing Rights

Academics who research and write about the visual world often complain about the way copyright law can hinder their scholarly endeavours, and with good reason. Writing about visual work without reproducing that work is an impoverished exercise, for both writer and reader. But reproducing visual work can trigger concerns on the part of the conscientious author or — more often — demands on the part of the publisher about the need to secure copyright permission. In this respect, comics scholarship is no different from any other field of visual or cultural studies. Clearing rights for publication can be a frustrating and time-consuming business, and academic publishers often manage the business of copyright clearance by making their contributors responsible for securing permissions. *European Comic Art* is typical: in its information for contributors, it sets out that '[u]pon acceptance [for publication], authors are required to submit copyright agreements and all necessary permission letters for reprinting or modifying copyrighted materials, both textual and graphic. The author is fully responsible for obtaining all permissions and clearing any associated fees.'[1]

---

1 'Information for Contributors: Copyright/Permissions', journals.berghahnbooks.com/eca/index.php?pg=notes. A declaration of a similar nature is set out on the 'Journal Contributors' Page' of the publisher's general website: 'When your article is accepted for publication, you must clear any required reproduction rights for any figures, photos, or text belonging to a third party, including any content found on the internet unless you can provide proof that no explicit permission is needed [...]. Your journal's Editor will require written correspondence attesting to the granting of permission. Should a fee be required, please first check that the quality of the materials you would receive is acceptable to the journal. Please also note that contributors are responsible for clearing any fees related to the reproduction of any copyrighted materials', journals.berghahnbooks.com/index.php?pg=authors. For another example, see also *Studies in Comics*, published by Intellectual Books; the journal's 'Notes for Contributors 2010' sets out that: 'Copyright clearance is the responsibility of the contributor and should be indicated by the contributor'.

8. *Comics, Copyright and Academic Publishing*   189

Not all publishers, however, adhere to such a black and white position. The *Journal of Graphic Novels and Comics* is published by Taylor & Francis. In the *Authors Services* section of its website, the publisher acknowledges that reproducing short extracts of text and other associated material 'for the purposes of criticism may be possible without formal permission'.[2]

---

2   See http://journalauthors.tandf.co.uk/copyright/usingThirdPartyMaterial.asp. Since first publication, the advice on the publisher's website has been revised. That said, the website still provides 'that the reproduction of short extracts of text and some other types of material may be permitted on a *limited basis* for the purposes of criticism and review without securing formal permission'. See http://authorservices.taylorandfrancis.com/using-third-party-material-in-your-article/

To better understand *when* permission is required, the publisher directs authors to the Publishers' Association *Permissions Guidelines*.³

To better understand *what rights* need to be cleared, Taylor & Francis direct authors to the publisher's own FAQs about using third-party copyright material in an academic article. There are twenty-two FAQs to which the publisher provides boilerplate responses.⁴ Of these, thirteen expressly relate to the reproduction of visual material. To the question, '[d]o I need permission' to reproduce the work?, the answer is typically: 'Yes'. Consider, for example, the following: 'Do I need permission if I use an image from the Internet? / Yes, you will need to find out the

---

3   Since first publication, the Publishers' Association have updated these guidelines. Their new 2016 *Permissions Guidelines* are available at http://www.publishers.org.uk/about-us/useful-links/pa-permissions-guidelines-2016/

4   At the time of preparing the 'Deluxe Edition' of this work, there are now only six FAQs on the publisher's website concerning the use of third-party material. They relate to the following: Do I need permission to reproduce text quotations from other sources? Do I need permission even if I have redrawn figures? Do I need permission if I have reused information and data from a table? Do I need permission is I use an image from the Internet? Do I need permission to reproduce the cover image of a book as part of a book review/ Do I need permission if I use material from my own work? See http://authorservices.taylorandfrancis.com/using-third-party-material-in-your-article/

status of the image and find out who owns the copyright (this may be the photographer, artist, agency, museum, or library). You will then need to get permission from the copyright holder to reproduce the image in a journal article'.[5] Indeed, only two of the thirteen FAQs relating to visual material acknowledge the potential to reproduce work without permission for the purpose of criticism or review; these relate to, respectively, the use of 'screenshots or grabs of film or video'[6] and the use of 'very old paintings'.[7]

What is not clear from this FAQs document is whether the publisher is purporting to accurately represent the law in this area. If so — as we shall see — the FAQs document is clearly deficient. If, however, the publisher is simply using the FAQs document to set out the parameters of its own editorial policy on the reproduction of copyright-protected third-party material, then so be it: the publisher is perfectly entitled to adopt such editorial guidelines as it sees fit. I would suggest, though, that in cleaving to an editorial policy that fails to take full advantage of the scope that the copyright regime allows for the lawful reproduction of copyright-protected material without need for permission, the publishers are missing an opportunity to enable their academic contributors to augment and enrich comics scholarship as a discipline.

---

5   Taylor & Francis, 'Using third-party material in your article: Frequently asked questions', https://authorservices.taylorandfrancis.com/using-third-party-material-in-your-article/. See also the stock responses to the questions: (i) Do I need permission even if I have redrawn figures? (ii) Do I need permission to reproduce the cover image of a book as part of a book review? (iii) Do I need permission if I use a facebook screenshot? (iv) Do I need permission to use an image from Flickr? (v) Do I need permission to use ClipArt? (vi) Do I need separate permission for an image that will appear on a journal cover? Other questions prompt a response that directs the potential contributor to other third-party guidelines: (i) Do I need permission to use an image from Google Earth? (ii) Do I need permission to use an image from Yahoo? (iii) Do I need permission to use a crown copyright image? (iv) May I describe and illustrate a patent in my article?

6   The FAQs response at the time of writing was as follows: 'Films stills, film clips, and extracts of video should be used specifically within the context of the article for criticism or review. Each clip should be no longer than is necessary to illustrate the point made in the text. You should always provide full credits for the source of every image or clip'. Ibid.

7   The FAQs response at the time of writing was as follows: 'In most cases, if the image you are using is specifically within the context of the article for criticism or review you should not need to get permission from the artist and the owner. However, some artwork falls under stringent copyright management. See www.dacs.org.uk/ for further help'. Ibid.

In this respect *The Comics Grid* is more ambitious and forward thinking: it actively promotes the lawful use of copyright-protected content for the purposes of academic scholarship. The journal's copyright policy sets out that third-party copyright material reproduced on the grounds of 'educational fair use', with readers and contributors directed to Columbia University Libraries' *Fair Use Checklist* for further information. This is a checklist that has been developed to help academics and other scholars make a reasonable and balanced determination about whether their use of copyright-protected work is permissible under s.107 of the US *Copyright Act* 1976: the *fair use* provision.

Obviously, the journal locates its copyright advice within the context of US copyright law. But, as a Belfast-based academic,[8] with an interest in both the history and the current state of the copyright regime, my focus within this essay concerns the extent to which UK-based academics — or indeed anyone interested in writing about comics — can rely upon the UK copyright regime to reproduce extracts and excerpts from published comics and graphic novels *without* having to ask the copyright owner of those works for permission.

To address that issue, we must consider three key questions. What constitutes *a work* protected by copyright within the context of comics publishing? What does it mean to speak of *insubstantial copying* from a copyright-protected comic? And, what scope do existing — and forthcoming — *exceptions to copyright* afford the academic in this regard? Where appropriate, we will also reflect upon how the PA *Guidelines* address these issues.

What is 'a Work'?

The CDPA, the Copyright, Designs and Patents Act, 1988[9] provides a detailed and exhaustive list of eight types of work that qualify for copyright protection within the UK (CDPA: s.1).[10] So, before we can

---

8 At the time of first publication, I was the Professor of Copyright Law at the University of Glasgow. I have since moved to Queen's University Belfast.
9 https://www.legislation.gov.uk/ukpga/1988/48/contents
10 Traditionally, it has always been thought that the list of protected work set out within s.1 of the CDPA was finite and exhaustive. That is, in order for something to be protected by copyright in the UK it had to fall within one of these eight prescribed categories. However, the idea that the list is exhaustive — or closed — has begun to be undermined by recent decisions of the Court of Justice of the European Union (the CJEU), through the Court's interpretation of various EU copyright

properly appreciate what latitude there exists within the copyright regime for the reproduction of copyright-protected work without permission, one must understand what constitutes 'a work'.[11] This is axiomatic: one can only sensibly and reasonably interrogate notions of substantial copying and fair dealing — about which more below — in relation to an identified 'work'. To be sure, for most copyright-protected content, to establish what constitutes a work will not present many conceptual challenges. The work is: the novel, the poem, the playtext, the score, the painting, the photograph, and so on. Like the proverbial elephant, we tend to assume to know the work when we see it. With the medium of comics, however, things are not always so straightforward.

One characteristic of comics is that individual stories are often presented to the reader, played out across a number of issues: similar to the serialisation of literary works — often published with accompanying illustrations — by Victorian novelists such as Charles Dickens and Wilkie Collins. If Dickens's work was still in copyright today would we regard, say, *Great Expectations* as 'a work', even though it was first published in serial form? Almost certainly yes; few would seek to argue otherwise. Should we read (certain) comics in a similar vein: that is, works first published in serial form?

Consider Dave Sim's *Cerebus the Aardvark*. Published over a period of nearly thirty years (1977–2004), this ground-breaking work is best understood as a series of ten 'novels' collected into sixteen 'books'. The third of these 'novels', *Church & State*, was first published across fifty-nine issues between 1983–1988 (Issues 52–111) before being collected and published in book form as two volumes (*Church & State Volume I*, and *Church & State Volume II*) in 1987 and 1988 respectively. So: for copyright purposes, what is the 'work'? Or what about Chester Brown's adaptation of the Gospel of Matthew (see Fig. 8.2)? Brown began his

---

directives. In short, the CJEU has suggested that literary and artistic works should be copyright-protected whenever they constitute an author's 'intellectual creation'. See, for example: *Bezpecnostni softwarova asociace* v *Ministerstvo kultury* (2010) C-393/09, http://curia.europa.eu/juris/liste.jsf?num=C-393/09 (concerning a graphic user interface), and *Nintendo* v *PC Box* (2014) C-355/12, http://curia.europa.eu/juris/liste.jsf?language=en&jur=C,T,F&num=c-355/12&td=ALL (concerning a video game). What impact these European decisions will have upon the concept of 'a work' within the context of the CDPA remains to be seen.

11   For a discussion of the concept of 'the work' within copyright discourse, see Brad Sherman, 'What is a Copyright Work?', *Theoretical Inquiries in Law*, 12.1 (2011), 99–121.

adaptation in *Yummy Fur*, Issue 15 (March 1989). It continued in the remaining issues of *Yummy Fur* (Issues 16–32), and then in Brown's next project: *Underwater* (11 issues, 1994–1997). The most recent instalment ('Chapter 20, verses 1–29') appeared in *Underwater* Issue 11 in October 1997 and, at the time of writing, Brown has yet to complete his work on the remaining eight chapters. But again: what, here, is the 'work', and does our understanding of 'the work' shift depending on what we know about the author's own creative process?

Fig. 8.2 Brown, *Yummy Fur* #21 (1990), p. 18/6.

8. *Comics, Copyright and Academic Publishing*   195

Brown, in this respect, provides an intriguing case study. In *Yummy Fur* Issue 20 he offers his readers an insight into the way he constructs his comics (at least, circa 1990) (see Fig. 8.3). Brown typically works with page layouts of between five and seven panels, which panels are rarely uniform in size or shape. But, whereas most comic artists sketch or draft a page of comic art as a single page, Brown draws each panel individually, on a separate sheet of paper (often 'cheap typewriting paper' (Matt 1991: 67/19)), and then assembles each 'page' of the comic by arranging these individual panels on a larger sheet. Given this, should we regard each of Brown's panels as a 'work'?

Fig. 8.3 Brown, *Yummy Fur* #20 (1990), pp. 5/1–4.

One final example: Chris Ware's *Building Stories*, an exquisite artefact, beautifully rendered by the artist, and luxuriously produced by the publisher. Its unconventional format challenges preconceptions that anyone — whether a long-standing comics fan or not — might have about the form and format of the comic. It consists of fourteen different types of printed work (individual books, newspapers and broadsheets, flip books, a poster, accordion-style fold-outs, and so on) which present the reader with a complex, multi-layered story centred around an unnamed female protagonist, but one that eschews narrative linearity. Produced over a period of ten years, these 'works' are collectively presented to the reader in an illustrated box: a format inspired by Marcel Duchamp's *Box in a Valise* (1935–1941). So, what is 'the work' that is the subject of copyright protection: the box and its contents? Should we understand each of the fourteen vignettes as separate works in themselves, rather than parts of a richer, more ambitious and intriguing narrative project? Is the box 'a work'?

My point here is not to make things more difficult for those writing about comics who are grappling with copyright clearance issues, or to further obfuscate an already problematic legal landscape; quite the reverse. But one cannot escape the fact that the very nature of comics problematise what are otherwise often simple, conceptual distinctions in other fields of literary and artistic publishing. And as we shall see, these definitions matter; for example, the courts routinely identify the *amount of the work that has been copied* as a significant factor in determining whether the unauthorised use of the work constitutes 'fair dealing'. To return to *Cerebus*: reproducing one page from *Church & State* — a work that runs to 1220 pages in its entirety — is a very different prospect to the reproduction of a single page from one of the 59 individual issues that progress the *Church & State* storyline (see Fig. 8.4). Quantitatively speaking, it is the difference between reproducing 5% of an individual comic and reproducing 0.08% of the *Church & State* novel.

But we will return to the concept of 'fair dealing' in due course. For now, it is enough to reiterate that identifying what constitutes 'a work' when dealing with comics is often conceptually problematic, which in turn blurs the boundaries of permissible and impermissible use for both copyright owner and user. Let us assume, however, that one can confidently identify the 'work' with which one is dealing; that being the case, there are three obvious strategies that an academic or researcher

Fig. 8.4 Sim, *Church & State Vol. I* (Windsor, Ontario: Aardvark-Vanaheim, 1989), p. 421.

might rely upon when reproducing material from that work without the need for permission from the copyright owner. They concern: (i) insubstantial copying; (ii) fair dealing for the purpose of non-commercial research; and, (iii) fair dealing for the purpose of criticism and review. We deal with each in turn.

Insubstantial Copying

Section 16 of the CDPA sets out the various 'acts restricted by copyright': that is, the different types of protected activity (copying, distributing, communicating online, and so on) that require permission from the copyright owner. The legislation provides, however, that the protection granted to copyright owners only extends 'to the work as a whole or any substantial part of it' (CDPA: s.16(3)(a)). Put another way: it is lawful to make use of another's copyright work, so long as you are not copying any more than a substantial part of the work. But where does one draw the line between substantial and insubstantial copying?

It is often said that the issue of substantiality depends upon the *quality* of what has been taken rather than the quantity (*Sillitoe* v *McGraw* 1983: 545), and courts of late have demonstrated a marked willingness to find infringement so long as the part used is not 'insignificant' or *de minimis* (per Lord Bingham, *Designers Guild* v *Russell Williams* 2001: 11). This would seem to militate against the likelihood of successfully relying upon an argument of insubstantial copying when reproducing any material — even a single panel — from a comic without permission. Without wishing to indulge in cliché, if there is any truth in the conceit that a picture paints a thousand words, the argument that reproducing even a single panel from a comic might be regarded as *qualitatively substantial copying* is likely to enjoy some traction.

8. Comics, Copyright and Academic Publishing 199

To understand what lawful insubstantial copying might mean in relation to a comic, one must understand *the comic as sequential art*, a term famously coined by Will Eisner in 1985. Scott McCloud develops the notion further in the landmark *Understanding Comics*. Of particular interest is what McCloud has to say about 'closure' (the experience of 'observing the parts but perceiving the whole'), a foundational concept in the psychology of narrative. McCloud argues that comics rely upon 'closure' as an agent of 'change, time and motion': a phenomenon that occurs in *the space between* comic panels, often referred to as 'the gutter.'[12] He writes as follows: 'Comics panels fracture both time and space, offering a jagged, staccato rhythm of unconnected moments. But closure allows us to connect these moments and mentally construct a continuous, unified reality'. And whereas closure in the context of film and television is 'continuous, largely involuntary and virtually imperceptible,'[13] with comics closure depends upon the active participation of the reader.

Consider the single panel from *Understanding Comics* (Fig. 8.5). If you are reading this essay online, then, with this panel, you are looking at a digital copy of a digital copy of a printed copy of an image that

---

12 Scott McCloud, *Understanding Comics: The Invisible Art* (Northampton, MA: Kitchen Sink Press, 1993), pp. 66–67.
13 Ibid., p. 68.

incorporates a drawing of an iconic twentieth century painting. By itself, the image is simply an image bearing as much significance (or not) as the observer cares to invest in the same. However, when presented as part of a sequence, as McCloud puts it, 'the image is transformed into something more: the art of comics.'[14] It is the *sequential nature* of the comic form that is imperative here and, I would suggest, when applying well-established principles of copyright law to the comic as 'a work', the law should be sensitive to the unique vocabulary and grammar of comics as an art form. That is, if the phenomenon of closure is as integral to the very nature of the comic as McCloud suggests, then — without a sequence, without the gutter — the reproduction of a single panel from a comic should not typically be regarded as an instance of substantial copying: at least not from a *qualitative* perspective.

Fig. 8.5 McCloud, *Understanding Comics* (*Understanding Comics: The Invisible Art*, Northampton, MA: Kitchen Sink Press, 1993), p. 25/6.

---

14   Ibid., p. 5.

There is, of course, something counterintuitive about this analysis: one presumes someone writing about a comic chooses to reproduce a specific panel from the comic *precisely because it is significant*. And, on its face, this logic appears to be at odds with my argument that a single panel from a comic should not be understood to be qualitatively substantial or significant. And yet, adhering to that argument does not mean that the panel cannot or should not be regarded as significant within the confines of a scholarly essay. In this respect, it is essential that we hold in mind — and clearly differentiate between — the two different contexts within which the image is reproduced: the comic as a copyright-protected 'work', and the scholarly essay. There is no contradiction in the idea that the same image might be *qualitatively insignificant* in the former context, while simultaneously being *intellectually or illustratively significant* in the latter.

Also, I make no claim here about whether a single panel from a comic may or may not be a *quantitatively* significant part of the comic within which it appears. That will always depend upon the individual circumstances under consideration. Quantitatively, for example, it is easy to see how reproducing a single panel from a three or four panel daily newspaper comic strip would amount to substantial copying. But consider again the panel from *Understanding Comics*: it is one of six panels from a page in a book of 215 pages. It represents approximately 0.1% of the work that is *Understanding Comics*. Does that amount to substantial copying — from a quantitative perspective — for the purposes of the CDPA?

Exceptions to Copyright

Fair Dealing ...

The concept of fair dealing is common to both the exception permitting non-commercial research and that concerning criticism and review. But what constitutes fair dealing with a work?

On the first point, I would offer a correction: fair dealing is *not* determined *subjectively* (that is, from the perspective of the claimant alleging copyright infringement). Time and again, the courts have stressed that the concept of fair dealing is to be tested *objectively*. Lord Justice Aldous put it very succinctly: 'the court must judge the fairness [of the use] by the *objective standard* of whether a fair minded and honest person would have dealt with the copyright work [in the same manner as the defendant]' (emphasis added) (*Hyde Park* v *Yelland* 2000: 38).

Otherwise, this is, in many respects, a reasonable, albeit brief summation of current copyright doctrine on the concept of fair dealing. Recent court decisions have indicated a number of factors worth bearing in mind that may be of relevance, many of which are alluded to in the PA *Guidelines*. For example, in 2001 Lord Phillips identified three considerations to be of particular importance (the so-called 'Laddie factors'): (i) commercial competition with the claimant; (ii) prior publication; (iii) the amount and importance of the work taken (Ashdown v Telegraph Group 2001: 66–77).[15] In 2005 Justice Mann stressed that the motives of the user are also important, as is the

---

15 See also HMSO, *Modernising Copyright: A Modern, Robust and Flexible Framework* (London: HMSO, 2012), p. 14, http://copyright-debate.co.uk/wp-content/uploads/Modernising-Copyright-a-modern-robust-and-flexible-framework-Government-

actual purpose of the new work that is being produced; in addition, he indicated that, depending on the circumstances, reproducing an original work *in its entirety* could be regarded as fair (*Fraser-Woodward v BBC* 2005: 55–70).

... For the Purpose of Non-Commercial Research (CDPA s.29)

Section 29(1) of the CDPA provides that fair dealing with a work for the purpose of non-commercial research does not infringe any copyright in the work. Before considering the internal logic and scope of s.29, is it worth considering what is meant by 'research'? In addressing this question, it is important to appreciate that the current exception was amended in 2003 to ensure compliance with A.5(3)(a) of the European *Information Society Directive* 2001.[16] Article 5 of the *Information Society Directive* sets out a list of mandatory and optional exceptions to copyright that Member States can incorporate within their national copyright regimes, and 5(3)(a) specifically establishes that Member States are entitled to provide for an exception 'for the sole purpose of illustration for teaching or *scientific research* [...] to the extent justified by the non-commercial purpose to be achieved' (emphasis added). And so: what bearing does the reference to 'scientific research' in A.5(3)(a) have on the meaning of 'research' within s.29? Influential opinions differ.

---

response.pdf (in which the government lists the same three factors as of relevance when determining whether a particular dealing with a work is fair or not).

16 The Patent Office, *EC Directive 2001/29/EC on the Harmonisation of Certain Aspects of Copyright and Related Rights in the Information Society: Consultation Paper on Implementation of the Directive in the United Kingdom* (London: Intellectual Property Office, 2001), p. 9.

Laddie, Prescott and Vitoria on Copyright suggests that, as the exceptions set out in the Directive are to be strictly interpreted (see: *Infopaq v DDF* 2009: 56), 'there would not appear to be any justification for interpreting the exception broadly to encompass matters which involve no enquiry or investigation which is scientific in nature';[17] this reading of the legislation was subsequently endorsed by Justice Arnold (*Forensic Telecommunications Service* 2011: 109), albeit as *obiter dictum*.[18] The authors of *Laddie* continue that, as such, research conducted in the arts and humanities 'could not by any stretch of the imagination be called scientific.'[19] Compare, however, the line taken in *Copinger on Copyright*: 'although the Directive refers to scientific research, it is reasonably clear that this includes the humanities.'[20] If the interpretation advanced in *Laddie* is correct, then s.29 would have almost no relevance for researchers and academics working outside explicitly scientific domains. That would be extremely unfortunate. From my perspective, if, as and when a court does hand down an express ruling on the meaning and scope of 'research' within the context of s.29(1), it is to be hoped that an interpretation is adopted that is as wide and as purposive as possible, albeit one that is consistent with the requirements of A.5(3)(a).

Turning to the arrangement of the exception, it will be useful to set out the relevant parts of s.29 at length: '(1) Fair dealing with a literary, dramatic, musical or artistic work for the purposes of research for a non-commercial purpose does not infringe any copyright in the work provided that it is accompanied by a sufficient acknowledgement. / (1B) No acknowledgement is required in connection with fair dealing for the purposes mentioned in subsection (1) where this would be impossible for reasons of practicality or otherwise. / (1C) Fair dealing with a literary, dramatic, musical or artistic work for the purposes of private study does not infringe any copyright in the work [...] (3) Copying by

---

17 M. Vitoria et al., *Laddie, Prescott and Vitoria: The Modern Law of Copyright and Designs*, 4th ed. (London: Lexis-Nexis, 2011), 21.33.

18 For the non-lawyer: *obiter dictum* refers to a remark or comment made by a judge which, although included in the main body of the court's opinion, does not constitute part of *the reason for the decision of the court* (what is referred to as the *ratio decidendi*). As such, comments that are *obiter* are not binding in any way upon the decisions of future courts, although they can be highly persuasive.

19 Vitoria et al., *The Modern Law of Copyright*, 21.33, n6.

20 K. Garnett et al., *Copinger and Skone James on Copyright*, 16th ed. (London: Sweet & Maxwell, 2010), pp. 9–30.

a person other than the researcher or student himself is not fair dealing if — [...] (b) [...] the person doing the copying knows or has reason to believe that it will result in copies of substantially the same material being provided to more than one person at substantially the same time and for substantially the same purpose.'[21]

Notice two things: first, the exception provides for two types of permissible copying in two separate sub-clauses: copying for non-commercial research (s.29(1)), and copying for private study (s.29(1C)); second, the lawfulness of fair dealing for non-commercial research turns upon the copying being 'accompanied by a sufficient acknowledgement', whereas copying for private study does not. Intuitively, this suggests two contrasting types of activity: one that has a purely internal or personal dynamic,[22] and one that anticipates external and public engagement.[23]

In relation to the latter, consider RCUK's *Policy on Open Access*, a policy developed to ensure that publicly funded research is as freely accessible as possible: 'the Research Councils take very seriously their responsibilities in making outputs from this research publicly available — not just to other researchers, but also to potential users in business, charitable and public sectors, and to the general public'.[24] Or

---

21 Since first publication, the exception has been amended to include all types of copyright work (effective: 1 October 2014). The exception now reads as follows: '(1) Fair dealing with a work for the purposes of research for a non-commercial purpose does not infringe any copyright in the work provided that it is accompanied by a sufficient acknowledgement. / (1B) No acknowledgement is required in connection with fair dealing for the purposes mentioned in subsection (1) where this would be impossible for reasons of practicality or otherwise. / (1C) Fair dealing with a work for the purposes of private study does not infringe any copyright in the work [...] (3) Copying by a person other than the researcher or student himself is not fair dealing if — [...] (b) [...] the person doing the copying knows or has reason to believe that it will result in copies of substantially the same material being provided to more than one person at substantially the same time and for substantially the same purpose.'
22 That is: copying for private study is *personal* to the student, the academic, the individual seeking to acquire knowledge. Note, however, that the CDPA further defines 'private study' to preclude 'any study which is directly or indirectly for a commercial purpose' (s.178).
23 As Burrell and Coleman put it: if the research exception does not extend to copying when a researcher's results are presented in an essay, a thesis, a published paper or a book, then 'the requirement of sufficient acknowledgement is anomalous'; R. Burrell and A. Coleman, *Copyright Exceptions: The Digital Impact* (Cambridge: Cambridge University Press, 2005), pp. 117–18.
24 Research Councils UK, *RCUK Policy on Open Access* (London: Research Councils UK, 2013), https://www.ukri.org/files/legacy/documents/rcukopenaccesspolicy-pdf/

what about the recent observations in the 2012 Finch Report on expanding access to published research findings: '[T]here is an increasing tendency across Government and other bodies, both in the UK and elsewhere, to regard information generated by researchers as a public good; and to promote the reduction, if not the complete removal, of barriers to access. [...] Also associated with such ideas is a recognition that *communication and dissemination are integral parts of the research process itself*.'[25] In short, research — as a concept within contemporary academia — is necessarily a public-facing activity, and the dissemination of research is a vital part of that activity.

That said, there is a cogent argument that the research exception does *not* enable the *dissemination* of research, but is instead largely confined to facilitating *access* to material for research purposes. The PA *Guidelines* suggest as much in offering that: 'As a general rule, [this] exception is limited to *personal* copying'.[26] The root of this argument lies in s.29(3)(b): that copying is not fair if it results in copies 'of substantially the same material being provided to more than one person at substantially the same time for substantially the same purpose'. On this provision, Burrell and Coleman write: 'It seems that this was intended to ensure that the research and private study exception could not be used to justify classroom copying, but its effect is to prevent entirely any reliance on the research exception to justify the inclusion of a substantial part of an earlier work in a published research paper.' The point is well taken, but I would offer a technologically-directed rejoinder.

Consider the difference between research that is published in print and born-digital form. If the essay that you are currently reading had been published in a traditional academic journal, physical copies of which were sent to as many research libraries as subscribe to the journal then, applied literally, s.29(3)(b) would likely preclude the lawful inclusion of copyright-protected material within this essay based on s.29(1). That is, more than one copy of the work will be distributed to more than one person (various subscribing libraries) at substantially the same time for substantially the same purpose.

---

25   Research Information Network, *The Finch Report: Report of the Working Group on Expanding Access to Published Research Findings* (London: Research Information Network, 2012), p. 53 (emphasis added), https://www.acu.ac.uk/research-information-network/finch-report-final
26   PA, *Guidelines*, p. 2 (emphasis added).

8. *Comics, Copyright and Academic Publishing* 207

However, the essay you are reading has not been published in a traditional academic journal. Rather, this essay, in its current incarnation, has been published by Open Book Publishers both as part of a print-on-demand edited collection (available in hardback and paperback), as well as online in a variety of file formats (HTML, XML, PDF, epub and mobi). In terms of publication in physical form, s.29(1) presents less of a problem here precisely because the works are published and distributed on demand: that is, only when an order is placed by a specific institution or individual will the material be supplied to that specific institution or individual. A similar logic applies to material that is made available to the public online. From a technical perspective, this essay is stored in PDF, epub and mobi versions on Open Book Publishers's server, and has also been archived with the British Library, Portico,[27] and the Internet Archive's WayBack machine.[28] Now: does that mean that copies of this essay 'are being provided to more than one person at substantially the same time'? Much would depend on what one understands by the phrase: 'at substantially the same time'. Are two people likely to access, or download, this essay simultaneously, or even nearly simultaneously?

One of the great advantages to communicating work online is that it facilitates *asynchronous engagement* with the work from a place and at a time individually determined by the reader. The flip side of this technological reality is that scholars who are minded to do so might be able to square Burrell and Coleman's circle by making informed choices about how and where they publish their research. That is: publishing in non-commercial, born digital journals such as *The Comics Grid* or with publishers such as Open Book — rather than more traditional, for profit, subscription-based print journals — might afford academics greater scope to rely upon s.29 to reproduce copyright-protected material without the need for permission from the owner(s). Put simply: it may be that there is wriggle-room for reliance upon s.29 when disseminating one's research, depending upon the *technique of dissemination*.[29]

But, as with my commentary on insubstantial copying, I do not want to labour the argument concerning the capaciousness of the research exception, and for two reasons: first, within the context of our current legal framework, there is a more obvious strategy that can be relied upon: fair dealing for the purpose of criticism and review; and second, as we shall see, the government are currently planning to introduce a new exception permitting quotation for any reason.[30]

---

27   Established in 2002, Portico is a digital preservation service provided by ITHAKA intended to help the academic community preserve the scholarly record. For further details, see: www.portico.org/digital-preservation/about-us/our-organization
28   For further information about the Internet Archive's WayBack Machine, see: https://archive.org/web/
29   Obviously, the argument regarding asynchronous engagement with online publications and the opportunity for availing of the exception for non-commercial research does not hold true when dealing with material published (and distributed) in print form by someone other than the researcher (for example, a university publisher). In this situation, print-based dissemination will more obviously depend on the exceptions for quotation, criticism and review, which are discussed next.
30   Since first publication, the new exception for quotation has been introduced (effective: 1 October 2014). See the next section — Current Proposals for Reform [in 2013] — for further commentary.

... Or, for the Purpose of Criticism and Review (s.30(1))

Section 30(1) permits fair dealing for the purposes of criticism and review, and sets out as follows: 'Fair dealing with a work for the purpose of criticism or review, of that or another work or of a performance of a work, does not infringe any copyright in the work provided that it is accompanied by a sufficient acknowledgement and provided that the work has been made available to the public.'[31] But what constitutes 'criticism and review'?

Consider again the PA *Guidelines*: that fair dealing with a work is permissible provided there is 'a significant element of actual criticism and review of the work being copied (i.e. substantial comment, as opposed to mere reproduction), although this is sometimes interpreted liberally.'[32] Unfortunately, the PA's suggestion that the criticism in question needs to be directed *at the work being copied* is out of step with both the literal wording of the CDPA and with existing copyright jurisprudence; in short, it is likely to mislead. The legislation is unambiguous that criticism can be concerned with 'the work', 'another work', or 'a performance of a work'. Moreover, the courts have established that the scope of the exception is not confined to a critique or review of the style or merit of a work or performance *per se*, but can extend to the ideas, doctrine, or philosophy underpinning the work (*Hubbard v Vosper* 1972), as well as to its social or moral implications (*Pro Sieben Media v Carlton* 1999). The comments of Lord Justice Robert Walker LJ provide a useful touchstone: that "criticism or review' [is an expression] of wide and indefinite scope'; that '[a]ny attempt to plot [its] precise boundaries is doomed to failure'; and that it is an expression 'which should be interpreted liberally' (*Pro Sieben Media v Carlton* 1999: 620). Without doubt, s.30(1) offers the academic working in the field of comics scholarship — as well as academic publishers — much greater scope for reproducing copyright-protected work than the PA *Guidelines* appear to suggest.

---

31   Since first publication, the exception has been amended (effective: 1 October 2014). The exception now reads as follows: 'Fair dealing with a work for the purpose of criticism or review, of that or another work or of a performance of a work, does not infringe any copyright in the work provided that it is accompanied by a sufficient acknowledgement (unless this would be impossible for reasons of practicality or otherwise) and provided that the work has been made available to the public.'

32   PA, *Guidelines*, p. 2.

Consider, for example, the various images that I have included within this essay. I have offered no criticism or review of the works from which these images have been taken. So: upon what basis do I reproduce them here? I could offer justifications that rely upon all three strategies discussed thus far: insubstantial copying; fair dealing for the purposes of non-commercial research; and fair dealing for criticism or review. The latter, I have suggested, provides me with my most robust defence, but what is 'the work' that I am critiquing or reviewing? Dear Reader, I have a number of 'works' in mind, including (but not limited to): *The Comics Grid*; Taylor & Francis's FAQs document concerning the use of third-party material in academic articles; the Publishers Association *Permissions Guidelines*; and the *Copyright Designs and Patents Act* (the Act is itself a copyright-protected work). Without hesitation, I would defend my reproduction of the copyright material reproduced within this essay as lawful, and without the need for securing permission from the relevant copyright owners concerned.

Only in relation to one illustration did I bother to seek permission from (what I took to be) the copyright owner: the two panels from *Crisis* Issue 31 (Fig. 8.1). Now, it is important to be clear that I did not seek permission because I considered it necessary. There is nothing about this illustration — when compared with the rest of the copyright-protected material that I have reproduced in this essay — that marks it out as warranting special attention or consideration (at least, not from a rights-clearance perspective). Rather, my motivation was far more self-regarding and mundane. Dear Reader, the young man in those panels is none other than myself.[33] That said, my experience in trying to clear rights in that particular image is one that will no doubt be familiar to many academics that write about visual culture. On 6 May 2013, I wrote to the Permissions Department at Egmont UK Ltd as follows:

---

[33] For those interested in how I came to feature in *Crisis* #31, the explanation is simple enough. Between the ages of 16 and 22 I worked in Northern Ireland's first comic shop — Dark Horizons — which, at that time was part-owned by John McCrea. When John was commissioned to illustrate 'Her Parents' he asked if he could draw me into the story (apparently the protagonist in Millar's story reminded him of me). Photographs were taken; the rest is history. (And yes, those are my actual clothes. I was a fan of a nice cardigan even at the tender age of 17.)

8. Comics, Copyright and Academic Publishing

Current Proposals for Reform [in 2013]: An Exception for Quotation

The decision to introduce the new exception for quotation is to be welcomed [indeed, since this work was first published, the new exception for quotation has been introduced].[34] Again: the government-funded UK Research Councils make clear that research should be relevant to society and wider societal concerns; it should engage the

---

34 The new exception for quotation was introduced as of 1 October 2014. This new exception (s.30(1ZA)) states as follows: 'Copyright in a work is not infringed by the use of a quotation from the work (whether for criticism or review or otherwise) provided that — (a) the work has been made available to the public, (b) the use of the quotation is fair dealing with the work, (c) the extent of the quotation is no more than is required by the specific purpose for which it is used, and (d) the quotation is accompanied by a sufficient acknowledgement (unless this would be impossible for reasons of practicality or otherwise).' The substance and scope of this new exception has little impact on the nature of the arguments set out within this section and the next.

public and empower people; it should have impact. It is right that the copyright regime should enable, not inhibit, those aspirations. And it is right that government should take advantage of the latitude afforded under the 2001 Directive, to ensure that both s.29 and the new quotation exception facilitate research endeavour, including the dissemination of that research, to the fullest possible extent, but without unduly compromising the economic interests of copyright owners.

Indeed, in this context, the IPO strike the right note in emphasising that the quotation of works should be permitted 'only to the extent necessary, and *without competing with sales of the original work*.'[35] And again: '[a]s this exception will be limited to "fair dealing" and extracts will be limited to the extent necessary to serve their purpose, works using extracts *will not substitute for, or complete with, originals*.'[36] This focus on the likely commercial competition between the two works in question accords with the first of the so-called 'Laddie factors' and underscores the extent to which quotation — within the context of academic scholarship and publishing — should generally be unburdened from the various costs (financial, administrative, and otherwise) associated with copyright clearance. Would anyone sensibly claim that the copyright-protected material that I have reproduced within this essay, without express permission, commercially competes with, or acts as a substitute for, any of the underlying works?

To be sure, a less nimble and less enlightened copyright regime — one that was less minded to enable freedom of expression — might

---

35 HMSO, *Modernising Copyright*, p. 1 (emphasis added).
36 Ibid., p. 2 (emphasis added).

legitimately require that users seek permission for all such quotations, and thus secure a potential revenue stream for copyright owners. But copyright has never been concerned solely with securing any and every potential revenue stream for copyright owners; nor should it. The type of use and quotation that we have discussed and envisaged within this essay is not such use as should require permission or payment. Put another way: these types of use fall outwith what might reasonably be regarded as the normal exploitation of copyright-protected work; neither do they unreasonably prejudice the legitimate interests of the authors concerned.[37]

Conclusion

Will these proposed reforms make a difference? Will the new quotation exception make it easier for academics writing about comics — or indeed any academic working in the digital humanities — to reproduce copyright-protected work within their published research without needing to clear rights in that work? Probably not: at least not in any meaningful way. Where they might make a difference is in relation to researchers who disseminate their work through websites and blogs, as well as other types of grey literature such as responses to government consultations or independent research reports. Rarely is the content of this type of material subject to editorial or other third-party intervention and as such researchers can choose to benefit from an exception that enables greater use of copyright-protected content without the need for formal permission.

But the mainstay of academic publication lies in books, book chapters, and journal articles, with journal publication firmly established as

---

[37] The Berne Convention (which originally dates to 1886) is an international agreement that requires the signatories to the Convention to recognise and confer copyright protection on the literary and artistic works of authors from other signatory countries. In this way the Convention enables the operation of the international copyright regime. In addition, the Convention sets out certain minimum criteria that signatory countries must ascribe to in their national copyright regimes. Article 9(2) of the Convention provides that '[i]t shall be a matter for legislation in the countries of [the Berne Union] to permit the reproduction of such works in certain special cases, provided that such reproduction does not conflict with a normal exploitation of the work and does not unreasonably prejudice the legitimate interests of the author'.

the predominant format across all disciplines, including the arts and humanities (a dominance that also appears to be increasing).[38] For so long as these types of output dominate the research landscape, academic publishers will remain the principal gatekeepers to the dissemination of scholarly research. And for so long as they do, any meaningful opportunity for researchers to benefit from the scope of these new exceptions is likely to be marginal, if not entirely bargained away as part of the publication process. We know that the Publishers Association interprets the existing exceptions far more narrowly than it needs to in the advice it gives its constituent members on copyright permissions. We also know that, in any event, academic publishers typically manage the business of copyright clearance by making their contributing authors responsible for securing permissions (even when the use of the material is covered by an exception). The imperatives underpinning those behaviours — maximising profit and minimising the risk (or fear) of copyright litigation — are entirely cogent, and they are unlikely to diminish in the mind of the publisher anytime soon. In short, it will make no difference to an academic that the copyright regime enables quotation from a work for purposes such as criticism and review, if the publisher chooses not to avail themselves of that exception. Rights will still have to be cleared, and fees might have to be paid.

And, of course, it is reasonable to ask: why shouldn't academic publishers seek to maximise profits and minimise their risks? The reality is that academic publishing is a global success story, one that should be celebrated and supported. In 2007, the estimated annual revenue generated by (English-language) scientific and scholarly journal publication was just under $8bn (or just over £4bn), the bulk of which revenue (68–75%) was generated through academic library subscriptions.[39]

---

38 Research Information Network, *Communicating Knowledge: How and Why UK Researchers Publish and Disseminate their Findings* (London: Research Information Network, 2009), pp. 13–27, https://dspace.lboro.ac.uk/dspace-jspui/bitstream/2134/5465/1/Communicating-knowledge-report.pdf

39 M. Ware and M. Mabe, *The STM Report: An Overview of Scientific and Scholarly Journal Publishing* (The Hague: IASTM Publishers, 2009; 3rd ed. 2012), p. 16, https://www.stm-assoc.org/2012_12_11_STM_Report_2012.pdf

Moreover, this is an industry that has sustained year on year growth throughout the current economic crisis.[40] By 2011, for example, the annual revenue generated by journal publishing had risen to $9.4bn.[41] (To contextualise that figure: in the same year the global revenue generated by the sale of recorded music (physical formats only) was just $10.4bn.[42])

To be sure, the nature of research communication is changing, but academic publishers will continue to perform an integral role in the future of scholarly endeavour and enterprise for many years to come. Indeed, it is important that they do so. They certify and review research, copy-edit, type-set and proof it for publication; they advertise, market and distribute the journals in which the research is published, develop new tools and platforms for engaging with that research, and archive and preserve it for the longer term (IASTM 2008). They add value in making our work easier to discover and navigate through citation linking and the allocation of persistent identifiers (digital object identifiers, or DOIs), coding for web dissemination, and other semantic publishing techniques (IASTM 2008; RIN 2012: 24–26). *How much value* academic publishers actually add is a question for debate, but certainly they do add value.

---

40   Ibid., p. 22.
41   Ibid., p. 19.
42   International Federation of the Phonographic Industry, *Digital Music Report* (London: UK IFPI, 2012), https://www.ifpi.org/content/library/DMR2012.pdf

8. Comics, Copyright and Academic Publishing

8. Comics, Copyright and Academic Publishing 221

Works Cited

Brown, C. (April 1990) *Yummy Fur* #20, Vortex Comics Inc.

— (June 1990) *Yummy Fur* #21, Vortex Comics Inc.

Burrell R. and A. Coleman (2005) *Copyright Exceptions: The Digital Impact* (Cambridge: Cambridge University Press).

Eisner, W. (2008) *Comics and Sequential Art: Principles and Practices from the Legendary Cartoonist* (New York and London: W. W. Norton & Co.).

Garnett K., et al. (2010) *Copinger and Skone James on Copyright*, 16th ed. (London: Sweet & Maxwell).

Gowers, A. (2006) *Gowers Review of Intellectual Property* (Norwich: HMSO), https://assets.publishing.service.gov.uk/government/uploads/system/uploads/attachment_data/file/228849/0118404830.pdf

Her Majesty's Government (2012) *Modernising Copyright: A Modern, Robust and Flexible Framework* (London: HMSO), http://copyright-debate.co.uk/wp-content/uploads/Modernising-Copyright-a-modern-robust-and-flexible-framework-Government-response.pdf

Intellectual Property Office (2012) *Exception for Use of Quotations or Extracts of Copyright Works*, IA No: BIS0310 (London: IPO), https://www.legislation.gov.uk/ukia/2014/275/pdfs/ukia_20140275_en.pdf

Intellectual Property Office (2014) *Technical Review of Draft Legislation on Copyright Exceptions: Government Response* (London: IPO), https://webarchive.nationalarchives.gov.uk/20140603102645/http:/www.ipo.gov.uk/response-copyright-techreview.pdf

International Association of Scientific, Technical and Medical Publishers (2008) *An Overview of Scientific, Technical and Medical Publishing and the Value it Adds to Research Outputs* (The Hague: IASTM Publishers), https://www.stm-assoc.org/2008_04_01_Overview_of_STM_Publishing_Value_to_Research.pdf

International Federation of the Phonographic Industry (2012) *Digital Music Report* (London: IFPI), https://www.ifpi.org/content/library/DMR2012.pdf

Matt, J. (1991) *Peepshow* (Princeton: Kitchen Sink Press).

McCloud, S. (1993) *Understanding Comics: The Invisible Art* (Northampton, MA: Kitchen Sink Press).

Millar, M, and J. McCrea (1989) 'Her Parents', *Crisis* #31, November, Fleetway Publications.

Patent Office, The (2001) *EC Directive 2001/29/EC on the Harmonisation of Certain Aspects of Copyright and Related Rights in the Information Society: Consultation Paper on Implementation of the Directive in the United Kingdom* (London: Intellectual Property Office).

Publishers' Association (2008) *PA Permissions Guidelines* (London: Publishers Association).

Research Councils UK (2013) *RCUK Policy on Open Access* (London: Research Councils UK), https://www.ukri.org/files/legacy/documents/rcukopenaccesspolicy-pdf/

Research Information Network (2012) *The Finch Report: Report of the Working Group on Expanding Access to Published Research Findings* (London: Research Information Network), https://www.acu.ac.uk/research-information-network/finch-report-final

— (2009) *Communicating Knowledge: How and Why UK Researchers Publish and Disseminate their Findings* (London: Research Information Network), https://dspace.lboro.ac.uk/dspace-jspui/bitstream/2134/5465/1/Communicating-knowledge-report.pdf

— (2008) *Activities, Costs and Funding Flows in the Scholarly Communications System* (London: Research Information Network), http://www.rin.ac.uk/system/files/attachments/Activites-costs-flows-report.pdf

Sherman, B. (2011) 'What is a Copyright Work?', *Theoretical Inquiries in Law* 12.1, 99–121, https://doi.org/10.2202/1565-3404.1264

Sim, D. (1987) *Church & State Volume I* (Windsor, Ontario: Aardvark-Vanaheim).

Tickell, A. (2016) 'Open Access to Research Publications: Independent Advice', London: Independent Report, Department for Business, Innovation and Skills, https://www.gov.uk/government/publications/open-access-to-research-independent-advice

Vaver, D. (2012) 'Harmless Copying', *Intellectual Property Journal* 19–28.

Vitoria M., et al. (2011) *Laddie, Prescott and Vitoria: The Modern Law of Copyright and Designs*, 4th ed. (London: Lexis-Nexis).

Ware C. (2012) *Building Stories* (London: Jonathan Cape).

Ware, M. and M. Mabe (2012) *The STM Report: An Overview of Scientific and Scholarly Journal Publishing* (The Hague: IASTM Publishers, 2009; 3rd ed.), https://www.stm-assoc.org/2012_12_11_STM_Report_2012.pdf

Cases

Ashdown v *Telegraph Group* [2001] EWCA Civ 1142.

Bezpecnostni softwarova asociace v *Ministerstvo kultury* [2010] C-393/09.

Designers Guild v *Russell Williams* [2001] FSR 11.

Forensic Telecommunications Services Limited v *The Chief Constable of West Yorkshire Police, Stephen Hirst* [2011] EWHC 2892.

Fraser-Woodward v *BBC* [2005] EMLR 22.

Hubbard v *Vosper* [1972] 2 QB 84.

Hyde Park v *Yelland* [2000] WL 462.

Infopaq International A/S v. *Danske Dagblades Forening* [2009] C-5/08.

Nintendo v *PC Box* [2014] C-355/12.

Pro Sieben Media AG v *Carlton UK Television Ltd* [1999] FSR 610.

Sillitoe v *McGraw-Hill Book Co (UK) Ltd* [1983] FSR 545.

From the Sketchbook of Jason Mathis

PART II

VIEWS FROM ELSEWHERE

9. Diversity or Die: How the Face of Book Publishing Needs to Change if it Is to Have a Future

Danuta Kean

Imagine the UK in twenty-five years' time. The average young person will be mixed race, female and, if things don't change soon, she will not be a reader. Why? Because the Office of National Statistics predicts that by then one in five of the population of Britain will be Black, Asian or Minority Ethnic (BAME). It is a statistic of which the UK publishing industry seemed ignorant in 2016 when, of the many thousands of new titles published, fewer than one hundred were by writers of colour. As for the future of the industry, its failure to reflect social change in Britain seemed set to ensure that its workforce would remain ninety per cent white, educated at independent schools and Oxbridge, publishing books by people just like them.[1]

As now, some Black and Asian authors will slip through the net, but they will be published as 'literary' fiction, which not only sells far less than genre fiction, but emphasises the Otherness of the writer and the world portrayed, a world dominated by themes of race and postcolonialism — essentially the intersection of white experience with that of other ethnicities — rather than wider, universal themes. It is a world that reflects white stereotypes of minority ethnic cultures.

---

1   Sarah Shaffi, 'Publishing Seeks to Address Industry's Lack of Diversity', *The Bookseller*, 4 November 2016, https://www.thebookseller.com/news/publishing-seeks-address-industry-s-lack-diversity-426031

This was a disturbing finding of *Writing the Future* (hereafter *WtF*), the 2016 report Mel Larsen and I were commissioned by Spread the Word to write about Black and Asian publishers and novelists in the UK marketplace.[2] The report was compiled over an eight month period and involved quantitative and qualitative research into the experiences of BAME writers and publishers, as well as the employment and publishing practices in the UK. It also covered the leading university courses and three biggest literary festivals.

I was chosen to head the research, because ten years earlier I edited *In Full Colour* (hereafter *IFC*), the first report into diversity in book publishing. Commissioned by decibel, an Arts Council diversity initiative, *IFC* found less than eight per cent of those working in publishing had a BAME background thanks to working practices that bred unconscious bias, actively excluded diverse people and, in some cases, tolerated outright racist attitudes. Black and Asian women workers reported colleagues' comments about their 'exoticism', while publishers commonly claimed that BAME people 'don't read' and don't engage with publishing either as readers or potential employees or novelists.

This puts into perspective what has happened since. When Mel Larsen and I began working on the new report, we expected to find that the diversity programmes set up ten years ago by decibel had matured and that percentages of BAME staff and writers on mainstream lists had significantly grown. This was because in the wake of *IFC* all the main publishers and publishing bodies, such as the Publishers Association, had committed to addressing the issue — not least because they recognised that by drawing in more BAME workers they would be better placed to reach BAME readers and take a share of their estimated £300bn in disposable income.

A networking organisation, prizes for culturally diverse writers and paid internships aimed at minority ethnic people were established quickly with Arts Council backing. With that level of support, it would be rational to expect that graduates from the earliest unpaid internship programmes had by now reached the boards of the main publishing houses.

---

2   Unless otherwise stated, statistics and interviews quoted in this chapter come from Danuta Kean and Mel Larsen (eds.), *Writing the Future* (hereafter *WtF*) (London: Spread the Word, 2016), https://www.spreadtheword.org.uk/wp-content/uploads/2016/11/Writing-the-Future-Black-and-Asian-Authors-and-Publishers-in-the-UK-Marketplace-May-2015.pdf

What we found was disappointing. Malorie Blackman, the former children's laureate and award-winning author, sums up the experience of those who have been around UK Books for the past twenty years. 'For the first few years of being published, I was always the sole face of colour at any publishing event I went to,' she recalled. 'About ten years ago that changed and there were a number of faces of colour at various events. It was wonderful. Progress was finally being made. But, over the last three or four years, I seem to have gone back to being the sole face of colour at literary events. What happened?'[3]

Bright hopes burned out quickly: not only had none of the earliest decibel internees reached board level, none remained in large houses, and those that remained in publishing had set up independent labels of their own rather than work for large publishers where they felt isolated. At entry level, the decibel unpaid internship programmes had fizzled out after the Arts Council withdrew match funding. Publishers claimed that in the post-recession environment, they simply didn't have the money to fully fund diversity-orientated paid internships.[4]

A handful of paid internships remained — notably at Profile Books, HarperCollins and at Penguin, through The Helen Fraser Fellowship. Of these only the latter was aimed at BAME candidates and, as far as I could ascertain, the graduates that had joined the programme had come from predominantly affluent backgrounds. This change coincided with a rapid rise in unpaid internships as a primary pipeline into book publishing and has formed a toxic combination that has undermined diversity, be that ethnic or social, in the industry (see Table 1).

Table 1. Survey of members of the Society of Young Publishers: 'How did you get your first paid job in publishing?' Source: *Writing the Future*, p. 24.

Through personal contact (i.e. family)	12.5%
Through industry contact	6.25%
Through unpaid internship	18.75%
Through paid internship	12.5%
Through job ad in trade press	18.75%
Declined to answer	31.25%

---

3   *WtF* 2015, 'Plus ça change', p. 13.
4   *WtF*, 'Could Do Better', pp. 21–24.

While paid internships, especially those aimed at minority ethnic candidates through the four-year-old Creative Access programme, were welcomed, they were no guarantee of opening up the trade to a wider talent pool. Like decibel, Creative Access interns are co-funded by publishers, and questions over its long term funding may mean the programme goes the same way as decibel.

These programmes proved a vital pipelines for BAME candidates: SYP members who responded to the *WtF* survey into access into the trade had worked as many as nine unpaid internships before securing paid employment. That is nine work experience placements that required them to self-fund living, food and transportation costs in London. It should be a matter of grave concern for the industry that a primary route into the business poses a significant barrier to those outside the affluent professional classes, and explains why the industry remains dominated by white, public-school-educated, Oxbridge graduates, even though this group represent a tiny fragment of the overall UK population — only seven per cent of the UK population attended public schools and less than one per cent of those attended Oxbridge (source: Social Mobility and Child Poverty Commission 2014). A report in 2010 by the Race for Opportunity Campaign shows how much this discriminates against BAME people: it found that only 11.1 per cent of Oxford students and 10.5 per cent of Cambridge students have a BAME background.

To be fair, there is recognition within the senior ranks of publishing that unpaid internships are iniquitous. 'I don't like unpaid internships. They prohibit people who don't live in London or who don't have parents to support them working in publishing,' said Ann Woodall, HR director at Little, Brown.[5] Over at Profile, founder and managing director Andrew Franklin did not mince his words: 'Unpaid internships are disgusting and should be banned.' Profile's commitment to diversity includes sponsoring a scholarship at City University, as well as paying all its internees the London Living Wage. As a result the small independent has an enviable record in recruiting diverse staff, though Franklin was not complacent. 'I'd like more, simple as that,' he added.

For those BAME publishers interviewed for *WtF*, there was a strong sense of isolation and a desire to network with others who understood the unique intersection of issues facing publishers and writers of colour.

---

5   *WtF*, 'No More Boom and Bust', pp. 26–29.

Even BAME internees complained about isolation. 'Everyone has been very nice, but you do look around and think you are the only one here who isn't like them,' one said. 'But they don't really get it, and sometimes they make you feel like you are a special case, as if you are only allowed in because you are Black or Asian and not for your skills. They don't realise how hard it was to get onto this scheme and how many people you had to compete against.'

In the wake of *IFC*, DipNet, the diversity networking organisation, had been set up by Black publishers Elise Dilsworth and the late Alison Morrison, but by the end of the decade it had faded through lack of top-line support within the industry. Furthermore, cultural awareness training that would tackle recruiters' unconscious bias and deal head on with exclusionist behaviour and outright racism, had been dropped due to financial pressures.

Again, the impact of this on senior management levels was visible: a survey of boards and, especially, the powerful C Circle of chief officers, revealed that the generational handover caused by the retirement of high-profile women such as Helen Fraser at Penguin and Gail Rebuck at Random House had not resulted in greater diversity. In fact, the recession appeared to have led to a retrenchment of white, middle class masculine power at the top level of publishing, with more white, public-school-educated men in the boardroom than had been seen for twenty years.

Interviews undertaken with senior personnel in all the biggest traditional publishing houses and a survey of Human Resources directors for *WtF* found that a step change took place after 2008. This change was not only fuelled by uncertainty over the economy, but over emerging digital formats for books and retail, as well as a fiercely competitive retail landscape that placed heavy pressure on publishers' already tight profit margins. Programmes to promote diversity and cultural awareness were seen as secondary to survival and were among the first things cut back in the recession. Though there is no firm evidence that this reflected a lack of commitment at senior level within publishing houses, it was taken that way by both writers and publishers of colour.[6]

Poor data collection at the most basic level in publishing houses offered further evidence of the failure by the industry to adequately own the problem of diversity and to recognise the considerable financial benefits

---

6   Ibid.

to having a diverse business. None of the HRs in the biggest publishing houses interviewed for the report had reliable data on diversity at recruitment level or higher, or on the number of writers of colour on their lists. The excuse given was that businesses relied on self-reporting and not every new employee wished to submit data. There was no data about the career progress of diverse employees or exit interviews that addressed any cultural issues that may have led employees to decide to leave.

As a result, HRs relied on educated guesses about the number of people of colour employed in-house. These guesses can be deemed reasonably accurate because the number of BAME publishers remains very low: between four and twelve per cent, still well below the forty per cent of minority ethnic people living in London, the hub of the British book trade.[7]

Within publishing there was widespread recognition among white and non-white staff that diversity is a problem (see Table 2 below), although it was only among white and BAME employees at middle and junior levels that it was regarded as symptomatic of a failure by directors, especially chief executive officers, to recognise the importance of diversity for more than ethical and PR value.

Typical of many in the trade was the comment of one white senior editor, who said: 'What we see time and again is a reaction to guilt privilege. The reason that these initiatives start up and then die again and again is that the issue of diversity is not taken up properly by those with strategic decision-making authority. They are paying lip service to the issue rather than bringing in effective change, because that could attack their privileged position.'

Table 2. 'How culturally diverse is the industry according to Publishers and Literary Agents?' Source: *Writing the Future*, p. 24.

	Publishers	Literary Agents
Very culturally diverse	3.13%	0%
Quite diverse	3.13%	0%
Moderately diverse	6.25%	0%
A little diverse	28.13%	45.95%
Not diverse at all	56.25%	51.35%
Don't know	3.13%	2.7%

---

7   *WtF*, 'Could Do Better', p. 23.

Well-meaning initiatives that shudder to a halt without bringing lasting change cause both minority-ethnic authors and publishers to be burned out by the fight for recognition. In-house, this plays out in the ignorance and even low-level racism experienced by many BAME publishers. One literary agent interviewed for *WtF* said: 'I recently had feedback on memoir by a Black author where several editors asked me — 'Do enough Black people buy books?' I was gobsmacked.' The problem, the agent said, was not limited to one publisher. It was endemic throughout the industry. 'The title didn't sell to a publisher,' he added.

One young publisher recalled that at the end of an interview for an entry-level job in editorial at a major house she was taken to one side by her interviewer, a senior publisher. She had failed the interview, for which the publisher apologised then offered advice that she hoped the candidate 'wouldn't take the wrong way'. 'If you don't mind me saying, if you want to get on in publishing, you need to lose your London accent.'[8]

Mel Larsen and I found that the impact of this lack of diversity is far greater than a handful of BAME employees feeling isolated: it affected how Black and Asian authors were treated. Many felt that the prevailing white, public school educated Oxbridge culture of the trade influences editorial decisions about their work and how it is marketed. That publishers are keenly aware of the problem is reflected in the anecdote told by one writer of colour: 'There is a story about one well known Asian author. Every time she goes in to meet her publisher, the accounts person comes along, because there are no other Asian or Black people working there.'

It also affects what appears in print and how it is marketed. Contends novelist and poet Bernardine Evaristo: 'Sometimes people assume that if you write stories about people of colour that you must be writing about racism, which is ridiculous.' The majority of published BAME novelists interviewed for *WtF* said they felt restricted by such expectations. One respected African Caribbean literary writer comments: 'There is a sense that if you are a Black writer, you should be writing about that [being Black]. I have heard publishers say: 'She's Black, what is she doing writing about Australia?''[9]

---

8   *WtF*, 'No More Boom and Bust', p. 26.
9   *WtF*, 'Plus ça change', pp. 13–16.

In part, she concedes, this reflects a risk-averse culture in publishing that focuses on the most obvious aspects of an author's life for marketing and publicity. 'There is a sense that there is now a certain book that they want from you,' adds the author, who has been publishing acclaimed novels for twenty years. 'So, no it hasn't changed. That is what was happening before when they were scrambling around for the next Walter Moseley or *Joy Luck Club*.'

BAME authors could be falling victim to the same marketing pressures as their white counterparts, driven by the demands of major retailers and under pressure to focus on obvious marketing tropes, such as the banyan tree at sunset that graces the cover of many books set in Africa. But the focus on ethnicity rather than universality makes writers of colour feel alienated from the wider commercial market. No-one interviewed was convinced that evidence exists for a market that separates Black and Asian readers from white ones, or that white readers only wanted to read about 'race' issues. 'There is an orthodoxy whereby the presumed reader is totally mono-cultural, white middle England,' said Arimatta Forma. 'We know from looking at Census data that that is a very outdated view. I think sometimes a paradigm gets created and everyone starts to subscribe to it.'

The impact of such thinking on Black and Asian novelists is that universality in their work is trumped by 'exoticism'. 'Colonialism is the lens through which they want to look at Africa and Asia, because it is all about them (white publishers and literary critics). It is not about us,' is the bitter commentary of one well-known name who asked to be kept anonymous. Writers at all stages in their career had experienced an expectation within the trade that they should reflect assumptions about race and colonialism — whether the tension of the ghetto or the fragrance of the mango grove. An ex-creative-writing student sums up the feeling: 'Maybe America is a slightly more liberal place towards the arts — there are writers there who are not white who don't 'have' to write about their race — but, I feel I'm supposed to be placed somehow because of my race and that I 'should' write about race, exoticism, immigrant stories.' This is why increasing numbers of BAME novelist are turning to US or Indian-sub-continent publishers to get book deals.[10]

---

10   Ibid.

The most pernicious way this stereotyping manifested itself was in the use of the word 'authentic' to either validate or dismiss a BAME writer's work. '"Authenticity" is used as an excuse to deny opportunities for people outside the cliché,' one respected literary name with an African heritage said. He added that the use of the word turns Black and Asian writers into totems for their communities, which emphasises the sense that they are outsiders to a white literary culture. 'Many of us simply wish to tell stories rather than represent our entire race,' the author claimed.

For many BAME novelists the word 'authentic' is interchangeable with 'exotic' — and is equally resented because it seems to emphasise difference rather than universality. 'If an unusual novel about minorities is an exposé of weird rituals or traditions it creates a special appeal: see also female infanticide, holy men molesting children, forced marriages, honour killings and so on. Add to that a thriller element, and you stand a much better chance of publication,' one established Indian author explains. 'If you have that, then your ethnicity becomes a license of "authenticity" and fair comment.'[11]

The most insidious use of the word we found when researching *WtF* was when it was used to undermine a Black or Asian author's ability to write about their community. For instance the critical reception of Gautam Malkani's *Londonstani*, a comic novel acquired with much brouhaha by Fourth Estate, included personal references to his education and supposed background. 'I'd open newspapers and I would actually hope for bad reviews of the book, because at least they'd be reviews of the book rather than a take-down of my publisher for being suckered by a 'brown phony' author who was too middle-class and too educated to meet the literary editor's criteria for being authentically Asian,' he recalled. Malkani could have pulled the 'right credentials' for his background: though he went to Cambridge, he is from a working class London family that struggled to get him there. He chose not to, because, he said: 'It was fiction for fuck's sake — Thomas Harris never had to prove he was an authentic cannibal serial killer.'[12]

Another consequence for Black and Asian novelists of this treatment of their work as Other, rather than genre, is that they are less likely to

---

11   Ibid., p. 14.
12   Ibid.

be published in the most commercial markets capable of sustaining a professional career. In the same survey for *WtF*, we found that forty-two per cent were published in literary fiction, compared to twenty-seven per cent of the white novelists who responded to our survey (See Table 3).[13]

Table 3. 'Under what genre is your work classified?' Source: *Writing the Future*, pp. 8–11.

Genre	BAME novelists	White novelists
Literary	42%	27%
Young adult (YA)	26%	23%
Romance / commercial women's	4%	16%
Crime	4%	16%
Other genres (science fiction and fantasy; erotica; historical; horror)	24%	18%

Spread the Word did not push against a closed door when it presented this research in April 2016. Already a number of tentative initiatives had begun, such as the Creative Access internships mentioned above and a company-wide diversity forum at HarperCollins to address the issue from all levels and seek out creative and lasting solutions.[14] Over at Hachette, which owns, among others, Little, Brown Book Group, Orion, Hodder and Headline, they had begun to run open days at non-Russell Group universities, which actively targeted non-English-Literature or History students.[15] In addition the Publishers Association had launched Equip, a charter to encourage diversity in book publishing, and to foster networking and best practice throughout the industry.[16]

---

13 *WtF*, 'Written off', pp. 8–11.
14 Natasha Onwuemezi, 'HarperCollins Honoured in Race and Inclusivity Awards', *The Bookseller*, 12 October 2016, https://www.thebookseller.com/news/hc-honoured-race-equality-awards-412516
15 Stephen Lawrence Charitable Trust, 'Hachette UK worked with the Stephen Lawrence Foundation's Graduate Career Pathway to Reach more Diverse Potential Recruits', http://www.stephenlawrence.org.uk/category/hachette-uk/
16 Publishers Association, 'PA Launches 10 Point Inclusivity Action Plan, https://www.publishers.org.uk/news/releases/2017/pa-launches-10-point-inclusivity-action-plan/

These initiatives were all aimed at entry level and not at tackling the problem of retention of BAME staff or drawing in more Black and Asian novelists. Significantly no publisher had introduced internal monitoring for unconscious bias that may explain why various initiatives had failed to bring lasting change to the publishing monoculture. On the evidence of the research for *WtF*, we felt it was crucial to recommend that publishers sign up to a cultural audit, which would monitor everything from recruitment and retention to promotion, pay and reward for staff. If the experiences of BAME staff proved to be very different to white staff, it would suggest there was a problem with either who was recruited or the culture of the employer, and that could then be addressed.[17]

This matters because the identity of the gatekeepers has a material impact on the diversity of lists and the ability of publishers to gauge and interact with diverse markets. 'If all the gatekeepers have a certain way of looking at things and they are all of a certain type, it's very hard,' one writer pointed out about the impact of the monoculture. 'If you are a Black person allowed in and are from a lower-middle-class background you have to know how to negotiate the class system as well and that is possibly harder than anything because it is really invisible and entrenched.'

Monocultures are self-perpetuating and, by concentrating at entry level rather than retention of existing staff, the trade is effectively failing to tackle any bias that undermines its relevance, longevity and profitability in the twenty-first century. Another way to ensure greater diversity within the industry is to address poor rates of pay in the lower ranks that affect the ability of employees to stay in the trade. Not only would this mean that unpaid internships are phased out, but that publishers would fund their own paid internships, rather than rely on third parties whose funding may be withdrawn, as happened with decibel.

The reaction from publishers has been mixed. At HarperCollins and Penguin Random House there has been a recognition that, in a global market, the industry needs staff whose strong cultural as well as linguistic ties underpin business relationships with emerging markets, notably India and China. There is also recognition that though UK Publishing PLC is a world leader, it needs to be 'future-fit' to compete with competition from emerging markets.

---

17   *WtF*, 'Key Recommendations', p. 37.

Writing the Future was published at a time when other sectors, notably in the financial sector, were beginning to recognise that diversity creates profitable future-proof twenty-first century businesses. In January 2016 the management consultants McKinsey released research comparing businesses in the US, UK and Brazil. It found that companies in the top quartile for diversity significantly outperformed their rivals. Gender diverse companies were 15% more likely to outperform those in the bottom quartile for diversity. Ethnically diverse companies were 35% more likely to outperform those in bottom quartile.

Those in the bottom quartile for diversity were also in the bottom quartile for profitability. In the US a direct relationship was found to exist between diversity and financial performance — for every 10 per cent increase in ethnic diversity at senior executive level, pre-tax profits are 0.8 per cent higher. Research by Harvard Business School found that 'employees at [diverse] companies are 45 per cent likelier to report that their firm's market share grew over the previous year and 70 per cent likelier to report that the firm captured a new market'.

The Harvard research also showed how diversity creates a virtuous circle. 'Without diverse leadership, women are 20 per cent less likely than straight white men to win endorsement for their ideas; people of color are 24 per cent less likely; and LGBTs are 21 per cent less likely,' it reported. It concluded: 'This costs their companies crucial market opportunities, because inherently diverse contributors understand the unmet needs in under-leveraged markets.'[18]

Widespread coverage of the report, which even reached the *New York Times*, seems to have galvanised some publishers into action. Spread the Word is working across the spectrum to bring about change. 'Overall, I think the research — and the justifiably forthright tone of the report — caught the industry on the back foot and they have been bounced or shamed into taking a hard look at how they can make changes — regarding their recruitment, staffing and promotion, but also in finding/publishing diverse authors,' said Eva Lewin, StW writer and development manager, who oversaw the report.

From a writers' perspective, the report created a stronger sense that there are other routes to publication and readership than exclusively

---

18 Vivian Hunt, Dennis Layton, and Sara Prince, 'Diversity Matters', McKinsey & Co., 2015, https://assets.mckinsey.com/~/media/857F440109AA4D13A54D9C496D86ED58.ashx

through mainstream trade publishing, as well as a sense that writers need to build their own profile (brand) through social media and so on, so that they have more control of how publishers mediate between them and the public when they do get a publishing deal.

At the time of writing this a number of more concrete initiatives had been announced by publishers. In February 2016 Penguin Random House launched its 'creative responsibility manifesto' based around a ten-point plan to improve the diversity of its workforce and lists. It was also introducing more robust diversity data-monitoring and training in unconscious bias. At HarperCollins, as well as existing schemes such as its joint venture with the disabled children's charity WhizzKidz to provide work experience and fundraising support[19] and a partnership programme aimed at disadvantaged children in Tower Hamlets, it introduced unconscious bias training and schemes to drive greater diversity across all areas, including a full staff survey.[20]

This is a snapshot of the findings and results of the research and impact of *Writing the Future*. There remains much to be done before UK publishing is future-fit. However it is encouraging that there has been a positive reaction in some quarters and that businesses finally seem to understand that diversity is not an option if they wish to survive. As the editor of *In Full Colour*, I know too well how easily early gains can be lost. But it feels as if *WtF* has focused minds more clearly on the business case for driving diversity, and that makes me cautiously optimistic about the ability of UK publishing to remain relevant to an increasingly diverse readership.

---

19 Natasha Onwuemezi, 'HarperCollins Partners with Whizz-Kidz', *The Bookseller*, 13 January 2016, https://www.thebookseller.com/news/hc-partner-disabled-childrens-charity-whizz-kidz-320294

20 'How HarperCollins is Setting the Diversity Standard within Publishing', *Vercida*, 7 July 2017, https://www.vercida.com/uk/articles/how-harpercollins-is-setting-the-diversity-standard-within-publishing

Works Cited

[n.a.] (7 July 2017) 'How HarperCollins is Setting the Diversity Standard within Publishing', *Vercida*, https://www.vercida.com/uk/articles/how-harpercollins-is-setting-the-diversity-standard-within-publishing

Hunt, Vivian, Dennis Layton, and Sara Prince (2015) 'Diversity Matters', McKinsey & Co., https://assets.mckinsey.com/~/media/857F440109AA4D13A54D9C496D86ED58.ashx

Kean, Danuta and Mel Larsen, eds. (2016) *Writing the Future* (London: Spread the Word), https://www.spreadtheword.org.uk/wp-content/uploads/2016/11/Writing-the-Future-Black-and-Asian-Authors-and-Publishers-in-the-UK-Marketplace-May-2015.pdf

Onwuemezi, Natasha (13 January 2016) 'HarperCollins Partners with Whizz-Kidz', *The Bookseller*, https://www.thebookseller.com/news/hc-partner-disabled-children-s-charity-whizz-kidz-320294

Onwuemezi, Natasha (12 October 2016) 'HarperCollins Honoured in Race and Inclusivity Awards', *The Bookseller*, https://www.thebookseller.com/news/hc-honoured-race-equality-awards-412516

Publishers Association (2017) 'PA Launches 10 Point Inclusivity Action Plan', https://www.publishers.org.uk/news/releases/2017/pa-launches-10-point-inclusivity-action-plan/

Shaffi, Sarah (4 November 2016), 'Publishing Seeks to Address Industry's lack of Diversity', *The Bookseller*, https://www.thebookseller.com/news/publishing-seeks-address-industry-s-lack-diversity-426031

Stephen Lawrence Charitable Trust [n.d.] 'Hachette UK Worked with the Stephen Lawrence Foundation's Graduate Career Pathway to Reach more Diverse Potential Recruits', http://www.stephenlawrence.org.uk/category/hachette-uk/

10. Writing on the Cusp of Becoming Something Else

J. R. Carpenter

As an academic writer, researcher, and educator I am necessarily invested in the rules of citation. As an author of three literary books published by small presses, with a fourth on the way, I am acutely aware of how little money there is to be made by all but a very few writers through the sale of books. As an artist and author of artist's books, zines, and web-based works of digital literature, I have made extensive use of 'found' materials. Over the past twenty years I have mixed my own writing, drawing, programming, and photography with images, texts, diagrams, and maps cut and copied from old magazines and textbooks, and source code 'borrowed' from dusty corners of the web. This chapter aims to reconcile these seemingly oppositional tendencies in two ways. First, by framing publication not as an end point but rather part of an on-going compositional process. And second, by framing the material appropriation of image and text both as integral to this compositional process and as a contribution to a larger cultural project. In making this argument this chapter draws upon performance-writing methodology. Performance writing takes a conceptually broad, historically long, and overtly interdisciplinary approach to considering the performance of text in relation to a wide range of social, cultural, material, mediatic, and disciplinary contexts. This contextual or pragmatic approach to writing is particularly well suited to expanding and adapting in order to accommodate new questions posed by new critical contexts. Digital writing, for example, presents complex new contexts for reading, writing, and publishing in which divisions between original and copy, user and product, reader and consumer, and author and publisher are becoming increasingly unclear.

Iteration

Writing is an iterative process. Written texts may start far from the page, as thoughts, sounds, smells, emotions, or spoken words. Written texts may go through many drafts, employing a plethora of writing media along the way. These media may include pencils, pens, paper, phones, computers, printers, digital networks, postal networks, USB memory sticks and other offline storage devices. Written texts may refer directly or indirectly to other texts, as well as to cultural outputs in other media, including films, visual art works, music, dance, architecture, or landscapes. Written texts may be translated into other languages and adapted for other media such as radio, stage, or film. I linger on the fluidity of the compositional process here, as it seems increasingly disassociated from the popular conception of the book as a finished product.

In order for a novel, memoir, or other monograph to become a print book a writer must aim for completion, resolution, a fixed, final, stable text. For centuries this condition, imposed by the materiality of print media, has aided and abetted the aims and objectives of academic literary scholarship and the publishing industry. Both of these fields remain heavily invested in the entwined notions of the originality of authorship and the fixity of text. These notions are reinforced by intellectual property law and the pervasiveness of Saussurian linguistic models, which conceive of language as a stable system, internal to itself, unconcerned by societal influences. Performance-writing methodology, with its insistence on contextual enquiry, continuously calls attention to the shifting societal, material, and temporal conditions in which texts are written and read. In *A Marxist Philosophy of Language*, Jean-Jacques Lecercle observes that, far from being stable, language is in fact a constructed system, 'constantly subject to historical change' and calls instead for a conception of 'language not as a stable, arrested system, but as a *system of variations*'.[1] Taking up this call, this chapter argues for

---

1   Jean-Jacques Lecercle, *A Marxist Philosophy of Language*, trans. by Gregory Elliott (Leiden: Brill, 2006), p. 11, emphasis in the original.

an updated conception of publishing better suited to iterative variable forms of writing that resist the fixity of the page.

Digital writing operates within and across a cacophony of code languages, operating systems, communication protocols, devices, and levels of encryption. These radically multimodal and atemporal reading and writing conditions make the constructed and variable nature of written language more readily apparent than in past print regimes. In 'The Time of Digital Poetry: From Object to Event' N. Katherine Hayles argues that, in digital media, the text 'ceases to exist as a self-contained object and instead becomes a process, an event brought into existence when the program runs'.[2] In 'What is Digital Materiality,' Johanna Drucker puts this more succinctly: 'Writing is an event, not an entity'.[3] In order for a digital text to perform across multiple platforms, browsers, and devices a digital writer must also be a performance writer, incorporating variability, instability, transformation, and change into the process of composition. Like all writing for live performance, digital writing is never fixed, final, or stable but rather, constantly subject to change. In this transformative spirit, the title of this chapter appropriates and adapts a line from John Hall's formative essay 'Thirteen Ways of Talking About Performance Writing': 'The performance writer writes the space between the writing and the performing, where the writing is always about to leave to become something else'.[4] Hall's essay, it must be noted, began as a talk presented at a live event and moved through a number of print iterations before becoming the text cited here.

Iterative or recursive writing repeatedly applies processes to successive results. Each new iteration allows for a new interrogation of the process of writing as it is unfolding, invites new ways of reading, and engenders new ways of writing. Texts resulting from an iterative compositional process bear the traces of their own making. For example, throughout my practice-led doctoral research[5] I performed the writing and rewriting,

---

[2] N. Katherine Hayles, 'The Time of Digital Poetry: From Object to Event' in Adelaide Morris and Thomas Swiss (eds.), *New Media Poetics: Contexts, Technotexts, and Theories* (Cambridge, MA: MIT Press, 2006), pp. 181–210 (pp. 181–82).

[3] Johanna Drucker, *What Is? Nine Epistemological Essays* (Berkley, CA: Cuneiform Press, 2013), p. 127.

[4] John Hall, *On Performance Writing, with Pedagogical Sketches: Essays on Performance Writing, Poetics and Poetry*, vol. 1 (Bristol: Shearsman Books, 2013), p. 24.

[5] J. R. Carpenter, 'Writing Coastlines: Locating Narrative Resonance in Transatlantic Communications Networks', PhD thesis, University of the Arts London and Falmouth University, 2015, http://ualresearchonline.arts.ac.uk/7825/

reading and rereading, sounding and resounding of texts through a continuum of forms and contexts. Many portions of the resulting thesis underwent multiple iterations. Passages were read, underlined, discussed, overheard, remembered, spoken, written by hand, typed, blogged, copied, pasted, tagged, encoded, animated, uploaded, downloaded, run, parsed, projected, published, presented in artist's talks, rewritten, presented in academic papers, read silently, read aloud, represented in a performance script, read aloud in multiple voices, listened to live, watched on screen, interacted with, edited, re-purposed, re-mixed, and so on. Methods for performing these individual tasks came from diverse fields of practice. For example, writing a computer program is a standard method in the field of digital literature. A contextual approach to writing and about writing computer programs goes further, situating the act of writing within a collaborative dialogic compositional process. The aim of writing a computer program may be articulated as the creation of a text that will only ever be read by humans in translation, through a web browser. A fixed source code may produce a highly unstable, variable text on screen. These concurrent texts may then be re-contextualised into non-digital contexts. A live performance iteration, for example, may result in the generation of a new text, such as a performance script. This contextual approach to reading and writing about digital text draws attention to the close association between the code languages and the natural languages they perform on screen. A pragmatic performance-writing-inflected methodology offers a fluid conceptual framework though which to observe and articulate the transformations a text undergoes and elicits as it moves through forms, methods, and modes of practice.

In 'What do we Mean by Performance Writing?' a keynote address delivered at the opening of the first Symposium of Performance Writing, which took place at Dartington College of Arts, 12 April 1996, Caroline Bergvall proposed that:

> the performance of writing would be this observation which seeks to locate expressedly [sic] the context and means for writing, both internal and external to language, whether these be activated for and through a stage, for and through a site, a time-frame, a performer's body, the body of a voice or the body of a page.[6]

---

6 Caroline Bergvall, 'What Do We Mean by Performance Writing?', keynote address delivered at the opening of the first Symposium of Performance Writing, Dartington

The democratic, inclusive and above all extensible nature of performance writing methodology allows, many years later, for the revising of Bergvall's statement for a digital literary landscape that barely existed at the time of her writing. In 'Performing Digital Texts in European Contexts,' a commentary column published in the online journal *Jacket2* in 2011, I re-framed Bergvall's statement as follows:

> The performance of digital texts both internal and external to code languages may be activated for and through a CPU, a network, a browser, a hand-held device, a <body> tag, a performer's body, the body of a voice or the body of a page.[7]

To further underline the iterative nature of the performance writing methodology employed in this chapter, I will note here that the above-cited adaptation of Bergvall's text was later integrated into 'Call and Response: Toward a Digital Dramaturgy,' a presentation paper co-written and co-presented by Barbara Bridger and myself at *Performance Writing Weekend 2012*, Arnolfini, Bristol UK, May 2012. That paper was then expanded by Bridger and myself into an article of the same name published in *Journal of Writing in Creative Practice*.[8] The text(s) in/and question(s) perform(s) differently in each of these contexts. Many other lines of text and of reasoning presented in this essay have been revised, re-framed, and adapted from elsewhere in my own writing in a similar though often less overtly acknowledged fashion.

Détournement

In *Poésies*, two small brochures self-published in Paris the spring of 1870, Isidore-Lucien Ducasse, the self-styled Le Comte de Lautréamont, famously wrote: 'Plagiarism is necessary. It is implied in the idea of progress. It clasps the author's sentence tight, uses her expressions, eliminates a false idea, replaces it with the right idea.' This quotation

---

College of Arts, 12 April 1996, http://www.carolinebergvall.com/content/text/BERGVALL-KEYNOTE.pdf

7   J. R. Carpenter, 'Performing Digital Texts in European Contexts', *Jacket2*, 2011, https://jacket2.org/commentary/performing-digital-texts-european-contexts

8   Barbara Bridger and J. R. Carpenter, 'Call and Response: Toward a Digital Dramaturgy', *Journal of Writing and Creative Practice*, 6.3 (2013), 373–86, https://doi.org/10.1386/jwcp.6.3.373_1

has been so widely reproduced in books and articles on- and off-line that I offer it here unabashedly devoid of proper page citation. In *The Beach Beneath the Street: The Everyday Life and Glorious Times of the Situationist International,* McKenzie Wark observes that in advocating for the elimination of false ideas in writing Lautréamont 'corrects, not back to a lost purity or some ideal form, but forward — to a new possibility'.[9] In this spirit, in quoting Lautréamont above I clasped the author's sentence tight and used his expressions, but eliminated the false idea of an assumed universal male author, replacing his 'his' with 'her'.

In the autumn of 1870 Lautréamont died of a fever at the age of twenty-four. His writing was rediscovered by the Belgian Symbolists in the 1890s and again independently in 1917 by the French Surrealists, who hailed him as a patron saint. In the early 1950s news broke that some of the most poetic passages of Lautréamont's most well-known work, *The Songs of Maldoror* (1869), had been plagiarised from old text books. I would love to claim that this is where I got the idea from, but I began plagiarising old text books long before I'd ever heard of Lautréamont. The Letterist International credited Lautréamont with the discovery of a new method of writing which they termed 'détournement'. To détourne is to detour, to lead astray, to appropriate — not a literary form, as in a style, a poetics, or a genre, but rather a material form, as in a sentence, a book, a film, a canvas. In this material approach to appropriation the Letterists lagged decades behind the Dadaist, Constructivist, and Surrealist collage and photomontage artists of the 1920s.

I went to art school, not law school. My aim is not to tear down the institution of citation but rather to offer some insight, to digital publishers and literary scholars in particular, into some of the compositional strategies currently employed in creating works of digital literature. I contend that these are not new strategies, but rather, that they have underpinned the transmutation of culture for thousands of years. Imagine, for example, if the Hesiod estate had sued Ovid for appropriation. Shakespeare would not have had the *Metamorphose* to borrow from so heavily.

I came to writing and publishing through the material practices of sewing, sawing, drawing, crochet, photography, photocopy, cutting

---

9   McKenzie Wark, *The Beach Beneath the Street: The Everyday Life and Glorious Times of the Situationist International* (London: Verso Books, 2011), p. 34.

10. Writing on the Cusp of Becoming Something Else

Fig. 10.1 Screenshot of J. R. Carpenter, *Mythologies of Landforms and Little Girls* (1996), http://luckysoap.com/mythologies

with scissors, and pasting with glue. In 1994 I began working on a non-linear, intertextual, multi-media short story that combined my own writing, in the form of a first-person fictional narrative, with diagrams and excerpts of technical writing form a civil engineering handbook published in the 1920s. The resulting story, *Mythologies of Landforms and Little Girls,* appeared in *Postscript, A Journal of Graduate Criticism and Theory* published by Memorial University in Newfoundland, Canada.[10] Although I was happy to have work published in an academic journal at the tender age of twenty-three, I remained dissatisfied with both the fixed linear order of what I thought of as a non-linear narrative and with the limited distribution of the print journal. Despite the general assumption that publication is an end point, for me the work just didn't seem finished. In 1996 I made a HTML version of *Mythologies of Landforms and Little Girls*.[11] The main page presented a map of Nova Scotia surrounded by small clickable icons. Readers had to choose how they entered and moved through the story. The deadpan engineering

---

10 J. R. Carpenter, 'Mythologies of Landforms and Little Girls,' *Postscript, A Journal of Graduate Criticism and Theory*, 2.1 (1995), 80–86, http://collections.mun.ca/cdm/compoundobject/collection/postscript/id/403/rec/3
11 J. R. Carpenter, 'Mythologies of Landforms and Little Girls', 1996, http://luckysoap.com/mythologies/

descriptions of dikes, groins and mattress work added a perverse sexual overtone to the otherwise chaste first-person narrative. Between the open-ended navigational structure, the diagrammatic images, and the enigmatic subtexts, a meta-narrative emerged. The tensions inherent in the story — between the absurd and the inarticulate, desire and loss, place and displacement — could finally co-exist.

My early adoption of the web as a medium was due in part to the ease with which one could combine image and text in a non-linear and intertextual context. I was also attracted to the speed and independence with which one could share web-based work with a wide audience. To this day, most of my web-based work is funded by and distributed through media art exhibitions and festivals rather than through literary publications. The art world, with its commissioning model, has proven more adept at supporting new and experimental work than the literary world, with its pay-per-unit-sold model. Jay David Bolter has suggested that the field of digital literary scholarship should look to art theory for more advanced thinking on medium and multimodality.[12] Thus far, art theory has shown little sign of looking toward digital literary theory for more advanced thinking on intertextuality, translation, and the performance of code languages in digital art work. Many useful points of entry into thinking and writing about iteration, appropriation, materiality, scale, and spatiality in works of digital literature may be found in the range of hybrid visual art practices loosely termed 'collage'. At *Wanderlust,* an exhibition of Joseph Cornell's work at the Royal Academy in London in 2015, I was delighted to discover that in an untitled collage from 1934 Cornell had appropriated a black and white image from a magazine of a girl balancing a stack of suitcases on her head. I must have had the same magazine. This same image is one of several that have graced the front page of my website for many years.

In 'Reorienting Narrative: E-lit as Psychogeography,' digital literary author and critic Illya Szilak turns to collage to address questions of place and spatiality in my web-based work, observing: 'Carpenter fabricates hybrid places that are both "virtual" and attached to real

---

12 Jay David Bolter, keynote presented at 'From the Page to the Screen to Augmented Reality: New Modes of Language-Driven Technology-Mediated Research,' roundtable event, Kingston University, London, 12 July 2010.

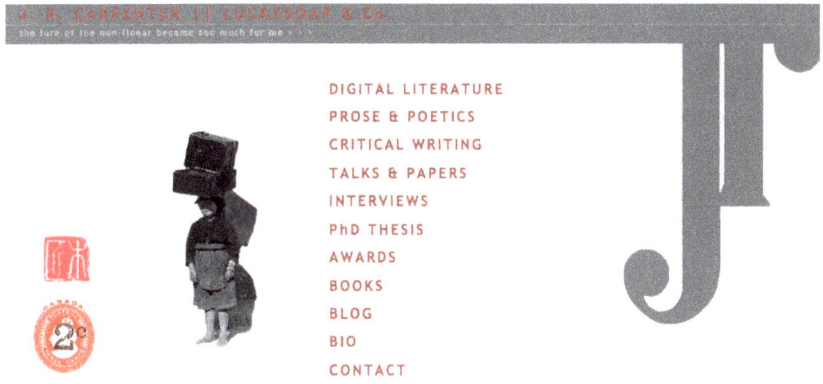

Fig. 10.2 Screenshot of J. R. Carpenter (1998–present), http://luckysoap.com

world locales'.[13] Szilak likens these 'hybrid places' to a Max Ernst collage called 'The Master's Bedroom — It's Worth Spending A Night There' (1920):

> In an elongated rectilinear view, we peer into a room populated with furniture and animals. Ernst copied these objects from a page in a teaching-aids catalog, preserving the spacing, but including only some of the objects. The result is disorienting. We cannot resolve the disparities in size within the Cartesian confines of the room. Despite the allusion to an intimate, familiar domestic space, we find ourselves in a very strange place.[14]

Reading and writing digital texts across multiple devices we find ourselves in very strange places: part visual, part textual, part material, part procedural, part embodied, part conceptual… Performance writing incorporates methods from visual, media, performance, and literary arts toward a conceptual framework within which we may consider these seemingly impossibly disparate elements all at once.

---

13   I. Szilak, 'Reorienting Narrative: E-lit as Psychogeography', *Huffington Post*, 11 June 2013, http://www.huffingtonpost.com/illya-szilak/mapping-the-virtual-elit_b_3409727.html

14   Ibid.

Transparency

For centuries the printed book operated as a closed system, invested in concealing the structural processes of writing from the reader. In the 1920s the Russian artist El Lissitzky wrote that after the revolution the book itself was revolutionised, 'torn in separate pages, enlarged a hundred-fold, colored for greater intensity, and brought into the street as a poster [...] meant for people who would stand up quite close and read it over and make sense of it'.[15] Throughout the 1970s Derrida insisted that, 'only in the book [...] could we indefinitely designate the writing beyond the book'.[16] By the time of his last book, *Paper Machine*, Derrida was writing of the World Wide Web as the ubiquitous book finally reconstituted, as 'electronic writing, traveling at top speed from one spot on the globe to another, and linking together, beyond frontiers'.[17] Though the shadow of the book still looms large over the fields of both digital literary scholarship and digital publishing, the web remains the most profoundly influential and accessible writing, publishing, and computing platform precisely because of its transparency. For most of the short history of the web, its pages have been read on desktop or laptop computers. Readers have had the option of right-clicking on any page and selecting View Page Source. From there readers can copy, paste, re-read, re-write, and re-publish the source code in their own web pages. In this manner, readers may become writers and writers may become publishers.

Like most authors, I learned to write by learning to read. I made my first web-based writing project during a visual arts thematic residency at The Banff Centre for the Arts in Canada in 1995. The theme of the residency was 'Telling Stories, Telling Tales'. In my application for the residency I wrote a fictional artist's statement in which I claimed to a writer, and they believed me. During the residency I tried to make a print book that told a circular story, but when people got to the end of the book they invariably stopped reading, because that's how books

---

15 I. Murray, 'Affirming the New: Art and Architecture in Soviet Avant-Garde Publications, 1918–1932', in *Architectural Drawings of the Russian Avant-Garde Publications 1917–1935* (Montreal: Canadian Centre for Architecture, 1991), pp. 7–8.
16 Jacques Derrida, *Writing and Difference*, trans. A. Bass (Chicago: University of Chicago Press, 1978), p. 294.
17 Jacques Derrida, *Paper Machine*, trans. Rachel Bowlby (Stanford: Stanford University Press, 2005), p. 15.

Welcome to my mini web para-site, devoted thus far to fishes and flying things, as they whir and flop in the night, in the spirit of desire in descriptive narrative.

In the Middle Ages, insects, worms, snails, and other creatures that were not clearly birds, beasts or fish presented some problems in classification. So did their products. Honey, for instance, comes under the weather phenomena in Book II of Conrad von Megenberg's *Buch der Natur*, 1475, right after the cause of mildew.

Fig. 10.3 Screenshot of J. R. Carpenter, *Fishes & Flying Things* (1995), http://luckysoap.com/butterflies/parasite.html

work. The artist in the studio next to mine informed me that if I wrote this story in HTML the last page could link to the first page and the reader could keep reading around and around. The web was simpler back then. This task was easily accomplished. The computer technician allowed me to upload the resulting work, *Fishes and Flying Things*,[18] directly from the web-server's Unix command line to The Banff Centre's public website. The paper book iteration of *Fishes and Flying Things* was printed from a QuarkExpress file stored on a 44 MB SyQuest cartridge, which I still own but the contents of which I can no longer access. The images in the print and web iterations were digital scans of photocopies of borrowed books no longer in my possession. The text was based on the title of an installation art exhibition I had on in Montreal at the time, of which, other than an event poster, no physical or documentary evidence remains. When I returned to Montreal after the residency my artist friends informed me that web-based work was elitist, because so

---

18 J. R. Carpenter, 'Fishes & Flying Things', 1995, http://luckysoap.com/butterflies/parasite.html

few people could access it, and my writer friends assured me that the Internet would never catch on. Over twenty-two years later, the web-based iteration of *Fishes and Flying Things* is still online and it still works.

The Internet has changed a lot since 1995. The more proprietary, predatory, and puerile a place the web becomes the more committed I am to using it in poetic, transformative, and transparent ways. In *Reading Writing Interfaces: From the Digital to the Bookbound*, Lori Emerson charts a critical shift in the meaning of 'transparency' away from a command line level of access to the machine's inner workings toward a 'user-friendly' graphic user interface (GUI) in which users have little or no comprehension of either the hardware or the software they consume. 'The user-friendly now takes the shape of keeping users steadfastly unaware and uninformed about how their computers, their reading/writing interfaces, work, let alone how they shape and determine their access to knowledge'.[19] The publishing industry has been keen to corner the market on new user-friendly digital reading devices in which the book in the guise of the ebook continues to operate as a closed system. It has been painfully slow to acknowledge, let alone adapt to new modes of reading and writing engendered by the data structure of the computer or the wider, wilder non-linear, intertextual, multi-media world of the open web.

Mainstream media has been similarly reluctant to recognise decades of technological experimentation and formal innovation undertaken by digital authors, preferring instead to herald the late-breaking efforts of digital publishers as 'world's first' and 'brand new'. Writers have been responding to the new formal possibilities presented by digital devices since the rise of the mainframe computer. Noah Wardrip-Fruin attributes the 'first experiment with digital literature and digital art of any kind'[20] to Christopher Strachey, who programmed the Manchester University Computer to randomly generate love letters in 1952. It has been over thirty years since Judy Malloy first began writing and publishing her ground-breaking hypertext novella *Uncle Roger*.[21] In an

---

19 Lori Emerson, *Reading Writing Interfaces: From the Digital to the Bookbound* (Minneapolis, MN: University of Minnesota Press, 2014), p. 49.
20 N. Wardrip-Fruin, 'Digital Media Archaeology: Interpreting Computational Processes', in Erkki Huhtamo and Jussi Parikka (eds.), *Media Archaeology: Approaches, Applications, and Implications* (Berkeley, CA and London: University California Press, 2011), pp. 302–22 (p. 302).
21 Judy Malloy, 'Uncle Roger,' *Electronic Literature Collection*, vol. 3, http://collection.eliterature.org/3/work.html?work=uncle-roger

interview published on *The Literary Platform* in 2014, Malloy stated: 'My vision was to create a computer-mediated novella in which the reader individually recreates a fictional environment by continually searching and retrieving narrative information'.[22] The formal structure of the work is intertwined with the narrative of Silicon Valley culture and semiconductor industry lore. Malloy has since adapted and altered the work a number of times to suit emerging media environments ranging from early newsgroups to BASIC, UNIX, and the World Wide Web. A recent iteration of *Uncle Roger* published in the *Electronic Literature Collection Volume 3* is accompanied by documentation of Malloy's extended compositional process.[23] Malloy has incorporated transformation and change into her process of composition, resulting in writing that is not fixed, final, or stable but rather, constantly subject to change.

Fig. 10.4 Screenshot of Judy Malloy, *Uncle Roger* (1986), http://collection.eliterature.org/3/works/uncle-roger/

---

22   Alice McKeever, 'Digital Literature Pioneers: Judy Malloy on "Narrabases"', *The Literary Platform*, 24 April 2014, http://theliteraryplatform.com/2014/04/digital-literature-pioneers-judy-malloy-on-narrabases-80s-silicon-valley-and-e-literature-today/

23   Malloy, 'Uncle Roger'.

It is hardly surprising that digital publishing has embraced the iPhone and the iPad as reading platforms. Emerson states: 'The iPad works because users can't know how it works'.[24] It is a read-only device. Reading the web on an iPhone, iPad, or similar device, readers do not have the option of viewing the page source. The iPad provides consumers with access to materials created by others, but cannot easily be used as a tool in the crafting of new materials. A writer can produce a novel without knowing how a printing press works. In order for a writer to produce a non-liner, multimodal, inter-textual, interactive, or variable digital text, she must have some idea of the codes and protocols, the possibilities and constraints that call such a text into being. Digital publishing platforms that deny readers access to the full text of a work of digital literature in the name of Digital Rights Management risk closing down a part of the learning process that has been vital to literacy since the invention of writing.

Making Public

In November 2012 *The Independent on Sunday* online published an article called 'The Blagger's Guide To: New Media Writing,'[25] by an anonymous author who shall be refereed to hereafter as The Blagger. Ostensibly a write-up of works shortlisted for the New Media Writing Prize 2012, the article took a sarcastic, condescending, and reactionary tone to discussing new media writing, asserting: 'It's still OK to love real books, though.' The link to this article was widely tweeted by the international digital literature community. A number of digital writers took exception to the post's characterisation of new media writing as being: 'a new generation of publisher-produced content.' As Andy ianCampbell of Dreaming Methods was quick to quip on Twitter:

> @dreamingmethods 25 November 2012 New Media Writing = 'a new generation of publisher-produced content'. Sorry? Did I miss something in the shortlist?, https://twitter.com/dreamingmethods/status/272672634678956032

---

24   Emerson, *Reading Writing Interfaces*, p. 15.
25   The Blagger, 'The Blagger's Guide To: New Media Writing', *Independent on Sunday*, 25 November 2012, https://www.independent.co.uk/arts-entertainment/books/features/the-blaggers-guide-to-new-media-writing-8348235.html

Indeed, none of the work on the shortlist came into the world through a publisher, at least not in the sense that we now understand that term. To publish is to make public, to issue, announce or proclaim. My own New Media Writing Prize 2012 shortlisted work, 'CityFish',[26] has been exhibited, published, performed, and in other ways publicly presented in journals, festivals, conferences, galleries, and museums in Canada, the US, the UK, Germany, Italy, and Australia, but its content was entirely independently produced. I offer the following discussion of the iterative and appropriative compositional process through which I created 'CityFish' as an example of writing on the cusp of becoming something else.

Fig. 10.5 Screenshot of J. R. Carpenter, *CityFish* (2010), http://luckysoap.com/cityfish

Over a fifteen-year period, 'CityFish' has been written and rewritten, edited, photographed, Photoshopped, filmed, edited, programmed, tested, exhibited, performed, published online by myself and by others, written about in print and online by myself and others, taught, studied, and, most recently, appropriated by students. The title détournes that of

---

26   J. R. Carpenter, 'CityFish', 2010, http://luckysoap.com/cityfish

Aesop's *Town Mouse Country Mouse* fable (sixth century BCE). 'CityFish' is a hybrid word, title of a hybrid work, tale of a hybrid creature. Part classical parable, part children's picture book, part literary fiction, part collage, part web art, 'CityFish' began in 1995 as a very short story told from the first-person point of view of a fish most unhappy about being caught, killed, and, piled unceremoniously in a heap on a sidewalk fishmonger's stall on a hot summer day, on a narrow, crowded street in Chinatown, New York. In 1998 I created a web-based iteration that incorporated a series of photographs shot on 35mm film in Chinatown, Toronto, circa 1996 and a line drawing of a fish with a tall building for a tail, drawn at around the same time. This web version was published in *IßWAS*, an exhibition at the Bavarian American Hotel in Nuremberg, Germany, in 1998. Twelve serially linked HTML pages each contained a small portion of text, an image, and a single navigational icon — a crudely drawn orange arrow. The arrow always pointed forward. No opportunities were offered for non-linear readings. As in the earlier example of *Mythologies of Landforms and Little Girls*, I remained dissatisfied with the linearity of the work. Even after it was published, I never quite felt it was finished.

'CityFish' continued to morph and expand over the years, as I sought its full extent, its proper shape. When the 'shape' of a work of literature is no longer defined in terms of the limits of the page or the size, length, or literary genre of a print book destined for a shop shelf, the compositional process becomes radically open-ended. The line drawing was made into a rubber stamp, a paper bookmark, and a transparent gif. The 35mm photographs were scanned and hundreds more digital photographs were taken in Chinatowns and fish markets in New York, San Francisco, Toronto, Montreal, and Barcelona. An eclectic archive of 'found images', maps, objects, video, source code, and quotations gradually accrued. A series of short videos were shot on location at Coney Island in 2005. They were edited during the 'Babel Babble Rabble: On Language and Art' visual arts thematic residency at The Banff Centre in Canada in 2006. The very short story expanded into a regular-sized short story during a writing residency at Yaddo in Saratoga Springs, New York, in 2007. The web implementation was undertaken with financial support from the Canada Council for the Arts. Funding the production of the work through fellowships, subsidised artist-in-residency programs, and public arts funding, and finding diverse modes of publicly disseminating the work as is was in a state of becoming allowed the work to evolve slowly over time. This exploratory process is especially vital in the composition of digital works. The constraints of the page are dissolving. The possibilities for non-linearity, multimodality, and interactivity are expanding rapidly. The digital author is tasked with finding the form of a story that is always on the cusp of becoming something else.

Returning to the Blagger's characterisation of digital writing as 'publisher-produced content' we must ask what differentiates writing from content in the digital age? This question is more elegantly posed by Alan Liu in the first paragraph of the introduction to his monumental book, *The Laws of Cool: Knowledge Work and the Culture of Information*: 'What is the future in general of the humanities and arts when the former seems destined only for what information industries call "content" and the latter for "multimedia entertainment"?'.[27] Within this paradigm, it would seem that writing becomes content when seen at a remove from a contextual awareness of the compositional process. Further, it would seem that the literary arts are already perceived by digital publishers as multimedia entertainment aimed not at making public the work of writers but rather at packaging the work of publishers for a consumer audience. Perhaps the distinction then, is that writing is read as process and content is consumed as product.

Now we may begin to approach the source of tension belied by The Blagger's assertion, 'It's still OK to love real books, though.' Traditional publishers must believe and litigiously assert that they can and do own the exclusive right to sell a contained unit of content in order to stay in business. In this, the ebook and the app function in exactly the same way as the print book. As writers make less and less money from the sale of books, ebooks, and apps, these long-held beliefs hold less and less sway. I am not suggesting that copyright is not necessary; simply that it may become less of a concern to writers who aren't making any money anyway. Writers working in any media who openly defy or problematize the 'sale by unit' publishing paradigm — by the acts of self-publishing, offering their work for free, offering multiple iterations,

---

27   Alan Liu, *The Laws of Cool: Knowledge Work and the Culture of Information* (Chicago, IL: University of Chicago Press, 2014), p. 1.

or inviting appropriation and remixing — may be perceived to be participating in the destruction of the cultural artefacts left by past generations. Yet the oft overlooked irony is, of course, that the bulk of those artefacts themselves contain the seeds of this destruction. Books are made of other books. Culture feeds on itself; culture is cannibalistic.

Liu suggests that cultural criticism and the creative arts have come to a conjuncture:

> Where once the job of literature and the arts was creativity, now, in an age of total innovation, I think it must be history [...] a special, dark kind of history [...] the history not of things created [...] but of things destroyed in the name of creation [...]. Whether it is expressed as appropriation, sampling, defacement, or hacking, there will be nothing more cool [...] than committing acts of destruction against what is most valued [...] the content, form, or control of information.[28]

We have of course come to this conjuncture many times before. Medieval Romans built blocks of flats in the ruins of once-great amphitheatres. Ovid and Virgil copied Hesiod. Early-modern English poets pillaged the epigrams of Roman satirists to flatter their patrons. Shakespeare was a known plagiarist, incorporating contemporary and classical sources alike. The Letterists and Situationists praised Lautréamont's praise of plagiarism as necessary for progress in order to advocate for creative destruction through détournement. Building on their work in *The Beach Beneath the Street*, half-way through a chapter on plagiarism McKenzie Wark states: 'Needless to say, the best lines in this chapter are plagiarized', brilliantly laying bare the process of his own writing as it is unfolding.[29]

As an author and scholar of digital writing I re-read, re-search, and re-write print books in digital literary spaces. I publish my own works multiple times in multiple formats as part of a compositional process engaged in finding new forms for longstanding literary preoccupations. Not content, as it were, to produce content in a format compatible with ensuring a publisher stays in business, I have had to develop other ways to support the production of this new writing. I do not consider these approaches to be acts of destruction but rather of creation. I must be very cool.

---

28   Ibid., p. 8.
29   Wark, *The Beach Beneath the Street*, p. 41.

Contributing to a Larger Cultural Project

Wark argues: 'For past works to become resources for the present requires [...] their appropriation as a collective inheritance, not as private property'.[30] Appropriation of past works was integral to the composition of 'CityFish'. Through a long and iterative and appropriative compositional process certain allegorical aspects of the story that had long been alluded to in the détourned title gradually became more apparent to me. As the point of view of the story shifted from first-person fish to third-person girl 'CityFish' became less about the fish and more about the city; it became a story of family, place, displacement, and difference emerging from immigration. The fish is still there, still pissed off, and still talking — an animal amongst humans, an impossible thinking speaking dead animal contesting the hot, smelly, stupid real. The fish operates on the threshold of language. What the country girl Lynne cannot speak, the city fish can think. None of the story's characters can hear the fish, but its readers can.

Aesop's fables often feature animals with human characteristics. Aesop himself is a quasi-mythical creature, part historical man, and part historical creation. He was almost certainly a slave in Greece in the mid-sixth century BCE. Aristotle, Herodotus and Plutarch each have him living and dying at different times and places. He was not born a slave; he became one by foreign capture. No one knows where he was captured from. No one knows if he wrote at all. The tales Aesop told may have been just that — told. Far too many have been attributed to him for them to have all originated from him. It may be that none originated from him. None of his writing survives, but many of the tales he told have been found on Egyptian papyri written between 800–1000 years before his time. A Mother Goose of the ancient world — a compiler, a re-teller, and an early practitioner of détournement — whether active or unwitting, Aesop was a central participant in the transmitting and transmuting of fables from ancient to modern, from oral into written forms.

'CityFish' furthers this process of transmutation of fable from oral to print in digital media. The digital text détournes lines spoken by my own family members, long since dead and attributes these lines to other family members entirely imaginary. Within the main body of 'CityFish'

---

30   Ibid., p. 37.

and again in its credits I acknowledge the authors whose texts I have appropriated without their publishers' permission. Détournement would go further; détournement would not name these authors at all. I do so in order to underline the additive nature of the material appropriation of texts. I have not taken the words or ideas of the authors as my own but rather used them as material to make transparent the force of my influences.

Embedded within the body of the text is a Google Maps satellite view of Coney Island. Embedded within this map are ten short videos containing images of strangers, none of whom have signed consent forms. I am allowed to quote satellite images owned by Google, but within the terms of use agreement Google make it clear that they can change their terms of use without my agreement at any time. Three weeks before the New Media Writing Prize 2012 short-list was announced, Superstorm Sandy dramatically altered the coastline depicted in the proprietary Google Maps satellite images embedded in 'CityFish'. Google has since updated these images, but for a brief period, within the already elegiac fictional terrain of a fabled story structure set in one past and evoking a past yet further distant, a storm-ravaged coastline remained pictorially pristine, eerily unchanged.

Something Else

The browser-based web as we know it has only been around for twenty-three years or so, at the time of this writing — a short amount of time in terms of both practice and discourse. It took much longer yet for photography to be written about 'not' in terms of painting, for cinema to be written about 'not' in terms of theatre. How long will it take for digital writing to be written about 'not' in terms of a publishing industry built on the back of the book as a contained unit of commodity? We don't quite know what we're writing yet; let alone how to write about it. Critical and creative focus within both academic digital literary scholarship and within digital publishing would benefit from studying and supporting the new structures for reading and writing that digital writers and their writing are revealing through as yet experimental processes. Writing performs differently on the page, on the screen, and online. We need to think and write about writing as not residing in any of these media but rather operating across and through multiple media at multiple times.

10. Writing on the Cusp of Becoming Something Else

This chapter has argued that iteration and détournement are methods central to digital authorship. Incorporating the cultural materials of the past into new contexts of reading and writing has been framed as part of an ongoing compositional process. This chapter has advocated for the preservation of transparency in publication platforms such as the open web, which allow readers to read both the source code and the text output on the screen, so that readers may become writers. All Internet-based writing and art works emerge from, refer to, and thus must be understood within the complex context of the Internet itself, which is in fact a conglomeration of contexts. For their function and for their intelligibility, Internet-based works are dependent upon the Internet and all its vagaries, from the constraints of its physical infrastructure to the menace of its many viruses, government spies, commercial trackers, cookies, and crawling bots, from the Babel babble of its multiple code languages to the competing visual and textual messages of its surface contents. How can works created for and within this highly provisional, seemingly immaterial, endlessly re-combinatory context be read, watched, interacted with, participated in, understood, or indeed commented upon in any other?

Working within the massively multi-authored context of the open web, the digital writer can and must incorporate iteration, appropriation, variation, and transformation into the processes of composition and publication. The result is writing that is never fixed, static, or stable but rather always simultaneously responding to past and current mediatic relations and correcting forward toward new possibilities. Rather than closing down these possibilities with proprietary platforms, we need to find new ways of funding and publicly presenting these new forms of writing, even as they are on the cusp of shifting and morphing into something else.

Works Cited

Bergvall, Caroline (12 April 1996) 'What Do We Mean by Performance Writing?', keynote address delivered at the opening of the first Symposium of Performance Writing, Dartington College of Arts, http://www.carolinebergvall.com/content/text/BERGVALL-KEYNOTE.pdf

Blagger, The (25 November 2012) 'The Blagger's Guide to New Media Writing,' *The Independent on Sunday*, http://www.independent.co.uk/arts-entertainment/books/features/the-blaggers-guide-to-new-media-writing-8348235.html

Bolter, Jay David (12 July 2010) Keynote, presented at 'From the Page to the Screen to Augmented Reality: New Modes of Language-Driven Technology-Mediated Research,' roundtable event, Kingston University, London.

Bridger, Barbara and J. R. Carpenter (2013) 'Call and Response: Toward a Digital Dramaturgy', *Journal of Writing and Creative Practice* 6.3., 373–86, https://doi.org/10.1386/jwcp.6.3.373_1

Carpenter, J. R. (2015) 'Writing Coastlines: Locating Narrative Resonance in Transatlantic Communications Networks', PhD thesis, University of the Arts London and Falmouth University, http://ualresearchonline.arts.ac.uk/7825/

— (2011) 'CityFish', in Lello Masucci and Giovanna Di Rosario (eds.), *Lavori del Convegno OLE Officina di Letteratura Elettronica, Palazzo Arti Napoli, 20–21 gennaio 2011* (Naples: Atelier Multimediale editrice).

— (2011) 'Performing Digital Texts in European Contexts', *Jacket2*, https://jacket2.org/commentary/performing-digital-texts-european-contexts

— (2010) 'CityFish', http://luckysoap.com/cityfish

— (1996) 'Mythologies of Landforms and Little Girls', http://luckysoap.com/mythologies/

— (1995) 'Fishes & Flying Things', http://luckysoap.com/butterflies/parasite.html

— (1995) 'Mythologies of Landforms and Little Girls,' *Postscript, A Journal of Graduate Criticism and Theory* 2.1, 80–86, http://collections.mun.ca/cdm/compoundobject/collection/postscript/id/403/rec/3

Derrida, Jacques (2005) *Paper Machine*, trans. Rachel Bowlby (Stanford, CA: Stanford University Press).

— (1978) *Writing and Difference*, trans. A. Bass (Chicago, IL: University of Chicago Press).

Drucker, Johanna (2013) *What Is? Nine Epistemological Essays* (Berkley, CA: Cuneiform Press).

Emerson, Lori (2014) *Reading Writing Interfaces: From the Digital to the Bookbound* (Minneapolis, MN: University of Minnesota Press).

Hall, John (2013) *On Performance Writing, with Pedagogical Sketches: Essays on Performance Writing, Poetics and Poetry*, vol. 1 (Bristol: Shearsman Books).

Hayles, N. Katherine (2006) 'The Time of Digital Poetry: From Object to Event' in Adelaide Morris and Thomas Swiss (eds.), *New Media Poetics: Contexts, Technotexts, and Theories* (Cambridge, MA: MIT Press), pp. 181–210.

Lea, Richard (3 February 2016) 'What Apps Next? Publishers and Developers Embrace "Unprintable" Fiction', *The Guardian*, http://www.theguardian.com/books/2016/feb/03/publishers-developers-digital-technology-unprintable-fiction-google-editions-play

Lecercle, Jean-Jacques (2006) *A Marxist Philosophy of Language*, trans. by Gregory Elliott (Leiden: Brill).

Liu, Alan (2014) *The Laws of Cool: Knowledge Work and the Culture of Information* (Chicago: University of Chicago Press).

Malloy, Judy (1986) 'Uncle Roger,' *Electronic Literature Collection*, vol. 3, Electronic Literature Organization, http://collection.eliterature.org/3/work.html?work=uncle-roger

McKeever, Alice (24 April 2014) 'Digital Literature Pioneers: Judy Malloy on "Narrabases"', *The Literary Platform*, http://theliteraryplatform.com/2014/04/digital-literature-pioneers-judy-malloy-on-narrabases-80s-silicon-valley-and-e-literature-today/

Murray, I. (1991) 'Affirming the New: Art and Architecture in Soviet Avant-Garde Publications, 1918–1932', in *Architectural Drawings of the Russian Avant-Garde Publications 1917–1935* (Montreal: Canadian Centre for Architecture), pp. 7–8.

New Media Writing Prize (2012), http://newmediawritingprize.co.uk/shortlist.html

Szilak, I. (11 June 2013) 'Reorienting Narrative: E-lit as Psychogeography', *Huffington Post*, http://www.huffingtonpost.com/illya-szilak/mapping-the-virtual-elit_b_3409727.html

Wardrip-Fruin, N. (2011) 'Digital Media Archaeology: Interpreting Computational Processes', in Erkki Huhtamo and Jussi Parikka (eds.), *Media Archaeology: Approaches, Applications, and Implications* (Berkeley, CA and London: University California Press), pp. 302–22.

Wark, McKenzie (2011) *The Beach Beneath the Street: The Everyday Life and Glorious Times of the Situationist International* (London: Verso Books).

11. Confronting Authorship, Constructing Practices (How Copyright is Destroying Collective Practice)

Eva Weinmayr

This chapter is written from the perspective of an artist who develops models of practice founded on the fundamental assumption that knowledge is socially constructed. Knowledge, according to this understanding, builds on imitation and dialogue and is therefore based on a collective endeavour. Although collective forms of knowledge production are common in the sciences, such modes of working constitute a distinct shift for artistic practice, which has been conceived as individual and isolated or subjective. Moreover, the shift from the individual to the social in artistic production — what has been called art's 'social turn'[1] — also shifts the emphasis from the artwork to the social processes of production and therefore proposes to relinquish 'the notion of the "work" as a noun (a static object)' and re-conceptualises 'the "work" as a verb (a communicative activity)'.[2] This shift from 'noun' to 'verb' promotes collective practices over authored objects and includes work such as developing infrastructures, organising events, facilitating, hosting, curating, editing and publishing. Such generative practices also question the nature of authorship in art.

---

1 https://www.tate.org.uk/art/art-terms/s/social-turn
2 Carys J. Craig, 'Symposium: Reconstructing the Author-Self: Some Feminist Lessons for Copyright Law', *American University Journal of Gender, Social Policy & the Law* 15. 2 (2007), 207–68 (p. 224).

Authorship is no doubt a method to develop one's voice, to communicate and to interact with others, but it is also a legal, economic and institutional construct, and it is this function of authorship as a framing and measuring device that I will discuss in this chapter. Oscillating between the arts and academia, I shall examine the concept of authorship from a legal, economic and institutional perspective by studying a set of artistic practices that have made copyright, intellectual property and authorship into their artistic material.

Copyright's legal definition combines authorship, originality and property. 'Copyright is not a transcendent moral idea', as Mark Rose has shown, 'but a specifically modern formation [of property rights] produced by printing technology, marketplace economics and the classical liberal culture of possessive individualism'.[3] Therefore the author in copyright law is unequivocally postulated in terms of liberal and neoliberal values. Feminist legal scholar Carys Craig argues that copyright law and the concept of authorship it supports fail to adequately recognise the essential *social nature* of human creativity. It chooses relationships qua private property instead of recognising the author as necessarily social situated and therefore creating (works) within a network of social relations.[4] This chapter tries to reimagine authorial activity in contemporary art that is not caught in 'simplifying dichotomies that pervade copyright theory (author/user, creator/copier, labourer/free-rider)',[5] and to examine both the blockages that restrict our acknowledgement of the social production of art and the social forces that exist within emancipatory collective practices.[6]

Copyright is granted for an 'original work [that] is fixed in any tangible medium of expression'. It is based on the relationship between

---

3   Mark Rose, *Authors and Owners, The Invention of Copyright* (Cambridge, MA and London: Harvard University Press, 1993), p. 142.
4   Craig, 'Symposium: Reconstructing the Author-Self', p. 261.
5   Ibid., p. 267.
6   See also cultural theorist Gary Hall's discussion of *Pirate Philosophy*, as a potential way forward to overcome such simplyfying dichotomies. 'How can we [theorists] operate differently with regard to our own work, business, roles, and practices to the point where we actually begin to confront, think through, and take on (rather than take for granted, forget, repress, ignore, or otherwise marginalize) some of the implications of the challenge that is offered by theory to fundamental humanities concepts such as the human, the subject, the author, the book, copyright, and intellectual property, for the ways in which we create, perform, and circulate knowledge and research?' Gary Hall, *Pirate Philosophy, for a Digital Posthumanities* (Cambridge, MA and London: The MIT Press, 2016), p. 16.

an 'originator', being imagined as the origin of the work,[7] and distinct products, which are fixed in a medium, 'from which they can be perceived, reproduced, or otherwise communicated, either directly or with the aid of a machine or device.'[8]

Practices, on the contrary, are not protected under copyright.[9] Because practice can't be fixed into a tangible form of expression, intellectual property rights are not created and cannot be exploited economically. This inability to profit from practice by making use of intellectual property results in a clear privileging of the 'outputs' of authored works over practice. This value system therefore produces 'divisive hierarchical splits between those who 'do' [practices], and those who write *about*, make work *about* [outputs]'.[10]

Media scholar Kathleen Fitzpatrick observes in her forthcoming book *Generous Thinking*:

> [H]owever much we might reject individualism as part and parcel of the humanist, positivist ways of the past, our working lives — on campus and off — are overdetermined by it. […] c. And the drive

---

[7] Here 'the producer is being imagined as the *origin* of the product'. (Strathern, p. 156). Therefore 'in law, originality is simply the description of a causal relationship between a person and a thing: to say that a work is original in law is to say nothing more than that it originates from [can be attributed to] its creator' (Barron, p. 56). And conversely, in law 'there can be no 'copyright work' […] without some author who can be said to originate it' (ibid., p. 55). Anne Barron, 'No Other Law? Author-ity, Property and Aboriginal Art', in Lionel Bently and Spyros Maniatis (eds.), *Intellectual Property and Ethics* (London: Sweet and Maxwell, 1998), pp. 37–88, and Marilyn Strathern, *Kinship, Law, and the Unexpected: Relatives Are Always a Surprise* (Cambridge: Cambridge University Press, 2005).
See also Mario Biagioli's and Marilyn Strathern's discussion of the author-work relationship as kinship in Mario Biagioli, 'Plagiarism, Kinship and Slavery', *Theory Culture Society* 31.2–3 (2014), 65–91, https://doi.org/10.1177/0263276413516372

[8] US Copyright Law, Article 17, §102 (a), amendment 2016, https://www.copyright.gov/title17/

[9] 'In no case does copyright protection for an original work of authorship extend to any idea, procedure, process, system, method of operation, concept, principle, or discovery, regardless of the form in which it is described, explained, illustrated, or embodied in such work.' US Copyright Law, Article 17, §102 (b), amendment 2016, https://www.copyright.gov/title17/

[10] Susan Kelly, '"But that was my idea!" Problems of Authorship and Validation in Contemporary Practices of Creative Dissent', *Parallax* 19.2 (2013), 53–69, https://doi.org/10.1080/13534645.2013.778496. All references to this text refer to the version published on academia.edu, which is slightly different: https://www.academia.edu/4485538/_But_that_was_my_idea_Problems_of_Authorship_and_Validation_in_Contemporary_Practices_of_Creative_Dissent_Parallax_Volume_19_2013, p. 6.

to compete [...] bleeds out into all areas of the ways we work, even when we're working together.' The competitive individualism that the academy cultivates makes all of us painfully aware that even our most collaborative efforts will be assessed individually, with the result that even those fields whose advancement depends most on team-based efforts are required to develop careful guidelines for establishing credit and priority.[11]

Artist and activist Susan Kelly expands on this experience with her observation that this regime of individual merit even inhibits us from partaking in collective practices. She describes the dilemma for the academic activist, when the demand for 'outputs' (designs, objects, texts, exhibitions), which can be measured, quantified and exploited by institutions (galleries, museums, publishers, research universities), becomes the prerequisite of professional survival.

> Take the young academic, for example, who spends evenings and weekends in the library fast tracking a book on social movements about which she cares deeply and wants to broaden her understanding. She is also desperate for it to be published quickly to earn her the university research points that will see her teaching contract renewed for the following year. It is likely that the same academic is losing touch with the very movements she writes about, and is no longer participating in their work because she is exhausted and the book takes time to write no matter how fast she works. On publication of the book, her work is validated professionally; she gets the university contract and is invited to sit on panels in public institutions about contemporary social movements. In this hypothetical case, it is clear that the academic's work has become detached from the movements she now writes and talks about, and she no doubt sees this. But there is good compensation for this uneasiness in the form of professional validation, invitations that flatter, and most importantly, an ease of the cycle of hourly paid or precarious nine-month contracts.[12]

---

11 Kathleen Fitzpatrick's working method with her book *Generous Thinking: A Radical Approach to Saving the University* (Baltimore: John Hopkins University Press, 2019) presents an interesting alternative to standard procedures in scholarly publishing. She published the draft of her book online, inviting readers to comment. This could potentially become a model for multiple authorship as well as an alternative to the standard peer review procedures. I am quoting from the published draft version: Kathleen Fitzpatrick, 'Critique and Competition' in *Generous Thinking: The University and the Public Good* (Humanities Commons, 2018), paragraph 1, https://generousthinking.hcommons.org/

12 Kelly, '"But that was my idea!"', p. 6.

11. Confronting Authorship, Constructing Practices

Kelly's and Fitzpatrick's examples describe the paradoxes that the demand for authorship creates for collective practices. But how can we actually escape regimes of authorship that are conceptualised and economised as 'cultural capital'?

Academic authorship, after all, is the basis for employment, promotion, and tenure. Also, arguably, artists who stop being 'authors' of their own work would no longer be considered 'artists', because authorship is one of art's main framing devices. In the following I will discuss three artistic practices that address this question — with, as we will see, very different outcomes.[13]

Authorship Replaces Authorship?

In 2011, American artist Richard Prince spread a blanket on a sidewalk outside Central Park in New York City and sold copies of his latest artwork, a facsimile of the first edition of J. D. Salinger's *The Catcher in The Rye*.[14] He did not make any changes to the text of the novel and put substantial effort into producing an exact replica in terms of paper quality, colours, typeset and binding, reproducing the original publication as much as possible except for several significant details. He replaced the author's name with his own. 'This is an artwork by Richard Prince. Any similarity to a book is coincidental and not intended by the artist', his colophon reads, concluding with '© Richard Prince'. Prince also changed the publisher's name, Little Brown, to a made-up publishing house with the name AP (American Place) and removed Salinger's photograph from the back of the dust cover.[15]

The artist's main objective appeared to be not to pirate and circulate an unauthorised reprint of Salinger's novel, because he did not present the book under Salinger's name but his own. Prince also chose a very limited circulation figure.[16] It is also far from conventional plagiarism,

---

13 I refer in this chapter to US copyright law, if not indicated otherwise.
14 He also released the book with Printed Matter at the New York Art Book Fair in 2011.
15 It took Prince and his collaborator John McWhinney over a year to find a printer with the guts to print this facsimile. The one he eventually found was based in Iceland.
16 Prince states in his blog entry 'Second Thoughts on Being Original', that he made 300 copies. 'My plan was to show up once a week, same day, same time, same

because hardly any twentieth century literature is more read and widely known than Salinger's *Catcher*. So the question is, why would Prince want to recirculate one of the most-read American novels of all time, a book available in bookshops around the world, with a total circulation of 65 million copies, translated into 30 languages?[17]

Prince stated that he loved Salinger's novel so much that 'I just wanted to make sure, if you were going to buy my *Catcher in the Rye*, you were going to have to pay twice as much as the one Barnes and Noble was selling from J. D. Salinger. I know that sounds really kind of shallow and maybe that's not the best way to contribute to something, but in the book-collecting world you pay a premium for really collectible books,' he explained in an interview with singer Kim Gordon.[18]

As intended, the work quickly turned into a collectible[19] and attracted lots of applause from members of the contemporary art world including, among others, conceptual writer Kenneth Goldsmith, who described the work as a 'terribly ballsy move'. Prince was openly 'pirating what is arguably the most valuable property in American literature, practically begging the estate of Salinger to sue him.'[20]

Who has the Power to Appropriate?

We need to examine Goldsmith's appraisal more closely. What is this 'ballsy move'? And how does it relate to the asserted criticality of appropriation artists in the late 1970s, a group of which Prince was part?

---

place, until all three hundred copies were gone.' *Birdtalk*, 13 April 2015, http://www.richardprince.com/birdtalk/ Booksellers' web pages, such as Printed Matter, N.Y. and richardprincebooks.com, list an edition of 500. See: https://www.printedmatter.org/catalog/31158

17 Mark Krupnick, 'JD Salinger Obituary', *The Guardian*, 28 January 2010, http://www.theguardian.com/books/2010/jan/28/jd-salinger-obituary

18 Kim Gordon, 'Band Paintings: Kim Gordon Interviews Richard Prince', *Interview Magazine*, 18 June 2012, http://www.interviewmagazine.com/art/kim-gordon-richard-prince#

19 The inside flap of his replica stated a price of $62. On this afternoon on the sidewalk outside Central Park, he sold his copies for $40. When I was browsing the shelves at the New York art bookshop Printed Matter in 2012 I saw copies for $200 and in 2018 it is priced at $1200 and $3500 for a signed copy on Abebooks, https://www.abebooks.co.uk/servlet/SearchResults?isbn=&an=richard%20prince&tn=catcher%20rye&n=100121503&cm_sp=mbc-_-ats-_-used

20 Kenneth Goldsmith, 'Richard Prince's Latest Act of Appropriation: The Catcher in the Rye', Harriet: A Poetry Blog, 19 April 2012, http://www.poetryfoundation.org/harriet/2012/04/richard-princes-latest-act-of-appropriation-the-catcher-in-the-rye/

Prince rose to prominence in New York in the late 1970s, associated with the Pictures generation of artists[21] whose appropriation of images from mass culture and advertising — Prince's photographs of Marlboro Man adverts, for example — examined the politics of representation.[22] Theorists and critics, often associated with the academic *October* journal,[23] interpreted the Pictures artists' 'unabashed usurpations of images as radical interrogations of the categories of originality and authenticity within the social construction of authorship. [...] The author had become irrelevant because the original gesture had become unimportant; the copy adequately stood in its place and performed its legitimising function.'[24]

Artist Sherrie Levine, one of the leading figures in American appropriation art, expresses the core theoretical commitment of this group of artists in her 1982 manifesto: 'The world is filled to suffocating. Man has placed his token on every stone. Every word, every image, is leased and mortgaged. [...] A picture is a tissue of quotations drawn from the innumerable centres of culture. We can only imitate a gesture that is always anterior, never original.'[25] This ostensive refusal of originality

---

21 In 1977 Douglas Crimp curated the exhibition 'Pictures' at Artists' Space in New York with artists Troy Brauntuch, Jack Goldstein, Sherrie Levine, Robert Longo and Philip Smith. Artist Cornelia Sollfrank interprets 'the non-specific title of the show' as a first indication of the aesthetic strategies presented in the exhibition. The presentation of reproduced visual materials marked, according to Sollfrank, 'a major challenge to the then predominant modernist discourse.' Cornelia Sollfrank, 'Copyright Cowboys Performing the Law', *Journal of New Media Caucus* 8.2 (2012), http://median.newmediacaucus.org/blog/current-issue-fall-2012-v-08-n-02-december-2nd-2012/copyright-cowboys-performing-the-law/

22 As Benjamin Buchloh writes 'these processes of quotation, excerption, framing and staging that constitute the strategies of the work [...] necessitate [the] uncovering strata of representation. Needless to say we are not in search of sources of origin, but of structures of signification: underneath each picture there is always another picture.' Benjamin Buchloh, 'Pictures', in David Evans (ed.), *Appropriation, Documents of Contemporary Art* (London: Whitechapel Gallery, 2009), p. 78. Originally published in *October* 8 (1979), 75–88.

23 *October*'s editors — including among others Rosalind Krauss, Hal Foster, Craig Owens, and Benjamin Buchloh — provided a theoretical context for this emerging art by introducing French structuralist and poststructuralist theory, i.e. the writings of Roland Barthes, Michel Foucault, and Jacques Derrida to the English speaking world.

24 Nate Harrison, 'The Pictures Generation, the Copyright Act of 1976, and the Reassertion of Authorship in Postmodernity', art&education.net, 29 June 2012, https://web.archive.org/web/20120701012619/artandeducation.net/paper/the-pictures-generation-the-copyright-act-of-1976-and-the-reassertion-of-authorship-in-postmodernity/

25 Sherrie Levine, 'Statement//1982', in David Evans (ed.), *Appropriation, Documents of Contemporary Art* (London: Whitechapel Gallery, 2009), p. 81.

poses, no doubt, a critique of the author who creates 'ex nihilo'. But does it really present a critique of authorship per se? I shall propose three arguments from different viewpoints — aesthetic, economic and legal — to explore the assumptions of this assertion.

From the aesthetic perspective, Prince and Levine are making formal choices in the process of appropriating already existing work. They re-photograph, produce photographic prints, make colour choices; they enlarge or scale down, trim the edges and take decisions about framing. Nate Harrison makes this point when he argues that 'Levine and Prince take individual control of the mass-authored image, and in so doing, reaffirm the ground upon which the romantic author stands.'[26] It is exactly this control of, and authority over, the signed and exhibited image that leads Prince and Levine to be validated as 'author[s] par excellence'.[27] Prince, for example, has been lauded as an artist who 'makes it new, by making it again'.[28] This 'making it again', a process that Hal Foster names 'recoding',[29] creates new meaning and must therefore be interpreted as an 'original' authorial act. Subsequently, this work has been validated by museums, galleries, collectors and critics. From an economic perspective one can therefore argue that Prince's numerous solo exhibitions in prestigious museums, his sales figures, and affiliation to commercial galleries are evidence that he has been ascribed artistic authorship as well as authorial agency by the institutions of the art world.[30]

---

26 Nate Harrison, 'The Pictures Generation, the Copyright Act of 1976, and the Reassertion of Authorship in Postmodernity', art&education.net, 29 June 2012, https://web.archive.org/web/20120701012619/artandeducation.net/paper/the-pictures-generation-the-copyright-act-of-1976-and-the-reassertion-of-authorship-in-postmodernity/

27 Ibid.

28 Quoting this line from Prince book, *Why I Go to the Movies Alone* (New York: Barbara Gladstone Gallery, 1994), the sponsor statement in the catalogue for Prince's solo show Spiritual America at The Guggenheim Museum in New York continues: 'although his [work is] primarily appropriated [...] from popular culture, [it] convey[s] a deeply personal vision. His selection of mediums and subject matter [...] suggest a uniquely individual logic [...] with wit and an idiosyncratic eye, Richard Prince has that rare ability to analyze and translate contemporary experience in new and unexpected ways.' Seth Waugh, 'Sponsor Statement', in The Solomon R. Guggenheim Foundation (ed.), *Richard Prince* (Ostfildern: Hatje Cantz, 2007).

29 See Hal Foster, '(Post)modern Polemics', in *Recodings: Art, Spectacle, Cultural Politics* (Port Townsend, WA: Bay Press, 1985).

30 See note 47.

Coming back to Prince's appropriation of *Catcher in the Rye*, his conceptual gesture employs necessarily the very rhetoric and conceptual underpinnings of legislation and jurisdiction that he seemingly critiques.[31] He declares 'this is an artwork by Richard Prince, © Richard Prince' and asserts, via claiming copyright, the concept of originality and creativity for his work. By this paradoxical gesture, he seemingly replaces 'authorship' with authorship and 'ownership' with ownership. And by doing so, I argue, he reinforces its very concept.

The legal framework remains conceptual, theoretical and untested in this case. But on another occasion, Prince's authorship *was* tested in court — and eventually legally confirmed to belong to him. This is crucial to my inquiry. What are we to make of the fact that Prince, who challenges the copyright doctrine in his gestures of appropriation, has been ascribed legitimate authorship by courts who rule on copyright law? It seems paradoxical, because as Elizabeth Wang rightly claims, 'if appropriation is legitimized, the political dimension of this act is

---

31 One might argue that this performative act of claiming intellectual property is an attempt to challenge J. D. Salinger's notorious protectiveness about his writing. Salinger sued the Swedish writer Fredrik Colting successfully for copyright infringement. Under the pseudonym John David California, Colting had written a sequel to *The Catcher in the Rye*. The sequel, *60 Years Later Coming Through The Rye*, depicts the protagonist Holden Caulfield's adventures as an old man. In 2009, the US District Court Judge in Manhattan, Deborah A. Batts, issued a preliminary injunction indefinitely barring the publication, advertising or distribution of the book in the US. See Sewell Chan, 'Judge Rules for J. D. Salinger in "Catcher" Copyright Suit', *The New York Times*, 1 July 2009, http://www.nytimes.com/2009/07/02/books/02salinger.html

'In a settlement agreement reached between Salinger and Colting in 2011, Colting has agreed not to publish or otherwise distribute the book, e-book, or any other editions of *60 Years Later* in the U.S. or Canada until *The Catcher in the Rye* enters the public domain. Notably, however, Colting is free to sell the book in other international territories without fear of interference, and a source has told *Publishers Weekly* that book rights have already been sold in as many as a half-dozen territories, with the settlement documents included as proof that the Salinger Estate will not sue. In addition, the settlement agreement bars Colting from using the title "Coming through the Rye"; forbids him from dedicating the book to Salinger; and would prohibit Colting or any publisher of the book from referring to *The Catcher in the Rye*, Salinger, the book being "banned" by Salinger, or from using the litigation to promote the book.' Andrew Albanese, 'J. D. Salinger Estate, Swedish Author Settle Copyright Suit', *Publishers Weekly*, 11 January 2011, https://www.publishersweekly.com/pw/by-topic/industry-news/publisher-news/article/45738-j-d-salinger-estate-swedish-author-settle-copyright-suit.html

excised'.³² And Cornelia Sollfrank argues 'the value of appropriation art lies in its illicitness. […] Any form of [judicial] legitimisation would not support the [appropriation] artists' claims, but rather undermine them.'³³

Authorship Defined by Market Value and Celebrity Status?

To illustrate this point I will briefly digress to discuss a controversial court case about Prince's authorial legitimacy. In 2009, New-York-based photographer, Patrick Cariou began litigation against Prince, his gallerist Larry Gagosian and his catalogue publisher Rizzoli. Prince had appropriated Cariou's photographs in his series *Canal Zone* which went on show at Gagosian Gallery.³⁴ A first ruling by a district judge stated that Prince's appropriation was copyright infringement and requested him to destroy the unsold paintings on show. The ruling also forbade those that had been sold from being displayed publicly in the future.³⁵

However Prince's eventual appeal turned the verdict around. A second circuit court decided that twenty-five of his thirty paintings fell under the fair use rule. The legal concept of fair use allows for copyright exceptions in order to balance the interests of exclusive right holders with the interests of users and the public 'for purposes such as criticism, comment, news reporting, teaching (including multiple copies for classroom use), scholarship, or research'.³⁶ One requirement to justify

---

32 Elizabeth H. Wang, '(Re)Productive Rights: Copyright and the Postmodern Artist', *Columbia-VLA Journal of Law & the Arts* 14.2 (1990), 261–81 (p. 281), https://heinonline.org/HOL/Page?handle=hein.journals/cjla14&div=10&g_sent=1&casa_token=&collection=journals
33 Sollfrank, 'Copyright Cowboys'.
34 Thirty paintings created by Prince contained forty-one of Cariou's photographs. The images had been taken from Cariou's book *Yes Rasta* (Brooklyn: powerHouse Books, 2000) and used by Prince in his painting series *Canal Zone*, which was shown at Gagosian Gallery, New York, in 2008.
35 It might be no coincidence (or then again, it might) that the district court judge in this case, Deborah Batts, is the same judge who ruled in the 2009 case in which Salinger successfully brought suit for copyright infringement against Swedish author Fredrik Colting for *60 Years Later Coming Through the Rye*, a sequel to Salinger's book. See note 31.
36 'In determining whether the use made of a work in any particular case is a fair use the factors to be considered shall include — (1) the purpose and character of the use, including whether such use is of a commercial nature or is for nonprofit educational purposes; (2) the nature of the copyrighted work; (3) the amount and substantiality

fair use is that the new work should be transformative, understood as presenting a new expression, meaning or message. The appeal's court considered Prince's appropriation as sufficiently transformative because a 'reasonable observer'[37] would perceive aesthetic differences with the original.[38]

Many artists applauded the appeal court's verdict, as it seemed to set a precedent for a more liberal approach towards appropriation art. Yet attorney Sergio Muñoz Sarmiento and art historian Lauren van Haaften-Schick voiced concerns about the verdict's interpretation of 'transformative' and the ruling's underlying assumptions.

The questions of 'aesthetic differences' perceived by a 'reasonable observer', Sarmiento rightly says, are significant. After all, Prince did not provide a statement of intent in his deposition[39] therefore the judges had to adopt the role of a (quasi) art critic 'employing [their] own artistic judgment[s]' in a field in which they had not been trained.[40]

---

of the portion used in relation to the copyrighted work as a whole; and (4) the effect of the use upon the potential market for or value of the copyrighted work.' US Copyright Act of 1976, amended 2016, https://www.copyright.gov/title17/

37 'What is critical is how the work in question appears to the reasonable observer, not simply what an artist might say about a particular piece or body of work.' Cariou v Prince, et al., court document, No. 11–1197-cv, page 14, http://www.ca2.uscourts.gov/decisions/isysquery/f6e88b8b-48af-401c-96a0-54d5007c2f33/1/doc/11-1197_complete_opn.pdf#xml=http://www.ca2.uscourts.gov/decisions/isysquery/f6e88b8b-48af-401c-96a0-54d5007c2f33/1/hilite/

38 The court opinion states: 'These twenty-five of Prince's artworks manifest an entirely different aesthetic from Cariou's photographs. Where Cariou's serene and deliberately composed portraits and landscape photographs depict the natural beauty of Rastafarians and their surrounding environs, Prince's crude and jarring works, on the other hand, are hectic and provocative. Cariou's black-and-white photographs were printed in a 9 1/2" x 12" book. Prince has created collages on canvas that incorporate color, feature distorted human and other forms and settings, and measure between ten and nearly a hundred times the size of the photographs. Prince's composition, presentation, scale, color palette, and media are fundamentally different and new compared to the photographs, as is the expressive nature of Prince's work.' Ibid., pp. 12–13.

39 Prince's deposition testimony stated that he 'do[es]n't really have a message,' that he was not 'trying to create anything with a new meaning or a new message,' and that he 'do[es]n't have any […] interest in [Cariou's] original intent.' Court Opinion, p. 13. For full deposition see Greg Allen (ed.), *The Deposition of Richard Prince in the Case of Cariou v. Prince et al.* (Zurich: Bookhorse, 2012).

40 The court opinion includes a dissent by Circuit Judge Clifford Wallace sitting by designation from the US Court of Appeals for the Ninth Circuit, 'I, for one, do not believe that I am in a position to make these fact- and opinion-intensive decisions on the twenty-five works that passed the majority's judicial observation. […] nor am I trained to make art opinions ab initio.' Ibid., p. 5.

Secondly, trying to evaluate the markets Cariou and Prince cater for, the court introduced a controversial distinction between celebrity and non-celebrity artists. The court opinion reasons: 'Certain of the *Canal Zone* artworks have sold for two million or more dollars. The invitation list for a dinner that Gagosian hosted in conjunction with the opening of the *Canal Zone* show included a number of the wealthy and famous such as the musicians Jay-Z and Beyoncé Knowles, artists Damien Hirst and Jeff Koons, [....] and actors Robert De Niro, Angelina Jolie, and Brad Pitt'.[41] Cariou, on the contrary, so the verdict argues, 'has not aggressively marketed his work', and has earned just over $8,000 in royalties from *Yes Rasta* since its publication.[42] Furthermore, he made only 'a handful of private sales [of his photographic prints] to personal acquaintances'.[43] Prince, by contrast, sold eight of his *Canal Zone* paintings for a total of $10,480,000 and exchanged seven others for works by canonical artists such as painter Larry Rivers and sculptor Richard Serra.[44]

The court documents here tend to portray Cariou as a sort of hobby artist or 'lower class amateur' in Sarmiento's words,[45] whereas Prince is described as a 'well-known appropriation artist'[46] with considerable success in the art market.[47] Such arguing is dangerous, because it brings social class, celebrity status and art market success into play as legal categories to be considered in future copyright cases and

---

'Furthermore, Judge Wallace questions the majority's insistence on analyzing only the visual similarities and differences between Cariou's and Prince's art works, "Unlike the majority, I would allow the district court to consider Prince's statements reviewing fair use ... I see no reason to discount Prince's statements as the majority does." In fact, Judge Wallace remarks that he views Prince's statements as "relevant to the transformativeness analysis." Judge Wallace does not believe that a simple visual side-by-side analysis is enough because this would call for judges to "employ [their] own artistic Judgment[s].'" Sergio Muñoz Sarmiento and Lauren van Haaften-Schick, citing court documents. 'Cariou v. Prince: Toward a Theory of Aesthetic-Judicial Judgements', Texas A&M Law Review, vol. 1, 2013–2014, p. 948.

41 Court opinion, p. 18.
42 Ibid., p. 17.
43 Ibid., pp. 4–5.
44 Ibid., p. 18.
45 Muñoz Sarmiento and van Haaften-Schick, 'Aesthetic-Judicial Judgements', p. 945.
46 Court opinion, p. 15.
47 The court opinion states: 'He is a leading exponent of this genre and his work has been displayed in museums around the world, including New York's Solomon R. Guggenheim Museum and Whitney Museum, San Francisco's Museum of Modern Art, Rotterdam's Museum Boijmans van Beuningen, and Basel's Museum für Gegenwartskunst.' Ibid., p. 5.

dismisses 'Cariou's claim as a legitimate author and artist'.[48] The parties eventually reached an out-of-court settlement regarding the remaining five paintings, and their infringement claim was returned to the district court meaning that no ruling had been issued. This pragmatic settlement can be interpreted as a missed opportunity for further clarification in the interpretation of fair use. No details about the settlement have been disclosed.[49]

Richard Prince presented himself in his court deposition as an artist, who 'do[es]n't really have a message,' and was not 'trying to create anything with a new meaning or a new message.'[50] Nevertheless the appeal court's ruling transforms the 'elusive artist not only into a subject, but also into an [artist] author'[51] — a status he set out to challenge in the first place. Therefore Richard Prince's ongoing games[52] might be entertaining or make us laugh, but they stop short of effectively challenging the conceptualisation of authorship, originality and property because they are assigned the very properties that are denied to the authors whose works are copied. That is to say, Prince's performative toying with the law does not endanger his art's operability in the art world. On the contrary, it constructs and affirms his reputation as a radical and saleable artist-author.

De-Authoring

A very different approach to copyright law is demonstrated by American artist Cady Noland, who employs the law to effectively endanger her art's operability in the art market. Noland is famously concerned with the circulation and display of her work with respect

---

48 Muñoz Sarmiento and van Haaften-Schick, 'Aesthetic-Judicial Judgements', p. 945.
49 *The New York Times* reports Prince had not to destroy the five paintings at issue. Randy Kennedy, 'Richard Prince Settles Copyright Suit With Patrick Cariou Over Photographs', *New York Times*, 18 March 2014, https://artsbeat.blogs.nytimes.com/2014/03/18/richard-prince-settles-copyright-suit-with-patrick-cariou-over-photographs/?_php=true&_type=blogs&_r=0
50 Court opinion, p. 13.
51 Sollfrank, 'Copyright Cowboys'.
52 In 2016 photographer Donald Graham filed a lawsuit against Prince with regard to Prince's use of Graham's Instagram pictures. Again, the image shows a photographic representation of Rastafarians. And similar to the Cariou case Prince appropriates Graham's and Cariou's cultural appropriation of Rastafarian culture.

to context, installation and photographic representation. Relatedly, she has also become very critical of short-term speculation on the art market. Noland has apparently not produced any new work for over a decade, due to the time she now spends pursuing litigation around her existing oeuvre.[53] In 2011, she strikingly demonstrated that an artist need not give up control when her work enters the commercial art market and turns into a commodity for short-term profit. She made probably one of the most important stands in modern art history when she 'de-authored' her work *Cowboys Milking* (1990), after it was put up for auction at Sotheby's with the consequence that the work could not be sold as a Cady Noland work anymore.

Swiss-born dealer Marc Jancou, based in New York and Geneva, had consigned the work to Sotheby's a few months after having purchased it for $106,500 from a private collector.[54] Jancou was obviously attracted by the fact that one of Noland's works had achieved the highest price for a piece by a living female artist: $6.6m.

At Noland's request, on the eve of the auction, Sotheby's abruptly withdrew the piece, a silkscreen print on an aluminium panel. The artist argued that it was damaged: 'The current condition [...] materially differs from that at the time of its creation. [...] [H]er honor and reputation [would] be prejudiced as a result of offering [it] for sale with her name associated with it.'[55] From a legal point of view, this amounts to a withdrawal of Noland's authorship. The US Visual Artists Rights Act of 1990, VARA, grants artists 'authorship' rights over works even after they have been sold, including the right to prevent intentional modification and to forbid the use of their name in association with

---

53 Cait Munro quotes Cady Noland from Sarah Thornton's book *33 Artists in 3 Acts*. Noland gave Thornton her first interview for twenty-four years: 'Noland, an extremely talented artist, has become so obsessed with her old work that she's been unable to create anything new in years. She admits to Thornton that 'I'd like to get into a studio and start making work,' but that tracking the old work has become a 'full-time thing'. Cait Munro, 'Is Cady Noland More Difficult To Work With Than Richard Prince?', *artNet news*, 10 November 2014, https://news.artnet.com/art-world/is-cady-noland-as-psychotic-as-richard-prince-162310;

54 Martha Buskirk, 'Marc Jancou, Cady Noland, and the Case of the Authorless Artwork', *Hyperallergic*, 9 December 2013, http://hyperallergic.com/97416/marc-jancou-cady-noland-and-the-case-of-an-authorless-artwork/

55 *Marc Jancou Fine Art Ltd. v Sotheby's, Inc.*, New York State Unified Court System, 2012 NY Slip Op 33163(U), 13 November 2012, http://cases.justia.com/new-york/other-courts/2012-ny-slip-op-33163-u.pdf?ts=1396133024

distorted or mutilated work.⁵⁶ Such rights are based on the premise that the integrity of a work needs to be guaranteed and a work of art has cultural significance that extends beyond mere property value.⁵⁷

Noland's withdrawal of authorship left Jancou with 'a Cady Noland' in his living room, but not on the market. In an email to Sotheby's, he complained: 'This is not serious! Why does an auction house ask the advise [sic] of an artist that has no gallery representation and has a biased and radical approach to the art market?'⁵⁸ Given that Noland is a long-standing and outspoken sceptic with respect to speculative dealing in art, he somewhat naively wonders why she would be able to exercise this degree of power over an artwork that had been entered into a system of commercial exchange. His complaint had no effect. The piece remained withdrawn from the auction and Jancou filed a lawsuit in February 2012 seeking $26 million in damages from Sotheby's.⁵⁹

From an economic perspective, both artists, Noland and Prince, illustrated powerfully how authorship is instituted in the form of the artist's signature, to construct (Prince's *Catcher in the Rye*) or destroy (Noland's *Cowboy Milking*) monetary value. Richard Prince's stated intention is to double the book's price, and by attaching his name to Salinger's book in a Duchampian gesture, he turns it into a work of art

---

56 'The author of a work of visual art — (1) shall have the right — (A) to claim authorship of that work, and (B) to prevent the use of his or her name as the author of any work of visual art which he or she did not create; (2) shall have the right to prevent the use of his or her name as the author of the work of visual art in the event of a distortion, mutilation, or other modification of the work which would be prejudicial to his or her honor or reputation; and (3) subject to the limitations set forth in section 113(d), shall have the right — (A) to prevent any intentional distortion, mutilation, or other modification of that work which would be prejudicial to his or her honor or reputation, and any intentional distortion, mutilation, or modification of that work is a violation of that right, and (B) to prevent any destruction of a work of recognized stature, and any intentional or grossly negligent destruction of that work is a violation of that right', from US Code, Title 17, § 106A, Legal Information Institute, Cornell Law School, https://www.law.cornell.edu/uscode/text/17/106A
57 Buskirk, 'Marc Jancou, Cady Noland'.
58 Ibid.
59 Jancou's claim was dismissed by the New York Supreme Court in the same year. The Court's decision was based on the language of Jancou's consignment agreement with Sotheby's, which gave Sotheby's the right to withdraw *Cowboys Milking* 'at any time before the sale' if, in Sotheby's judgment, 'there is doubt as to its authenticity or attribution.' Tracy Zwick, 'Art in America', 29 August 2013, https://www.artinamericamagazine.com/news-features/news/sothebys-wins-in-dispute-with-jancou-gallery-over-cady-noland-artwork/

authored and copyrighted by Prince. Noland, on the contrary lowers the value of her artwork by removing her signature and by asserting the artist-author's (Noland) rights over the dealer-owner's (Jancou).[60]

However, from a legal perspective I would argue that both Noland and Prince — in their opposite approaches of removing and adding their signatures — affirm authorship as it is conceptualised by the law.[61] After all 'copyright law is a system to which the notion of the author appears to be central — in defining the right owner, in defining the work, in defining infringement.'[62]

Intellectual Property Obsession Running Amok?

Intellectual property — granted via copyright — has become one of the driving forces of the creative economy, being exploited by

---

60   It might be important here to recall that both Richard Prince and Cady Noland are able to afford the expensive costs incurred by a court case due to their success in the art market.

61   The legal grounds for Noland's move, the federal Visual Artists Rights Act of 1990, is based on French moral rights or author rights (*droit d'auteur*), which are inspired by the humanistic and individualistic values of the French Revolution and form part of European copyright law. They conceive the work as an intellectual and creative expression that is directly connected to its creator. Legal scholar Lionel Bently observes 'the prominence of romantic conceptions of authorship' in the recognition of moral rights, which are based on concepts of the originality and authenticity of the modern subject (Lionel Bently, 'Copyright and the Death of the Author in Literature and Law', *Modern Law Review*, 57 (1994), 973–86 (p. 977)). 'Authenticity is the pure expression, the expressivity, of the artist, whose soul is mirrored in the work of art.' (Cornelia Klinger, 'Autonomy-Authenticity-Alterity: On the Aesthetic Ideology of Modernity' in *Modernologies*: *Contemporary Artists Researching Modernity and Modernism*, exhibition catalogue (Barcelona: Museu d'Art Contemporani de Barcelona, 2009), pp. 26–28 (p. 29)) Moral rights are the personal rights of authors, which cannot be surrendered fully to somebody else because they conceptualize authorship as authentic extension of the subject. They are 'rights of authors and artists to be named in relation to the work and to control alterations of the work.' (Bently, 'Copyright and the Death of the Author', p. 977) In contrast to copyright, moral rights are granted in perpetuity, and fall to the estate of an artist after his or her death.

Anglo-American copyright, employed in Prince's case, on the contrary builds the concept of intellectual property mainly on economic and distribution rights, against unauthorised copying, adaptation, distribution and display. Copyright lasts for a certain amount of time, after which the work enters the public domain. In most countries the copyright term expires seventy years after the death of the author. Non-perpetual copyright attempts to strike a balance between the needs of the author to benefit economically from his or her work and the interests of the public who benefit from the use of new work.

62   Bently, 'Copyright and the Death of the Author', p. 974.

corporations and institutions of the so-called 'creative industries'. In the governmental imagination, creative workers are described as 'model entrepreneurs for the new economy'.[63] Shortly after the election of New Labour in the UK in 1997, the newly formed Department of Culture, Media and Sport established the *Creative Industries Mapping Document* (CIMD 1998) and defined the 'Creative Industries' primarily in relation to creativity and intellectual property.[64] According to the Department for Culture Media and Sport the creative industries have 'their origin in individual creativity, skill and talent, which have a potential for wealth and job creation through the generation and exploitation of intellectual property.'[65] This exploitation of intellectual property as intangible capital has been taken on board by institutions and public management policymakers, which not only turn creative practices into private property, but trigger working policies that produce precarious self-entrepreneurship and sacrifice in pursuit of gratification.[66]

We find this kind of thinking reflected for instance on the website built by the University of the Arts London to give advice on intellectual property — which was until recently headlined 'Own It'.[67] Here, institutional policies privilege the privatisation and propertisation of creative student work over the concept of sharing and fair use.

There is evidence that this line of thought creates a self-inflicted impediment for cultural workers inside and outside art colleges. The College Art Association, a US-based organization of about fourteen

---

63 Geert Lovink and Andrew Ross, 'Organic Intellectual Work', in Geert Lovink and Ned Rossiter (eds.), *My Creativity Reader: A Critique of Creative Industries* (Amsterdam: Institute of Network Cultures, 2007), pp. 225–38 (p. 230), http://networkcultures.org/_uploads/32.pdf

64 UK Government Department for Digital, Culture, Media and Sports, *The Creative Industries Mapping Document*, 1998, https://www.gov.uk/government/publications/creative-industries-mapping-documents-1998

65 UK Government, Department for Media, Culture & Sport, *Creative Industries Economic Estimates January 2015*, https://www.gov.uk/government/publications/creative-industries-economic-estimates-january-2015/creative-industries-economic-estimates-january-2015-key-findings

66 See critical discussion of the creative industries paradigm and the effects of related systems of governance on the precarisation of the individual: Lovink and Rossiter, *My Creativity*, and Isabell Lorey, *State of Insecurity: Government of the Precarious* (London: Verso, 2015).

67 University of the Arts London, 'Intellectual Property Know-How for the Creative Sector'. This site was initially accessed on 30 March 2015. In 2018 it was taken down and integrated into the UAL Intellectual Property Advice pages. Their downloadable PDFs still show the 'Own-it' logo, https://www.arts.ac.uk/students/student-careers/freelance-and-business-advice/intellectual-property-advice

thousand artists, arts professionals, students and scholars released a report in 2015 on the state of fair use in the visual arts.[68] The survey reveals that 'visual arts communities of practice share a great deal of confusion about and misunderstanding of the nature of copyright law and the availability of fair use. [...] Formal education on copyright, not least at art colleges, appears to increase tendencies to overestimate risk and underuse fair use.' As a result, the report states, the work of art students 'is constrained and censored, most powerfully by themselves, because of that confusion and the resulting fear and anxiety.'[69]

This climate even results in outright self-censorship. The interviewees of this study 'repeatedly expressed a pre-emptive decision not to pursue an idea'[70] because gaining permission from right holders is often difficult, time consuming or expensive. The authors of this report called this mindset a 'permissions culture', giving some examples. 'I think of copyright as a cudgel, and I have been repeatedly forestalled and censored because I have not been able to obtain copyright permission', stated one academic, whose research did not get approval from an artist's estate. He added: 'For those of us who work against the grain of [the] market-driven arts economy, their one recourse for controlling us is copyright.' Another said: 'In many cases I have encountered artists' estates and sometimes artists who refuse rights to publish (even when clearly fair use) unless they like the interpretation in the text. This is censorship and very deleterious to scholarship and a free public discourse on images.'[71] One scholar declared that copyright questions

---

68 Patricia Aufderheide, Peter Jaszi, Bryan Bello, and Tijana Milosevic, *Copyright, Permissions, and Fair Use Among Visual Artists and the Academic and Museum Visual Arts Communities: An Issues Report* (New York: College Art Association, 2014).
69 Ibid., p. 5.
70 Sixty-six percent of all those who reported that they had abandoned or avoided a project because of an actual or perceived inability to obtain permissions said they would be 'very likely' to use copyrighted works of others more than they have in the past were permissions not needed. Ibid., p. 50.
71 The *Copyright, Permissions, and Fair Use Report* gives some intriguing further observations: 'Permissions roadblocks result in deformed or even abandoned work. Exhibition catalogues may be issued without relevant images because rights cannot be cleared. Editors of art scholarship reported journal articles going to print with blank spots where reproductions should be, because artists' representatives disagreed with the substance of the article; and one book was published with last-minute revisions and deletions of all images because of a dispute with an estate — with disastrous results for sales. Journal editors have had to substitute articles or go without an article altogether because an author could not arrange

overshadowed his entire work process: 'In my own writing, I'm worrying all the time.'[72] In such a climate of anxiety 'editors choose not to publish books that they believe might have prohibitive permission costs; museums delay or abandon digital-access projects', as Ben Mauk comments in the *New Yorker Magazine*.[73]

The language of law does harm because it has the rhetorical power to foreclose debate. Legal and political science scholar Jennifer Nedelsky traces the problem to the fact 'that many right claims, such as "it's my property", have a conclusory quality. They are meant to end, not to open up debate', therefore 'treating as settled, what should be debated'.[74]

In a similar vein, political scientist Deborah Halbert describes how her critique of intellectual property took her on a journey to study the details of the law. The more she got into it, so she says, the more her own thinking had been 'co-opted' by the law. 'The more I read the case law and law journals, the more I came to speak from a position inside the status quo. My ability to critique the law became increasingly bounded by the law itself and the language used by those within the legal profession to discuss issues of intellectual property. I began to speak in terms of incentives and public goods. I began to start any discussion of intellectual property by what was and was not allowed under the law. It became clear that the very act of studying the subject had transformed my standpoint from an outsider to an insider.'[75]

---

permissions in time for publication. In one case, after an author's manuscript was completed, an estate changed position, compelling the author both to rewrite and to draw substitute illustrations. Among other things, the cost of permissions leads to less work that features historical overviews and comparisons, and more monographs and case studies. Scholarship itself is distorted and even censored by the operation of the permissions culture. [...] In some cases, the demands of rights holders have extended to altering or censoring the scholarly argument about a work. Catalogue copy sometimes is altered because scholarly arguments and perspectives are unacceptable to rights holders.' These actions are in some cases explicitly seen as censorship. Ibid., p. 52.

72 Ibid., p. 51.
73 Ben Mauk, 'Who Owns This Image?', *The New Yorker*, 12 February 2014, http://www.newyorker.com/business/currency/who-owns-this-image
74 Jennifer Nedelsky, 'Reconceiving Rights as Relationship', in *Review of Constitutional Studies / Revue d'études constitutionnelles* 1.1 (1993), 1–26 (p. 16), https://www.law.utoronto.ca/documents/nedelsky/Review1.1Nedelsky.pdf
75 Deborah J. Halbert, *Resisting Intellectual Property* (London: Routledge, 2005), pp. 1–2.

The Piracy Project — Multiple Authorship or 'Unsolicited Collaborations'?

A similar question of language applies to the term 'pirate'.[76] Media and communication scholar Ramon Lobato asks whether the language of piracy used by the critical intellectual property discourse 'should be embraced, rejected, recuperated or rearticulated'? He contends that reducing 'piracy' to a mere legal category — of conforming, or not, with the law — tends to neglect the generative forces of piracy, which 'create its own economies, exemplify wider changes in social structure, and bring into being tense and unusual relationships between consumers, cultural producers and governments.'[77]

When the word pirate first appeared in ancient Greek texts, it was closely related to the noun 'peira' which means trial or attempt. 'The 'pirate' would then be the one who 'tests', 'puts to proof', 'contends with', and 'makes an attempt'.[78] Further etymological research shows that from the same root stems *pira*: experience, practice [πείρα], *pirama*: experiment [πείραμα], *piragma*: *teasing* [πείραγμα] and *pirazo*: tease, give trouble [πειράζω].[79]

This 'contending with', 'making an attempt' and 'teasing' is at the core of the Piracy Project's practice, whose aim is twofold: firstly, to gather and study a vast array of piratical practices (to test and negotiate the complexities and paradoxes created by intellectual property for artistic practice); and secondly to build a practice that is itself collaborative and generative on many different levels.[80]

---

76 See for example Amedeo Policante examining the relationship between empire and pirate, claiming that the pirate can exist only in a relationship with imperial foundations. 'Upon the naming of the pirate, in fighting it and finally in celebrating its triumph over it, Empire erects itself. There is no Empire without a pirate, a terrorizing common enemy, an enemy of all. At the same time, there is no pirate without Empire. In fact, pirates as outlaws cannot be understood in any other way but as legal creatures. In other words, they exist only in a certain extreme, liminal relationship with the law.' Amedeo Policante, *The Pirate Myth, Genealogies of an Imperial Concept* (Oxford and New York: Routledge, 2015), p. viii.

77 Ramon Lobato, 'The Paradoxes of Piracy', in Lars Eckstein and Anja Schwarz (eds.), *Postcolonial Piracy: Media Distribution and Cultural Production in the Global South* (London and New York: Bloomsbury, 2014), pp. 121–34 (pp. 121, 123).

78 Daniel Heller-Roazen, *The Enemy of All: Piracy and the Law of Nations* (New York: Zone Books, 2009), p. 35, as cited by Gary Hall, *Pirate Philosophy*, p. 16.

79 'Etymology of Pirate', in *English Words of (Unexpected) Greek Origin*, 2 March 2012, http://ewonago.wordpress.com/2009/02/18/etymology-of-pirate

80 The Piracy Project is a collaboration between AND Publishing and Andrea Francke initiated in London in 2010.

The Piracy Project explores the philosophical, legal and social implications of cultural piracy and creative modes of dissemination. Through an open call, workshops, reading rooms and performative debates as well as through our research into international pirate book markets[81] we gathered a collection of roughly 150 copied, emulated, appropriated and modified books from across the world. Their approaches to copying vary widely, from playful strategies of reproduction, modification and reinterpretation of existing works; to acts of civil disobedience circumventing enclosures such as censorship or market monopolies; to acts of piracy generated by commercial interests. This vast and contradictory spectrum of cases, from politically motivated bravery as well as artistic statements to cases of hard-edged commercial exploitation, serves as the starting point to explore the complexities and contradictions of authorship in debates, workshops, lectures and texts, like this one.

In an attempt to rearticulate the language of piracy we call the books in the collection 'unsolicited collaborations'.[82] *Unsolicited* indicates that the makers of the books in the Piracy Project did not ask for permission — Richard Prince's 'Catcher in the Rye' is one example.[83] *Collaboration* refers to a relational activity and re-imagines authorship

---

81   Andrea Francke visited pirate book markets in Lima, Peru in 2010. The Red Mansion Prize residency enabled us to research book piracy in Beijing and Shanghai in 2012. A research residency at SALT Istanbul in 2012 facilitated field research in Turkey.

82   See also Stephen Wright's *Towards a Lexicon of Usership* (Eindhoven: Van Abbemuseum, 2013) proposing to replace the term (media) 'piracy' with 'usership'. He explains: 'On the one hand, the most notorious and ruthless cultural pirates today are Google and its subsidiaries like YouTube (through the institutionalized rip-off of user-generated value broadly known as Page-Rank), Facebook, and of course Warner Bros etc., but also academic publishers such as the redoubtable Routledge. On the other hand, all the user-run and user-driven initiatives like aaaaarg, or pad.ma, or until recently the wonderful Dr Auratheft. But, personally, I would hesitate to assimilate such scaled-up, de-creative, user-propelled examples with anything like "cultural piracy". They are, through usership, enriching what would otherwise fall prey to cultural piracy.' Email to the author, 1 August 2012.
See also: Andrea Francke and Eva Weinmayr (eds.), *Borrowing, Poaching, Plagiarising, Pirating, Stealing, Gleaning, Referencing, Leaking, Copying, Imitating, Adapting, Faking, Paraphrasing, Quoting, Reproducing, Using, Counterfeiting, Repeating, Translating, Cloning* (London: AND Publishing, 2014).

83   Richard Prince's 'Catcher in the Rye' forms part of the Piracy Collection. Not the book copy priced at £1,500, just an A4 colour printout of the cover, downloaded from the Internet. On the shelf it sits next to Salinger's copy, which we bought at Barnes and Noble for £20.

not as proprietary and stable, but as a dialogical and generative process. Here, as feminist legal scholar Carys Craig claims, 'authorship is not originative but participative; it is not internal but interactive; it is not independent but interdependent. In short, a dialogic account of authorship is equipped to appreciate the derivative, collaborative, and communicative nature of authorial activity in a way that the Romantic [individual genius] account never can.'[84]

Such a participatory and interdependent conceptualisation of authorship is illustrated and tested in the Piracy Project's research into reprinting, modifying, emulating and commenting on published books. As such it revisits — through material practice — Michel Foucault's critical concept of the 'author function' as the triggering of a discourse, rather than a proprietary right.[85]

This becomes clearer when we consider that digital print technologies, for example through print on demand and desktop publishing, allow for a constant re-printing and re-editing of existing files. The advent and widespread accessibility of the photocopy machine in the late 1960s allowed the reader to photocopy books and collate selected chapters, pages or images in new and customised compilations. These new reproduction technologies undermine to an extent the concept of the printed book as a stable and authoritative work,[86] which had prevailed since the mass production of books on industrial printing presses came into being. Eva Hemmungs Wirtén describes how the widespread availability of the photocopier[87] has been perceived as a threat to the authority of the text and cites Marshall McLuhan's address at the Vision 65 congress in 1965:

> Xerography is bringing a reign of terror into the world of publishing because it means that every reader can become both author and publisher. [...] Authorship and readership alike can become production-oriented under xerography. Anyone can take a book apart, insert parts of other

---

84 Craig, 'Symposium: Reconstructing the Author-Self', p. 246.
85 Michel Foucault, 'What Is an Author?', in Donald F. Bouchard (ed.), *Language, Counter-Memory, Practice: Selected Essays and Interviews* (Ithaca, NY: Cornell University Press, 1977), pp. 113–38.
86 See The Piracy Project, 'The Impermanent Book', *Rhizome*, 19 April 2012, http://rhizome.org/editorial/2012/apr/19/impermanent-book/
87 It might be no coincidence that Roland Barthes' seminal short essay 'Death of the Author' was published in the magazine *Aspen* at the same time, when photocopy machines were beginning to be widely used in libraries and offices.

books and other materials of his own interest, and make his own book in a relatively fast time. Any teacher can take any ten textbooks on any subject and custom-make a different one by simply xeroxing a chapter from this one and from that one.[88]

One example of a reprinted and modified book in the Piracy Project is *No se diga a nadie* ('Don't tell anyone').[89] It is an autobiographical novel by Peruvian journalist and TV presenter Jaime Bayli. The pirate copy, found by Andrea Francke on Lima's pirate book markets, is almost identical in size, weight, and format and the cover image is only slightly cropped. However, this pirate copy has two extra chapters. Somebody has infiltrated the named author's work and sneaked in two fictionalised chapters about the author's life. These extra chapters are well written, good enough to blend in and not noticeable at first glance by the reader.[90]

The pirates cannot gain any cultural capital here, as the pirating author remains an anonymous ghost. Equally there is no financial profit to be made, as long as the pirate version is not pointed out to readers as an extended version. Such act is also not framed as a conceptual gesture, as it is the case with Prince's *Catcher in the Rye*. It rather operates under the radar of everyone, and moreover and importantly, any revelation of this intervention or any claim of authorship would be counterproductive.

---

[88] Eva Hemmungs Wirtén, *No Trespassing, Authorship, Intellectual Property Rights and the Boundaries of Globalization* (Toronto: University of Toronto Press, 2004), p. 66.

[89] See *No se diga a nadie*, The Piracy Project Catalogue, http://andpublishing.org/PublicCatalogue/PCat_record.php?cat_index=99

[90] In an essay in *Granta Magazine*, Daniel Alarcon explains the popularity of book piracy in Peru due to the lack of formal distribution. 'Outside Lima, the pirate book industry is the only one that matters' explains Alarcon. Iquitos, the largest city in the Peruvian Amazon, with nearly 400,000 residents, had until 2007 no formal bookstore and in 2010 only two. Trujillo, the country's third largest city, has one. According to Alarcon, an officially produced book costs twenty percent of an average worker's weekly income, therefore the pirate printing industry fills this gap — an activity that is not seriously restricted by the state. In fact, Alarcon claims that the government is involved in the pirate printing industry as a way to control what is being read. Pirated books are openly sold in book markets and by street vendors at traffic crossings, therefore they 'reach sectors of the market that formal book publishers cannot or don't care to access. In a similar vein, the few prestigious private universities' book check-out time is exactly twenty-four hours, the very turnaround for the copy shops in the neighbourhood to make a photocopied version of the checked-out library books. Daniel Alarcon, 'Life Amongst the Pirates', *Granta Magazine*, 14 January 2010, https://granta.com/life-among-the-pirates/

This example helps us to think through concepts of the authoritative text and the stability of the book. Other cases in the Piracy Project find similar ways to queer the category of authorship and the dominant modes of production and dissemination.[91] Our practice consists of collecting; setting up temporary reading rooms to house the collection; and organising workshops and debates in order to find out about the reasons and intentions for these acts of piracy, to learn from their strategies and to track their implications for dominant modes of production and dissemination.[92]

This discursive practice distinguishes the Piracy Project from radical online libraries, such as aaaaarg.fail or memoryoftheworld.org.[93] While we share similar concerns, such as distribution monopolies, enclosure and the streamlining of knowledge, these peer-to-peer (p2p) platforms mainly operate as distribution platforms, developing strategies to share intact copies of authoritative texts. Marcell Mars, for example, argues against institutional and corporate distribution monopolies when he states 'when everyone is a librarian, [the] library is everywhere'. Mars invites users of the online archive memoryoftheworld.org to upload their scanned books to share with others. Similarly, Sean Dockray, who initiated aaaaarg.fail, a user generated online archive of books and texts, said in an interview: 'the project wasn't about criticising institutions, copyright, authority, and so on. It was simply about sharing knowledge. This wasn't as general as it sounds; I mean literally the sharing of knowledge between various individuals and groups that

---

91 A discussion of the vast variety of approaches here would exceed the scope of this text. If you are interested, please visit our searchable Piracy Collection catalogue, which provides short descriptions of the pirates' approaches and strategies, http://andpublishing.org/PublicCatalogue/PCat_thumbs.php

92 For the performative debate *A Day at the Courtroom* hosted by The Showroom in London, the Piracy Project invited three copyright lawyers from different cultural and legal backgrounds to discuss and assess selected cases from the Piracy Project from the perspective of their differing jurisdictions. The final verdict was given by the audience, who positioned the 'case' on a colour scale ranging from illegal (red) to legal (blue). The scale replaced the law's fundamental binary of legal — illegal, allowing for greater complexity and nuance. The advising scholars and lawyers were Lionel Bently (Professor of Intellectual Property at the University of Cambridge), Sergio Muñoz Sarmiento (Art and Law, New York), Prodromos Tsiavos (Project lead for Creative Commons, England, Wales and Greece). *A Day at the Courtroom*, The Showroom London, 15 June 2013. See a transcript of the debate in Francke and Weinmayr, *Borrowing, Poaching, Plagiarising*.

93 Aaaaaarg.fail operates on an invitation only basis; memoryoftheworld.org is openly accessible.

I was in correspondence with at the time but who weren't necessarily in correspondence with each other.'[94]

Practising Critique — Queering Institutional Categories

In contrast to online p2p sharing platforms, the Piracy Project took off in a physical space, in the library of Byam Shaw School of Art in London. Its creation was a response to restrictive university policies when, in 2010, the management announced the closure of the art college library due to a merger with the University of the Arts London. A joint effort by students and staff, supported by the acting principal, turned Byam Shaw's art college library into a self-organised library that remained public, as well as intellectually and socially generative.[95]

As a result of the college taking collective ownership over the library and its books, the space opened up. It had been a resource that was controlled and validated by institutional policies that shaped crucial decisions about what went on the shelves, but it became an assemblage of knowledge in which potentially obscure, self-published materials that were not institutionally validated were able to enter.

For example, artist and writer Neil Chapman's handmade facsimile of Gilles Deleuze's *Proust and Signs*[96] explored the materiality of print and related questions about the institutional policies of authorisation. Chapman produced a handmade facsimile of his personal paperback copy of Deleuze's work, including binding mistakes in which a few

---

94 Julian Myers, *Four Dialogues 2: On AAAARG*, San Francisco Museum of Modern Art — Open Space, 26 August 2009, https://openspace.sfmoma.org/2009/08/four-dialogues-2-on-aaaarg/. This constructive approach has been observed by Jonas Andersson generally with p2p sharing networks, which 'have begun to appear less as a reactive force (i.e. breaking the rules) and more as a proactive one (setting the rules). [...] Rather than complain about the conservatism of established forms of distribution they simply create new, alternative ones.' Jonas Andersson, 'For the Good of the Net: The Pirate Bay as a Strategic Sovereign', *Culture Machine* 10 (2009), p. 64.

95 This process was somewhat fraught, because at the same time David Cameron launched his perfidious 'Big Society' concept, which proposed that members of the community should volunteer at institutions, such as local public libraries, which otherwise could not survive because of government cuts.

96 See the Piracy Project catalogue: Neil Chapman, *Deleuze, Proust and Signs*, http://andpublishing.org/PublicCatalogue/PCat_record.php?cat_index=69

pages were bound upside down, by scanning and printing the book on his home inkjet printer. The book is close to the original format, cover and weight. However, it has a crafty feel to it: the ink soaks into the paper creating a blurry text image very different from a mass-produced offset printed text. It has been assembled in DIY style and speaks the language of amateurism and makeshift. The transformation is subtle, and it is this subtlety that makes the book subversive in an institutional library context. How do students deal with their expectations that they will access authoritative and validated knowledge on library shelves and instead encounter a book that was printed and assembled by hand?[97] Such publications circumvent the chain of institutional validation: from the author, to the publisher, the book trade, and lastly the librarian purchasing and cataloguing the book according to the standard bibliographic practices.[98] A similar challenge to the stability of the printed book and the related hierarchy of knowledge occurred when students at Byam Shaw sought a copy of Jacques Ranciere's *Ignorant Schoolmaster* and found three copied and modified versions. In accordance with, or as a response to, Ranciere's pedagogical proposal, one copy featured deleted passages that left blank spaces for the reader to fill and to construct their own meaning in lieu of Ranciere's text.[99]

---

97 Of course unconventional publications can and are being collected, but these are often more arty objects, flimsy or oversized, undersized etc. and frequently end up in the special collections, framed and categorised 'as different' from the main stack of the collections.
98 When The Piracy Project was invited to create a reading room at the New York Art Book Fair in 2012, a librarian from the Pratt Institute dropped by every single day, because she was so fixed on the questions, the pirate books and their complex strategies of queering the category of authorship posed to standardised bibliographic practices. Based on this question we organised a cataloguing workshop 'Putting the Piracy Collection on the shelf' at *Grand Union* in Birmingham, where we developed a new cataloguing vocabulary for cases in the collection. See https://grand-union.org.uk/gallery/putting-the-piracy-collection-on-the-shelves/
See also Karen Di Franco's reflection on the cataloguing workshop 'The Library Medium' in Francke and Weinmayr, *Borrowing, Poaching, Plagiarising*.
99 See Piracy Project catalogue: Camille Bondon, *Jacques Rancière: le maître ignorant*, http://andpublishing.org/PublicCatalogue/PCat_record.php?cat_index=19. Rancière's pedagogical proposal suggests that 'the most important quality of a schoolmaster is the virtue of ignorance'. (Rancière, 2010, p. 1). In his book *The Ignorant Schoolmaster: Five Lessons in Intellectual Emancipation* Jacques Rancière uses the historic case of the French teacher Joseph Jacotot, who was exiled in Belgium and taught French classes to Flemish students whose language he did not know

This queering of the authority of the book as well as the normative, institutional frameworks felt like a liberating practice. It involved an open call for pirated books, a set of workshops and a series of lectures,[100] which built a structure that allowed the Piracy Project to share concerns about the wider developments at the university and the government's funding cuts in education, while the project could at the same time playfully subvert the dire and frustrating situation of a library that is earmarked for closure.

The fact that the library's acquisition budget was cut made the pirating action even more meaningful. Many books were produced on the photocopy machine in the college. Other copies were sent to the project by artists, writers, curators and critics who responded to the international call. The initial agreement was to accept any submission, no matter how controversial, illegal or unethical it might be. This invited a variety of approaches and contradicting voices, which were not muted by the self-censorship of their originators, nor by the context in which they circulated. By resisting generalised judgments, the project tried to practice critique in Judith Butler's sense. For Butler 'judgments operate [...] as ways to subsume a particular under an already constituted category, whereas critique asks after the occlusive constitution of the field of categories themselves. [...] Critique is able to call foundations into question, denaturalise social and political hierarchy, and even establish perspectives by which a certain distance on the naturalised world can be had.'[101]

To create such a space for the critique of the naturalisation of authorship *as* intellectual property was one of the aims of the Piracy

---

and vice versa. Reportedly he gave his students a French text to read alongside its translation and, without mediation or explanation, let the students figure out the relationship between the two texts themselves. By intentionally using his ignorance as teaching method, Rancière claims, Jacotot removed himself as the centre of the classroom, as the one who knows. This teaching method arguably destabilises the hierarchical relationship of knowledge (between student and teacher) and therefore 'establishes equality as the centre of the educational process'. Annette Krauss, 'Sites for Unlearning: On the Material, Artistic and Political Dimensions of Processes of Unlearning', PhD, Academy of Fine Arts Vienna, 2017, p. 113. Jacques Rancière, *Education, Truth and Emancipation* (London: Continuum, 2010). Jacques Rancière, *The Ignorant Schoolmaster: Five Lessons in Intellectual Emancipation* (Stanford: University Press California, 1987).

100 'AND Publishing announces The Piracy Lectures', *Art Agenda*, 4 May 2011, http://www.art-agenda.com/shows/and-publishing-announces-the-piracy-lectures/

101 Judith Butler, 'What is Critique? An Essay on Foucault's Virtue', *Transversal* 5 (2001), http://eipcp.net/transversal/0806/butler/en

Project: firstly by understanding that there is always a choice through discovering and exploring other cultures and nations dealing with (or deliberately suspending) Western copyright, and secondly through the project's collective practice itself.

Collective Authorship, Institutional Framing

The collaborative mode and collectivity within the Piracy Project differentiates its artistic strategy in principle from Prince's or Noland's approaches, who both operate as individuals claiming individual authorship for their work.

But how did the Piracy Project deal with the big authorship question? There was an interesting shift here: when the project still operated within the art college library, there was not much need for the articulation of authorship because it was embedded in a community who contributed in many different ways. Once the library was eventually shut after two years and the project was hosted by art institutions, a demand for the definition and framing of authorship arose.[102] Here the relationship between the individual and the collective requires constant and careful negotiation.[103] Members of collectives naturally develop different priorities and the differences in time, labour and thought invested by individuals makes one contributor want to claim 'more authorship' than another. These conflicts require trust, transparency and a decision

---

102 Institutions that hosted long and short-term reading rooms or invited us for workshops included: The Showroom London, Grand Union Birmingham, Salt Istanbul, ZKM Academy for Media Arts Cologne, Kunstverein Munich. The Bluecoat Liverpool, Truth is Concrete, Steirischer Herbst Graz, Printed Matter New York, New York Art Book Fair at MoMA PS1, 281 Vancouver, Rum 46 Aarhus, Miss Read, Kunstwerke Berlin. Institutions that invited us for talks or panel discussions included: Whitechapel Art Gallery, Open Design Conference Barcelona, Institutions by Artists Vancouver, Academy of Fine Arts Leipzig, Freie University Berlin, and various art academies and universities across Europe.

103 At times, we signed 'the Piracy Project' (the title) under our own names (the artist-authors), because it felt suitable to take the credit for all our personal work, instead of strengthening the 'umbrella organisation' AND. When the editor of *Rhizome* asked us to write about the project, we authored the jointly written text as 'by Piracy Project'. On other occasions we framed it 'The Piracy Project is a collaboration of the artists x and y, as part of AND Publishing's research program.' At some point, the Piracy Project outgrew AND Publishing because it took up all our time, and we began to question whether the Piracy Project was part of AND, or whether AND was part of the Piracy Project.

to value the less glamorous, more invisible and supportive work needed to maintain the project as much as the authoring of a text or speaking on a panel.[104] We also do not necessarily speak with one voice. Andrea grew up in Peru and Brazil, and I in Germany, so we have different starting points and experiences: 'we' was therefore sometimes a problematic category.

Our Relationships Felt Temporarily Transformed

Walter Benjamin, in his text 'The Author as Producer', rightly called on intellectuals to take into account the means of production as much as the radical content of their writings.[105] In theoretical writing, modes of production are too often ignored, which means in practice that theorists uncritically comply with the conventional micropolitics of publishing and dissemination. In other words, radical men and women write radical thoughts in books that are not radical at all in the way they are produced, published and disseminated. Cultural philosopher Gary Hall recounts with surprise a discussion headlined 'Radical Publishing: What Are We Struggling For?' that was held at the Institute of Contemporary Arts (ICA) in London in 2011. The invited panel speakers — Franco 'Bifo' Berardi, David Graeber, Peter Hallward, and Mark Fisher among others — were mostly concerned with, as Hall remembers,

> political transformations elsewhere: in the past, the future, Egypt, [....] but there was very little discussion of anything that would actually affect the work, business, role, and practices of the speakers themselves: radical ideas of publishing with transformed modes of production, say. As a result, the event in the end risked appearing mainly to be about a few publishers, including Verso, Pluto, and Zero Books, that may indeed publish radical political content but in fact operate according to quite traditional business models […] promoting their authors and products and providing more goods for the ticket-paying audience to buy. If the content of their publications is politically transformative, their publishing models certainly are not, with phenomena such as the student

---

104 This less glamourous work includes answering emails, booking flights, organising rooms and hosting, in short the administrative work required to run and maintain such a project. The feminist discourse of domestic and reproductive labour is relevant here, but a more detailed discussion exceeds the scope of this text.
105 Walter Benjamin, 'The Author as Producer', *New Left Review* 1.62 (1970), 83–96. See also Hall, *Pirate Philosophy*, pp. 127–232.

protests and ideas of communism all being turned into commodities to be marketed and sold.[106]

That truly radical practices are possible is demonstrated by Susan Kelly, when she reflects on her involvement in collective practices of creative dissent during the austerity protests in the UK in 2010 — roughly at the same time and in the same climate that the panel at the ICA took place.[107] Kelly describes occasions when artists and activists who were involved in political organising, direct action, campaigning, and claiming and organising alternative social and cultural spaces, came together. She sees these occasions as powerful moments that provided a glimpse into what the beginnings of a transversal and overarching movement might look like.[108] It was an attempt to

> devise the new modes of action, and new kinds of objects *from* our emerging analyses of the situation while keeping the format open, avoiding the replication of given positions, hierarchies and roles of teachers, students, artists, onlookers and so on. [...] We met people we had never met before, never worked with or known, and for many of us, our relationships felt temporarily transformed, our vulnerabilities exposed and prior positions and defenses left irrelevant, or at least suspended.[109]

---

106 Ibid., p. 129.
107 Several gatherings, such as 'Direct Weekend' and 'Long Weekend' at various art colleges in London involved Precarious Workers Brigade, Carrot Workers, tax evasion campaigners, UK Uncut, alternative media groups, feminist alliances, anti-poverty groups. See Precarious Workers Brigade, 'Fragments Toward an Understanding of a Week that Changed Everything...', *e-flux* 24 (April 2011), http://www.e-flux.com/journal/24/67844/fragments-toward-an-understanding-of-a-week-that-changed-everything/
108 Susan Kelly describes Felix Guattari's use of the term transversality 'as a conceptual tool to open hitherto closed logics and hierarchies and to experiment with relations of interdependency in order to produce new assemblages and alliances [...] and different forms of (collective) subjectivity that break down oppositions between the individual and the group.' Susan Kelly, 'The Transversal and the Invisible: How do You Really Make a Work of Art that Is not a Work of Art?', *Transversal* 1 (2005), http://eipcp.net/transversal/0303/kelly/en. See also Gerald Raunig's description of transversal activist practice: as 'There is no longer any artificially produced subject of articulation; it becomes clear that every name, every linkage, every label has always already been collective and must be newly constructed over and over again. In particular, to the same extent to which transversal collectives are only to be understood as polyvocal groups, transversality is linked with a critique of representation, with a refusal to speak for others, in the name of others, with abandoning identity, with a loss of a unified face, with the subversion of the social pressure to produce faces.' Gerald Raunig, 'Transversal Multitudes', *Transversal* 9 (2002), http://eipcp.net/transversal/0303/raunig/en
109 Kelly, '"But that was my idea!"', p. 3.

Exactly because these moments of protest produced actions and props that escaped authorship, it was even more alienating for the participants when a collectively fabricated prop for a demonstration, a large papier-mâché carrot[110] that became a notorious image in the press at the time, was retrospectively ascribed in an Artforum interview to be the 'authored' work of an individual artist.[111]

Kelly, correctly, is highly critical of such designation, which re-erects the blockages and boundaries connected to regimes of authorship that collective action aimed to dismantle in the first place. It is vital not to ignore the 'complex set of open and contingent relationships, actions and manifestations that composed this specific collective political work.' We would have to ask, to which of the activities in the making of the papier-mâché carrot would we attribute authorship? Is it the paper sourcing, the gluing, the painting, the carrying or the communicative work of organising the gatherings? What if the roles and practices are fluid and cannot be delimited like this?

How Not to Assign Authorship?

What about this text you are reading now? It is based on a five-year collaboration to which numerous people contributed. Pirated books were given to the Piracy Project as well as arguments, ideas, questions, knowledge and practices in the form of conversations and workshops.

In that regard, this text is informed by a myriad of encounters in panel discussions and debates, as well as in the classrooms supported by institutions, activist spaces and art spaces.[112] All these people donated their valuable ideas to its writing. Various drafts have been read and commented on by friends, PhD supervisors and an anonymous peer

---

110 The carrot is used as 'a symbol of the promise of paid work and future fulfilment made to those working under conditions of free labour in the cultural sector.' Ibid.
111 In an interview published in *Artforum*, David Graeber says: 'Another artist I know, for example, made a sculpture of a giant carrot used during a protest at Millbank; I think it was actually thrown through the window of Tory headquarters and set on fire. She feels it was her best work, but her collective, which is mostly women, insisted on collective authorship, and she feels unable to attach her name to the work.' 'Another World: Michelle Kuo Talks with David Graeber', *Artforum International* (Summer 2012), p. 270, https://www.artforum.com/print/201206/michelle-kuo-talks-with-david-graeber-31099
112 Artist Rosalie Schweiker, who read a draft of this text, suggested that I make a list of the name of every person involved in the project in order to demonstrate this generative and expansive mode of working.

reviewer, and it has been edited by the publishers in the process of becoming part of the anthology you now hold in your hands or read on a screen. In that light, do I simply and uncritically affirm the mechanisms I am criticising by delivering a single-authored text to be printed and validated within the prevailing audit culture?

What if I did not add my name to this text? If it went unsigned, so to speak? If anonymity replaced the designation of authorship? The text has not been written collectively or collaboratively, despite the conventional processes of seeking comments from friendly and critical readers. This is my text, but what would happen if I did not assert my right to be its named author?

How would the non-visibility of the author matter to the reader? We are used to making judgements that are at least partially based on the gender, status, authority and reputation of a writer. There are also questions of liability and accountability with respect to the content of the text.[113] Given the long struggle of women writers and writers of colour to gain the right to be acknowledged as author, the act of not signing my text might be controversial or even counter productive. It would also go against the grain of scholarship that aims to decolonise the canon or fight against the prevailing gender inequality in scholarly publishing.[114] And more, we have to ask who is actually in a position to afford not to assign individual names to works given that authorship — as discussed above — is used as a marker for professional survival and advancement.

In this specific context however, and as practice based research, it would be worth testing out practically what such a text orphan would trigger within dominant infrastructures of publishing and validation. How would bibliographers catalogue such a text? How could it be referenced and cited? And how would it live online with respect to

---

113 Such an action might even infringe legal requirements or contracts. Open Book Publishers' contract, for example, states: 'The author hereby asserts his/her right to be identified in relation to the work on the title page and cover and the publisher undertakes to comply with this requirement. A copyright notice in the Author's name will be printed in the front pages of the Work.' Open Book Publishers, *Authors' Guide*, p. 19, https://www.openbookpublishers.com/shopimages/resources/OBP-Author-Guide.pdf

114 For a discussion of gender inequality in recent scholarly publishing see Chad Wellmon and Andrew Piper 'Publication, Power, Patronage: On Inequality and Academic Publishing', *Critical Inquiry* (21 July 2017), http://criticalinquiry.uchicago.edu/publication_power_and_patronage_on_inequality_and_academic_publishing/

search engines, if there is no searchable name attached to it? Most of our current research repositories don't allow the upload of author-less texts, instead returning error messages: 'The author field must be completed'. Or they require a personalised log-in, which automatically tags the registered username to the uploaded text.

What if I used a pseudonym, a common practice throughout literary history?[115] Multiple identity pseudonyms, such as 'Karen Eliot' or 'Monty Cantsin' used by the Neoist movement in the 1980s and 1990s could be interesting as they provide a joint name under which anybody could sign her or his work without revealing the author's identity.[116] This strategy of using a multi-identity avatar is currently practiced by a decentralised, international collective of hacktivists operating under the name 'Anonymous'. The 'elimination of the persona [of the author], and by extension everything associated with it, such as leadership, representation, and status, is', according to Gabriella Coleman, 'the primary ideal of Anonymous.'[117]

What if we adopted such models for academia? If we unionised and put in place a procedure to collectively publish our work anonymously, for example under a multi-identity avatar instead of

---

115 See Gérard Genette's discussion of the 'pseudonym effect' as conceptual device. He distinguishes between the reader not knowing about the use of the pseudonym and the conceptual effect of the reader having information about the use of a pseudonym. Gérard Genette, *Paratexts, Thresholds of Interpretation* (Cambridge University Press, 1997).

116 The Neoist movement developed in Canada, North America and Europe in the late 1970s. It selected one signature name for multiple identities and authors, who published, performed and exhibited under this joint name. It is different from a collective name, as any person could sign her or his work with these joint names without revealing the author's identity. See letter exchanges between cultural theorist Florian Cramer and artist and writer Stewart Home: 'I would like to describe "Monty Cantsin" as a multiple identity, "Karen Eliot" as a multiple pen-name and, judging from the information I have, "Luther Blissett" as a collective phantom.' Florian Cramer, 2 October 1995, in Stewart Home and Florian Cramer, *House of Nine Squares: Letters on Neoism, Psychogeography & Epistemological Trepidation*, https://www.stewarthomesociety.org/neoism/ninesq.htm. See also Nicholas Thoburn's research into the political agency of anonymous authorship. Nicholas Thoburn, *Anti-Book, On the Art and Politics of Radical Publishing* (Minneapolis and London: University of Minnesota Press, 2016) pp. 168–223.

117 Anonymous started on 4chan, an online imageboard where users post anonymously. 'The posts on 4chan have no names or any identifiable markers attached to them. The only thing you are able to judge a post by is its content and nothing else.' Gabriella Coleman, *Hacker, Hoaxer, Whistleblower, Spy: The Many Faces of Anonymous* (London and New York: Verso, 2014), p. 47.

individual names — how would such a text, non-attributable as it is, change the policies of evaluation and assessment within the knowledge economy? Would the lack of an identifiable name allow the text to resist being measured as (or reduced to) a quantifiable auditable 'output' and therefore allow the issue of individualistic authorship to be politicised? Or would it rather, as an individual and solitary act, be subjected — again — to the regimes of individualisation? It seems that only if not assigning individual authorship became a widespread and unionised practice could procedures be put in place that acknowledged non-authored, collective, non-competitive practices.[118]

However, as tempting and urgent as such a move might appear in order to allow individualistic authorship to be politicised, such a step also produces a challenging double bind. According to Sara Ahmed it actually does matter who is speaking. 'The 'who' does make a difference, not in the form of an ontology of the individual, but as a marker of a specific location from which the subject writes'.[119]

From a feminist and postcolonial perspective, the detachment of writing from the empirical body is problematic. Ahmed points out: 'The universalism of the masculine perspective relies precisely on being disembodied, on lacking the contingency of a body. A feminist perspective would surely emphasise the implication of writing in embodiment, in order to re-historicise this supposed universalism, to locate it, and to expose the violence of its contingency and particularity (by declaring some-body wrote this text, by asking which body wrote this text).'[120] Gayatri Spivak for example insists on marking the positionality

---

118 I thank Susan Kelly for making this point while reviewing my text.
119 It is interesting to come back to Foucault's text 'What is an author' and complicate his own position as authorial subject. Referring to Naomi Schor and Gayatri Spivak, Sara Ahmed suggests, that 'Foucault effaces the sexual specificity of his own narrative and perspective as a male philosopher. The refusal to enter the discourse as an empirical subject, a subject which is both sexed and European, may finally translate into a universalising mode of discourse, which negates the specificity of its own inscription (as a text)'. See Naomi Schor, 'Dreaming Dissymmetry: Barthes, Foucault and Sexual Difference', in Elizabeth Weed (ed.), *Coming to Terms: Feminism, Theory, Politics* (London: Routledge, 1989), pp. 47–58; and Gayatry Chakravorty Spivak, 'Can the Subaltern Speak?', in Cary Nelson and Lawrence Grossberg (eds.), *Marxism and the Interpretation of Culture* (Urbana, IL: University of Illinois Press, 1988), pp. 271–313.
120 Sara Ahmed, *Differences That Matter, Feminist Theory and Postmodernism* (Cambridge, UK: Cambridge University Press, 2004) p. 125.

of a speaking subject in order to account for the often unacknowledged eurocentrism of western philosophy.[121]

If we acknowledged this double bind, we might eventually be able to invent modes of being and working together that recognise the difference of the 'who' that writes, and at the same time might be able to move on from the question 'how can we get rid of the author' to inventing processes of subjectivation that we want to support and instigate.

---

121 Spivak, 'Can the Subaltern Speak?', pp. 271–313.

Works Cited

(2 March 2012), 'Etymology of Pirate', in *English Words of (Unexpected) Greek Origin*, http://ewonago.wordpress.com/2009/02/18/etymology-of-pirate

Ahmed, Sara (2004) *Differences That Matter, Feminist Theory and Postmodernism* (Cambridge: Cambridge University Press).

Alarcon, Daniel (14 January 2010) 'Life Among the Pirates', *Granta Magazine*, https://granta.com/life-among-the-pirates/

Albanese, Andrew (11 January 2011) 'J. D. Salinger Estate, Swedish Author Settle Copyright Suit' in *Publishers Weekly*, https://www.publishersweekly.com/pw/by-topic/industry-news/publisher-news/article/45738-j-d-salinger-estate-swedish-author-settle-copyright-suit.html

Allen, Greg, ed. (2012) *The Deposition of Richard Prince in the Case of Cariou v. Prince et al.* (Zurich: Bookhorse).

AND Publishing (4 May 2011) 'AND Publishing announces The Piracy Lectures', *Art Agenda*, http://www.art-agenda.com/shows/and-publishing-announces-the-piracy-lectures/

Andersson, Jonas (2009) 'For the Good of the Net: The Pirate Bay as a Strategic Sovereign', *Culture Machine* 10, 64–108.

Aufderheide, Patricia, Peter Jaszi, Bryan Bello and Tijana Milosevic (2014) *Copyright, Permissions, and Fair Use Among Visual Artists and the Academic and Museum Visual Arts Communities: An Issues Report* (New York: College Art Association).

Barron, Anne (1998) 'No Other Law? Author–ity, Property and Aboriginal Art', in Lionel Bently and Spyros Maniatis (eds.), *Intellectual Property and Ethics* (London: Sweet and Maxwell), pp. 37–88.

Barthes, Roland (1967) 'The Death of the Author', *Aspen*, [n.p.], http://www.ubu.com/aspen/aspen5and6/threeEssays.html

Benjamin, Walter (1970) 'The Author as Producer' in *New Left Review* 1.62, 83–96.

Bently, Lionel (1994) 'Copyright and the Death of the Author in Literature and Law', *Modern Law Review* 57, 973–86.

— Andrea Francke, Sergio Muñoz Sarmiento, Prodromos Tsiavos and Eva Weinmayr (2014) 'A Day at the Courtroom', in Andrea Francke and Eva Weinmayr (eds.), *Borrowing, Poaching, Plagiarising, Pirating, Stealing, Gleaning, Referencing, Leaking, Copying, Imitating, Adapting, Faking, Paraphrasing, Quoting, Reproducing, Using, Counterfeiting, Repeating, Translating, Cloning* (London: AND Publishing), pp. 91–133.

Biagioli, Mario (2014) 'Plagiarism, Kinship and Slavery', *Theory Culture Society* 31.2/3, 65–91, https://doi.org/10.1177/0263276413516372

Buchloh, Benjamin (2009) 'Pictures', in David Evans (ed.), *Appropriation, Documents of Contemporary Art* (London: Whitechapel Gallery), originally published in *October* 8 (1979), 75–88.

Buskirk, Martha (9 December 2013) 'Marc Jancou, Cady Noland, and the Case of the Authorless Artwork', *Hyperallergic*, http://hyperallergic.com/97416/marc-jancou-cady-noland-and-the-case-of-an-authorless-artwork/

Butler, Judith (2001) 'What is Critique? An Essay on Foucault's Virtue', *Transversal* 5, http://eipcp.net/transversal/0806/butler/en

Cariou, Patrick (2009) *Yes Rasta* (New York: powerHouse Books).

Chan, Sewell (1 July 2009) 'Judge Rules for J. D. Salinger in "Catcher" Copyright Suit', *New York Times*, http://www.nytimes.com/2009/07/02/books/02salinger.html

Coleman, Gabriella (2014) *Hacker, Hoaxer, Whistleblower, Spy: The Many Faces of Anonymous* (London and New York: Verso).

Corbett, Rachel (14 November 2012) *New York Supreme Court Judge Dismisses Marc Jancou's Lawsuit Against Sotheby's*, https://web.archive.org/web/20121123082543/http://blogs.artinfo.com/artintheair/2012/11/14/new-york-supreme-court-judge-dismisses-marc-jancou%E2%80%99s-lawsuit-against-sotheby%E2%80%99s/

Cariou v Prince, et al., No. 11–1197-cv. http://www.ca2.uscourts.gov/decisions/isysquery/f6e88b8b-48af-401c-96a0-54d5007c2f33/1/doc/11-1197_complete_opn.pdf#xml=http://www.ca2.uscourts.gov/decisions/isysquery/f6e88b8b-48af-401c-96a0-54d5007c2f33/1/hilite/

Craig, Carys J. (2007) 'Symposium: Reconstructing the Author-Self: Some Feminist Lessons for Copyright Law', *American University Journal of Gender, Social Policy & the Law* 15.2, 207–68.

Di Franco, Karen (2014) 'The Library Medium', in Andrea Francke and Eva Weinmayr (eds.), *Borrowing, Poaching, Plagiarising, Pirating, Stealing, Gleaning, Referencing, Leaking, Copying, Imitating, Adapting, Faking, Paraphrasing, Quoting, Reproducing, Using, Counterfeiting, Repeating, Translating, Cloning* (London: AND Publishing), pp. 77–90.

Fitzpatrick, Kathleen (2018) 'Generous Thinking The University and the Public Good', *Humanities Commons*, https://generousthinking.hcommons.org/

Foster, Hal (1985) '(Post)modern Polemics', in *Recodings: Art, Spectacle, Cultural Politics* (Port Townsend, WA: Bay Press), pp. 121–38.

Foucault, Michel (1977) 'What Is an Author?', in Donald F. Bouchard (ed.), *Language, Counter-Memory, Practice: Selected Essays and Interviews* (Ithaca, NY: Cornell University Press), pp. 113–38.

Genette Gérard (1997) *Paratexts, Thresholds of Interpretation* (Cambridge: Cambridge University Press).

Goldsmith, Kenneth (19 April 2012) 'Richard Prince's Latest Act of Appropriation: The Catcher in the Rye', *Harriet, A Poetry Blog*, http://www.poetryfoundation.org/harriet/2012/04/richard-princes-latest-act-of-appropriation-the-catcher-in-the-rye/

Gordon, Kim (18 June 2012) 'Band Paintings: Kim Gordon Interviews Richard Prince', *Interview Magazine*, http://www.interviewmagazine.com/art/kim-gordon-richard-prince#

Halbert, Deborah J. (2005) *Resisting Intellectual Property* (London: Routledge).

Hall, Gary (2016) *Pirate Philosophy, for a Digital Posthumanities* (Cambridge, MA and London: The MIT Press).

Harrison, Nate (29 June 2012) 'The Pictures Generation, the Copyright Act of 1976, and the Reassertion of Authorship in Postmodernity', *art&education.net*, https://web.archive.org/web/20120701012619/artandeducation.net/paper/the-pictures-generation-the-copyright-act-of-1976-and-the-reassertion-of-authorship-in-postmodernity/

Heller-Roazen, Daniel (2009) *The Enemy of All*: *Piracy and the Law of Nations* (New York: Zone Books).

Hemmungs Wirtén, Eva (2004) *No Trespassing, Authorship, Intellectual Property Rights and the Boundaries of Globalization* (Toronto: University of Toronto Press).

Home, Stewart and Florian Cramer (1995) *House of Nine Squares*: *Letters on Neoism, Psychogeography & Epistemological Trepidation*, https://www.stewarthomesociety.org/neoism/ninesq.htm

Kelly, Susan (2005) 'The Transversal and the Invisible: How do You Really Make a Work of Art that Is not a Work of Art?', *Transversal* 1, http://eipcp.net/transversal/0303/kelly/en

Kelly, Susan (2013) '"But that was my idea!" Problems of Authorship and Validation in Contemporary Practices of Creative Dissent', *Parallax* 19.2, 53–69, https://doi.org/10.1080/13534645.2013.778496

Kennedy, Randy (2014) 'Richard Prince Settles Copyright Suit With Patrick Cariou Over Photographs', *New York Times* 18 March, https://artsbeat.blogs.nytimes.com/2014/03/18/richard-prince-settles-copyright-suit-with-patrick-cariou-over-photographs/?_php=true&_type=blogs&_r=0

Klinger, Cornelia (2009) 'Autonomy-Authenticity-Alterity: On the Aesthetic Ideology of Modernity' in *Modernologies*: *Contemporary Artists Researching Modernity and Modernism* (Barcelona: Museu d'Art Contemporani de Barcelona), pp. 26–28.

Krauss, Annette (2017) 'Sites for Unlearning: On the Material, Artistic and Political Dimensions of Processes of Unlearning', PhD thesis, Academy of Fine Arts Vienna.

Krupnick, Mark (28 January 2010) 'JD Salinger Obituary', *The Guardian*, http://www.theguardian.com/books/2010/jan/28/jd-salinger-obituary

Kuo, Michelle and David Graeber (Summer 2012) 'Michelle Kuo Talks with David Graeber', *Artforum International*, https://www.artforum.com/print/201206/michelle-kuo-talks-with-david-graeber-31099

Levine, Sherrie (2009) 'Statement//1982', in David Evans (ed.), *Appropriation, Documents of Contemporary Art* (London: Whitechapel Gallery), p. 81.

Lobato, Ramon (2014) 'The Paradoxes of Piracy', in Lars Eckstein and Anja Schwarz (eds.), *Postcolonial Piracy: Media Distribution and Cultural Production in the Global South* (London and New York: Bloomsbury), pp. 121–34, https://publishup.uni-potsdam.de/opus4-ubp/frontdoor/deliver/index/docId/7218/file/ppr89.pdf

Lorey, Isabell (2015) *State of Unsecurity: Government of the Precarious* (London: Verso).

Lovink, Geert and Ross, Andrew (eds.) (2007) 'Organic Intellectual Work', in *My Creativity Reader: A Critique of Creative Industries* (Amsterdam: Institute of Network Cultures), pp. 225–38, http://networkcultures.org/_uploads/32.pdf

Marc Jancou Fine Art Ltd. v Sotheby's, Inc. (13 November 2012) New York State Unified Court System, 2012 NY Slip Op 33163(U), http://cases.justia.com/new-york/other-courts/2012-ny-slip-op-33163-u.pdf?ts=1396133024

Mauk, Ben (2014) 'Who Owns This Image?', *The New Yorker* 12 February, http://www.newyorker.com/business/currency/who-owns-this-image

McLuhan, Marshall (1966) 'Address at Vision 65', *American Scholar* 35, 196–205.

Memory of the World, https://marcell.memoryoftheworld.org/

Muñoz Sarmiento, Sergio and Lauren van Haaften-Schick (2013–2014) 'Cariou v. Prince: Toward a Theory of Aesthetic-Judicial Judgements', in *Texas A&M Law Review*, vol. 1.

Munro, Cait (10 November 2014) 'Is Cady Noland More Difficult To Work With Than Richard Prince?', *artNet news*, https://news.artnet.com/art-world/is-cady-noland-as-psychotic-as-richard-prince-162310

Myers, Julian (26 August 2009) *Four Dialogues 2: On AAAARG*, San Francisco Museum of Modern Art — Open Space, https://openspace.sfmoma.org/2009/08/four-dialogues-2-on-aaaarg/

Nedelsky, Jennifer (1993) 'Reconceiving Rights as Relationship', *Review of Constitutional Studies / Revue d'études constitutionnelles* 1.1, 1–26, https://www.law.utoronto.ca/documents/nedelsky/Review1.1Nedelsky.pdf

Open Book Publishers *Authors' Guide*, https://www.openbookpublishers.com/shopimages/resources/OBP-Author-Guide.pdf

Piracy Project Catalogue. *No se diga a nadie*, http://andpublishing.org/PublicCatalogue/PCat_record.php?cat_index=99

Piracy Project Catalogue / Camille Bondon, *Jacques Rancière: le maître ignorant*, http://andpublishing.org/PublicCatalogue/PCat_record.php?cat_index=19

Piracy Project Catalogue / Neil Chapman, *Deleuze, Proust and Signs*, http://andpublishing.org/PublicCatalogue/PCat_record.php?cat_index=69

Piracy Project (19 April 2012) 'The Impermanent Book', *Rhizome*, http://rhizome.org/editorial/2012/apr/19/impermanent-book/

Policante, Amedeo (2015) *The Pirate Myth, Genealogies of an Imperial Concept* (Oxford and New York: Routledge).

Precarious Workers Brigade (24 April 2011) 'Fragments Toward an Understanding of a Week that Changed Everything...', *e-flux*, http://www.e-flux.com/journal/24/67844/fragments-toward-an-understanding-of-a-week-that-changed-everything/

Prince, Richard (13 April 2015) *Birdtalk*, http://www.richardprince.com/birdtalk/

Rancière, Jacques (2010) *Education, Truth and Emancipation* (London: Continuum).

— (2008) *The Ignorant Schoolmaster: Five Lessons in Intellectual Emancipation* (Stanford: University Press California)

Raunig, Gerald (2002) 'Transversal Multitudes', *Transversal* 9, http://eipcp.net/transversal/0303/raunig/en

Rose, Mark (1993) *Authors and Owners, The Invention of Copyright* (Cambridge MA and London: Harvard University Press).

Schor, Naomi (1989) 'Dreaming Dissymmetry: Barthes, Foucault and Sexual Difference', in Elizabeth Weed (ed.), *Coming to Terms: Feminism, Theory, Politics* (London: Routledge), pp. 47–58.

Sollfrank, Cornelia (2012) 'Copyright Cowboys Performing the Law', *Journal of New Media Caucus* 8.2, http://median.newmediacaucus.org/blog/current-issue-fall-2012-v-08-n-02-december-2nd-2012/copyright-cowboys-performing-the-law/

Spivak, Gayatry Chakravorty (1988) 'Can the Subaltern Speak?', in Cary Nelson and Lawrence Grossberg (eds.), *Marxism and the Interpretation of Culture* (Urbana: University of Illinois Press), pp. 271–313.

Strathern, Marilyn (2005) *Kinship, Law, and the Unexpected: Relatives Are Always a Surprise* (Cambridge: Cambridge University Press).

Thoburn, Nicholas (2016) *Anti-Book, On the Art and Politics of Radical Publishing* (Minneapolis and London: University of Minnesota Press).

UK Government, Department for Digital, Culture, Media and Sport (2015) *Creative Industries Economic Estimates January 2015*, https://www.gov.uk/government/publications/creative-industries-economic-estimates-january-2015/creative-industries-economic-estimates-january-2015-key-findings

— (1998) *The Creative Industries Mapping Document*, https://www.gov.uk/government/publications/creative-industries-mapping-documents-1998

US Copyright Act (1976, amended 2016), https://www.copyright.gov/title17/

Wang, Elizabeth H. (1990) '(Re)Productive Rights: Copyright and the Postmodern Artist', *Columbia-VLA Journal of Law & the Arts* 14.2, 261–81, https://heinonline.org/HOL/Page?handle=hein.journals/cjla14&div=10&g_sent=1&casa_token=&collection=journals

Waugh, Seth (2007) 'Sponsor Statement', in The Solomon R. Guggenheim Foundation (ed.), *Richard Prince* (Ostfildern: Hatje Cantz).

Wellmon, Chad and Andrew Piper (21 July 2017) 'Publication, Power, Patronage: On Inequality and Academic Publishing', *Critical Inquiry*, http://criticalinquiry.uchicago.edu/publication_power_and_patronage_on_inequality_and_academic_publishing/

Wright, Stephen (2013) *Towards a Lexicon of Usership* (Eindhoven: Van Abbemuseum).

Zwick, Tracy (29 August 2013) 'Art in America', https://www.artinamericamagazine.com/news-features/news/sothebys-wins-in-dispute-with-jancou-gallery-over-cady-noland-artwork/

12. Ethical Scholarly Publishing Practices, Copyright and Open Access: A View from Ethnomusicology and Anthropology[1]

Muriel Swijghuisen Reigersberg

Introduction

Whose book is it anyway? Whose research is it really? If musical experience and meaning are co-created through listening and performative participation and a form of embodied knowledge, what does this mean in terms of copyright, cultural ownership, epistemologies and the academic enterprise of writing about the music of others? Who owns musical experience? Who, if anyone, has the right to write about shared musical experience, and then sell this writing, or gain a doctorate from it? Has written musical experience in Western academe, however incomplete and personal, become a commodity that can be copyrighted and sold or bartered for employment? Is this selling and bartering ethical or is it exploitative and ethnocentric, particularly when working outside Western European frameworks of knowledge production, cultural ownership and copyright?

---

1   This chapter was both blind peer-reviewed and put out for open peer review via Figshare and Google Docs. During the process of open peer review, some colleagues added their suggestions on the Google Docs document, whereas others preferred to send their comments via email. I am especially grateful to Alex Rodriguez, Patrick Egan, Lin, Wei Ya and the Society for Ethnomusicology for offering to comment on this chapter before it went to blind review.

© 2019 Muriel Swijghuisen Reigersberg, CC BY 4.0   https://doi.org/10.11647/OBP.0159.12

The above concerns have occupied me and other ethnomusicologists and anthropologists for some time. In this chapter I will explore some of these questions in relation to copyright and how they in turn have the potential to influence new debates around publishing ethics, open access dissemination, co-authorship and new technologies. Firstly, I will briefly describe what ethnomusicologists research and how they research it, demonstrating that ethnomusicology's inherent interdisciplinarity and academic practice focus make it an ideal discipline for exploring copyright and open access topics in the arts, humanities and social sciences. This will be followed by a quick outline of recent developments within the global open access movement to date and the unity of purpose that links what is quite a diverse grouping. This discussion foregrounds the more in-depth enquiry as to why rights of authorship and copyright should be accorded to creative practitioners when they help inform academic monographs through practice and participation. Through problematising Foucault's concept of authorship,[2] I shall discuss how ethical guidelines, definitions of open access, technical developments and copyright legislation either hinder or facilitate the possibility of sharing authorship rights. In conclusion, I will propose a variety of ways in which we might actively develop the ideas proposed here, turning them into applied action that critically engages with the academic responsibility of sharing research ethically, and all that this entails.

Ethnomusicology, Anthropology and Open Access

Definitions of what ethnomusicology is, and what ethnomusicologists do, have been widely debated by ethnomusicologists themselves. Trends also vary depending on where researchers are active in the world and which ethnomusicological intellectual 'lineage' they subscribe to.[3] What is certain, though, is that ethnomusicology no longer restricts itself to studying non-Western music through transcription and participant

---

2   M. Foucault, 'What is an Author?', in P. Rabinow (ed.), *The Foucault Reader: An Introduction to Foucault's Thought* (London: Penguin Group, 1984), pp. 101–20.

3   Cf. H. Stobart (ed.), *The New (Ethno) Musicologies (Europea: Ethnomusicologies and Modernities)* (Lanham, MD: Scarecrow Press, 2008) and Bruno Nettl, *The Study of Ethnomusicology: Thirty-One Issues and Concepts* (Champaign, IL: University of Illinois Press, 2005).

observation in remote places. Although originally an interdiscipline based in Western academic theory and practice, ethnomusicology now includes many non-European researchers internationally who capture in culturally specific ways musical practices using a multitude of methods in a variety of locations. Some ethnomusicologists work in their home communities, others further afield. Generally speaking what differentiates ethnomusicologists from musicologists are the methodologies used. Ethnomusicologists use social-science approaches, usually taken from anthropology. The boundaries between musicology and ethnomusicology have become blurred however. Researchers of music have come to acknowledge that the prefix 'ethno' is unhelpful, leading some eminent musicologists to wonder whether perhaps we are all either ethnomusicologists or musicologists now:[4] after all, all people have an ethnicity and music is a human practice.

Ethnomusicology is an interdiscipline. Its scholars study a wide variety of musical topics using an even more diverse set of methods. These methods include: practice research through musical learning, education and performance; applied research, advocacy and activism; musical transcription; cultural policy analysis and formation; historical and musical archival investigations; interviewing, creative writing; filming and photography. Increasingly, digital approaches to music documentation, composition, performance, sharing and management are being adopted due to rapid technological developments. Recording digitally and streaming digital content have become affordable and easy to achieve technologically. The quality of sound- and video recordings and the size and portability of devices, combined with the rapid rise of social media platforms, have meant that digital ethnomusicological data can include, but is not limited to: audio-visual recordings of (co-) created works of (musical) art; conversations and interviews; images of persons, instruments and locations; ethnographies; co-edited volumes and much else. Additionally, many field interlocutors with whom ethnomusicologists engage have also begun documenting their own practices and sharing these.

For ethnomusicologists, the scholarly practice of data generation, processing and publishing is intimately related to deliberations

---

4   Cf. Nicholas Cook, 'We Are All (Ethno) Musicologists Now', in H. Stobart (ed.), *The New (Ethno)Musicologies*, pp. 48–70.

around authorship, cultural ownership and representation, copyright, intellectual property, Indigenous rights to culture, academic practice (and promotions) and ethics,[5] all of which are also relevant to current open access debates. Within ethnomusicology, therefore, there lies latent the opportunity to become a fertile 'test-bed' for open access initiatives, debate and responsible sharing of creative practices. The discipline could help inform: social science and arts and humanities research data management practices; copyright debates; policy development; academic publishing practices and ethical codes of research conduct.

Ethnomusicologists thus far, however, have been slow to recognise their discipline's potential for informing open access developments, at least in writing. They have not yet published extensively on the theoretical and scholarly implications of open access for their discipline. An exception here is a series of short contributions to the open access journal *Ethnomusicology Review*[6] 'Ethnomusicological Perspectives on Open Access' (2014).[7] These papers are based on a round table held at the Society for Ethnomusicology's (SEM)[8] 2014 annual conference in Pittsburgh, organised by Alex Rodriguez and Darren Mueller. They provide an insight in to how open access is being used, especially by graduate students. In practice ethnomusicologists have, however, engaged with open access more actively. Jeff Todd Titon, for example has a long-standing and well-respected academic Sustainable Music Blogspot,[9] where, on the subject of commonwealth and culture, he writes:

---

[5] B. Nettl, *The Study of Ethnomusicology: Thirty-Three Discussions* (Champaign, IL: University of Illinois Press, 2015), p. 212 and A. N. Weintraub and B. Yung (eds.), *Music and Cultural Rights* (Chicago, IL: University of Illinois Press, 2009).

[6] https://ethnomusicologyreview.ucla.edu/

[7] Darren Mueller, J. Schell, W. Hsu, J. R. Cowdery, A. W. Rodriguez, and G. P. Ramsey, 'Ethnomusicological Perspectives on Open Access Publication', *Ethnomusicology Review* 19 (2014), 1–21, http://ethnomusicologyreview.ucla.edu/sites/default/files/er_volume_19_2014.pdf

[8] The SEM is a US-based learned society for ethnomusicology that has an international membership and publishes one of the leading journals in the field: *Ethnomusicology*. The SEM is not the only learned ethnomusicological society. Others include the British Forum for Ethnomusicology (BFE), which publishes its journal *Ethnomusicology Forum* via Taylor and Francis in hardcopy and electronically on JSTOR. Membership benefits include copies of the journal. There is also the International Council for Traditional Music (ICTM) which publishes its *Yearbook for Traditional Music*, available via JSTOR and in print. Membership benefits include a hard copy of the journal. The journal is currently transitioning to Cambridge University Press to facilitate open access publishing options.

[9] Jeff Todd Titon, 'The Commonwealth of Culture', Sustainable Music: A Research Blog on the Subject of Sustainability, 31 December 2013, https://sustainablemusic.blogspot.com.au/search/label/ownership

Commonwealth is therefore allied with the notion of a cultural commons, the domain of ideas and performance which folklorists like to think of as a group's expressive culture. Much in the air today are arguments over enclosures such as copyright that limit the free flow of ideas in the digital, cultural, and/or creative commons. Folklorists, who have a long history of considering culture as a common group possession, have a great deal to contribute to this discussion. Commons thinking is one means of theorizing folklore and cultural sustainability […].

Other colleagues have begun their own open access journal, such as the *International Journal of Traditional Arts* (first issue June 2017),[10] whilst Orsini and Butler Schofield (eds.) published an open access volume entitled *Tellings and Texts*: *Music, Literature and Performance in North India* via Open Book Publishers.[11] Butler Schofield commented that her reason for publishing open access was to promote access for her North Indian readers.[12] Some open access publications are available online, such as the *Ethnomusicology Review*, or can be downloaded or ordered as print on demand via publishers such as Open Book. Open Book texts can also be accessed online in HTML and, in many cases XML editions.

No in-depth, full-length ethnomusicological analysis to date has been written, however, on how open access and academic publishing relate to copyright, ethics and Indigenous performative and creative knowledge-sharing in the field. Theoretical discussions and panels at ethnomusicological conferences to date have not critically examined the challenges that open access (monograph and article) publishing poses with regards to managing research and cultural data ethically and how this weighs up against the benefits of being able to share work more easily. Questions have been surfacing that are intimately related to open access, however. Nettl, for example, queries whether the discipline of ethnomusicology should begin considering what he labels 'econo-musicology'. Econo-musicology might specifically study concepts of musical ownership (individual as well as communal), sharing, musical practice, distribution and the economics of

---

10 This journal uses a Gold open access model, offers researchers a choice of licences and safeguards submissions via the LOCKSS system, http://tradartsjournal.org/index.php/ijta/about/editorialPolicies#openAccessPolicy
11 Francesca Orsini and Katherine Butler Schofield (eds.), *Tellings and Texts: Music, Literature and Performance in North India* (Cambridge: Open Book Publishers, 2015), https://doi.org/10.11647/OBP.0062; https://www.openbookpublishers.com/product/311
12 Personal communication, 29 May 2017.

distribution and relative value of sharing patterns cross-culturally.[13] Open access, with its technological opportunities and challenges, would need to feature as an intimate part of such an enquiry due to the economies of scale and value attribution practices involved. As early as 2001, Anthony McCann also highlighted the potential of the creative commons to influence gifting and sharing practices in Irish Traditional music and how these relate to copyright and ownership questions.[14]

In terms of academic publishing practise, the SEM's journal *Ethnomusicology* is available in print, on JSTOR and has a Green open access policy whereby after a twelve-month embargo period, readers can access the peer-reviewed author-created manuscript for free. This also provides journal access to field interlocutors after the work has been published. It is up to individual authors to determine how they wish to engage with their field interlocutors pre-publication during the processes of writing and allocation of copyright and IP. The Society's subscription funding model includes access to the journal. Therefore, the SEM leadership feels it is not yet able to proceed to a fully open access model, free to all readers with Internet access. There is also overwhelming support for the retention of a printed version of the journal among SEM membership.[15] Responses to my request for information via the SEM list-serv indicated too, that discussions about open access are occurring among SEM members, especially graduate students and early-career researchers. Responses called for increased use of Internet-based, digital, multimodal approaches to ethnomusicological publishing and advocated for a journal that was open to all readers with an Internet connection. Whilst publications in ethnomusicology

---

13 Nettl, *Thirty-Three Discussions*, pp. 216–18.
14 Anthony McCann, 'All That Is not Given is Lost: Irish Traditional Music, Copyright and Common Property', *Ethnomusicology* 45.1 (2001), 89–106, https://doi.org/10.2307/852635.
15 According to SEM leadership, 78% of respondents to the SEM membership survey indicated they wanted print copies of the journal. However, it was acknowledged that this might change in future and that (research) students undertook all their research digitally. The SEM leadership continues to monitor the situation (personal communication with SEM leadership December 2016–June 2017). I suggest that the demand for digital resources is likely to grow, not decrease, driving a future membership-led need to increase digital, Internet-based tools and multimodal, visually appealing approaches to sharing ethnomusicological learning.

have included images of musicians, instruments and musical notation for quite some time, and cassette tapes and 33-1/3 Long Play records have accompanied texts for decades, the younger generation and open access advocates are lobbying for media that are Internet-based, digital and also free to access via commonly available, freely downloadable software, such as YouTube. Not many ethnomusicological publications however, encapsulate or summarise current ethnomusicological discussion around open access publishing.

Anthropologists have considered the implications of open access more thoroughly. They have explored its influence on scholarly practices and related it back to business models and academic cultures.[16] They have also questioned the desirability of 'openness' from an Indigenous perspective.[17] Additionally, some identified very early on the potential of open access for multimodal presentations of culture and different ways of reading, learning and engaging with knowledge construction.[18]

As I will show below, ethnomusicological and anthropological studies and theory around copyright,[19] archiving[20] authorship and

---

16 Cf. J. B. Jackson and R. Anderson, 'Anthropology and Open Access', *Cultural Anthropology* 29.2 (2014), 236–63, https://doi.org/10.14506/ca29.2.04; C. M. Kelty, M. M. J. Fischer, A. R. Golub, et al., 'Anthropology of/in Circulation: The Future of Open Access and Scholarly Societies', *Cultural Anthropology* 23.3 (2008), 559–88, https://www.jstor.org/stable/20484516

17 K. Christen, 'Does Information Really Want to be Free? Indigenous Knowledge Systems and the Question of Openness', *International Journal of Communication* 6 (2012), 2870–93, https://ijoc.org/index.php/ijoc/article/view/1618

18 A. Howard, 'Hypermedia and the Future of Ethnography', *Cultural Anthropology* 3.3 (1988), 304–15, https://doi.org/10.1525/can.1988.3.3.02a00060

19 A. Seeger, 'Ethnomusicology and Music Law', *Ethnomusicology*, 36.3 (1992), 345–59, https://doi.org/10.2307/851868; A. Seeger and S. Chaudhuri, 'The Contributions for Reconfigured Audiovisual Archives to Sustaining Tradition', *The World of Music. Special Issue on Sound Futures: Exploring Contexts for Music Sustainability*, 4.1 (2015), 21–34; S. Feld, 'Pygmy POP. A Genealogy of Schizophonic Mimesis', *Yearbook for Traditional Music* 28 (1996), 1–35, https://doi.org/10.2307/767805; C. M. Kelty, 'Beyond Copyright and Technology: What Open Access Can Tell Us about Precarity, Authority, Innovation, and Automation in the University Today', *Cultural Anthropology* 29.2 (2014), 203–15, https://doi.org/10.14506/ca29.2.02; S. Mills, 'Indigenous Music and the Law: An Analysis of National and International Legislation', *Yearbook of Traditional Music*, 28 (1996), 57–86, https://doi.org/10.2307/767807; G. Booth, 'Copyright Law and the Changing Economic Value of Popular Music in India', *Ethnomusicology* 59.2 (2015), 262–87, https://doi.org/10.5406/ethnomusicology.59.2.0262

20 A. Seeger, 'Ethnomusicology and Law'; A. Seeger and S. Chaudhuri, 'The Contributions for Reconfigured Audiovisual Archives to Sustaining Tradition'.

writing,[21] 'ownership' of culture[22] and open access[23] are extremely relevant to open access debates. They can help support the formation of an ethical approach to sharing creative practice.

This chapter's contribution is therefore twofold: firstly, it complements other work in this volume by offering an alternative perspective on copyright from a specific discipline, ethnomusicology, and its related discipline, anthropology. By focussing on ethnomusicology's questions of authorship, international copyright, archiving and ethics, I seek to broaden the copyright debate, illustrating how complexities are multiplied when we examine these topics from a cross-cultural, creative perspective. I will argue that ethical sharing and culturally appropriate approaches to open access, authorship and copyright negotiations are required. Ethnomusicologists have an important educative, advocacy role to play in this sphere which can inform the open access movement at large. Secondly, I will be contributing to the body of knowledge within ethnomusicology itself, which has not published on open access in any detail. Consequently, (inter)national open access mandates have, by and large, been generated without ethnomusicological input.[24] It is critical that ethnomusicologists do involve themselves, however, as these mandates

---

21 M. Kisliuk, *Seize the Dance! BaAka Musical Life and Ethnography of Performance* (Oxford: Oxford University Press, 1998); K. Hagedorn, *Divine Utterances: The Performance of Afro-Cuban Santeria* (Washington: Smithsonian Books, 2001); J. Clifford and G. Marcus (eds.), *Writing Culture: The Poetics and Politics of Ethnography* (Berkeley: University of California Press, 1986); G. E. Marcus and M. M. Fischer, *Anthropology as a Cultural Critique*, 2nd ed. (Chicago and London: The University of Chicago Press, 1999); E. Lassiter, C. Ellis and R. Kotay, *The Jesus Road: Kiowas, Christianity, and Indian Hymns* (Lincoln: University of Nebraska Press, 2002); E. Lassiter, H. Goodall, E. Campbell and N. M. Johnson, *The Other Side of Middletown: Exploring Muncie's African American Community* (Walnut Creek: AltaMira Press, 2004); E. Lassiter, 'Collaborative Ethnography and Public Anthropology', *Current Anthropology* 46.1 (2005), 83–106, https://doi.org/10.1086/425658

22 M. F. Brown, *Who Owns Native Culture?* (Cambridge, MA: Harvard University Press, 2003); T. Janke, *Our Culture, Our Future: Report on Australian Cultural and Intellectual Property Rights* (Report for the Australian Institute of Aboriginal and Torres Strait Islander Studies and the Australian and Torres Strait Islander Commission, 1998), http://www.cdu.edu.au/sites/default/files/Our%20culture%20our%20future%20report[2]%20copy.pdf; T. Janke, *Who Owns Story*, presented at Sydney Writers' Festival 2010, http://aiatsis.gov.au/sites/default/files/docs/asp/who-owns-story.pdf.

23 Jackson and Anderson, 'Anthropology and Open Access'; Kelty, Fischer, Golub, et al., 'Anthropology of/in Circulation'.

24 I say 'by and large' because as an ethnomusicologist and research development professional I was involved in the OAPEN-UK monograph project (http://oapen-uk.jiscebooks.org/), contributing to two of their workshops: one in my capacity as an

have significant, sometimes potentially negative, implications for the wellbeing of those they work with as well as ethnomusicological academic practice.[25] The discipline of ethnomusicology has much to offer the open access movement when exploring how copyright and rights to culture intersect. This chapter thus aims to begin a conversation about open access publishing and ethics within ethnomusicology itself, stimulating engagement and thought. It is not designed to be the definitive last word on this subject. Neither are the recommendations made here exhaustive, but they do provide interested colleagues with a starting point.

Open Access: Unity in Diversity

Before going any further, it is useful to briefly outline the nature of open access as a movement and its diversity. There is currently not one definition of open access that is preferred by all stakeholders. The open access movement is extremely diverse. It now includes, for example, librarians, technicians, occasionally traditional publishers and academics from a wide variety of disciplines, including increasingly the arts, humanities and social sciences. The implications of open access for academic, publishing and sharing traditions vary from one discipline to another. Scientists for example, are less concerned with the copyright of creative outputs than arts, humanities and social sciences colleagues as scientists tend not to include the creative outputs of others in scientific publications. Already, there is available a considerable body of literature that focusses on open access, documenting the movement's *raison d'etre* and progress.[26] I therefore need not discuss this here in any detail. Instead, I will restrict myself to examining definitions, hallmarks

---

      ethnomusicological author and early-career researcher and one on Green Open Access monographs as a research development professional.

25 Nettl, *Thirty-Three Discussions*, pp. 218–22.

26 Cf. G. Crossick, 'Monographs and Open Access: A Report to HEFCE. Higher Education Funding Council for England', 2015, https://webarchive.nationalarchives.gov.uk/20180322112445tf_/http://www.hefce.ac.uk/media/hefce/content/pubs/indirreports/2015/Monographs,and,open,access/2014_monographs.pdf; M. Eve, *Open Access in the Arts and Humanities: Contexts, Controversies and the Future* (Cambridge: Cambridge University Press, 2014), https://doi.org/10.1017/CBO9781316161012; K. Fitzpatrick, *Planned Obsolescence: Publishing, Technology and the Future of the Academy* (New York: New York University Press, 2011); P. Suber, *Open Access (the book)* (Cambridge, MA: MIT Press, 2012), https://cyber.harvard.edu/hoap/Open_Access_(the_book)

and the impact of open access on ethnomusicology and how these relate to copyright and authorship.

This chapter also will not delve into the economic minutia of open access publishing or funding mechanisms and their sustainability. Such discussions are peripheral to the subject matter at hand and will only be alluded to briefly when related to, for example, peer reviewing and making ethical writing and publishing choices. Neither should this chapter's discussion on open access be interpreted as being uncritically in agreement with any specific (inter)national policies designed to encourage the implementation of open access publishing and sharing practices. Like Eve I view thinking about publishing (and especially writing) praxis as a form of reflexive critique of academic practice.[27] Specifically, from an ethnomusicological perspective, I would also argue that thinking about how and what we publish allows us to further examine the ways in which we accord particular values to specific modes of knowledge creation and dissemination, whether they be in written formats or audio-visual, creative and practice-based ones. This is especially relevant for a discipline like ethnomusicology, which employs practice research methodologies and champions embodied and non-text-based modes of knowledge creation.

Epistemologies, Definitions of Authorship and Publishing Ethics

Practice research has been embedded within ethnomusicological methodology for many decades. Mantle Hood was the first researcher to develop a performative, embodied approach to ways of knowing in a formal educational setting. He believed that 'the training of ears, eyes, hands and voice and fluency gained in these skills assure a real comprehension of theoretical studies.'[28] As well as writing about the importance of becoming bi-musical[29] (or multi-musical) to gain

---

27　Eve, *Open Access in the Arts and Humanities*, p. 138.
28　Quoted in K. Shelemay, 'The Ethnomusicologist and the Transmission of Tradition', *The Journal of Musicology* 14.1 (1996), 33–51 (p. 37), https://doi.org/10.1525/jm.1996.14.1.03a00020
29　The term bi-musicality was originally coined by Mantle Hood in his 1960 journal article 'The Challenge of "Bi-Musicality"', *Ethnomusicology* 4.2 (1960), 55–59. Hood describes bi-musicality as the ability to fluently perform in more than one musical

cross-cultural musical knowledge, Hood established a university curriculum at UCLA that included native performers as instructors.[30] Although the concept of bi-musicality was first theorised by Hood in 1960, Shelemay points out that well before the concept became established, ethnomusicologists had actively participated in the transmission and perpetuation of musical traditions through performance.[31] John Lomax, for example, during his early studies of cowboy songs and frontier ballads actively fed back song lore into the stream of oral tradition.[32]

Ethnomusicologists have also incorporated anthropological thinking and ethical approaches to fieldwork. Musical experiences, ethnomusicologists say, are influenced by individual musical backgrounds and personal skill, and are often co-created. Musical performance, so ethnomusicologists argue, is also a potent way in which other socio-cultural knowledge is acquired and perpetuated.[33] The logical implication of this reasoning is that creators of music are also creators and performers of (new) socio-cultural as well as musicological knowledge.

Although musical experiences and knowledge are often co-created by the ethnomusicologist and their interlocutors in the field context,[34] it is frequently, (though not always), only the researcher who receives the rights to authorship and later copyright during the publication process of any subsequent ethnographies. This copyright in a written text, which will include the musicological materials of others, is then 'ceded' to a publishing house of choice and the academic subsequently receives a doctorate, promotion, a job or, much more rarely in the arts and

---

tradition, observing that Japanese musicians of the Imperial Household were accomplished in both Japanese Gaguku music and the Western classical tradition (p. 55). Of course, many musicians are fluent in more than two musical traditions, so bi-musical may be best described as multi-musical in some cases.

30   Shelemay, 'The Ethnomusicologist and the Transmission of Tradition', p. 37.
31   Ibid., passim.
32   Ibid., p. 48.
33   Cf. T. Rice, 'Reflections on Music and Identity in Ethnomusicology', *Muzikologjia*, 7 (2007), 17–38, https://doi.org/10.2298/muz0707017r; M. Stokes, *Ethnicity, Identity and Music: The Musical Construction of Place* (London: Berg Publishers, 2010).
34   Fieldwork interlocutors will vary from one context to another. Ethnomusicological fieldwork sites can be close to home or further afield. They need not be remote. There are many ethnomusicologists conducting fieldwork in their own communities and/ or urban areas. The musical materials learnt, performed, studied and historicised nowadays have come to include popular, classical and liturgical music genres amongst others.

humanities, some small royalties for a book's publication.[35] Dynamics between publishers, editors and author(s) and the services and input that editors and publishers provide also raise questions of ownership and authorship. Good editors, reviewers and publishing houses can and do offer significant input in shaping the work of academic authors. Other critical factors in determining how authorship is attributed and royalties disseminated include: the variegated permissions that can or cannot be negotiated with publishing houses in terms of royalty-return to communities and the possible sharing arrangements or owning of copyright; publishing open access; and intellectual property negotiations. Authors are encouraged to explore in advance of signing a contract whether the sharing of royalties is possible and how this is accomplished to ensure it meets the needs of all contributors. With the advent of open access a wealth of economic and licencing models have appeared, some probably based on more sustainable financial models than others. The future will determine which ones succeed, but it would still behove ethnomusicologists to familiarise themselves with the variety of options available and to consider carefully where they publish, if their desire is to share equitably the authorship and possible royalties and licences of their work.

This, I would add, is a state of affairs not uncommon in other disciplines as well, and in part the result of restrictive copyright licensing and conservative academic practices that hamper the decolonisation of the academy, as we will see later. I will explore here how these issues can be examined in new ways through open access publishing practices and new technologies, beginning my discussion by exploring definitions of 'authorship' using Foucault.

Foucault unpacks the definition of what an author is and proposes a broadening of the definition, suggesting that:

> Certainly the author function in painting, music, and other arts should have been discussed, but even supposing that we remain within the world of discourse, as I want to do, I seem to have given the term 'author'

---

35 Cf. P. Torres, 'Interested in Writing about Indigenous Australians?', *Australian Author* 26.3 (1994), 24–25, http://search.informit.com.au/documentSummary;dn=950504428;res=IELAPA; Nettl, *Thirty-Three Discussions*, p. 221; A. Heiss, 'Australian Copyright v/s Indigenous Cultural Property Rights: A Discussion Paper' (Strawberry Hills, Australia: Australian Society of Authors, 2010), https://www.asauthors.org/products/info-papers/australian-copyright-vs-indigenous-intellectual-and-cultural-property-rights

much too narrow a meaning. I have discussed the author only in the limited sense of a person to whom the production of a text, a book, or a work can be legitimately attributed[.][36]

If we define authorship as Foucault has whilst continuing to accord epistemological value to co-created performative and embodied musical experiences and representations thereof, it becomes critical to include ethnomusicological data in our discussions of attribution, copyright and open access.[37] Ethnomusicological data might include musical, photographic, interview-based, audio-visual, and dance-related materials. Since it is often co-created[38] it must be attributable to field interlocutors and therefore they should also receive some share of, for example, a monograph's royalties.

Very seldom, if ever, however, are field interlocutors named as co-authors when they contribute creative outputs and performative knowledge to research texts, for it is this need for 'legitimate attribution', which is influenced by legal, political and economic power structures in Foucauldian terms, which forms the crux of the issue under examination. Interlocutors may receive an acknowledgement and word of 'thanks' and they are nowadays cited and accredited for having helped researchers with their work. However, not many arts and humanities researchers go as far as naming their co-creators as co-authors. Some argue that this is because academic writing is not motivated by monetary gain. Eve (himself a Professor of Literature, Technology and Publishing) references Stevan Harnad (a leading figure in the open access movement) who writes that what makes open access possible:

> is that the economic situation of the academy is different from other spheres of cultural production. Academics are, in Harnad's view,

---

36   Foucault in Rabinow (ed.), *The Foucault Reader*, p. 113.
37   Others have also explored this issue. McQueen (2012) for example, examines film adaptations of literary genres in relation to Foucault's definition. He explores what questions the adaptation process raises for definitions of authorship. S. McQueen, 'Michel Foucault's "What is an Author?" and Adaptation', *COLLOQUY text theory and critique* 24 (2012), 60–77, http://artsonline.monash.edu.au/wp-content/arts-files/colloquy/colloquy_issue_twenty-four_/mcqueen.pdf
38   All forms of scholarship are in fact co-created as Craig, Turcotte, Coombe (2011) have argued in relation to open access and copyright. C. J. Craig, J. F. Turcotte, and R. J. Coombe, 'What's Feminist About Open Access? A Relational Approach to Copyright in the Academy', *feminist@law* 1.1 (2011), 1–35, http://journals.kent.ac.uk/index.php/feministsatlaw/article/view/7

'esoteric' authors whose primary motivation is to be read by peers and the public, rather than to sell their work. While the labour of publishing still needs to be covered (and these costs cannot be denied), this situation potentially enables academics employed at universities to give their work to readers for free; this specific subset of researchers are paid a salary, rather than earning a living by selling their specialist outputs[.][39]

Whilst Harnad and Eve view esoteric authorship practices and motivations as an economic opportunity for open access, these same esoteric publishing practices are also a double-edged sword. Researchers may not publish for money, but they do gain other benefits, unlike their interlocutors.[40]

This fact has been acknowledged by anthropologists. Some, such as Lassiter, in attempting to redress the balance, have collaboratively co-authored texts with their interlocutors. Lassiter painstakingly read and wrote alongside his Native and African American interlocutors to create texts that would both fulfil the requirements of scholarly rigour and address issues of authorship attribution and representation. Lassiter has described and problematized the various forms that collaborative ethnography might take. The last form of collaborative ethnography Lassiter mentions is that of co-authorship:

> Collaboratively written texts can take a variety of forms. Ethnographers and their interlocutors bring diverse skills and experience to any given ethnographic project. While all collaborative ethnography is arguably *coauthored*, not all collaborative ethnography can be *cowritten* (Hinson 1999) [...].[41] In other coauthored collaborative texts, consultants have had an even more direct role in the writing of the text, contributing their own writings. In 'The Other Side of Middletown,' some consultants responded to the students' chapter drafts by presenting texts of their own, which the students then integrated into their chapters (see, e.g., Lassiter et al. 2004: 186–87).[42]

---

39 M. Eve, *Open Access in the Arts and Humanities*.
40 Cf. Torres, 'Interested in Writing about Indigenous Australians?', p. 25 and Nettl, *Thirty Three Discussions*, p. 221.
41 G. Hinson, '"You've Got to Include an Invitation": Engaged Reciprocity and Negotiated Purpose in Collaborative Ethnography', paper presented at the 98th annual meeting of the American Anthropological Association, Chicago, Illinois, November 1999.
42 Luke E. Lassiter, 'Collaborative Ethnography and Public Anthropology', *Current Anthropology* 46.1 (2005), 83–106 (p. 96), https://doi.org/10.1086/425658; the quoted reference is to Luke E. Lassiter, H. Goodall, E. Campbell and N. M. Johnson, *The*

Using Field's anthropological work as an example, Lassiter acknowledges that written co-authorship may not suit all working relationships between anthropologists and their field interlocutors. Field felt that the 'experiment in co-authorship is nothing if not fraught with contradictions and dangers'.[43] He candidly acknowledged:

> I have not individually listed these Nicaraguans as coauthors of the book, because that would misrepresent how the book was written. I organized, edited, conceptualized, and wrote the vast majority of this book, and I claim its overall authorship. On the other hand, I have tried to navigate a blurry middle ground between treating the essays written by my friends as rich ethnographic material, with which I can support my own points, and handling them as I would a text written by another academic.[44]

Lassiter[45] uses this point to argue that co-authorship is dependent on linguistic, training and power differences and relationships between researchers and their interlocutors. He shows though, how anthropologists, at least, are willing to consider co-authorship options.

Ethnomusicologists, who draw heavily on anthropological theory, have followed suit at least in terms of adapting their approaches to writing in order to more accurately capture musical experience, whilst acknowledging that musical experience is co-created. The work of anthropologists Clifford and Marcus[46] and Marcus and Fischer[47] has been influential. These authors argue for an interpretive anthropology, providing the context for addressing the so-called crisis of representation within the discipline. This crisis emerged due to postmodern critiques of the ethnographic genre. It embraced feminist, humanistic, symbolic and cognitive anthropology — all of which had variously struggled with objectivity and experimented with the limitations of the ethnographic craft in representing the lived complexities of culture and experience from the 'native point of view'. As performers and academics, ethnomusicologists co-create

---

Other Side of Middletown: Exploring Muncie's African American Community (Walnut Creek: AltaMira Press, 2004), pp. 186–87.
43   L. Field, *The Grimace of Macho Ratón: Artisans, Identity, and Nation in Late-Twentieth-Century Western Nicaragua* (Durham, N.C.: Duke University Press, 1999), p. 20.
44   Field, *The Grimace of Macho Ratón*, p. 20, in Lassiter, 'Collaborative Ethnography', p. 96.
45   Lassiter, 'Collaborative Ethnography'.
46   Clifford and Marcus (eds.), *Writing Culture*.
47   Marcus and Fischer, *Anthropology as a Cultural Critique*.

and record music and knowledge and some also co-author works with their field interlocutors. Kisliuk[48] and Hagedorn[49] have experimented with poetic and creative writing styles to capture the nature of musical co-creation and in Hagedorn's case trance-like musical experiences, which are difficult to convey in standard academic prose. Co-authorship in a written form is employed in Barney's 2014 selection of essays,[50] which includes several co-authored chapters examining applied ethnomusicological research approaches with Indigenous Australians. In my own work, I have woven Indigenous Australian written questionnaire responses into the narrative of performative choral experiences in a prison and an Indigenous rehabilitation centre (Swijghuisen Reigersberg),[51] whilst Araújo,[52] when he was unable to list all his student-colleagues as authors and co-producers of knowledge on the publisher's header, made a point to add an extensive footnote explaining that the text was collaboratively produced. Others, such as Diamond,[53] acknowledged other scholars for their editorial and intellectual input into her chapter on Indigenous knowledge and intellectual property.

Ethical guidelines are also provided by specific learned societies and organisations, which recommend that researchers carefully consider how they manage and negotiate their authorship attributions. The American Anthropological Association's (AAA) ethical code of conduct[54] reads:

---

48   M. Kisliuk, *Seize the Dance! BaAka Musical Life and Ethnography of Performance* (Oxford: Oxford University Press, 1998).
49   K. Hagedorn, *Divine Utterances: The Performance of Afro-Cuban Santeria* (Washington: Smithsonian Books, 2001).
50   K. Barney (ed.), *Collaborative Ethnomusicology: New Approaches to Music Research between Indigenous and Non-Indigenous Australians* (Melbourne: Lyrebird Press, 2014).
51   M. E. Swijghuisen Reigersberg, 'Choral Singing and the Construction of Australian Aboriginal Identities: An Applied Ethnomusicological Study in Hopevale, Northern Queensland, Australia' (unpublished doctoral thesis, University of Surrey, Roehampton University, 2009).
52   S. Araújo, 'Conflict and Violence as Theoretical Tools in Present-Day Ethnomusicology: Notes on a Dialogic Ethnography of Sound Practices in Rio de Janeiro', *Ethnomusicology* 50.2 (2006), 287–313.
53   B. Diamond, A. Corn, F. Fjleheim, et al., 'Performing Protocol: Indigenous Traditional Knowledge as/and Intellectual Property', in J. C. Post (ed.), *Ethnomusicology: A Contemporary Reader*, vol. 2 (New York and London: Routledge, 2017), pp. 17–34.
54   AAA Ethics Forum, 'Principles of Professional Responsibility' (2012), http://ethics.americananthro.org/category/statement/

> Anthropologists have an ethical obligation to consider the potential impact of both their research and the communication or dissemination of the results of their research […]. Explicit negotiation with research partners and participants about data ownership and access and about dissemination of results, may be necessary before deciding whether to begin research.

The ethical guidelines of the Australian Institute of Aboriginal and Torres Strait Islander Studies (AIATSIS) state that researchers must:

> Ensure familiarity with laws, administrative arrangements and other developments relevant to Indigenous traditional knowledge and cultural expressions as well as intellectual property rights. Include attention to actual and/or potential implications of digitisation on research processes and outputs.
>
> Discuss co-ownership of intellectual property, including co-authorship of published and recorded works and performances, shared copyright, future management of the resources collected, and proper attribution and notices.[55]

An example of policy addressing the ethical and legal recommendations covering ownership, IP and copyright is the United Nations' 2007 *Declaration on the Rights of Indigenous Peoples*, Article 31:[56]

> Indigenous people have the right to maintain, control and develop their cultural heritage, traditional knowledge and traditional cultural expressions, as well as the manifestations of their sciences, technologies and cultures, including human and genetic resources, seeds, medicines, knowledge of the properties of fauna and flora, oral traditions, literatures, designs, sport and traditional games and visual and performing arts. They also have the right to maintain, control, protect and develop their intellectual property over such cultural heritage, traditional knowledge, and traditional cultural expressions.

Independent organisations such as the UK Research Integrity Office (UKRIO) have also acknowledged in their *Code of Practice for Research*[57]

---

55 Australian Institute of Torres Strait Islander Studies, *Guidelines for Ethical Research in Australian Indigenous Studies* (2012), http://aiatsis.gov.au/sites/default/files/docs/research-and-guides/ethics/gerais.pdf, p. 6.
56 United Nations (UN), *Declaration on the Rights of Indigenous Peoples* (2007), https://www.un.org/development/desa/indigenouspeoples/wp-content/uploads/sites/19/2018/11/UNDRIP_E_web.pdf, pp. 22–23.
57 UKRIO, 'Code of Practice for Research' (2009), http://ukrio.org/publications/code-of-practice-for-research/

that negotiations with international colleagues should be approached paying particular attention to variances in national laws and social protocol. UKRIO specify that researchers should aim to seek agreement on intellectual property, publication and the attribution of authorship early on, whilst acknowledging that the roles and contributions of researchers may evolve over the course of research projects. They recommend that all sources of knowledge are systematically acknowledged and that researchers should seek the necessary permissions if significant portions of another person's work are used. UKRIO's guidance also stipulates that all people listed as an author should be prepared to take a public responsibility for the accuracy of a published piece of work (UKRIO Ethical Guidelines sections 3.5.1 to 3.15.7).

These generic UKRIO guidelines, designed for consideration at UK research active organisations, offer no prescriptive methods as aids to determining the value and nature of authorship contributions, and refer regularly to 'published' work as written work, not making allowances for other creative outputs. UKRIO's *Code of Practice for Research* also operates using Western concepts of copyright law. It may not be possible for field interlocutors and potential co-authors to publicly vouch for the accuracy of the knowledge created about them, as they might not be able to access it. It is clear however, that the attribution of authorship rights is an important practice that has ethical, legal and practical implications, some of which can be explored through open access publishing and new technologies.

New Technologies, Open Access and the Potential for Increased Equity

Open access writing, publishing and peer reviewing methods have the potential to inform these practical and ethical considerations in a way that is better suited to recording the contributions made by field interlocutors and the inclusion of non-Western epistemological processes. Where co-authorship is concerned, open access offers interesting technological opportunities for innovation, which may help authors explore attribution rights and how they are awarded. New software such as Authorea[58] is making it possible to track co-author interventions electronically. The

---

58 https://www.authorea.com/

software logs different author contributions and revisions, allows for real-time communication with co-authors and can be used to resolve authorship disagreements. The Authorea system retains no ownership of the authors' copyright or data and could be used where interlocutors are able to contribute to academic writing and editing. However, copyright and licensing may impact on the collaboration, as the system operates under the local copyright law of the author, which might be problematic if musical materials are owned by a group of people or music is conceived of as a social currency that should not be indiscriminately shared, as we shall see later. The system is also predominantly geared towards scientific journal publishing and not set up to handle multimedia well. The free account only allows users to work on 1 article and offers 100 MB of file space, which might not be useful for larger audio-visual files. So, whilst Authorea can facilitate co-authorship, it might not work well for multimodal approaches.

Figshare[59] is better for sharing audio-visual data and offers opportunities for collaborative writing and content sharing. The platform deals well with larger files and arts and humanities outputs, allowing for a variety of formats and 5GB files to be uploaded, as well as 20GB for private storage space on free individual accounts. This allowance will facilitate the uploading of single, short samples of musical material for journal articles and papers, the average length of a short four-minute audio recording being about 10MB. The Music Archive at Monash University in Australia, for example, has used the system to upload some Indonesian gamelan music collected by Kartomi in 1983.[60] Copyright licencing, again, proves problematic in that all works are managed under EU copyright and UK laws. Figshare also only allows for CC-BY and CC0 Creative Commons licences,[61] which

---

59 https://figshare.com/about
60 Margaret Kartomi, 'Field trip Liwa 1983 — Sound recordings — Gamolan Excerpt' (1983), https://figshare.com/articles/Field_trip_Liwa_1983_Sound_recordings_Gamolan_Excerpt/2001246
    In this example, however, we are not given sufficient metadata about the recording in Figshare to tell us about the contributing artists, so if ethnomusicologists are to use Figshare it would be advisable to offer more metadata about the recording before sharing.
61 Creative Commons licenses provide a simple standardized way for individual creators, companies and institutions to share their work with others on flexible terms without infringing copyright. The licenses allow users to reuse, remix and share the content legally. Work offered under a Creative Commons license does

facilitate free sharing and reuse without remuneration to the creators of musical works. This may not always be appropriate where musical performance forms part of a musician's regular livelihood.

Some journal publishing systems allow for open peer review, recording information about the comments made about and amendments made to texts. For example, Fitzpatrick, a leading thinker on publishing technologies who questions the anti-collaborative nature of arts and humanities research, experimented with online peer review and made her text available through CommentPress[62] (a WordPress[63] Plugin), before having it published by New York University Press.[64] She found this process to be helpful. Fitzpatrick obtained the types of feedback she needed to improve her text, whilst having a record of the comments received and her responses to them. She acknowledges, however, that the software formatting was time consuming and that the need to rapidly respond to comments requires authors to be electronically connected on an ongoing basis. The system is also most effective when there is a pre-existing interested, knowledgeable community available willing to offer useful and constructive advice. Systems such as CommentPress, Figshare or Authorea may therefore not suit field interlocutors who, for example, have no access to the Internet, are unfamiliar with digital tools, do not write, or are not proficient in the language or disciplinary jargon used by the academic writer. However, this type of electronic approach facilitates the tracking of multiple contributions to texts, making the valuable input of good editors, reviewers, collaborators and field interlocutors more visible. This in turn can inform the attribution

---

        not remove copyright from the author. Instead it permits users to make use of digital materials in a variety of ways, under certain conditions, determined by the type of license: http://creativecommons.org.au/learn/licences/. As early as 2001, McCann explored aspects of Common Property theory and their implications for discussions around copyright, Irish traditional music and definitions of musical gifting, ownership and sharing practices, whilst Diamond et al. (2017) also discuss the sharing and gifting of song as social practice among Native American communities. A. McCann, 'All That Is Not Given is Lost: Irish Traditional Music, Copyright and Common Property', *Ethnomusicology* 45.1 (2001), 89–106, https://doi.org/10.2307/852635; D. Diamond, A. Corn, F. Fjleheim, et al., 'Performing Protocol: Indigenous Traditional Knowledge as/and Intellectual Property', in J. C. Post (ed.), *Ethnomusicology: A Contemporary Reader*, vol. 2 (New York and London: Routledge, 2017), pp. 17–34 (pp. 27–28).

62   www.futureofthebook.org/commentpress
63   https://wordpress.com/
64   Fitzpatrick, *Planned Obsolescence*, pp. 109–20.

of authorship rights and offer insights into how new knowledge is created and interpreted in culturally specific ways. They are also not the only systems available.

Others, which may be useful to some researchers, could include Annotation Studio,[65] a student-centred project led by MIT, which allows for the electronic and critical reading and annotation of texts and the formation of discussions. Another platform, Scalar,[66] seeks to close the gap between scholarly publishing and digital visual archives by enabling researchers to work more organically with archival materials. Scalar seeks to create interpretive pathways through archival materials such as video and sound recordings, enabling new forms of analysis. Each system however, will have its strengths and weaknesses. Researchers should carefully explore what these are before deciding on their suitability in the context of their own research projects. As scholars in the digital humanities have suggested more broadly, rather than debating 'who is in and who is out' we should instead ask how the creation and deployment of digital tools perform distinct, but equally useful functions in the analysis of research data, writing and materials.[67]

Additionally, a note of caution is warranted. As with the new financial models being developed and trialled to support open access publishing initiatives, it is by no means certain that all new technologies supporting co-authorship or open access publishing will prove to be sustainable or long-lived. This may therefore jeopardise the continued access that researchers and interlocutors need. Technological obsolescence is a real challenge for publishers, archivists, librarians and researchers alike. Researchers would do well to familiarise themselves with, for example, the LOCKSS system (Lots of Copies Keeps Stuff Safe — system),[68] a low cost, open source, digital preservation tool designed by Stanford University that provides persistent access to digital content. The rate of technological change makes the threat of obsolescence very real and must be factored in to any publishing or sharing choice.

That said; open access and new technologies provide us with new means to explore the structuring of academic 'texts' so that these reflect

---

65 http://www.annotationstudio.org/project/background/
66 https://scalar.me/anvc/about/
67 L. F. Klein and M. K. Gold, 'Digital Humanities: The Expanded Field' (2016), http://dhdebates.gc.cuny.edu/debates
68 https://www.lockss.org/

the epistemological pathways of our field interlocutors. As early as 1988 Howard, for example, proposed that the inclusion of hypermedia would make it possible to remove the hierarchical structuring of texts such as chapters, subsections, and paragraphs. Instead he suggests that ethnographers generate an elaborate series of digital knowledge networks, which readers can enter at any point to explore their own interests.[69] Some of these networked journeys could be structured using multimodal formats so that they reflect the epistemological journeys and experiences of field interlocutors, facilitating comparisons and promoting experiential understanding. In this way, open access and digital approaches to creation, writing, structuring, publishing and peer review could become related to a social science method called triangulation or inter/ intra-cultural feedback, in which experts and field interlocutors discuss and interpret the new information gathered, which, in the case of ethnomusicologists, includes recorded musical practices and cultural customs as well as written texts. Others have already commenced exploring applied anthropological approaches, such as Gubrium and Harper.[70] Employing these methods, when they are appropriate and workable, I argue, will make for a more equitable, decolonised academe.

To summarise then, open access and new technologies make it possible to capture authorship contributions, but all have their limitations. It is advisable that ethnomusicologists interested in exploring collaborative authorship and ethical sharing familiarise themselves with the terms and conditions of any platform vis-à-vis platform sustainability, copyright, intellectual property and data ownership before deciding whether to use a specific digital tool. New technologies provide a means for supporting the accreditation of non-academic contributors and allow us to rethink the ways in which knowledge is created and constructed in culturally and person-specific ways. This is desirable because it addresses the need to remedy the power imbalances that still inherently exist in the academic enterprise, namely that: (a) field interlocutors often cannot access or comment on the knowledge that is created about them; (b) academic authors receive (in)direct monetary rewards for publishing materials

---

69 Howard, 'Hypermedia and the Future of Ethnography', pp. 308–09.
70 A. Gubrium and K. Harper, 'Visualizing Change: Participatory Digital Technologies in Research and Action', *Practising Anthropology* 31.4 (2009), 2–4, https://doi.org/10.17730/praa.31.4.t6w103r320507394

based on the (creative) knowledge provided by field interlocutors, which are not always shared; and (c) the new knowledge created about field interlocutors may not accurately reflect Indigenous epistemologies and experiences.[71] Whilst, theoretically, researchers have been aware of these ethical problems for some time and guidelines do exist to promote ethical approaches to publishing and attribution, various practices have hampered the decolonisation of the academy, including conservative publishing and peer review practices, citation metrics and publisher hierarchies, and a focus on arbitrary and inaccurate assessments of 'research excellence' rather than equity.[72] As I have shown, however, electronic co-creation and co-authorship are not always possible or for that matter ethically desirable, depending on the nature of the research enquiry. There is also another matter that considerably complicates open sharing: copyright.

Copyright, Open Access and Ethnomusicology

Copyright remains a contentious issue in the dissemination of cultural, musical and other creative knowledge.[73] It is intimately tied to ethical questions that touch on rights to cultural ownership, group ownership and co-creation (cf. Diamond et al. 2017). Copyright negotiations are affected by differences that exist between cultural sharing practices globally, some of which stipulate that free and open sharing might not be appropriate since they impact on an academic's ability to publish certain content in open access formats, especially if they are

---

71 Cf. L. Tuhiwai Smith, *Decolonizing Methodologies: Research and Indigenous Peoples*, 2nd ed. (London: Zed Books, 2012); M. Nakata, *Disciplining the Savages: Savaging the Disciplines* (Canberra: Aboriginal Studies Press, 2007); N. Pearson, '"Ngamu-ngaadyarr, Muuri-bunggaga and Midha Mini" Guugu Yimidhirr History (Dingoes, Sheep and Mr Muni in Guugu Yimidhirr History). Hope Vale Lutheran Mission 1900–1950' (unpublished bachelor's dissertation, University of Sydney, History Department, 1986); B. Brabec de Mori, 'What Makes Natives Unique? Overview of Knowledge Systems among the World's Indigenous People', *Taiwan Journal of Indigenous Studies* 8 (2016), 43–61.

72 Cf. S. Moore, C. Neylon, and M. Eve, et al., 'Excellence R Us: University Research and the Fetishisation of Excellence', *Palgrave Communications* 3 (2017), 2–13, https://doi.org/10.1057/palcomms.2016.105; J. Wilsdon, L. Allen, E. Belfiore, et al., *The Metric Tide: Report of the Independent Review of the Role of Metrics in Research Assessment and Management* (2015), https://doi.org/10.13140/RG.2.1.4929.1363.

73 Cf. R. Coombe, *The Cultural Life of Intellectual Properties: Authorship, Appropriation and the Law* (Durham, N.C. and London: Duke University Press, 1998).

multimodal.[74] Careful consideration needs to be given on a case-by-case basis to how copyright issues and the sharing of cultural content are approached and negotiated. The Crossick report on open access monograph publishing states that 'the fact that monographs in a significant number of disciplines depend on reproducing, analysing and building upon existing material, such as images and musical quotations, which are covered by copyright means that the challenges to open access publishing have for some seemed insuperable.'[75] whilst Diamond et al. explored how Indigenous native American communities distinguished between collective ownership and individual authorship where the rights of both are not perceived as conflicting in nature.[76]

This need for caution when sharing knowledge is where anthropologists, folklorists and ethnomusicologists have most to contribute to the open access movement. The importance of sharing ethically and perhaps, therefore, selectively is not always fully understood by other open access supporters, some of whom lobby for the open sharing of all academic content, including data, especially in the sciences. Given that many open access treaties and statements are based on scientific approaches to and preferences for sharing, this blanket 'openness' requires careful examination. The 2003 *Berlin Declaration on Open Access to Knowledge in the Sciences and Humanities*,[77] for example, states that holders of cultural heritage should be encouraged to support open access by providing their resources on the Internet. In some cases, however, the secret, sacred, community-owned or copyrighted nature of musical data makes it ethically inappropriate to share widely. Free and open sharing has, in some cases, promoted the exploitative appropriation of Indigenous cultural heritage, whereby Western artists gained large sums of money through sampling open access materials in their new work, without offering recompense to the originating

---

74 Cf. Christen, 'Does Information Really Want to be Free?'.
75 This report was commissioned by the Higher Education Funding Council for England (HEFCE) and in partnership with the Arts and Humanities and Economic and Social Research Councils (AHRC and ESRC) to help inform national open access agendas and policies (2015), p. 10, https://webarchive.nationalarchives.gov.uk/20180322112445tf_/http://www.hefce.ac.uk/media/hefce/content/pubs/indirreports/2015/Monographs,and,open,access/2014_monographs.pdf
76 Diamond, Corn, Fjleheim, et al., 'Performing Protocol', p. 22.
77 'Berlin Declaration on Open Access to Knowledge in the Sciences and Humanities' (2003), https://openaccess.mpg.de/Berlin-Declaration

community. I shall provide some examples of these practices below and I shall also offer some Indigenous responses to this.

Some open access statements acknowledge the problematic nature of copyright law and state that attributions will not be governed by it, such as the Bethesda Statement 2003 on open access. The Statement stipulates that 'Community standards, rather than copyright law, will continue to provide the mechanism for enforcement of proper attribution and responsible use of the published work, as they do now'.[78] This however, can be difficult to negotiate because copyright legislation is not always attuned to cross-cultural understandings of sharing and ownership. Who becomes 'the community' by which we must set our standards? Is it the academic community or that of the field interlocutor's? What if this community is not in agreement either about how academic attributions should be managed? How do we negotiate potential disputes, which might be difficult to resolve, using the Euro- and Western-centric notions of ownership and concepts of artistry that do not allow for there to be multiple copyright holders?[79] Royalties and proceeds might be shared, but copyright may not.

To acknowledge the complex and sensitive nature of sharing knowledge responsibly, many ethical guidelines and UNESCO's 2005 *Convention on the Protection and Promotion of Diversity of Cultural Expression*[80] refer to some of the challenges that communities face in relation to new technologies and the sharing of their heritage in ways that are equitable. UNESCO's Convention states that processes of globalization have facilitated the rapid sharing of information and development of new technologies, but that this brings with it certain challenges for cultural diversity. Imbalances in wealth impact on people's ability to engage with new technologies and may reduce their resources to combat the misappropriation of their cultural heritage.[81]

---

78 'Bethesda Statement on Open Access Publishing' (2003), http://legacy.earlham.edu/~peters/fos/bethesda.htm

79 Diamond et al. also observe that ethnomusicologists' studies of Indigenous performing protocol can have use beyond the academy, allowing for shifts in frameworks and conversations that better align with the efforts of Indigenous scholars who are working to define the best strategies for cultural resurgence ('Performing Protocol', p. 20).

80 UNESCO, 'Convention on the Protection and Promotion of the Diversity of Cultural Expressions (mul)' (2005), http://unesdoc.unesco.org/images/0014/001429/142919e.pdf

81 See also Nettl, *Thirty Three Discussions*.

The American Anthropological Association (AAA) also notes that sometimes limitations on dissemination may be appropriate. In some cases, in fact, preventing dissemination might be the most ethical option.[82] I shall now explore how ethnomusicologists and other creative artists have documented and theorised these issues and refer to the inclusion of creative materials in written texts and authorship.

In his 1996 article, Feld explores how ethnomusicological recordings, deemed not to be under copyright but within the public domain, were used to generate multi-million-dollar recordings for which the originating communities received no or very little compensation.[83] A striking example was that of the eponymous album *Deep Forest*, released in 1992. The album featured digitally sampled, mixed sounds from ethnographic materials recorded in a variety of African locations as performed by pygmy communities. Some samples were part of ethnomusicological research undertaken by Simha Arom. Apart from the album itself being hugely successful, the disco-dance artists also received income through licensing for television commercials, which advertised big brands such as Sony, The Body Shop, and Porsche. Whilst a small portion of the album's proceeds went to the Pygmy Fund, further scrutiny revealed that in fact the monies were sent to a pygmy community whose music was not sampled on the successful album.[84] This example has meant that some ethnomusicologists have become cautious about openly sharing creative outputs provided by their field interlocutors, which impacts on their willingness to engage with open access formats.

Cultural and creative artefacts may also have great non-monetary significance. In the Australian Aboriginal culture, for example, Janke asks: 'Who owns story?'[85] She argues that traditional Indigenous stories help shape local identities. They have been part of an oral tradition that communicates knowledge about ways of life, including food collection and preparation, knowledge of healing plants and kinship patterns. To Indigenous people these stories contain vital information about

---

82   AAA Ethics Forum, 'Principles of Professional Responsibility'.
83   Feld, 'Pygmy POP.'.
84   Ibid., p. 26. For further examples also see Mills, 'Indigenous Music and the Law'.
85   This reference is an excerpt from *Who Owns Story*, by Terri Janke presented at Sydney Writers Festival in 2010. It is copyrighted and reproduced with kind permission of the author by the Australian Institute of Torres Strait Islander Studies (AIATSIS), https://aiatsis.gov.au/sites/default/files/docs/asp/who-owns-story.pdf.

understanding their place in the world and how to survive, sometimes quite literally. Not all stories are secular, and all are a currency of a kind: 'the title deeds to a culture'. Indigenous clans have ownership of particular stories under Indigenous custom. The right to tell stories and to tap into specific histories, locations, connections and people is an Indigenous cultural right. Many of these stories also have affiliated musical, painting and dance genres, which allow for sacred stories to be performed into being, honouring Country and kin.[86] The wide and indiscriminate sharing of this material through open access may not be culturally appropriate or ethical. Once in a monograph, it may also be legally 'owned' by a publisher under copyright law, depending on contract stipulations. Authors should make it a habit to cross check what the copyright arrangements for their preferred publisher are to ensure these meet the needs of all contributors.

Janke goes on to list several areas where she has identified Western European copyright laws are incommensurate with oral Indigenous practices of creation, concepts of ownership and spirituality. Firstly, she suggests that stories do not meet the material form requirement of the Copyright Act, which stipulates that the person who writes down a story into material form owns the copyright and the expression of that story. In the case of oral Indigenous stories, there is no legal requirement to get the prior informed consent of a 'story owner' to write their story. Secondly, the finite nature of copyright protection is problematic. It does not take into consideration the antiquity of Indigenous stories, which places them outside copyright and therefore in the public domain, opening them up to free use. Consequently, copyright laws do not protect sacred stories from being published. Under Indigenous customary laws, however, the unauthorised dissemination of sacred or secret knowledge to the uninitiated is a serious breach of cultural laws and in some cases deemed harmful or hurtful. Janke then points out that 'without copyright, there are no moral rights of attribution or integrity'. These moral rights are especially important in Indigenous

---

86 Cf. F. Dussart, *The Politics of Ritual in an Aboriginal Settlement: Kinship, Gender and the Currency of Knowledge* (Washington: Smithsonian Institution Press, 2005); A. Grau, 'Sing a Dance, Dance a Song: The Relationship between Two Types of Formalised Movements and Music Among the Tiwi of Melville and Bathurst Islands, North Australia', *Dance Research: The Journal of the Society for Dance Research* 1.2 (1983), 32–44, https://doi.org/10.2307/1290759; A. Marett, *Songs, Dreamings, and Ghosts: The Wangga of North Australia* (Middletown: Wesleyan University Press, 2005).

communities, where ownership rights are communal. This brings us to the problem that copyright acknowledges the rights of individuals without recognising that stories are collectively owned by the family or community and told and retold for the benefit of future generations.[87] The same is true for other creative outputs generated by and with Indigenous people in Australia such as music, dance and painting.[88]

Whilst in cases such as those in Aboriginal Australia copyright is problematic and directly opposes Indigenous sharing practices, other countries have implemented approaches that engage with copyright debates in culturally specific ways. In her 1996 article[89] for example, Mills shows how, at least in 1996, Senegal nationalized its traditional music to protect it, whilst Brazil embraced the concept of 'cultural self-determination', surrendering control over the music to the originating communities. In the final section of her work she examines what laws and protections exist that deal with traditional music, concluding that such international legislation is very rare. Where it does exist, it usually indicates that it is an individual country's responsibility to determine the laws they deem appropriate. This has not changed significantly since 1996. However, Indigenous activism has led in 2009 to the establishment of the Intergovernmental Committee on Intellectual Property and Genetic Resources, Traditional Knowledge and Folklore in 2009, under the auspices of the World Intellectual Property Organization (WIPO).[90] This committee includes in its remit all traditional forms of creativity, oral history and folklore and seeks to 'protect traditional remedies and indigenous art and music against misappropriation, and enable communities to control and benefit collectively from their commercial exploitation.'[91] Within ethnomusicological and folkloric discussions the jury is still out on whether the copyrighting and prescriptive ownership of intellectual property and culture is desirable. Titon, in his blog on the commonwealth of culture, suggests that historically the discipline of folklore studies lends weight to the argument that nobody must 'own' culture if we are to steward it appropriately. He observes, however, that

---

87 Janke, *Who Owns Story*, p. 2.
88 Cf. Janke, *Our Culture, Our Future*.
89 Mills, 'Indigenous Music and the Law'.
90 See WIPO's pages, https://www.wipo.int/tk/en/igc/
91 Reporting on the progress of this committee and their actual impact is beyond the scope of this chapter but would be worth further attention in future.

folklorists are very much involved in international efforts to propertise culture in seeking to protect it:

> But thinking of culture as intellectual property, and thinking of groups as possessing cultural rights in this property, while it may seem attractive in the short run, is a losing strategy in the long term, for by putting a price on expressive culture it degrades and transforms it into commodity, thereby furthering the mistaken project of economic rationality.[92]

This then brings us to ask: What of academic publishing, which includes musical materials by more than one author or often, not always, will ask that authors relinquish their copyright to the publisher? These recent developments and international variances in the copyright laws of music have not yet been absorbed into standard academic publishing, policy and ethical considerations on open access, but should be as they have bearing on how and where academics decide to publish and inform decisions on whether open access is the best format or not.

It is to the areas of copyright and responsible sharing then, that researchers, open access publishers, archives, archivists, librarians and data managers might wish to pay special attention. Whilst the Creative Commons licences offer a variety of options for sharing works and are designed to deter inappropriate use of creative and other works online, the licences do not technologically prevent the sampling of digital data. Creative Commons licences allow authors to indicate via logos how they would like their work to be shared. Some licences are very restrictive and do not allow sharing or duplication, even if the work is correctly attributed to authors. Technologically however, it is still possible to copy and replicate the digital data. The licence icons offer no digital protection against data mining. Additionally, it is not possible to entirely prevent inappropriate sampling altogether, without there being a reduction in openness. To complicate matters, with sharing mandates being implemented by research funders, governments, and institutions, it is becoming increasingly likely that research information and data of creative kinds will be handled, managed and stored by non-experts who may not be trained in the variances in sharing practice across the world. To conclude then, I will suggest a few ways in which the open access community might engage with these debates, taking on board some of the ethnomusicological and anthropological thinking.

---

92 Titon, 'The Commonwealth of Culture'.

Conclusion: Suggested Ways of Engagement

To share ethically it is necessary that the sector become more attuned to the cultural sensitivities around sharing creative practice and how these differ from one community and person to another. Researchers should actively collaborate with specialist archivists[93] university librarians, funders and publishers to ensure that ethical guidelines, reporting requirements and dissemination mandates allow for sensitive sharing practices. They must also proactively inform themselves and their students about what technologies are able to offer and what their shortfalls might be. It should become commonplace for funders and policymakers to consider these matters carefully and in consultation with researchers by designing sensitive data management and dissemination protocols and expectations that cater to a variety of disciplines, including the arts, humanities and social sciences. Whilst this is already occurring in the UK with, for example, the Research Councils UK's Concordat on Open Research Data[94] much still needs to be done at a local, practical level to ensure the recommendations in Concordats such as these are implemented.

Researchers should be encouraged to consider and discuss allocating authorship to creative practitioners and Indigenous contributors when publishing. In some cases, contributors may be able to acquire ORCIDs[95] and creative outputs can be stamped with digital object identifier (DOI) numbers, to help digitally cement the links between authors and digital objects, where this is appropriate. Metadata records could also be created and maintained to show which researchers are linked to which DOI numbers. This may allow for some discoverability options and accreditation even if copyright is prohibitive. Where open access models are being explored, copyright in audio-visual files, images and song texts etc. can be carefully negotiated and levels of openness

---

93   Cf. Seeger, 'Ethnomusicology and Law'; Seeger and Chaudhuri, 'The Contributions for Reconfigured Audiovisual Archives to Sustaining Tradition'.
94   Research Councils UK, *Concordat on Open Research Data* (2016), https://www.ukri. org/files/legacy/documents/concordatonopenresearchdata-pdf/
95   www.orcid.org: ORCID provides persistent digital identifiers that distinguish individual researchers from one another. Through their integration in key research workflows such as manuscript and grant submissions, ORCID supports automated linkages between researchers and their professional activities, ensuring their work is recognized.

agreed before, during and after the research process. This can ensure that all parties involved are aware of the economies of scale involved and the implications of the methods used. (Ethno)musicologists, legal and digital experts might combine forces with economists and publishers to explore Nettl's 'econo-musicologies' to investigate the relative social and financial cost of open access musical sharing practices internationally. This process will require that researchers familiarise themselves with open access options and that institutions, funding bodies and government organisations find ways to support this through infrastructure, funding, staff training and development. Learning opportunities will be time consuming and resource intensive as well as influenced by local, financial, and other priorities, but if such opportunities can be made available, they will be worthwhile from an equity perspective at the very least

Funders might carefully consider whether mandating open access is always appropriate ethically and journals should explore whether in some cases academic retention of copyright and intellectual property rights to their data during the publishing process may be preferable if Indigenous or other collaborators are involved. Some researchers may also like to consider collaborating with organisations such as WIPO to help inform debates on copyright legislation. This may speed up positive legislative change, promoting equity.

Researchers, institutions and publishers may wish to critically review their overreliance on outmoded peer reviewing practices and consider innovating through technologies that allow creative practitioners and/ or Indigenous contributors to have an input into the writing and editorial processes where this is ethically appropriate and practically possible. In turn, less emphasis might be placed on the production of single-authored manuscripts in the arts and humanities for promotion purposes. Instead the concept of research 'soundness' might be more appropriate.[96] Through this concept it becomes ethically sound to award co-authorship to creative contributors. Academic authors must not to be penalised for publishing ethically.

Learned societies and ethics specialists are also well placed to design publishing guidance that includes references to Indigenous

---

96   Moore, Neylon and Eve, et al., 'Excellence R Us'.

rights to culture and intellectual property rights. This could encourage researchers to feel supported in their bid to adopt ethical publishing practices. Such ethical guidance might also be used to teach research students and university staff, the latter having a role to play in supporting researchers to publish their work and manage their data.

Lastly, open access definitions in relation to copyright could to be adjusted to ensure that they are receptive and open to Indigenous and creative participation globally where this is ethically appropriate.

No doubt acting on all these suggestions will take time, collaboration and negotiation. Some changes are small and can be implemented easily. Others will take more time in that they require expertise, training and resources and the raising of general levels of awareness and sensitivity. What is least likely to change is copyright legislation due to its role in supporting monetary rewards for creative practice. However, it might be possible in some cases, through sustainable, non-profit open access publishing models, to shift some of the economic drivers that perpetuate inequalities in the copyright domain, ensuring that the greater participation of field interlocutors in knowledge creation, and the satisfactory acknowledgement of their role, is achieved in future.

Works Cited

American Anthropological Association (AAA) Ethics Forum (2012) 'Principles of Professional Responsibility', http://ethics.americananthro.org/category/statement/

Araújo, S. (2006) 'Conflict and Violence as Theoretical Tools in Present-Day Ethnomusicology: Notes on a Dialogic Ethnography of Sound Practices in Rio de Janeiro', *Ethnomusicology* 50.2, 287–313.

Australian Institute of Torres Strait Islander Studies. (2012) *Guidelines for Ethical Research in Australian Indigenous Studies*, http://aiatsis.gov.au/sites/default/files/docs/research-and-guides/ethics/gerais.pdf

Barney, K. (ed.) (2014) *Collaborative Ethnomusicology: New Approaches to Music Research between Indigenous and Non-Indigenous Australians* (Melbourne: Lyrebird Press).

Berlin Declaration on Open Access to Knowledge in the Sciences and Humanities (2003), https://openaccess.mpg.de/Berlin-Declaration

Bethesda Statement on Open Access Publishing (2003), http://legacy.earlham.edu/~peters/fos/bethesda.htm

Booth, G. (2015) 'Copyright Law and the Changing Economic Value of Popular Music in India', *Ethnomusicology* 59.2, 262–87, https://doi.org/10.5406/ethnomusicology.59.2.0262

Brabec de Mori, B. (2016) 'What Makes Natives Unique? Overview of Knowledge Systems among the World's Indigenous People', *Taiwan Journal of Indigenous Studies* 8, 43–61.

Brown, M. F. (2003) *Who Owns Native Culture?* (Cambridge, MA: Harvard University Press).

Christen, K. (2012) 'Does Information Really Want to be Free? Indigenous Knowledge Systems and the Question of Openness', *International Journal of Communication* 6, 2870–93, https://ijoc.org/index.php/ijoc/article/view/1618

Clifford, J. and G. Marcus (eds.) (1986) *Writing Culture: The Poetics and Politics of Ethnography* (Berkeley: University of California Press).

Cook, N. (2008) 'We Are All (Ethno) Musicologists Now', in H. Stobart (ed.), *The New (Ethno)Musicologies* (Lanham, MD: Scarecrow Press), pp. 48–70.

Coombe, R. (1998) *The Cultural Life of Intellectual Properties: Authorship, Appropriation and the Law* (Durham, N.C. and London: Duke University Press).

Craig, C. J., J. F. Turcotte, and R. J. Coombe. (2011) 'What's Feminist about Open Access? A Relational Approach to Copyright in the Academy', *feminist@law* 1.1, 1–35 http://journals.kent.ac.uk/index.php/feministsatlaw/article/view/7

Crossick, G. (2015) 'Monographs and Open Access: A Report to HEFCE. Higher Education Funding Council for England', https://webarchive.nationalarchives.gov.uk/20180322112445tf_/http://www.hefce.ac.uk/media/hefce/content/pubs/indirreports/2015/Monographs,and,open,access/2014_monographs.pdf

Diamond, D., A. Corn, F. Fjleheim, et al. (2017) 'Performing Protocol: Indigenous Traditional Knowledge as/and Intellectual Property', in J. C. Post (ed.), *Ethnomusicology: A Contemporary Reader*, vol. 2 (New York and London: Routledge), pp. 17–34.

Dussart, F. (2005) *The Politics of Ritual in an Aboriginal Settlement: Kinship, Gender and the Currency of Knowledge* (Washington: Smithsonian Institution Press).

Eve, M. (2014) *Open Access in the Arts and Humanities: Contexts, Controversies and the Future* (Cambridge: Cambridge University Press), https://doi.org/10.1017/CBO9781316161012

Feld, S. (1996) 'Pygmy POP. A Genealogy of Schizophonic Mimesis', *Yearbook for Traditional Music* 28, 1–35, https://doi.org/10.2307/767805

Field, L. (1999) *The Grimace of Macho Ratón: Artisans, Identity, and Nation in Late-Twentieth-Century Western Nicaragua* (Durham: Duke University Press).

Fitzpatrick, K. (2011) *Planned Obsolescence: Publishing, Technology and the Future of the Academy* (New York: New York University Press).

Grau, A. (1983) 'Sing a Dance, Dance a Song: The Relationship between Two Types of Formalised Movements and Music among the Tiwi of Melville and Bathurst Islands, North Australia', *Dance Research: The Journal of the Society for Dance Research* 1.2, 32–44, https://doi.org/10.2307/1290759

Gubrium, A. and K. Harper (2009) 'Visualizing Change: Participatory Digital Technologies in Research and Action', *Practising Anthropology* 31.4, 2–4, https://doi.org/10.17730/praa.31.4.t6w103r320507394

Hagedorn, K. (2001) *Divine Utterances: The Performance of Afro-Cuban Santeria* (Washington: Smithsonian Books).

Heiss, A. (2010) 'Australian Copyright v/s Indigenous Cultural Property Rights: A Discussion Paper' (Strawberry Hills, Australia: Australian Society of Authors), https://www.asauthors.org/products/info-papers/australian-copyright-vs-indigenous-intellectual-and-cultural-property-rights

Hinson, G. (November 1999) '"You've Got to Include an Invitation": Engaged Reciprocity and Negotiated Purpose in Collaborative Ethnography', paper presented at the 98th annual meeting of the American Anthropological Association, Chicago, IL.

Hood, M. (1960) 'The Challenge of Bi-Musicality', *Ethnomusicology* 4.2, 55–59, https://doi.org/10.2307/924263

Howard, A. (1988) 'Hypermedia and the Future of Ethnography', *Cultural Anthropology* 3.3, 304–15, https://doi.org/10.1525/can.1988.3.3.02a00060

Jackson, J. B. and R. Anderson. (2014) 'Anthropology and Open Access', *Cultural Anthropology* 29.2, 236–63, https://doi.org/10.14506/ca29.2.04

Janke, T. (2010) *Who Owns Story*, http://aiatsis.gov.au/sites/default/files/docs/asp/who-owns-story.pdf

— (1998) 'Our Culture, Our Future: Report on Australian Cultural and Intellectual Property Rights', report for the Australian Institute of Aboriginal and Torres Strait Islander Studies and the Australian and Torres Strait Islander Commission, http://www.cdu.edu.au/sites/default/files/Our%20culture%20our%20future%20report[2]%20copy.pdf

Kelty, C. M. (2014) 'Beyond Copyright and Technology: What Open Access Can Tell Us about Precarity, Authority, Innovation, and Automation in the University Today', *Cultural Anthropology* 29.2, 203–15, https://doi.org/10.14506/ca29.2.02

— M. M. J. Fischer, A. R. Golub, et al. (2008) 'Anthropology of/in Circulation: The Future of Open Access and Scholarly Societies', *Cultural Anthropology* 23.3, 559–88, https://www.jstor.org/stable/20484516

Kisliuk, M. (1998) *Seize the Dance! BaAka Musical Life and Ethnography of Performance* (Oxford: Oxford University Press).

Klein, L. F. and M. K. Gold. (2016) 'Digital Humanities: The Expanded Field', http://dhdebates.gc.cuny.edu/debates.

Lassiter, Luke, E., H. Goodall, E. Campbell and N. M. Johnson, *The Other Side of Middletown*: *Exploring Muncie's African American Community* (Walnut Creek: AltaMira Press).

Lassiter, Luke, E. (2005) 'Collaborative Ethnography and Public Anthropology', *Current Anthropology* 46.1, 83–106, https://doi.org/10.1086/425658

Lassiter, E., C. Ellis and R. Kotay (2002) *The Jesus Road*: *Kiowas, Christianity, and Indian Hymns* (Lincoln: University of Nebraska Press).

Marcus, G. E. and M. M. Fischer (1999) *Anthropology as a Cultural Critique*, 2nd ed. (Chicago and London: The University of Chicago Press).

Marett, A. (2005) *Songs, Dreamings, and Ghosts*: *The Wangga of North Australia* (Middletown: Wesleyan University Press).

McCann, A. (2001) 'All That Is Not Given is Lost: Irish Traditional Music, Copyright and Common Property', *Ethnomusicology* 45.1, 89–106, https://doi.org/10.2307/852635

McQueen, S. (2012) 'Michel Foucault's "What Is an Author?" and Adaptation', *COLLOQUY text theory and critique* 24, 60–77, http://artsonline.monash.edu.au/wp-content/arts-files/colloquy/colloquy_issue_twenty-four_/mcqueen.pdf

Mills, S. (1996) 'Indigenous Music and the Law: An Analysis of National and International Legislation', *Yearbook of Traditional Music* 28, 57–86, https://doi.org/10.2307/767807

Moore, S., C. Neylon, and M. Eve, et al. (2017) 'Excellence R Us: University Research and the Fetishisation of Excellence', *Palgrave Communications* 3, 1–13, https://doi.org/10.1057/palcomms.2016.105

Mueller, D., J. Schell, and W. Hsu, et al. (2014) 'Ethnomusicological Perspectives on Open Access Publication', *Ethnomusicology Review* 19, 1–21, http://ethnomusicologyreview.ucla.edu/sites/default/files/er_volume_19_2014.pdf

Nakata, M. (2007) *Disciplining the Savages: Savaging the Disciplines* (Canberra: Aboriginal Studies Press).

Nettl, B. (2005; 3rd ed. 2015) *The Study of Ethnomusicology: Thirty-One Issues and Concepts* (Champaign, IL: University of Illinois Press).

Orsini, F. and K. Butler Schofield (eds.) (2015) *Tellings and Texts: Music, Literature and Performance in North India* (Cambridge, UK: Open Book Publishers), https://doi.org/10.11647/obp.0062

Pearson, N. (1986) '"Ngamu-ngaadyarr, Muuri-bunggaga and Midha Mini" Guugu Yimidhirr History (Dingoes, Sheep and Mr Muni in Guugu Yimidhirr History). Hope Vale Lutheran Mission 1900–1950' (unpublished bachelor's dissertation, University of Sydney, History Department).

Rabinow, P. (ed.) (1984) *The Foucault Reader: An Introduction to Foucault's thought* (London: Penguin Group).

Research Councils UK (2016) *Concordat on Open Research Data*, https://www.ukri.org/files/legacy/documents/concordatonopenresearchdata-pdf/

Rice, T. (2007) 'Reflections on Music and Identity in Ethnomusicology', *Muzikologjia* 7, 17–38, https://doi.org/10.2298/muz0707017r.

Seeger, A. (1992) 'Ethnomusicology and Music Law', *Ethnomusicology* 36.3, 345–59, https://doi.org/10.2307/851868

— and S. Chaudhuri (2015) 'The Contributions for Reconfigured Audiovisual Archives to Sustaining Tradition', *The World of Music. Special Issue on Sound Futures: Exploring Contexts for Music Sustainability* 4.1, 21–34.

Shelemay, K. (1996) 'The Ethnomusicologist and the Transmission of Tradition', *The Journal of Musicology* 14.1, 33–51, https://doi.org/10.1525/jm.1996.14.1.03a00020

Stobart, H. (ed.) (2008) *The New (Ethno)Musicologies* (*Europea: Ethnomusicologies and Modernities*) (Lanham, MD: Scarecrow Press).

Stokes, M. (2010) *Ethnicity, Identity and Music: The Musical Construction of Place* (London: Berg Publishers).

Swijghuisen Reigersberg, M. E. (2009) 'Choral Singing and the Construction of Australian Aboriginal Identities: An Applied Ethnomusicological Study in Hopevale, Northern Queensland, Australia' (unpublished doctoral thesis, University of Surrey, Roehampton University).

Suber, P. (2015) *Open Access Overview*, http://legacy.earlham.edu/~peters/fos/overview.htm

— (2012) *Open Access (the book)* (Massachusetts: MIT Press), https://cyber.harvard.edu/hoap/Open_Access_(the_book)

Titon, J. T. (31 December 2013) 'The Commonwealth of Culture', *Sustainable Music: A Research Blog on the Subject of Sustainability*, https://sustainablemusic.blogspot.com.au/search/label/ownership

Torres, P. (1994) 'Interested in Writing About Indigenous Australians?', *Australian Author* 26.3, 24–25, http://search.informit.com.au/documentSummary;dn=950504428;res=IELAPA

Tuhiwai Smith, L. (2012) *Decolonizing Methodologies: Research and Indigenous Peoples*, 2nd ed. (London: Zed Books).

United Kingdom Research Integrity Office (UKRIO) (2009) 'Code of Practice for Research', http://ukrio.org/publications/code-of-practice-for-research/

United Nations (UN) (2007) *Declaration on the Rights of Indigenous Peoples*, https://www.un.org/development/desa/indigenouspeoples/declaration-on-the-rights-of-indigenous-peoples.html

United Nations Educational, Scientific and Cultural Organization (UNESCO) (2005) *Convention on the Protection and Promotion of Diversity of Cultural Expression*, http://unesdoc.unesco.org/images/0014/001429/142919e.pdf

Weintraub, A. N. and B. Yung (eds.) (2009) *Music and Cultural Rights* (Chicago, IL.: University of Illinois Press).

Wilsdon, J., L. Allen, E. Belfiore et al. (2015) *The Metric Tide: Report of the Independent Review of the Role of Metrics in Research Assessment and Management*, https://doi.org/10.13140/RG.2.1.4929.1363.

13. Show me the Copy! How Digital Media (Re)Assert Relational Creativity, Complicating Existing Intellectual Property and Publishing Paradigms[1]

Joseph F. Turcotte

Introduction

It is important to recognize that emerging technological changes, especially communications media, are reciprocally engaged with changing social, economic, political, and cultural dynamics — even those that have a long history.[2] This relationship needs to be understood in order to address the myriad ways that long-standing social and economic practices in developed countries are being reoriented alongside the rise of digital and networked communication technologies. In particular,

---

1   This chapter develops arguments made elsewhere (cf. Carys Craig and Joseph F. Turcotte with Rosemary J. Coombe, 'What's Feminist About Open Access? A Relational Approach to Copyright in the Academy', *feminists@law*, 1.1 (2011), 1–35) and presented on the panel 'Agency and Ethics: Media and Communications in the Digital Era' at the Canadian Communication Association Annual Meeting at Congress of the Humanities and Social Sciences, Wilfrid Laurier University and University of Waterloo, Waterloo, ON, 30 May 2012. The author would like to acknowledge and thank Professors Carys J. Craig and Rosemary J. Coombe for their formative work in these areas and the helpful comments of the anonymous reviewers.

2   Cf. Harold A. Innis, *Political Economy in the Modern State* (Toronto: University of Toronto Press, 2018).

digital technologies are giving new life to socio-cultural practices based on the appropriation and recombination of already existing cultural resources, and extending creative practices developed with the earlier advent of electronic technologies. Prior to digitization, electronic media enabled recombinant forms of cultural production: from Canadian pianist Glenn Gould's use of electronic media to the outer boroughs of New York City where the pioneers of hip-hop music used turntables and vinyl records to create a new art form, electronic technologies facilitated emerging and innovative creative practices while simultaneously rekindling marginalized forms of social and cultural production.

The rise of digital technologies has similarly contributed to the birth of a so-called remix culture, wherein the appropriation and recombination of existing texts and cultural works is deployed in novel and potentially transformative ways.[3] Such practices demonstrate the vitality of relational creativity[4] and should not be viewed in isolation, as they and contribute to the re-emergence of socially embedded forms of knowledge production, dissemination, and collaboration. However, dominant economic and legal systems, such as intellectual property (IP) law, in general, and copyright law, in particular, potentially impede these types of creativity, as they remain grounded on normative foundations that privilege Romantic conceptions of individual genius and creativity rather than relational and appropriative forms of creation.[5] The extension of IP law into international trade and transnational economic realms extends this disjuncture globally, shifting normative positions surrounding whether 'bad artists copy — good artists steal'[6] to punitive concerns and affirmations that 'to copy is to steal'.[7]

---

3   Lawrence Lessig, *Remix: Making Art and Commerce Thrive in the Hybrid Economy* (New York: Penguin Press, 2008), https://doi.org/10.5040/9781849662505
4   Carys J. Craig, *Copyright, Communication, and Culture: Towards a Relational Theory of Copyright* (Cheltenham and Northampton, MA: Edward Elgar, 2011), https://doi.org/10.4337/9780857933522
5   Cf. Martha Woodmansee and Peter Jaszi (eds.), *The Construction of Authorship: Textual Appropriation in Law and Literature*, 3rd ed. (Durham, N.C.: Duke University Press, 1994).
6   Debra L. Quentel, 'Bad Artists Copy-Good Artists Steal: The Ugly Conflict between Copyright Law and Appropriationism', *UCLA Entertainment Law Review*, 4 (1996), 39–80.
7   Graham Dutfield, 'To Copy is to Steal: TRIPS, (Un)free Trade Agreements and the New Intellectual Property Fundamentalism', *Journal of Information, Law & Technology*, 1 (2006), 1–13.

This chapter seeks to find a middle ground, arguing that existing IP law does not properly align with how human creativity increasingly occurs and fails to reflect the emerging conditions of knowledge production facilitated by digital technologies and the reassertion of relational creativity. The chapter begins by re-presenting earlier arguments on relational creativity[8] to demonstrate how knowledge production and creativity are necessarily socio-cultural processes that depend upon already existing works. Using the writing and publication processes surrounding scholarly research as an exemplar, this chapter highlights how authors and collaborators work within and beyond relationships with other researchers and existing bodies of work to generate novel insights. Next, the chapter employs feminist legal critique to demonstrate how copyright law obscures this relational creativity by privileging authorial categories based on Romantic notions of individuated creative practice. It then demonstrates how digital technologies and attendant practices are reasserting relational creativity in academic scholarship through open access movements, which complicate existing IP and academic publishing paradigms. By way of conclusion, the chapter discusses recent copyright developments in Canada, including rulings by the Supreme Court of Canada (SCC) as well as changes to Canada's *Copyright Act*, which seemingly recognize and validate the necessity of relational creativity in academic contexts, in particular, in the form of users' rights. In light of the such affirmation of fair dealing and user rights, especially in academic and research contexts, more open forms of knowledge production and exchange need to be viewed as complex and dialectical resources, which can be simultaneously commodified as intellectual goods, through copyright and related law, while serving to threaten proprietary publishing paradigms in that they facilitate alternative social and economic relationships — including unauthorized and illicit means of distributing and sharing knowledge-based resources.

---

8   cf. Craig, *Copyright, Communication, and Culture*; Carys J. Craig, 'Reconstructing the Author-Self: Some Feminist Lessons for Copyright Law', *Journal of Gender, Social Policy and the Law*, 15.2 (2007), 207–68; Craig, Turcotte with Coombe, 'What's Feminist About Open Access?'.

Relational Creativity and Socio-Cultural Authorship

IP and copyright law depend upon authorial categories that are premised upon individuated forms of creation and creative expression.[9] From such perspectives, individual creators work independently or in small groups and are necessarily entitled to gain from their creative works due to moral claims based on Lockean conceptions of just reward.[10] Furthermore, state governments grant proprietary rights to these expressions and inventions through IP law as a means to incentive such creativity: by fusing ideals of individual entitlement with utilitarian views of economic rationality and self-interest,[11] legislators seek to benefit both the author(s) and the general public through the creation and dissemination of useful knowledge. Authors are regarded as individuated, rights-bearing legal and economic subjects under this calculus and they are afforded the right of exclusivity over the expressions of their creativity. This exclusivity rests, in part, on the belief that incentives are necessary to encourage authors to produce expressions of knowledge and information,[12] thus contributing to the public good. This incentive theory is combined with a belief that such creative expression occurs independently and originally — further necessitating the granting of the right(s) to exclude others and the public from appropriating creative works.[13] However, as legal scholars

---

9 Cf. Craig, *Copyright, Communication, and Culture*; Craig, Turcotte with Coombe, 'What's Feminist About Open Access?'; Woodmansee and Jaszi, *The Construction of Authorship*; C. B. Macpherson, *The Political Theory of Possessive Individualism: Hobbes to Locke* (Oxford: Oxford University Press, 1962).

10 Yacine Dottridge, 'Creative Exploitation: Intellectual Property as a Form of Neoliberal Cultural Policy', Master of Arts, Major Research Paper (Toronto: Ryerson University and York University, 2012), https://digital.library.ryerson.ca/islandora/object/RULA:3210; Lawrence Liang, 'The Man Who Mistook His Wife for a Book', in Gaëlle Krikorian and Amy Kapczynski (eds.), *Access to Knowledge in the Age of Intellectual Property* (New York: Zone Books, 2010), pp. 277–92, https://mitpress.mit.edu/books/access-knowledge-age-intellectual-property

11 Edwin C. Hettinger, 'Justifying Intellectual Property Rights', *Philosophy and Public Affairs*, 18.1 (1989), 31–52 (p. 50); Christopher May, *The Global Political Economy of Intellectual Property Rights: The New Enclosures*, 2nd ed. (London and New York: Routledge, 2010), pp. 7–8, https://doi.org/10.4324/9780203873816

12 David Vaver, *Intellectual Property Law*, 2nd ed. (Concord: Irwin Law, 2011), p. 22, https://digitalcommons.osgoode.yorku.ca/faculty_books/134

13 Grantland S. Rice, *The Transformation of Authorship in America* (Chicago: University of Chicago Press, 1997), p. 76.

Martha Woodmansee and Peter Jaszi demonstrate, this liberal-economic construction of authorship is a distinctly Modern conception.

Despite its seemingly universal and natural position in contemporary society, the concept of the Modern author presupposed by IP law 'is a relatively recent formation — the result of a quite radical reconceptualization of the creative process that culminated less than 200 years ago in the heroic self-presentation of Romantic poets'.[14] This shift altered the authoritative claims of literature and the production of knowledge away from imitation and relational forms of creation towards a 'valorization of originality'.[15] Moral as well as political and economic claims from — or on behalf of — the individual became rooted in liberal-Romantic conceptions of the essence of human expression. Through this Romantic lens, 'worthwhile' productivity is viewed as acts that are 'authentic' and 'original' to the individual author; acts of imitation, therefore, are disparaged as of a lesser quality, not necessarily deserving of moral worth. Copying, appropriating, or imitating are consequently regarded 'as evidence of a lesser state of human civilization and development'.[16] IP regimes based upon these premises, especially copyright, reinforce these assumptions, introducing them into industrial and economic relationships that privilege claims of 'possessive individualism'[17] over other creative processes that based on dialogue and intrapersonal communication.

The dominant liberal, Modern, Romantic conception of authorship does not necessarily reflect how creation and innovation always occur. A return to acknowledging relational forms of creativity is found in literary philosopher Roland Barthes' declaration of the 'death of the author',[18] which argues creativity remains inherently and necessarily imbued within external and social relationships that contribute to the development of ideas and creations. From this perspective, acts of creativity are not wholly original but necessitate many acts of adaptation, appropriation, and derivation of other texts that form a reserve-source of ideas and inventions that contribute directly to future innovations.

---

14   Supra note 5, p. 3.
15   Marilyn Randall, *Pragmatic Plagiarism: Authorship, Profit and Power* (Toronto: University of Toronto Press, 2001), p. 47, https://doi.org/10.3138/9781442678736
16   Craig, Turcotte with Coombe, 'What's Feminist About Open Access?', p. 6.
17   Macpherson, *The Political Theory of Possessive Individualism*, p. 3.
18   Roland Barthes, *Image, Music, Text* (London: Fontana Press, 1977), pp. 142–48.

As copyright scholar Jessica Litman describes, this includes 'a process of adapting, transforming, and recombining what is already "out there" in some other form.'[19] Creativity is, therefore, a relational activity that includes 'a combination of absorption, astigmatism, and amnesia'.[20] Yet, through enduring beliefs in possessive individualism, external relationships are obscured or forgotten in favour of ideas about creative inspiration occurring within the originator — which are then backed through the force of copyright and IP law.

The processes behind the production of scholarly literature and research demonstrate the reductionist nature of possessive individualism — a perspective that overlooks the relational activity that underscores creative endeavours. As Barthes elaborates, '[t]he text is a tissue of quotations drawn from the innumerable centres of culture [...] [T]he writer can only imitate a gesture that is always anterior, never original. His (sic) only power is to mix writings, to counter the ones with the others, in such a way as never to rest on any one of them.'[21] Researchers and scientists are implicated within these external relational activities, whether knowingly or not:

> the production of information works in a circle. An existing horizon of knowledge [...] is the raw material to which human creativity or innovation is applied. The resulting product is then passed back into this horizon of knowledge as raw material for other acts of creativity, and the circle begins again. With each cycle, something new is created, but this new product always carries a trace of the earlier innovations on which it builds.[22]

Creative production, or the generation of 'new' knowledge and information, is based on recombinant processes that appropriate existing knowledge-based resources to create new informational outputs.[23] Research and science depend on these interactions: existing hypotheses and methods are appropriated and deployed to test, confirm, or challenge existing findings and ways of thought. In this sense, 'academics actively

---

19 Jessica Litman, 'The Public Domain', *Emory Law Journal*, 39 (1990), 965–1024 (p. 967).
20 Ibid., p. 1011.
21 Supra note 18, p. 137.
22 Arun Kundnani, 'Where Do You Want to Go Today? The Rise of Informational Capital', *Race & Class*, 40.2–3 (1998/99), 49–71 (p. 56).
23 Marcus Boon, *In Praise of Copying* (Cambridge, MA: Harvard University Press, 2010), http://www.hup.harvard.edu/features/in-praise-of-copying/

engage in knowledge construction as members of professional groups [...] their discoursal decisions are socially grounded, influenced by the broad inquiry patterns and knowledge structures of their disciplines'.[24] This form of relational creativity 'insists upon the practical impossibility of independent creation and declares that all texts are necessarily reproductions of [parts of] other texts: it is in the nature of expression and cultural development that the new builds upon the old'.[25]

Relational creativity does not discount the individual's contribution to creativity. Instead, it works to destabilize Romantic authorial categories, foregrounding relational and constructivist positions. Feminist political and legal theory offers an instructive conception of the self that does not preclude these socially related impulses: 'relational feminism' offers a map for resolving the liberal privileging of authorship with a social constructivist position.[26] This position affords 'attention both to the individuality of human beings and to their essentially social nature',[27] highlighting that 'autonomy itself is understood in relational terms; if we take as a starting point the intrinsic sociality of human beings'.[28]

From this perspective, individual texts or academic scholarship are not necessarily the product of individuated labour and inspiration. Instead, these acts are part of broader social, cultural, economic, and political relationships that infuse an individual's understanding with external influences. While an individual's *expression* of creativity may be articulated as an authorial concept based in originality, the expression is always already implicated within external networks of *ideas* that fundamentally contribute to the development of subsequent innovations and creations. The relational perspective of creativity and authorship recognizes the duality inherent in such actions. Rather than either obscuring the individual component of authorship — the ability to appropriate various sources for new ends — or the relational aspects of creativity — the imbedded and interconnected nature of human expression — the relational perspective offers a way of articulating the

---

24 Ken Hyland, 'Academic Attribution: Citation and the Construction of Disciplinary Knowledge', *Applied Linguistics*, 20.3 (1999), 341–67 (p. 362).
25 Craig, *Copyright, Communication, and Culture*, p. 16.
26 Craig, Turcotte with Coombe, 'What's Feminist About Open Access?', p. 3.
27 Jennifer Nedelsky, 'Reconceiving Autonomy: Sources, Thoughts and Possibilities', *Yale Journal of Law & Feminism*, 1 (1989), 7–36 (p. 27), https://pdfs.semanticscholar.org/4fca/3904f6b21b83b5cb2030e569415390011491.pdf
28 Craig, Turcotte with Coombe, 'What's Feminist About Open Access?', p. 11.

necessarily entangled and interrelated aspects that contribute to creative and innovative advances. As the next section will demonstrate, however, the relational nature of creativity and scholarly research is obscured by contemporary IP law based on the liberal, Modern, Romantic ideal of an individuated 'author' working apart from external, social relationships.

Authorship, Control and Intellectual Property

Throughout history, emerging communications, media, and transportation technologies have had the tendency to disrupt the social, cultural, and political relations and hierarchies of the societies to which they are introduced. Since Ancient Greek times, the ability of emerging technologies to facilitate changes in social relationships has been a point of discussion: for example, Plato depicts Socrates viewing the advent of writing as a potentially destabilizing influence with the potential to undermine the capacities of memory and learning.[29] Similarly, subsequent technological developments, including the printing press and electronic broadcasting, in the forms of radio and television, gave rise to optimism and concern over the impact of media devices.[30] From this perspective, the ongoing maturation of the Internet and associated digitally networked technologies contribute to shifting social, cultural, political, and economic dynamics.[31] The potential for technologically facilitated disruption has caused existing hierarchies of power to find ways to mitigate these changes to maintain their advantages. Under the auspices of an emerging 'informational economy',[32] established economic and political actors have become increasingly attuned to the ways that digitally networked technologies threaten business models and economic rationales based upon the creation, control, and

---

29   Plato, trans. by Alexander Nehamas and Paul Woodruff, 'Phaedrus', in John M. Cooper (ed.), *Plato: Complete Works* (Indianapolis, IN and Cambridge, MA: Hackett Publishing Company, 1997).

30   Cf. Marshall McLuhan, *The Gutenberg Galaxy: The Making of Typographic Man* (Toronto: University of Toronto Press, 1962); Neil Postman, *Amusing Ourselves to Death* (New York: Viking, 1985).

31   Manuel Castells, *The Rise of Network Society*, 2nd ed. (Oxford: Blackwell, 2009), https://doi.org/10.1002/9781444319514

32   Manuel Castells and Peter Hall, 'Technopoloes: Mines and Foundries of the Informational Economy', in Manuel Castells and Peter Hall (eds.), *Technopoles of the World: The Making of 21st Century Industrial Complexes* (New York: Routledge, 1994), pp. 1–11.

dissemination of content and informational goods and services. Debates about IP law have become key sites where the disruptive potential of emerging technologies is actively resisted.

In recent years, debates surrounding IP law have moved increasingly into popular forums and become topics of critical discussion.[33] This politicization of IP law is in line with historic developments, which are replete with theoretical and legal contestation.[34] Historically, the development of Modern, (neo)liberal IP regimes has had two parallel threads. The first is a debate over whether IP is best understood as an extension of an individual's moral rights or whether the rights granted through IP law are utilitarian privileges afforded to the rights holder in order to spur creativity, which will, ultimately, serve the public good.[35] This debate revolves around the questions of authorship discussed above; the former position presupposes the author as an individual creating apart from social and cultural influence, whereas the latter conceives of the author as an individual working within social and cultural practices to which she is indebted and to which she contributes.

The second strand that has shaped the development of IP regimes revolves around technology: more specifically, how emerging technologies enable the ability to copy, appropriate, and reproduce works in previously impossible ways. This technological component has been fundamental to the make-up of IP laws since their inception. From this perspective, the first examples of Modern IP, the Venetian patent statutes of 1474 and Britain's Statute of Anne (1710) covering copyright, emerge out of the desire to address emerging technological capabilities to copy, appropriate, and disseminate inventions and creative works in new ways. These Statutes also represent the beginning of an international IP regime. They construct the notion of IP — more specifically, patents and copyright — in terms of an individuated author who is provided with

---

33 Sebastian Haunss, *Conflicts in the Knowledge Society: The Contentious Politics of Intellectual Property* (Cambridge, UK: Cambridge University Press, 2013), https://doi.org/10.1017/cbo9781139567633

34 Adrian Johns, *Piracy: The Intellectual Property Wars from Gutenberg to Gates* (Chicago: University of Chicago Press, 2010), https://doi.org/10.7208/chicago/9780226401201.001.0001; Susan K. Sell and Christopher May, 'Moments in Law: Contestation and Settlement in the History of Intellectual Property', *Review of International Political Economy*, 8.3 (2001), 467–500.

35 Cf. David Vaver, 'Intellectual Property: Is It Still A 'Bargain'?', *Intellectual Property Journal*, 24 (2012), 143–58.

the legal right to determine how his or her works are appropriated and reproduced. The adoption of the printing press in Europe facilitated the emergence of an industry devoted to the reproduction of 'unauthorized' texts, highlighting the interrelated nature of emerging technologies and IP. As English scholar Mark Rose argues:

> The institution of copyright is the child of technology. Without printing technology — without the means of multiplying copies of a book more readily and easily than by hand copying of manuscripts — there would be no need for copyright. Anglo-American copyright has its roots in 16th- and 17th-century guild practices that served to preserve order in the book trade and to protect booksellers' investments.[36]

In the realm of copyright, the enactment of the Statute of Anne was in response to this technological advance. Tellingly, concerns over the ownership and reproduction of creative works are stated in the first section of the Statute:

> Whereas Printers, Booksellers, and other Persons, have of late frequently taken the Liberty of Printing, Reprinting, and Publishing, or causing to be Printed, Reprinted, and Published Books, and other Writings, without the Consent of the Authors or Proprietors of such Books and Writings, to their very great Detriment, and too often to the Ruin of them and their Families […].[37]

Thus, the interest of individual authors to own and transfer the rights over their works as well as to manage the appropriation and reproduction of texts became a central tenet of IP law.

This technological concern has remained a priority throughout subsequent developments of IP law: as technologies have developed and enabled the reproduction of creative works through various media forms, IP law has been adjusted accordingly. Subsequent technologies such as photography, recorded music, radio and video have resulted in changes to IP law in order to maintain the position of rights holders and the individuated author.[38] The moral rights of the individuated author

---

36 Mark Rose, 'Technology and Copyright in 1735: The Engraver's Act', *The Information Society*, 21 (2005), 63–66 (p. 63).

37 *The Statute of Anne: An Act for the Encouragement of Learning, by Vesting the Copies of Printed Books in the Authors or Purchasers of Such Copies, During the Times Therein Mentioned*, 8 Anne, c. 19 (1710), The Avalon Project: Documents in Law, History and Diplomacy, http://avalon.law.yale.edu/18th_century/anne_1710.asp

38 Cf. Mark Rose, 'Mothers and Authors: *Johnson v. Calvert* and the New Children of Our Imaginations', *Critical Inquiry*, 22 (Summer) (1996), 613–33 (pp. 614–15).

were prioritized in order to ensure that the fruits of one's 'own' labour were legally protected, so that the rights holders were able to profit from their creative works.

However, there is another important theory that has undergirded the development of IP law: a balance between the private rights of individual owners and the benefit of the public good through access to knowledge and information.[39] This public-private balance foregrounds an awareness of the relational nature of creativity, by attempting to encourage individuated forms of creativity based upon access to socially disseminated cultural products. Specifically in the American context, IP law developed with a concern for balancing private and public rights. Arguments persisted between those who viewed IP as another form of private property and others who envisioned that access to information and knowledge was a social good. As literature scholar Lewis Hyde describes it:

> One side argued that the history of the common law showed that authors and inventors had a natural right to their work, and that like other such rights it should exist in perpetuity; the other side replied that the common law contained no such record, that copyrights and patents 'were merely privileges, which excludes the idea of a right,' that such privileges come from statutes rather than nature and that they could and should be limited in term.[40]

This debate was ultimately resolved and intellectual property laws sought to balance the two positions. Authors, inventors and rights holders were afforded a limited-term monopoly over the control of their works, after which these works would enter the public domain where subsequent creators could freely appropriate them.[41]

However, since at least the negotiations surrounding the World Trade Organization (WTO) and the Trade-Related Aspects of Intellectual Property (TRIPS) Agreement,[42] this balance has been disrupted, as these

---

39 Gaëlle Krikorian and Amy Kapczynski (eds.), *Access to Knowledge in the Age of Intellectual Property* (New York: Zone Books, 2010), https://mitpress.mit.edu/books/access-knowledge-age-intellectual-property; Sara Bannerman, *International Copyright and Access to Knowledge* (Cambridge, UK: Cambridge University Press, 2016), https://doi.org/10.1017/CBO9781139149686

40 Lewis Hyde, *Common as Air: Revolution, Art and Ownership* (New York: Farrar, Straus and Giroux, 2010), pp. 86–87.

41 Cf. Johns, *Piracy: The Intellectual Property Wars*.

42 Cf. Peter Drahos with John Braithwaite, *Information Feudalism* (London: Earthscan Publications, Ltd., 2002), https://doi.org/10.4324/9781315092683

limited-term monopolies have grown longer: 'The story of copyright law in the twentieth [and now early twenty-first] century has been the process of expanding, lengthening, and strengthening [...]'.[43] This expansion and deepening of the international IP regime, in terms of protectable subject matter and the duration of the terms of protection,[44] distorts the historical balances that informed the creation of these legal structures.[45]

This history of IP reform reveals tension between private and public interests, and how these concerns intersect with conceptions of the author as an individuated being who does her work separate from, or at least with no obligation to, external cultural influences. Under this view, it is the right of authors — and subsequent rights holders — to determine how their works are appropriated and reproduced. Technological innovations have played a central role in these discussions as subsequent technologies have made replication easier, thus threatening the control that rights holders have over the works in question. In particular, digital uses of published content create antagonisms between authors, publishers, and users,[46] with each group seeking to access and control published content for their own benefit.

The debate between private and public interest conceptions of IP centres on the role and nature of the author or creator. The private property perspective, which is largely ingrained in contemporary IP law, presupposes an individuated form of authorship and creativity.[47] The subject and property become intimately intertwined and are inseparable unless transferred elsewhere, as the object 'must become the production of the subject in order for it to be protected by law'.[48] The object is only afforded the status and protection of property if it is created by, and can be attributed, to a nameable author. In this way, IP

---

43 James Boyle, *The Public Domain: Enclosing the Commons of the Mind* (New Haven: Yale University Press, 2008), p. 4, http://thepublicdomain.org/thepublicdomain1.pdf

44 Susan K. Sell, *Private Power, Public Law: The Globalization of Intellectual Property Rights* (Cambridge, UK: Cambridge University Press, 2003), https://doi.org/10.1017/cbo9780511491665

45 Bannerman, *International Copyright and Access to Knowledge*.

46 Cf. Giuseppina D'Agostino, *Copyright, Contracts, Creators: New Media, New Rules* (Cheltenham and Northampton: Edward Elgar, 2010), p. 19, https://doi.org/10.4337/9781849805209

47 Cf. Woodmansee and Jaszi, *The Construction of Authorship*.

48 Bernard Edelman, *Ownership of the Image: Elements of a Marxist Theory of Law* (London: Routledge, 1979), p. 45.

law facilitates the mis- and over-appropriation of creative works and privileges the interests of the individuated author over relational and discursive forms of creativity.[49] As legal scholar Shelley Wright offers:

> The existing definition of copyright [...] presupposes that individuals live in isolation from one another, that the individual is an autonomous unit who creates artistic works and sells them, or permits their sale by others, while ignoring the individual's relationship with others within her community, family, ethnic group, religion — the very social relations out of which and for the benefit of whom the individual's limited monopoly rights are supposed to exist.[50]

However, the public good notion of intellectual activity points to a more collaborative form of creative action, described above. This perspective asserts that creativity is based upon social relationships and interactions. This collaborative interpretation of creativity demonstrates the interconnected nature of the human subject. Rather than being separated from social interactions, this view recognizes how human subjects, as authors, work within networks of associated beings and ideas. From this relational perspective, creation does not happen in spaces of isolated individual brilliance. Instead, creativity is the result of complex relationships between sources of inspiration. Therefore, the public, or community, plays an integral role in creative activity.

Historic debates over the public-private nature of IP law demonstrates the influence that relational forms of creativity have in articulating balanced means for protecting and incentivizing creative endeavours. Although this balanced approach undergirds the historic development of IP regimes, the entrenchment of IP into international trade via the TRIPS Agreement has coincided with a disruption of the public-private balance in favour of models of IP regulation based upon the interests of entrenched industries and the economic rationales of large, IP-trading states. As IP and law scholars Peter Drahos and John Braithwaite demonstrate, the negotiations surrounding an international IP regime governed through the WTO via TRIPS focused on perpetuating the business models of content providers.[51] Leading

---

49   Ibid., p. 70.
50   Shelley Wright, 'A Feminist Exploration of the Legal Protection of Art,' *Canadian Journal of Women and the Law*, 7 (1994), 59–96 (pp. 73–74).
51   Supra note 42.

up to and following the negotiations, lobbyists from the entertainment industry — predominately in the US — worked to advance IP provisions that strengthened the positions of IP rights holders, often at the disservice of emerging creative and innovative industries.

Following the adoption of the TRIPS Agreement, lobbyists for IP rights holders have continued to work and promote the extension of these rights and provisions elsewhere, while simultaneously extending the scope and duration of these rights through so-called TRIPS-plus agreements, which are often conducted at the bilateral or regional level.[52] International trade negotiations work to strengthen the rights afforded to content creators and distributors in order to safeguard their business models against future, technologically facilitated threats and disruptions. These efforts have gone so far that they are increasingly drawing criticism from a disparate group of governments of developing nations, as well as concerned civil society actors. The rationale behind these anti-IP movements lies in a belief that these agreements and their IP provisions represent an overreach based upon the desires of certain corporate industries, which do a disservice to emerging industries and the development of domestic, local, and community-based socio-economic alternatives.[53] Importantly, the proprietary norms expanded through the international IP regime rest upon the rationale of possessive individualism mentioned above.[54] In doing so, TRIPS-plus IP law further subverts and obscures the relational aspects of creativity in favour of individuated forms of economic growth.

Relational creativity, however, remains an integral component of existing practices and emerging social circumstances. The opposition to further IP expansion from developing and indigenous communities serves to demonstrate this. From the perspective of developing states, the current international IP regime is ill-suited for the needs of countries at disparate levels of socio-economic development.[55] IP expansion from

---

52 Supra note 44.
53 Amy Kapczynski, 'The Access to Knowledge Mobilization and the New Politics of Intellectual Property,' *Yale Law Journal*, 117.5 (2008), 839–51; Krikorian and Kapczynski, *Access to Knowledge in the Age of Intellectual Property*.
54 Sharmishta Barwa and Shirin M. Rai, 'Knowledge and/as Power: A Feminist Critique of Trade Related Intellectual Property Rights', *Gender, Technology and Development*, 7.1 (2003), 91–113.
55 Boatema Boateng, *The Copyright thing doesn't Work here: Adinkra and Kente Cloth and Intellectual Property in Ghana* (Minneapolis, MN: University of Minnesota Press,

largely developed states and their international and corporate allies does little to address the needs of countries facing problems associated with health, food security, education, and environmental concerns.[56] Indigenous communities rooted in more collaborative histories of knowledge production similarly dispute advances in international IP regimes that are based upon liberal, Romantic, and Enlightenment ideals. For these communities, legal regimes based upon the private ownership of information-based goods do not cohere with traditional and historic relationships that valorise the community and an interconnection with external influences including the environment.[57] Adding to these oppositional forces is an increasingly assertive lobby group comprising businesses and civil society actors that base their claims upon emerging socio-technological realities facilitated by digital and information communication technologies.[58] In the same way that Indigenous communities oppose international IP expansion, in part, because it does not cohere with relational forms of knowledge maintenance and production, digital technologies are facilitating the rise of communities that privilege relational creative practices in academic contexts.

Digitization, Open Access and the (Re)Emergence of Relational Creativity

The ongoing development of the Internet and associated digital, networked technologies continues to recast our social, cultural, political, and economic landscape. At the same time, these technological

---

2011), https://doi.org/10.5749/minnesota/9780816670024.001.0001; Miranda Forsyth and Sue Farran, *Weaving Intellectual Property Policy in Small Island Developing States* (Cambridge, UK: Intersentia, 2015), https://doi.org/10.1017/9781780685731

56 Duncan Matthews, *Intellectual Property, Human Rights and Development: The Role of NGOs and Social Movements* (Cheltenham: Edward Elgar, 2011), https://doi.org/10.4337/9780857931245; Krikorian and Kapczynski, *Access to Knowledge in the Age of Intellectual Property*; Tzen Wong and Graham Dutfield (eds.), *Intellectual Property and Development: Current Trends and Future Scenarios* (Cambridge, UK: Cambridge University Press, 2011), https://doi.org/10.1017/cbo9780511761027

57 Kathy Bowery and Jane Anderson, 'The Politics of Global Information Sharing: Whose Cultural Agendas Are Being Advanced?', *Social and Legal Studies*, 18.4 (2009), 479–504; Madhavi Sunder, 'The Invention of Traditional Knowledge', *Law and Contemporary Problems*, 70.2 (2007), 97–124.

58 Jyh-An Lee, *Non-Profit Organizations and the Intellectual Commons* (Cheltenham: Edward Elgar, 2012), https://doi.org/10.4337/9781781001585

advances are reasserting creative methods that have been previously obscured by modern, liberal conceptions of the individuated author. Digital technologies foreground the recursive and relational nature of creativity, highlighting how previous ideas, texts, and forms are appropriated during the creation of derivative and innovative works. Legal scholar Lawrence Lessig describes how these technologies facilitate creative activities based on combining previous cultural texts in new ways.[59] While these acts appear unprecedented and rooted in the socio-technological circumstances of the time, Lessig argues that only the techniques of this relational 'read-write (RW)' are novel and that recombinant creativity harkens back to previous eras in which information was shared and passed along to new generations through primarily oral means.[60] Literary theorist Thomas Pfau reminds us that nineteenth-century authors and artists regularly used recombinant techniques and allusion to generate new writings and creative works.[61] Emerging digital technologies reassert this relational past, demonstrating the recursive nature of human expression and creativity.

The historic development of the Internet revolved around a focus on open access and information sharing being fundamental for spurring new ideas and creative expressions. The open and collaborative nature of the early Internet was ingrained in the technical apparatuses and internal coding of the network's infrastructure. Interoperability and enhanced accessibility were privileged in order to facilitate information sharing and collaboration across varying distances. Aspirational rhetoric accompanied this, promoting a belief that increased communication and information sharing could facilitate '[a]n enduring peace, an unprecedented rise in prosperity, an era of comfort, convenience and ease and a political world without politics or politicians — these were the hopes that cultivated a wave of belief in the magically transforming power of technology'.[62] Facilitating possibilities for interaction, collaboration, and information sharing

---

59 Supra note 3.
60 Ibid., p. 82.
61 Thomas Pfau, 'The Pragmatics of Genre: Moral Theory and Lyric Authorship in Hegel and Woodsworth', in Martha Woodmansee and Peter Jaszi (eds.), *The Construction of Authorship: Textual Appropriation in Law and Literature* (Durham: Duke University Press, 1994), pp. 133–58.
62 James W. Carey, 'Historical Pragmatism and the Internet', *New Media & Society*, 7.4 (2005), 443–55 (p. 445), https://doi.org/10.1177/1461444805054107

were regarded as means for pursuing a techno-utopian ideal based upon vibrant intellectual activity and innovation. While subsequent changes to the Internet's architecture as well as IP law in the name of commercial progress have led to the Internet being remade and recoded to facilitate informational capitalist expansion by increasing security and dissuading supposedly illicit acts of information sharing,[63] digitally networked technologies continue to enable creative agents to appropriate, combine, and recast cultural texts and ideas.

As the Internet and world-wide web have matured, various technological fixes have been developed to re-introduce forms of artificial scarcity over digital goods. In particular, digital technological protection measures (TPM) techniques are often used to affix so-called digital locks to media files as a way of prescribing, via code, terms of use and access.[64] The blockchain, a distributed ledger for verifying and circulating digital assets such as Bitcoin, is also increasingly used by producers and distributors of digital goods and assets to maintain control over the use and circulation of digital files online, with the promise of providing fair remuneration to artists and creators.[65] These technologies themselves further exemplify the public-private tensions within IP law and the culture industries. TPM and blockchain-based technologies seek to maintain the commercial and financial aspects of cultural texts and works, whether as goods in and of themselves or as assets for creator and/or rights-holder. In particular, TPMs have been added to TRIPS-plus trade agreements requiring signatory countries to prohibit anti-circumvention even when done for legitimate purposes.[66] The viability of technological controls such as these remain to be seen, especially in environments outside of the closed systems they depend

---

63 Lawrence Lessig, *Code and Other Laws of Cyberspace* (New York: Basic Books, 1999).
64 Stefan Bechtold, 'The Present and Future of Digital Rights Management — Musings on Emerging Legal Problems', in Eberhard Becker, Willms Buhse, Dirk Günnewig, and Niels Rump (eds.), *Digital Rights Management: Technological, Economic, Legal and Political Aspects* (Berlin: Springer Science & Business Media, 2003), pp. 597–654, https://doi.org/10.1007/10941270_36
65 Cf. Rachel O'Dwyer, 'Limited Edition: Producing Artificial Scarcity for Digital Art on the Blockchain and its Implications for the Cultural Industries', *Convergence: The International Journal of Research into New Media Technologies* (2018), 1–21, https://doi.org/10.1177/1354856518795097; Martin Zeillinger, 'Digital Art as "Monetised Graphics": Enforcing Intellectual Property on the Blockchain', *Philosophy & Technology*, 31.1 (2018), 15–41.
66 Christopher May, 'Digital rights management and the breakdown of social norms', *First Monday*, 8.11 (2003), https://doi.org/10.5210/fm.v8i11.1097

on. If, for example, this artificial scarcity is lost once a file is transferred into a non-TPM format or a file that can be circulated on the broader world-wide-web.

In response to the growing commercialization and prioritization of the Internet and digital content, a host of online activists are working to retain the accessible nature of the digital realm. Anthropologist Christopher Kelty describes the 'open source' software movement as an initiative committed to developing and disseminating digital code and technologies that retain the Internet's open ethos.[67] The open source movement is a reaction against perceived overreach of private ownership over IP, rooted in the belief that an open and accessible Internet benefits from the creative potential of increased collaboration and relational creativity. Others describe open source as 'an oasis of anarchist production'.[68] Rather than 'locking in' content and information via digital code, open source initiatives allow their creative works to be freely accessible so that subsequent programmers can fix problematic elements of the software and create new and improved uses as well as possibilities. Various quasi-legal elements, such as Creative Commons licenses and the GNU General Public License, employ basic IP concepts such as attribution while enabling rights holders to easily and identifiably share their works with like-minded users. While such licenses are based upon the individuated authorship paradigm ingrained in the IP regimes that they are based upon, these tools implicitly recognize the relational nature of creativity by facilitating greater accessibility to knowledge and the creation of derivative works.

The Open Society Institute, a social justice initiative founded by billionaire George Soros, describes the basic tenets of this open and accessible Internet:

> By 'open access' [...] we mean its free availability on the public internet, permitting any users to read, download, copy, distribute, print, search, or link to the full texts of these articles, crawl them for indexing, pass them as data to software, or use them for any other lawful purpose, without

---

67 Christopher Kelty, 'Geeks, Social Imaginaries and Recursive Publics', *Cultural Anthropology*, 2.2 (2008), 185–214; Christopher Kelty, *Two Bits: The Cultural Significance of Free Software* (Durham, N.C.: Duke University Press, 2008), https://doi.org/10.1215/9780822389002

68 Yochai Benkler, 'Freedom in the Commons: Towards a Political Economy of Information', *Duke Law Journal*, 52 (2003), 1245–76 (p. 1246).

financial, legal, or technical barriers other than those inseparable from gaining access to the internet itself. The only constraint on reproduction and distribution, and the only role for copyright in this domain, should be to give authors control over the integrity of their work and the right to be properly acknowledged and cited.[69]

This approach seeks to mesh existing IP and authorial categories with (re)emerging relational creative practices: 'Open access principles seek instead to maintain and contribute to a vibrant public sphere based upon public domain, accessible and/or re-useable materials, thereby leveraging the enormous possibilities for innovation and exchange that online, networked communication technologies afford'.[70] Technological advances are transforming ingrained hierarchies of knowledge production, protection, and promotion and (re)asserting interconnected conceptions of authorship and creativity.

Since at least the early 2000s, many librarians and academics have worked to advance a movement towards open access in scholarly publishing, which seeks to publish literary and scholarly works in ways free from proprietary IP regimes. For example, the 2003 Berlin Declaration on Open Access to Knowledge and Information in the Sciences and Humanities,[71] have helped to advance the cause of access to knowledge in educational and scientific settings. The Berlin Declaration seeks to address concerns raised by practitioners in the library and archive communities over issues including restrictive user rights and prohibitively expensive licensing regimes.[72] The Berlin Declaration[73] follows two other open access statements of principle — the Budapest Open Access Initiative (2002)[74] and the Bethesda Statement on Open Access Publishing (2003)[75] — and states:

---

69 Cited in Ann Bartow, 'Open Access, Law, Knowledge, Copyrights, Dominance and Subordination', *Lewis & Clark Law Review*, 10.4 (2006), 869–84 (pp. 873–74).
70 Craig, Turcotte with Coombe, 'What's Feminist About Open Access?', p. 20.
71 Max Planck Society and Max Planck Institute for the History of Science, *Berlin Declaration on Open Access to Knowledge in the Sciences and Humanities*, 22 October 2003, http://openaccess.mpg.de/Berlin-Declaration
72 Peggy E. Hoon, 'Who Woke the Sleeping Giant?: Libraries, Copyrights, and the Digital Age', *Change*, 35.6 (2003), 28–33.
73 Supra note 71.
74 Leslie Chan, et al., *Budapest Open Access Initiative*, 2002, https://www.budapestopenaccessinitiative.org/read
75 Patrick Brown, et al., *Bethesda Statement on Open Access Publishing*, 2003, http://legacy.earlham.edu/~peters/fos/bethesda.htm

> Our mission of disseminating knowledge is only half complete if the information is not made widely and readily available to society. New possibilities of knowledge dissemination not only through the classical form but also and increasingly through the open access paradigm via the Internet have to be supported. We define open access as a comprehensive source of human knowledge and cultural heritage that has been approved by the scientific community.[76]

The Berlin Declaration, the Budapest Open Access Initiative, and the Bethesda Statement have collectively helped to develop an increasing open access movement[77] within academia and beyond.

According to the Budapest Open Access Initiative, open access relates, in part, to scholarly literature that is difficult to easily or affordably access due to burdensome and prohibitively expensive proprietary licensing regimes. It recognizes that copyright and IP law enable profit-oriented academic publishers to sequester large segments of academic scholarship[78] behind so-called paywalls and other technological protection measures, which reduce the availability of scholarly literature — especially in developing or historically marginalized locales.[79] These proprietary practices disrupt the relational nature of academic scholarship by adding financial burdens to access critical research and scholarly texts, which may impair use by other academics and scholars as well as broader communities of interest.

From the dominant IP perspective, the tools and resources that individuals use to orient themselves and engage in creative activity are regarded as market goods that must be purchased and/or licensed accordingly. The public good is subverted in order to privilege private gain, resulting in 'an exploitative situation in which academic authors and the institutions for which they work are paying the costs of publication but losing control over their published works'.[80] In

---

76 Supra note 71.
77 Charles W. Bailey Jr., *What Is Open Access?*, preprint (2006), http://digital-scholarship.org/cwb/WhatIsOA.htm
78 Vincent Larivière, Stefanie Haustein, and Philippe Mongeon, 'The Oligopoly of Academic Publishers in the Digital Era', *PloS one*, 10.6 (2015), 1–15.
79 Manon A. Ress, 'Open-Access Publishing: From Principles to Practice', in Gaëlle Krikorian and Amy Kapczynski (eds.), *Access to Knowledge in the Age of Intellectual Property* (New York: Zone Books, 2010), pp. 475–96, https://mitpress.mit.edu/books/access-knowledge-age-intellectual-property
80 Nicholas Bramble, 'Preparing Academic Scholarship for an Open Access World', *Harvard Journal of Law & Technology*, 20.1 (2006), 209–33 (p. 217).

response, open access initiatives have been created, which seek to return public interest concerns to the fore[81] and reflect the relational creativity inherent in academic scholarship and publishing. Such initiatives include practices of self-archiving in open online archives as well as the use of freely accessible open access online journals.[82] Other open access initiatives use online message boards, indexable and searchable hashtags, and so-called shadow libraries to allow users to request and share scholarly texts more easily.[83] For the most part, such open access communities attempt to work alongside — or at least not to openly contradict — existing copyright and IP law; however, a guerrilla open access movement has also developed, which openly confronts the restrictive nature of proprietary scholarly publishing practices by openly flouting copyright and IP law by providing shadow libraries of paywall-protected texts.[84] Regardless of the practices employed to facilitate access, such practices represent a reassertion of the norms of relational creativity necessary to participate in academic research, scholarship, and writing.

Consultant, writer, and entrepreneur Matt Mason has labelled such situations as 'the Pirate's Dilemma'.[85] Mason's work charts the ways in which emerging cultural groups from reggae to disco to punk rock and through to hip-hop have destabilized existing cultural norms by appropriating existing knowledge and information in new ways. The sharing of digital works in explicitly legal or potentially illicit ways, then, is an example of subversive countercultural elements challenging existing norms in the hopes of generating new social alternatives. The challenge for governments and industry is to adapt to and capitalize upon these changing circumstances. The appropriation of countercultural elements to become commodified goods and marketing opportunities

---

81 Peter Suber, *Knowledge Unbound: Selected Writings on Open Access, 2002–2011* (Cambridge, MA: MIT Press, 2016), https://mitpress.mit.edu/books/knowledge-unbound
82 Craig, Turcotte with Coombe, 'What's Feminist About Open Access?', p. 24.
83 Guillaume Cabanac, 'Bibliogifts in LibGen? A Study of a Text-Sharing Platform Driven by Biblioleaks and Crowdsourcing', *Science and Technology*, 67.4 (2016), 874–84.
84 Balázs Bodó, 'Pirates in the Library — An Inquiry into the Guerilla Open Access Movement', in 8th Annual Workshop of the International Society for the History and Theory of Intellectual Property, CREATe, University of Glasgow, 2016.
85 Matt Mason, *The Pirate's Dilemma: How Youth Culture is Reinventing Capitalism* (New York: Free Press, 2008).

throughout all of the musical epochs mentioned above demonstrates the resilience of the capitalist system to incorporate potentially destabilizing elements. In terms of digital disruption, businesses that were slow to adapt to changing technological circumstances during the rise of Napster and other peer-to-peer (p2p) networks have turned to legal and legislative means to ingrain their vested interests and historic business practices. From a socio-legal perspective, the evolution of law to reflect changing circumstances is an expected development. However, by often privileging the interests and business models of existing industry over emerging alternatives as well as social rights based claims, ongoing IP expansion threatens to prevent innovative forms of creativity.

Conclusion: Canada's 'Copyright Pentalogy' and the Affirmation of Fair Dealing

Content-based industries, most noticeably those based in developing countries, are, in part, responding to the social and technological changes facilitated by digital media with increased lobbying campaigns devoted to extending and projecting individuated forms of IP protection globally via trade-based mechanisms.[86] This has caused a global 'ratcheting up' of IP law in terms of breadth and scope.[87] However, as has been explored elsewhere,[88] these primarily economically motivated lobbies overlook the significant social, cultural, and political implications of IP law. IP regimes do not exist in purely economic realms as they enable and constrain access to social and cultural goods that are fundamental for human expression as well as political and cultural life. What is more, subsequent invention and creativity require access to the knowledge produced previously so that it may be refined, reworked, and redeployed. The primacy of individuated authorial rights within copyright law and international

---

86 Supra note 42.
87 Susan K. Sell, 'The Global IP Upward Ratchet, Anti-Counterfeiting and Piracy Enforcement Efforts: The State of Play', *PIJIP Research Paper no. 15* (Washington: American University Washington College of Law, 2010), http://digitalcommons.wcl.american.edu/research/15
88 Rosemary J. Coombe and Joseph F. Turcotte, 'Cultural, Political, and Social Implications of Intellectual Property Law in an Informational Economy', in UNESCO-EOLSS Joint Committee (ed.), *Encyclopedia of Life Support Systems (EOLSS): Culture, Civilization and Human Society* (Oxford: EOLSS Publishers, 2012), pp. 1–33.

trade agreements has contributed to a chilling effect whereby academic institutions and scholars are wary of asserting their relational creativity by sharing scholarly texts out of the fear of costly litigation and damages from rights holders.[89] Such fears limit the potential of relational creativity and the maintenance of a robust reservoir of knowledge and information for subsequent discovery and creativity.

Legal reform is one potential avenue for embracing the reassertion of relational creativity. Changes to Canada's copyright regime in 2012 demonstrate this: through the SCC's 'copyright pentalogy' of rulings[90] and the changes to Canada's *Copyright Act* contained in the Copyright Modernization Act, Bill C-11 (*Copyright Act*), Canada's domestic copyright regime was altered to accommodate more collaborative and open forms of knowledge creation and distribution. Importantly, in rulings on five copyright-related cases, the SCC 'provided an unequivocal affirmation that copyright exceptions such as fair dealing should be treated as users' rights';[91] and, in Bill C-11 Canada's fair dealing provisions were expanded to include education, parody, and satire. These developments help bring greater clarity to the legal situation in Canada, where the success of a fair dealing argument was relatively uncertain and 'rather than engaging in risky copying activities, authors, publishers, creators, and users chose to, or were advised to, err on the side of caution'.[92]

In addition the SCC's rulings helped to affirm fair dealing as not merely exceptions to copyright law but integral components of it.[93] When fair

---

89 Samuel E. Trosow, 'Bill C-32 and the Educational Sector: Overcoming Impediments to Fair Dealing' in Michael Geist (ed.), *From 'Radical Extremism' to 'Balanced Copyright': Canadian Copyright and the Digital Agenda* (Toronto: Irwin Law, 2010), pp. 541–68, https://www.irwinlaw.com/content_commons/from_radical_extremism_to_balanced_copyright

90 Michael Geist, 'Introduction', in Michael Geist (ed.), *The Copyright Pentalogy: How the Supreme Court of Canada Shook the Foundations of Canadian Copyright Law* (Ottawa: University of Ottawa Press, 2013), pp. ii–xii, https://doi.org/10.26530/oapen_515360

91 Ibid., p. iii.

92 Rosemary J. Coombe, Darren Wershler, and Martin Zeilinger, 'Introducing Dynamic Fair Dealing: Creating Canadian Digital Culture', in Rosemary J. Coombe, Darren Wershler and Martin Zeilinger (eds.), *Dynamic Fair Dealing: Creating Canadian Culture Online* (Toronto: University of Toronto Press, 2014), pp. 3–42 (p. 9), https://doi.org/10.3138/9781442665613-001; for an overview of fair dealing in Canada, see Ariel Katz, 'Fair Use 2.0: The Rebirth of Fair Dealing in Canada', in Michael Geist (ed.), *The Copyright Pentalogy: How the Supreme Court of Canada Shook the Foundations of Canadian Copyright Law* (Ottawa: University of Ottawa Press, 2013), pp. 93–156, https://doi.org/10.26530/oapen_515360

93 Cf. David Vaver, 'User Rights', *Intellectual Property Journal*, 25 (2013), 106–10.

dealing is conceived of as a user's right[94] the attendant permissibility of the appropriation of copyright-protected content helps restore the so-called balance between creators and users — or private and public rights — that IP historically considered. For example, in *CCH v. Law Society of Upper Canada*, the SCC asserted the importance of users' rights in fair-dealing contexts.[95] Recognizing the existence of rights and obligations for both copyright owners and users, the SCC stated that, 'In order to maintain the proper balance between the rights of a copyright owner and users' interests, [fair dealing] must not be interpreted restrictively' (at Para. 48). In addition, '"research" must be given a large and liberal interpretation in order to ensure that users' rights are not unduly constrained' (at Para. 51).

Similarly, in SOCAN v. Bell Canada, the SCC reaffirmed the central role that fair dealing plays in Canadian copyright law:

> One of the tools employed to achieve the proper balance between protection and access in the Act is the concept of fair dealing, which allows users to engage in some activities that might otherwise amount to copyright infringement. In order to maintain the proper balance between these interests, the fair dealing provision 'must not be interpreted restrictively'.[96]

The SCC's reaffirmation of the importance of fair dealing as well as the changes to the *Copyright Act* provide greater legal clarity for academic institutions and researchers to employ relational creativity through fair dealing exceptions. The SCC's rulings also stand apart from the rulings of courts in other countries, which 'have typically referred to exceptions to copyright infringements as defences that cannot form the basis of a legal claim'.[97] These developments may also provide greater clarity for Canadian academic institutions and libraries when considering their copyright and acquisition policies: under Canadian copyright law, educational copying will pass the fair dealing 'first stage purposes test' and then will be judged according to the 'second stage six part test'

---

94 David Vaver, 'Copyright Defenses as User Rights', *Journal of the Copyright Society of the USA* 60.4 (2013), 661–72.

95 Giuseppina D'Agostino, 'The Arithmetic of Fair Dealing at the Supreme Court of Canada' in Michael Geist (ed.), *The Copyright Pentalogy: How the Supreme Court of Canada Shook the Foundations of Canadian Copyright Law* (Ottawa: University of Ottawa Press, 2013), pp. 187–211 (p. 187), https://doi.org/10.26530/oapen_515360

96 Society of Composers, Authors and Music Publishers of Canada v. Bell Canada, 2012 SCC 36, [2012] 2 S.C.R. 326 at Para. 11 (SOCAN v. Bell), https://scc-csc.lexum.com/scc-csc/scc-csc/en/item/9996/index.do

97 Pascale Chapdelaine, 'Copyright User Rights and Remedies: An Access to Justice Perspective', *Laws*, 7.3 (2018), 24–50 (p. 25).

of the 1) purpose, 2) character, 3) amount, and 4) alternatives to the copying as well as the 5) nature of the work and 6) effect of the work being copied.[98] However, the reliance on the Six-Part Test may, itself, lead to unintended consequences.[99]

For authors and scholars engaged in academic publishing, the affirmation of fair dealing as a user's right is welcome news. As legal scholar Samuel Trosow argues:

> At least with respect to the use of copyrighted materials in the educational and library context, the combined message from these measures is unmistakable and clear: users' rights are now firmly entrenched as core principles in Canadian copyright law, and the central policy tool to realize this principle is fair dealing.[100]

For open access advocates in Canada, the SCC and Bill-C11 have provided legal mechanisms through which they can develop and deploy their normative claims around increasing access to scholarly texts. The reaffirmation and expansion of fair dealing in Canada enables innovative cultural and creative practices to develop with reduced fear of litigation or damages from rights holders as long as their uses of copyright-protected works accord with fair dealing.

However, the breadth and strength of users' rights remain contested in domestic and international contexts. In particular, the treatment of fair dealing as a users' right in Canadian law is not matched by recourse for users who have these rights impeded, such as through TPMs.[101] Internationally, the inclusion of anti-circumvention provisions that privilege TPMs in international trade agreements over legitimate uses such as fair dealing for education purposes undermines the balance affirmed by the SCC and seemingly reflected elsewhere in Bill-C11. While recent Canadian free trade agreements such as the Canada-European Union Comprehensive Economic and Trade Agreement[102] contain

---

98 Supra note 90.
99 Cf. supra note 95.
100 Samuel E. Trosow, 'Fair Dealing Practices in the Post-Secondary Education Sector After the Pentalogy', in Michael Geist (ed.), *The Copyright Pentalogy: How the Supreme Court of Canada Shook the Foundations of Canadian Copyright Law* (Ottawa: University of Ottawa Press, 2013), pp. 213–33 (p. 213), https://doi.org/10.26530/oapen_515360
101 Supra note 97, p. 30.
102 Canada-European Union Comprehensive Economic and Trade Agreement, 30 October 2016, 20.9, http://international.gc.ca/trade-commerce/trade-agreements-accords-commerciaux/agr-acc/ceta-aecg/text-texte/toc-tdm.aspx?lang=eng

flexibilities regarding legitimate circumvention of TPMs, Canadian law does not reflect this. The Government of Canada is currently reviewing Bill-C11 and Canada's copyright law as part of the legislation's mandated five-year review. Whether any new legislation will affirm fair dealing as an appropriate limitation of TPMs in educational and research situations, at the least, remains to be seen.

Relational creativity, digital technologies, and the open access movement demonstrate the necessity of accounting for the various interests of rights holder and users in scholarly publishing contexts. The SCC's 'pentalogy' of rulings, as well as the expansion of fair dealing exemptions in the *Copyright Act* work to reaffirm the fundamental importance of allowing for relational creativity alongside copyright protections. Rather than viewing appropriation and inspiration as negative aspects of creativity, the ability of users to build from previously published work — even if copyright protected — serves an integral role in the generation and dissemination of subsequent knowledge and information. Canada's copyright framework and fair dealing provisions are a small step towards recognizing a proper calibration of competing rights and obligations around the 'copy' inherent to both copyright law and digital technologies.

Works Cited

Bailey Jr. Charles W. (2006) *What Is Open Access?*, preprint, http://digital-scholarship.org/cwb/WhatIsOA.htm

Bannerman, Sara (2016) *International Copyright and Access to Knowledge* (Cambridge, UK: Cambridge University Press), https://doi.org/10.1017/CBO9781139149686

Barthes, Roland (1977) *Image, Music, Text* (London: Fontana Press).

Bartow, Ann (2006) 'Open Access, Law, Knowledge, Copyrights, Dominance and Subordination', *Lewis & Clark Law Review* 10.4, 869–84.

Barwa, Sharmishta and Shirin M. Rai (2003) 'Knowledge and/as Power: A Feminist Critique of Trade Related Intellectual Property Rights', *Gender, Technology and Development* 7.1, 91–113.

Benkler, Yochai (2003) 'Freedom in the Commons: Towards a Political Economy of Information', *Duke Law Journal* 52, 1245–76.

Max Planck Society and Max Planck Institute for the History of Science (22 October 2003) *Berlin Declaration on Open Access to Knowledge in the Sciences and Humanities*, http://openaccess.mpg.de/Berlin-Declaration

Boateng, Boatema (2011) *The Copyright Thing Doesn't Work Here: Adinkra and Kente Cloth and Intellectual Property in Ghana* (Minneapolis, MN: University of Minnesota Press), https://doi.org/10.5749/minnesota/9780816670024.001.0001

Bodó, Balázs (2016) 'Pirates in the Library — An Inquiry into the Guerilla Open Access Movement', in 8th Annual Workshop of the International Society for the History and Theory of Intellectual Property, CREATe, University of Glasgow.

Boon, Marcus (2010) *In Praise of Copying* (Cambridge, MA: Harvard University Press), http://www.hup.harvard.edu/features/in-praise-of-copying/

Bowery, Kathy and Jane Anderson (2009) 'The Politics of Global Information Sharing: Whose Cultural Agendas Are Being Advanced?', *Social and Legal Studies* 18.4, 479–504.

Boyle, James (2008) *The Public Domain: Enclosing the Commons of the Mind* (New Haven: Yale University Press), http://thepublicdomain.org/thepublicdomain1.pdf

Cabanac, Guillaume (2016) 'Bibliogifts in LibGen? A Study of a Text-Sharing Platform Driven by Biblioleaks and Crowdsourcing', *Science and Technology* 67.4, 874–84.

Carey, James W. (2005) 'Historical Pragmatism and the Internet', *New Media & Society* 7.4, 443–55, https://doi.org/10.1177/1461444805054107

Castells, Manuel (2009) *The Rise of Network Society*, 2nd ed. (Oxford: Blackwell), https://doi.org/10.1002/9781444319514

Castells, Manuel and Peter Hall (1994) 'Technopoles: Mines and Foundries of the Informational Economy', in Manuel Castells and Peter Hall (ed.), *Technopoles of the World*: *The Making of 21st Century Industrial Complexes* (New York: Routledge), pp. 1–11.

Coombe Rosemary J., and Darren Wershler, Martin Zeilinger (2014) 'Introducing Dynamic Fair Dealing: Creating Canadian Digital Culture', in Rosemary J. Coombe, Darren Wershler and Martin Zeilinger (eds.), *Dynamic Fair Dealing*: *Creating Canadian Culture Online* (Toronto: University of Toronto Press), pp. 3–42, https://doi.org/10.3138/9781442665613-001

Coombe Rosemary J., and Joseph F. Turcotte (2012) 'Cultural, Political, and Social Implications of Intellectual Property Law in an Informational Economy', in UNESCO-EOLSS Joint Committee (ed.), *Encyclopedia of Life Support Systems (EOLSS)*: *Culture, Civilization and Human Society* (Oxford: EOLSS Publishers), pp. 1–33.

Craig, Carys J. (2011) *Copyright, Communication, and Culture*: *Towards a Relational Theory of Copyright* (Cheltenham and Northampton, MA: Edward Elgar), https://doi.org/10.4337/9780857933522

— (2007) 'Reconstructing the Author-Self: Some Feminist Lessons for Copyright Law', *Journal of Gender, Social Policy and the Law* 15.2, 207–68.

— and Joseph F. Turcotte with Rosemary J. Coombe. (2011) 'What's Feminist About Open Access? A Relational Approach to Copyright in the Academy', *feminists@law* 1.1, 1–35.

D'Agostino, Giuseppina (2010) *Copyright, Contracts, Creators*: *New Media, New Rules* (Cheltenham & Northampton: Edward Elgar), https://doi.org/10.4337/9781849805209

— (2013) 'The Arithmetic of Fair Dealing at the Supreme Court of Canada' in Michael Geist (ed.), *The Copyright Pentalogy*: *How the Supreme Court of Canada Shook the Foundations of Canadian Copyright Law* (Ottawa: University of Ottawa Press), pp. 187–211, https://doi.org/10.26530/oapen_515360

Dottridge, Yacine (2012) 'Creative Exploitation: Intellectual Property as a Form of Neoliberal Cultural Policy', Master of Arts, Major Research Paper (Toronto: Ryerson University and York University), https://digital.library.ryerson.ca/islandora/object/RULA:3210

Drahos, Peter with John Braithwaite (2002) *Information Feudalism* (London: Earthscan Publications, Ltd.), https://doi.org/10.4324/9781315092683

Dutfield, Graham (2006) 'To Copy is to Steal: TRIPS, (Un)free Trade Agreements and the New Intellectual Property Fundamentalism', *Journal of Information, Law & Technology* 1, 1–13.

Forsyth, Miranda and Sue Farran (2015) *Weaving Intellectual Property Policy in Small Island Developing States* (Cambridge, UK: Intersentia), https://doi.org/10.1017/9781780685731

Foucault, Michel (1984) 'What Is an Author?', in Paul Rabinov (ed.), *The Foucault Reader* (New York: Pantheon Books), pp. 101–19.

Geist, Michael (2013) 'Introduction', in Michael Geist (ed.), *The Copyright Pentalogy: How the Supreme Court of Canada Shook the Foundations of Canadian Copyright Law* (Ottawa: University of Ottawa Press), pp. ii–xii, https://doi.org/10.26530/oapen_515360

Haunss, Sebastian (2013) *Conflicts in the Knowledge Society: The Contentious Politics of Intellectual Property* (Cambridge, UK: Cambridge University Press), https://doi.org/10.1017/cbo9781139567633

Hettinger, Edwin C. (1989) 'Justifying Intellectual Property Rights', *Philosophy and Public Affairs* 18.1, 31–52.

Hoon, Peggy E. (2003) 'Who Woke the Sleeping Giant?: Libraries, Copyrights, and the Digital Age', *Change* 35.6, 28–33.

Hyde, Lewis (2010) *Common as Air: Revolution, Art and Ownership* (New York: Farrar, Straus and Giroux).

Hyland, Ken (1999) 'Academic Attribution: Citation and the Construction of Disciplinary Knowledge', *Applied Linguistics* 20.3, 341–67.

Jaszi, Peter (1994) 'On the Author Effect: Contemporary Copyright and Collective Creativity', in Martha Woodmansee and Peter Jaszi (eds.), *The Construction of Authorship: Textual Appropriation in Law and Literature* (Durham, N.C.: Duke University Press), pp. 29–56.

Johns, Adrian (2010) *Piracy: The Intellectual Property Wars from Gutenberg to Gates* (Chicago: University of Chicago Press), https://doi.org/10.7208/chicago/9780226401201.001.0001

Kapczynski, Amy (2008) 'The Access to Knowledge Mobilization and the New Politics of Intellectual Property,' *Yale Law Journal* 117.5, 839–51.

Katz, Ariel (2013) 'Fair Use 2.0: e Rebirth of Fair Dealing in Canada', in Michael Geist (ed.), *The Copyright Pentalogy: How the Supreme Court of Canada Shook the Foundations of Canadian Copyright Law* (Ottawa: University of Ottawa Press), pp. 93–156, https://doi.org/10.26530/oapen_515360

Krikorian, Gaëlle and Amy Kapczynski (eds.) (2010) *Access to Knowledge in the Age of Intellectual Property* (New York: Zone Books), https://mitpress.mit.edu/books/access-knowledge-age-intellectual-property

Kelty, Christopher (2008) 'Geeks, Social Imaginaries and Recursive Publics', *Cultural Anthropology* 2.2, 185–214.

— (2008) *Two Bits: The Cultural Significance of Free Software* (Durham, N.C.: Duke University Press), https://doi.org/10.1215/9780822389002

Larivière, Vincent, Stefanie Haustein, and Philippe Mongeon (2015) 'The Oligopoly of Academic Publishers in the Digital Era', *PloS one* 10.6, 1–15.

Lee, Jyh-An (2012) *Non-Profit Organizations and the Intellectual Commons* (Cheltenham: Edward Elgar), https://doi.org/10.4337/9781781001585

Lessig, Lawrence (1999) *Code and Other Laws of Cyberspace* (New York: Basic Books).

— (2008) *Remix: Making Art and Commerce Thrive in the Hybrid Economy* (New York: Penguin Press), https://doi.org/10.5040/9781849662505

— (2010) 'The Man Who Mistook His Wife for a Book', in Gaëlle Krikorian and Amy Kapczynski (eds.), *Access to Knowledge in the Age of Intellectual Property* (New York: Zone Books), pp. 277–92, https://mitpress.mit.edu/books/access-knowledge-age-intellectual-property

Litman, Jessica (1990) 'The Public Domain', *Emory Law Journal* 39, 965–1024.

Macpherson, C. B. (1962) *The Political Theory of Possessive Individualism: Hobbes to Locke* (Oxford: Oxford University Press).

Mason, Matt (2008) *The Pirate's Dilemma: How Youth Culture is Reinventing Capitalism* (New York: Free Press).

Matthews, Duncan (2011) *Intellectual Property, Human Rights and Development: The Role of NGOs and Social Movements* (Cheltenham: Edward Elgar), https://doi.org/10.4337/9780857931245

May, Christopher (2010) *The Global Political Economy of Intellectual Property Rights: The New Enclosures*, 2nd ed. (London and New York: Routledge), https://doi.org/10.4324/9780203873816

McLuhan, Marshall (1962) *The Gutenberg Galaxy: The Making of Typographic Man* (Toronto: University of Toronto Press).

Nedelsky, Jennifer (1989) 'Reconceiving Autonomy: Sources, Thoughts and Possibilities', *Yale Journal of Law & Feminism* 1, 7–36, https://pdfs.semanticscholar.org/4fca/3904f6b21b83b5cb2030e569415390011491.pdf

Pfau, Thomas (1994) 'The Pragmatics of Genre: Moral Theory and Lyric Authorship in Hegel and Woodsworth', in Martha Woodmansee and Peter Jaszi (eds.), *The Construction of Authorship: Textual Appropriation in Law and Literature* (Durham, N.C.: Duke University Press), pp. 133–58.

Plato, trans. by Alexander Nehamas and Paul Woodruff (1997) 'Phaedrus', in John M. Cooper (ed.), *Plato: Complete Works* (Indianapolis and Cambridge, MA: Hackett Publishing Company).

Postman, Neil (1985) *Amusing Ourselves to Death* (New York: Viking).

Randall, Marilyn (2001) *Pragmatic Plagiarism: Authorship, Profit and Power* (Toronto: University of Toronto Press), https://doi.org/10.3138/9781442678736

Ress, Manon A. (2010) 'Open-Access Publishing: From Principles to Practice', in Gaëlle Krikorian and Amy Kapczynski (eds.), *Access to Knowledge in the Age of Intellectual Property* (New York: Zone Books), pp. 475–96, https://mitpress.mit.edu/books/access-knowledge-age-intellectual-property

Rice, Grantland S. (1997) *The Transformation of Authorship in America* (Chicago: University of Chicago Press).

Rose, Mark (1996) 'Mothers and Authors: *Johnson v. Calvert* and the New Children of Our Imaginations', *Critical Inquiry* 22 (Summer), 613–33.

— (2005) 'Technology and Copyright in 1735: The Engraver's Act', *The Information Society* 21, 63–66.

Sell, Susan K. (2010) 'The Global IP Upward Ratchet, Anti-Counterfeiting and Piracy Enforcement Efforts: The State of Play', *PIJIP Research Paper no. 15* (Washington: American University Washington College of Law), http://digitalcommons.wcl.american.edu/research/15

— (2003) *Private Power, Public Law*: *The Globalization of Intellectual Property Rights* (Cambridge, UK: Cambridge University Press), https://doi.org/10.1017/cbo9780511491665

— and Christopher May (2001) 'Moments in Law: Contestation and Settlement in the History of Intellectual Property', *Review of International Political Economy* 8.3, 467–500.

Statute of Anne, The: *An Act for the Encouragement of Learning, by Vesting the Copies of Printed Books in the Authors or Purchasers of Such Copies, During the Times Therein Mentioned,* 8 Anne, c. 19 (1710), The Avalon Project: Documents in Law, History and Diplomacy, http://avalon.law.yale.edu/18th_century/anne_1710.asp

Suber, Peter (2016) *Knowledge Unbound*: *Selected Writings on Open Access, 2002–2011* (Cambridge, MA: MIT Press), https://mitpress.mit.edu/books/knowledge-unbound

Sunder, Madhavi (2007) 'The Invention of Traditional Knowledge', *Law and Contemporary Problems* 70.2, 97–124.

Trosow, Samuel E. (2013) 'Fair Dealing Practices in the Post-Secondary Education Sector After the Pentalogy', in Michael Geist (ed.), *The Copyright Pentalogy*: *How the Supreme Court of Canada Shook the Foundations of Canadian Copyright Law* (Ottawa: University of Ottawa Press), pp. 213–33, https://doi.org/10.26530/oapen_515360

— (2010) 'Bill C-32 and the Educational Sector: Overcoming Impediments to Fair Dealing' in Michael Geist (ed.), *From 'Radical Extremism' to 'Balanced Copyright'*: *Canadian Copyright and the Digital Agenda* (Toronto: Irwin Law), pp. 541–68, https://www.irwinlaw.com/content_commons/from_radical_extremism_to_balanced_copyright

Quentel, Debra L. (1996) 'Bad Artists Copy-Good Artists Steal: The Ugly Conflict between Copyright Law and Appropriationism', *UCLA Entertainment Law Review* 4, 39–80.

Vaver, David (2013) 'User Rights', *Intellectual Property Journal* 25, 106–10.

— (2013) 'Copyright Defenses as User Rights', *Journal of the Copyright Society of the USA* 60.4, 661–72.

— (2012) 'Intellectual Property: Is It Still A 'Bargain'?', *Intellectual Property Journal* 24, 143–58.

— (2011) *Intellectual Property Law*, 2nd ed. (Concord: Irwin Law), https://digitalcommons.osgoode.yorku.ca/faculty_books/134

Wong, Tzen and Graham Dutfield (eds.) (2011) *Intellectual Property and Development: Current Trends and Future Scenarios* (Cambridge, UK: Cambridge University Press), https://doi.org/10.1017/cbo9780511761027

Woodmansee, Martha and Peter Jaszi (eds.) (1994) *The Construction of Authorship: Textual Appropriation in Law and Literature*, 3rd ed. (Durham, N.C.: Duke University Press).

Wright, Shelley (1994) 'A Feminist Exploration of the Legal Protection of Art,' *Canadian Journal of Women and the Law* 7, 59–96.

14. Redefining Reader and Writer, Remixing Copyright: Experimental Publishing at if:book Australia

Simon Groth

Remixing Clarke

> 'Lines of text gradually blur until *almost* illegible.'
>
> — *Notes for the designer from the manuscript for* Hunted Down and Other Tales

Even at first blush, *Hunted Down and Other Tales by Marcus Clarke* is anything but an ordinary book. It is a slim volume, barely one hundred pages, in a small form factor. It declares its price of 'one shilling' directly on the front and fills its back cover with breathless descriptions of recently published books (with illustrations, available from the low price of 9d.). Its first few pages are filled with advertisements: an oyster saloon bar, a shipping insurance broker, a brewery and 'wine merchant', and more. Though part of an experimental literary remix project, at this point, *Hunted Down and Other Tales* is nothing more than pitch-perfect mimicry and a loving paean to books first published in the 1870s in colonial Australia. Even the ads are genuine, lifted from a contemporary edition for *Queensland Figaro and Punch* from 1872.

© 2019 Simon Groth, CC BY 4.0   https://doi.org/10.11647/OBP.0159.14

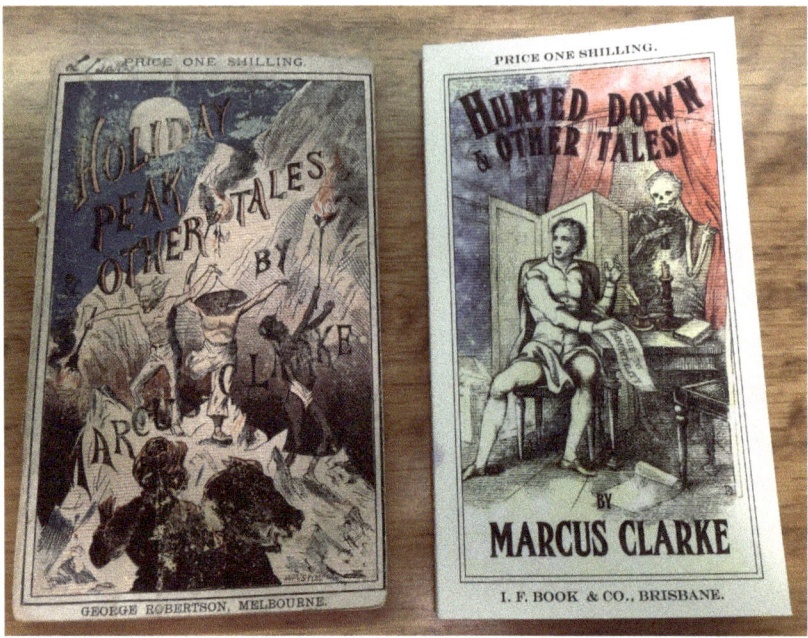

Fig. 14.1 Proof copy of *Hunted Down and Other Tales* (ISBN: 9780994471925) alongside an original copy of Clarke's 1871 title *Holiday Peak and Other Tales*.

A literary remix modifies its source material in a way that seeks to bring a new artistic perspective and creates a new co-authored work in the process. In the case of *Hunted Down*, it is not until the third story — 'How the Circus Came to Bullocktown' — that the twenty-first century begins to disrupt the nineteenth.

In my original manuscript, every page is littered with notes, instructions and asides intended for the book's designer George Saad. In the quote above, I suggest a design to accompany a section of the story in which the entire populace of Bullocktown gets uproariously drunk. My initial instinct was to modify the printed page in the way that is only possible from a digital source, with an eye to taking the reader more deeply into story. The modifications in 'Bullocktown' come thick and fast: Clarke's text is divided into eight shorter sections, each of which is variously annotated, flanked by posters and advertisements, formed into textual puzzles, faded to grey, and so on.

In the example above, rather than follow my design suggestion, George took the 'drunk' narrative and stretched and squashed it into a wobbling, nauseous block of text that, by its conclusion, stumbles off the page altogether. This is typesetting that would have been unimaginable in the 1870s and is today possible only with a battery of digital tools.

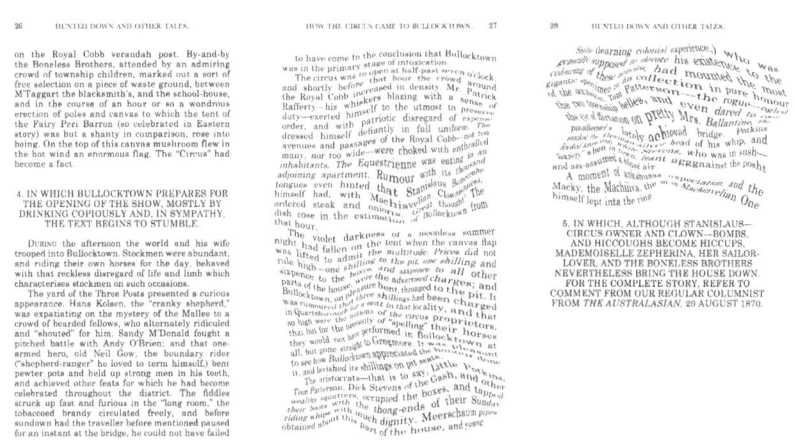

Fig. 14.2 The 'drunk' text from *Hunted Down and Other Tales* mirrors the narrative as its characters become increasingly intoxicated.

In *Hunted Down and Other Tales*, these tools are applied in the service of introducing to a contemporary audience a lesser-known work from an author widely regarded as one of the finest our nation has produced. It is also a work that challenges underlying assumptions of original work, copyright, and intellectual property. It is as good an introduction as any to if:book Australia's often heady blend of art, design, and narrative: technologies and techniques that acknowledge the rich heritage of literature's past while challenging the assumptions of the present in the interests of leaning into the future.

if:book Australia

Based in Brisbane and linked to an international fellowship of organisations exploring book futures, if:book Australia (the Institute for the Future of the Book) explored new forms of digital literature and investigated the changing relationship between writer and reader. Its explorations at the intersection of technology and publishing took the form of writing, teaching, and experimenting. From 2010 to 2016, if:book Australia published tens of thousands of words from some of the nation's best writers and thinkers on book futures, delivered workshops from Perth to Canberra to Alice Springs, helped authors create live writing inspired by an audience, and remixed lost nineteenth-century Australian fiction. Working at the blurred boundaries of what qualifies as 'the book', if:book made fascinating and instructive observations on how writers and readers interact and what kind of stories can be told.

If we remove the medium altogether and define the book as a type of interaction, a relationship, between reader and writer, then we can ask a series of pertinent questions:

- What is the purpose of the book in a connected, participatory reading and writing culture?
- What are the new forms that continue to emerge that take advantage of how ideas and stories are discovered and shared?
- How can the technologies for old and new media interact to create new work?
- What does that mean for how that work might be read?
- What changes when we change the book and what remains the same?

Though not addressed directly in the organisation's brief, assumptions around copyright and intellectual property were regularly questioned and challenged by if:book's experimental projects.

Copyright and Medium

Copyright law, in the words of Jonathan Zittrain, Harvard Professor of Internet Law, 'was written with a particular form of industry in mind,'[1] specifically publishing through the medium of print. Indeed, the publishing industry's long history and recent disruption at the hands of digital media makes the book a particularly apt lens through which to observe the challenges of copyright to a form of intellectual property that until relatively recently existed only in physical media. Although copyright today covers a range of rights and licensing laws beyond a

---

1   Quoted in Matthew Rimmer, *Digital Copyright and the Consumer Revolution* (Cheltenham, UK: Edward Elgar Publishing, 2007).

set of rules that govern the ability to make copies of a given work, the notion of the 'copy' and the assumptions that underlie it remain central to the disruption of traditional copyright at the hands of digital media.

To make an unauthorised copy of a printed book takes dedication, resources, time, and money. Even to plagiarise from a print work requires a certain amount of intellectual and physical labour. For these labours and costs to be worthwhile, the act of copying is assumed to be accompanied by some kind of benefit: credit for the plagiarist and profit for the pirate. In a world of print media, the path of least resistance to obtain a work for most readers is to purchase or borrow through established and legal means. Even with modern home scanning and printing technology, the process of making a copy of even a modestly sized novel, for example, would be interminable and unlikely to deliver a reading experience that matches the original. The effort one must go to in order to copy a print book is prohibitive without a means of profiting from it.

Things are very different in the networked world of ones and zeros.

One of the early touted benefits of electronic digital media was its capacity to effortlessly create perfect copies of content. Entire digital files can be replicated with drag-and-drop ease. Similarly, the content within those files can be copied and pasted, replicating it perfectly into a new file. Operating systems and software such as word processors have made such ease a virtue: keyboard shortcuts for cut, copy and paste appeared as early as 1983 on Apple's Lisa and Macintosh systems before becoming computing standards.

With the Internet, that ease of data replication becomes linked to a vast distribution network in which 'copying' content has become second nature, to the point of being invisible to the end user. To view a single page of web content, a reader requests data from a remote server. On its way from server to user, each packet of that data passes through a series of routers, which not only direct Internet traffic but which also make temporary copies of everything that passes through. When the transmitted data is reassembled into content on the viewer's screen, the web browser automatically copies information from the page to a local cache on the reader's device. Calling up a browser page necessarily requires making a copy of its content. Another example is the case of email. The humble act of sending an email attachment results in a bloom of copies: dragging a document from the file system to the mail client saves a copy in the local messages system; another copy is uploaded and stored on the sender's IMAP server; another is stored at the receiver's mail server, which is then downloaded to their mail client, and which they may then save to a specific location in their own file system. Of course, many of us access messages on a number of devices (each of which stores another copy). In both of these examples, much of this copying takes place without the intervention or even awareness of the individual user or reader. One of the reasons the Internet can be thought of as, in the words of Cory Doctorow, 'the world's most efficient copying machine'[2] is that accurate and automated copying is an essential part of its machinery. In a world of digital media on interconnected devices, making a copy of any given set of data is not just easy; it's as natural and as unconscious as taking a breath.

It is here that the digital disruption of copyright is at its starkest. Original works should certainly be protected from individuals who seek to benefit from them without fair compensation to the creator. But an underlying assumption of copyright law — that the act of copying is difficult and must therefore be accompanied by a profit motive or intent for intellectual deception — cannot be applied universally to digital media on networked devices.

A set of rules that govern property in the physical world has proven an awkward fit for the digital environment and has often led to overreach by rights holders: artificial geoblocks or punitive restrictions on how content can be stored and accessed (restrictions that have no parallel in the physical world). Equating unauthorised copying of intellectual property with theft and shoplifting strains credulity and the frequently heavy-handed responses of rights holders treat their audience as criminals first and audience second.

Indeed, audiences are well aware that digital media is fundamentally different to physical media. After observing the shortcomings of existing copyright law, Professor Zittrain continued: 'the flourishing of information technology gives amateurs and home-recording artists powerful tools to build and share interesting, transformative, and socially valuable art drawn from pieces of popular cultures. There's no place to plug such an important cultural sea change into the current legal regime.'

---

2   Cory Doctorow, *About Little Brother* (2008), http://craphound.com/littlebrother/about/

While audiences have demonstrated little sympathy for corporate 'rights holders', the community regularly expresses support for artists, authors, and other creative people and the work they produce. For an audience steeped in digital media, this love for a creative work is not a passive experience. The logical extension of that love then is the ability to copy and paste, to quote, sometimes to absorb, adapt and modify, and most importantly to share. if:book's experimental work around the future of the book and the nexus of technology and publishing has actively sought new ways to define the central relationship between writer and reader, to blur their roles, and to examine models of copyright that embrace rather than resist the capabilities and culture of digital media.

Lifting the Veil, Inviting Contributions

Revealing the process of writing and opening it up to the scrutiny of readers has been a major component of many if:book projects.

The '24-Hour Book' was a live writing event that brought a team of writers, editors, designers, and technologies together to complete the production of a book in both print and digital formats — from concept to finished product — within a single twenty-four-hour period. The book was written using an online book production tool, Pressbooks, to expedite writing and editing and to handle typesetting for print and coding for digital. Created in if:book's office in Brisbane, Australia, the first copy of the project's resulting book, *Willow Pattern*, rolled off an Espresso Book Machine in Brooklyn, NY approximately twenty-three hours and forty minutes after commencement.

Fig. 14.3 The authors meet to discuss progress during the 24-Hour Book (left), Bronwen Blaney of On Demand Books presents the first copy of *Willow Pattern* (ISBN: 9780987251435) from an Espresso Book Machine (right).

During the live event, the project's nine authors published their work in progress online. Readers were encouraged to follow the stories throughout the day and to interact with the writers and each other via comments and social media. This created a dynamic in which the reader was not only able to observe the creative process in action (for better and for worse) but also potentially to influence the writing that emerged. A number of authors played up to this dynamic, directly soliciting ideas and contributions from readers, some of which made their way into the final text. It was this dynamic that led to the creation of another if:book project based around live writing.

'Memory Makes Us' is an event that challenges writers to create a new work using as their inspiration memories collected from the general public. Where the live component of the '24-Hour Book' was primarily an online reading experience, 'Memory Makes Us' happens both online and in a physical space. Over the last three years, the project has taken place at writers' festivals throughout Australia and in the US. At each event, up to three writers occupy a public space at a festival or other event to create a new work live before the audience. The writers work at notebook computers connected both to a display monitor at the venue and fed live to the project website. From a predetermined theme, each writer invites contributions and inspiration from audience members in the form of 'memories'. Memory texts can be recorded in one of two ways: by filling in a form on the project website or by using one of the manual typewriters provided at the venue.

Fig. 14.4 Writer Kate Pullinger (left) and participants recording memories (right) at the first *Memory Makes Us* event in Brisbane, 2013.

As the number of collected contributions grows throughout the day, each typewritten 'memory' is attached to the authors' table, eventually reaching the floor and 'flowing' out towards the audience, both marker of progress and visual flourish. This is writing as a performance, but one distinct from other performative aspects of literature: it is not a reading of a prepared work, nor is it freestyle poetry or 'improv'. It is improvisation not with speech but with text and the tools of contemporary writing: keyboard and cut-and-paste.

It is also a project that deliberately blurs the roles of reader and writer, in which the audience contributes to a singularly authored work, and in which permission to co-opt memories and emotions is consciously granted.

Grappling with the Remix as a Literary Act

Alongside open demonstrations of the creative process and blurring the roles of artist and audience, if:book has run a series of projects that explore the remix as a distinct literary art form. 'Remix' is an umbrella term for a range of forms and techniques that use existing creative work as source material to be modified in a way that seeks to bring a new artistic perspective.

The term itself originates from its more familiar use in popular music. Though its antecedents are as old as artistic expression itself — from the collages and 'readymades' of Dadaists that played with the malleability of meaning all the way back to the limitlessly fluid oral storytelling tradition — the distinguishing feature of remixing is that it presupposes a recorded source work that can be divided into smaller components capable of manipulation, manoeuvring, and recombination. It also relies on technologies and tools to enable this.

In this sense, remix can be considered a digital art form.

In music, the remix is distinct from the 'cover version' or reinterpretation. The advent of editable magnetic tape and multitrack recording — in which individual instruments and sounds can be isolated from the whole — first enabled the concept of remixing. More recent digital recording tools and techniques offer a greater palette for sound manipulation than traditional analogue tapes.

Use of the specific term 'remix' in relation to literature is a relatively recent phenomenon (see Mark Amerika's 'Remix the Book' from 2011). As with music, the literary remix relies on and benefits from an increasing sophistication in digital tools. Where the typewriter breaks literature into smaller components, the word processor and its twin concepts of the software 'document' and cut, copy and paste make the movement and recombination of text blocks an essential skill for contemporary writers. In the remix, cut-and-paste becomes a transformative act, a performance, something magnified by the plethora of Internet-based digital tools and the real-time distribution it enables.

An important distinction to make, especially in literature, is between a remix and an edit. An edit seeks to strengthen and clarify the original author's intention. A remix is made with the understanding that the remixer will intentionally change the original work as a creative act. Remixing is also an inherently critical act. The choices made by a remixer — the choices of what to keep and what to change — necessarily counter the original author's vision for the work. Several authors who have participated in if:book's remixing projects have struggled with the thought that they might be making value judgements on the quality of the source material. But, unlike an edit, a remix need not be considered an improvement or detraction from the original. A remix does not replace its source material, but exists as a distinct entity, linked but independent: a new version.

Early Experiments with Remix

The first of if:book's remix projects grew directly from the '24-Hour Book'. The primary motivation to adopt the online publishing system, Pressbooks, was to find a convenient way to reach readers during the writing and to speed up the process of typesetting and internal design. Pressbooks is based on the open source Wordpress blogging tool and its writing and editing backend created an opportunity to extend the '24-Hour Book' beyond its initial scope. As well as providing a platform on which the authors and editors could work, Pressbooks also created an extensive database of backups: every time an author or editor saved their work in progress (and at regular intervals in between) the system stored a complete snapshot of the text, including metadata such as the login details of the person making the save and a time stamp. What emerged at the end of the initial project was a database that recorded the complete creation of a book, from the first word to the final edit.

Throughout 2013 and 2014, if:book opened that database to public scrutiny, creating an interface at *willowpatterns.net* that enables readers to browse, search, and download the complete editing data. The project also turned the editing data over to four Australian poets for the purpose of creating new works of remix to be published on the project website. Their responses varied from meticulously referenced cento poetry to a video-based work that reproduces, once, all the words used throughout the entire the project.

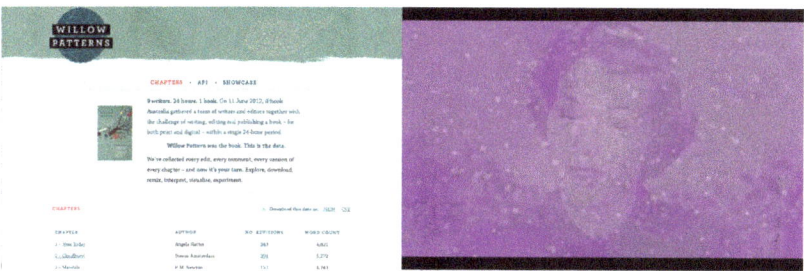

Fig. 14.5 Home page of book database *willowpatterns.net* (left), and a still from *I Will Say This Only Once*, a database remix by Pascalle Burton.

The project explored the relationship between narrative and data and the artistic responses of the project were based on the story of how the '24-Hour Book' was made, rather than on the stories contained within it.

The next stage in exploring the literary remix combined cut-and-paste transformation with the personal and intimate craft of memoir. 'Lost in Track Changes' was a project that asked five writers to create a short piece of memoir, a vignette. Each of these pieces was passed on to another author within the group tasked with remixing it into a new work. The remixes would then be passed along to another author and again and again until each of the pieces had been remixed by all five authors in series. In the background, if:book tracked all the changes between each of these transformations.

Featuring the talents of Cate Kennedy, Ryan O'Neill, Krissy Kneen, Robert Hoge, and Fiona Capp, the result is a curious artefact produced for print and digital media: frequently subtle and nuanced in its treatment of source material, but peppered by lurching shifts in style, form, and perspective. In just one series of stories a heartfelt recollection of growing up becomes dystopian sci-fi which becomes a dictionary entry which becomes a poem in requiem for an imaginary writer.

Unlike remixes from the '24-Hour Book', the source material for 'Lost in Track Changes' was written specifically with its subsequent transformation in mind. The effect on its authors varied: for Ryan O'Neill, well versed in the postmodern short story, the most difficult part of the project was writing the initial memoir piece; Fiona Capp's writing represented a progression from subtle, editorial-style changes for the first remix to wholesale rewriting and a change of narrator in the project's final 'round'.

The print title created by the project actively encourages its reader to continue modifying the work within, both directly in its introductory text and, more subtly, in its design cues. The pages are laid out with wide margins and line spacing and the book itself is wire bound in the style of a notepad.

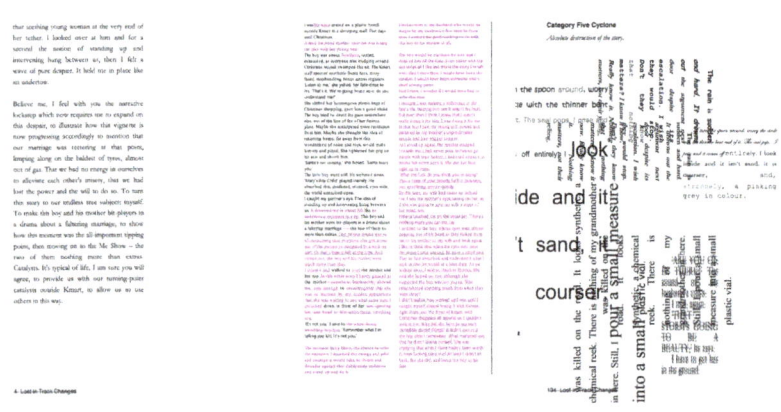

Fig. 14.6 Pages from *Lost in Track Changes* (ISBN: 9780992373733) showing wide margins, 'track changes' layout, and remixed story layout.

Rumours of my Death

Where 'Lost in Track Changes' commissioned new short-form works for the specific purpose of remixing, the follow up project, 'Rumours of My Death' targeted established long-form literary works as its

14. Redefining Reader and Writer, Remixing Copyright

source material to create extended works of remix. Again borrowing the parlance of popular music, such extended works of remix are called 'mashups'. The project challenged three Australian authors — Mez Breeze, Christopher Currie, and myself — to each select a lesser-known work from the public domain and, using it as source material, to create a new remixed work for a range of contemporary media. Where prior popular literary mashups blend seemingly incompatible genres for comic effect, 'Rumours of My Death' was intended as an exploration of Australian times and culture and to highlight works and authors that had fallen into relative obscurity.

'Rumours of My Death' consists of three distinct works.

A [[Non]] Guardian Age was written by Mez Breeze and based on *The Guardian: A Tale*, an 1838 novel by Anna Maria Bunn. Despite being both the first Australian novel published on mainland Australia and the first by a female author, Bunn's only literary work is not widely known. It is an unusual novel that itself 'mashes' gothic romance with comedy of errors in an awkward and uneven story. Shortlisted for the 2016 Western Australian Premier's Book Awards, *A [[Non]] Guardian Age* is a web-based book created using mixed media that mashes prose with poetry and code while it 'refashions' Bunn's novel, passing commentary as it goes: on time, on the country, and on the original work itself.

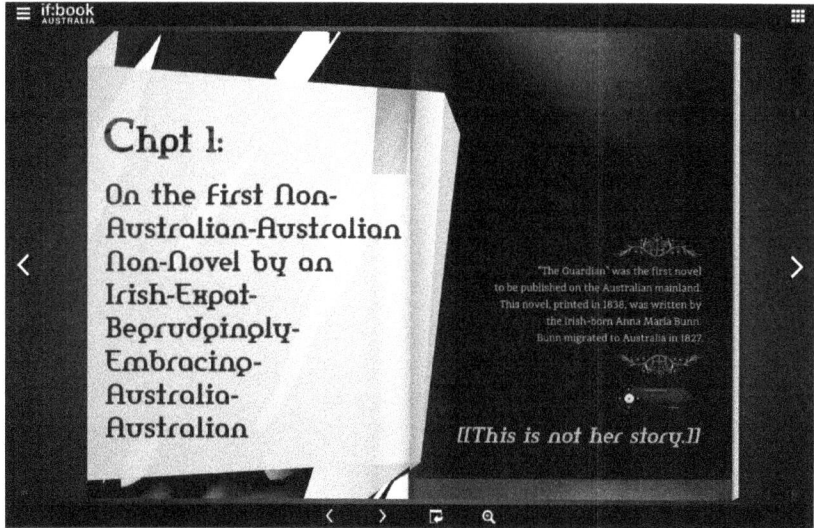

Fig. 14.7 Sample page from *A [[Non]] Guardian Age*, by Mez Breeze.

The Tweets of @HenrySavery was written by Christopher Currie and based on *Quintus Servinton*, by Henry Savery, the first novel published in Australia (in 1830). The piece took place live on Twitter as 'Savery' — twice-convicted forger, one-time novelist, gossip columnist, and ne'er-do-well about town — took up a digital residency at the 2015 Brisbane Writers Festival. Via the handle @HenrySavery, the piece tracked the author's week-long journey from Tasmania's Isle of the Dead to Brisbane, creating a comic array of characters and situations along the way. Throughout the festival Currie attended events and commented anonymously in character (mimicking and sometimes quoting from Savery's breathless and dense prose), chatting with the authors and attendees, making observations on contemporary writing and publishing culture, and nursing hangovers.

Fig. 14.8 Tweet from @HenrySavery during the 2015 Brisbane Writers Festival.

The final work from 'Rumours of My Death' is *Hunted Down and Other Tales*, the print book introduced at the outset of this chapter that collects and remixes three stories by Marcus Clarke. Clarke is the celebrated author of the classic novel *His Natural Life*, but *Hunted Down* focuses instead on his lesser-known short fiction. Superficially, the book directly mimics the size and visual style of the short story anthologies Clarke originally published in the 1870s: pocket-size editions of around 100 pages sold from newsstands and were filled with advertisements for local businesses alongside the fiction. It begins with two original stories by Clarke. The title story (which itself directly references Dickens) appears under its original title and in its original length for the first time since its publication in *The Australasian* newspaper on 6 May 1871. The remixes begin with the third story in the collection. 'How the Circus Came to Bullocktown', already a wild and chaotic story, has a toolbox of visual remix techniques thrown at it: the text is annotated, faded almost to the point of deletion, formed into typographic puzzles. Several times, the text 'breaks out' from the page and onto a series of paper inserts: flyer, newspaper clipping, business card and beer coaster. The final two stories are remixed versions of the first two: relocating Clarke's stories to contemporary Australia. The book's advertisements are also given the remix treatment: actual ads from the 1870s give way to mashups of contemporary products presented in an old-fashioned style to mimicry of online recommendations and customer reviews.

Fig. 14.9 Progression of 'advertisements' through *Hunted Down and Other Tales*, from original nineteenth-century copy to contemporary buyer recommendations and customer reviews.

Audience as Co-Creator: Copyright Status of Audience Contributions

For a project such as 'Memory Makes Us', audience members who contribute do so expressly for the purpose of having their words and images adapted or copied directly into another person's creative work. The project's privacy statement states:

> By submitting your work to this site, you assert that you own the rights to the material and grant to if:book Australia the non-exclusive right to use this work for the duration of the project Memory Makes Us.
>
> Your text and images may be edited and published to the if:book web site for the duration of the Memory Makes Us project and may also be displayed at events related to the project. If we wish to reproduce your work in other forms, we will ask first. The copyright in all work submitted to Memory Makes Us remains with its author.

To reinforce the status of audience contributions, the website and the subsequent print edition of the project include the following text in their copyright notices:

> Your memories are your own.

The primary purpose of seeking audience contributions to any if:book project is to create a depth of connection between the 'writer' and 'reader' that goes beyond the traditional reading experience. The effect can be profound, especially for a project like 'Memory Makes Us' in which the personal and private is subtly made public. This is something to which I can attest from my own experience as a contributor: seeing my own words and a memory from my own experience suddenly dropped into someone else's work and displayed on a giant screen in Melbourne's Federation Square is not easily forgotten. At the time, I looked up, recognised my words, then watched in mild dismay as author Paddy O'Reilly highlighted and deleted the entire passage, save for a single word: 'sunscreen'. My private sense of ownership over that word and the pleasure of its presence in the final work is an experience shared by many of the contributors and authors who have participated in the project. It is an experience that relies on a shared understanding and mutual respect between author and contributor.

Works published by if:book are licensed under Creative Commons (Attribution, NonCommercial 4.0 International Licence, abbreviated as BY-NC-4.0). Creative Commons describes itself as 'a worldwide non-profit organisation that provides copyright owners with free licences allowing them to share, reuse and remix their material, legally.'[3] This licence details for an audience in plain language the extent to which a work can be copied, distributed and modified. It reads as follows:

You are free to:

- *Share — copy and redistribute the material in any medium or format*
- *Adapt — remix, transform, and build upon the material*

The licensor cannot revoke these freedoms as long as you follow the license terms. Under the following terms:

- *Attribution — You must give appropriate credit, provide a link to the license, and indicate if changes were made. You may do so in any reasonable manner, but not in any way that suggests the licensor endorses you or your use.*
- *NonCommercial — You may not use the material for commercial purposes.*

No additional restrictions — You may not apply legal terms or technological measures that legally restrict others from doing anything the license permits.

Especially for a project such as 'Memory Makes Us', which relies on freely shared public contributions, this licence provides an important acknowledgement to the audience and returns the favour, turning the completed work back to the people who helped create it.

Remix and Copyright Law in Australia

For its various remix projects, if:book has relied on two categories of source material: work commissioned specifically to be remixed and out-of-copyright work drawn from the public domain. In part, this is a choice born from necessity: the organisation chooses to use its limited

---

3   Creative Commons Australia, http://creativecommons.org.au/learn/

resources for creative work rather than licensing from publishers or other third-party rights holders. Australian copyright law allows for the use of material that remains under copyright to be used without permission in remix, mashup and even memes under specific circumstances, in particular if the amount of source material used is not 'substantial'. But the definition of 'substantial' is subjective and open to interpretation and challenge. The law also makes special provisions for parody or satire within the concept of 'fair dealing' (exceptions under copyright law that differ from the US 'fair use' provisions).[4] The law also takes into account if the remixed work has no commercial element to its creation or distribution.[5] But proceeding with a remix under these provisions means inevitably testing the law's definitions.

For an Australian literary remixer to stay within the law, seeking permission for remix purposes may be the most prudent approach. However using material that requires explicit permission and licensing means tracking down current rights holders who may or may not be the actual creator of the work and striking an agreement under a set of rules that are complex, often subjective, and not static over time.

As a small organisation, the legal costs of exploring the use of fair dealing exceptions are too high to justify expanding the range of works we might use.

The choice of source material is also stylistic, intended to expand the writer's craft and to explore wider cultural questions. For the authors of 'Lost in Track Changes', the project represented their first experience of writing material in the full knowledge that their work would be modified by others. 'Rumours of My Death' made a virtue of restricting its source material, focusing on lesser-known works and using the project to observe and comment on the changes in Australian life and culture since its early days.

Even a focus on out-of-copyright works, though, means addressing complexities in the law and problems of representation and access. Until 1 January 2005, the duration of Australia's copyright protection was the

---

4   Debate is currently underway as to whether Australia should adopt the broader fair use exceptions.
5   Australian Copyright Council, 'Mashups, Memes, Remixes & Copyright (Information sheet G118v04)', 2014, https://www.copyright.org.au/ACC_Prod/ACC/Information_Sheets/Mashups__Memes__Remixes___Copyright.aspx

life of the author plus fifty years. On that date, protection was extended to life plus seventy years, under the terms of a free trade agreement with the US,[6] a ruling that effectively means no works published in Australia will enter the public domain until 2025. For now, a rule of thumb for determining the copyright status of a work therefore is to determine the date of publication and date of the author's death: if both fall prior to 1955, the work is out of copyright. This applies only to published written work, meaning remixers who wish to work with images, sound or film must consider separate provisions.

In literature, Australia's public domain contains barely a century's worth of works and significant biases and omissions. Though printing presses had been established from the earliest days of the colonies, Australian literature took many years to become established. *Quintus Servinton*, Australia's first novel, was published in Tasmania in 1830 while *The Guardian*, the first published on the mainland, did not emerge until 1838. Since copyright relies on works first being published, many important voices, in particular those of Aboriginal and Torres Strait Islander people, are absent from the public domain.

Access to works may also prove problematic. Major resources such as the National Library's digitisation and search tool Trove and Project Gutenberg provide access to digitised collections (an essential resources for 'Rumours of My Death'), but coverage is far from universal. *The Guardian*, for example, has not been digitised in any form and its remix involved transcribing text from a print edition, rather than cut and paste. It is unfortunate that the first novel published on mainland Australia and also the first by a female author is less accessible than other literary works of historical significance, something the project was able to highlight, although this was not part of its original intention.

Remix as an Experiment in Copyright

Remix shatters the assumption that copying is necessarily a nefarious act, concealed from an audience in order to gain unfair advantage. In

---

6 Australian Copyright Council, 'Duration of Copyright (Information sheet G023v17)', 2014, https://www.copyright.org.au/acc_prod/ACC/Information_Sheets/Duration_of_Copyright.aspx

best practice, remix happens openly, drawing attention to its process and to the original work from which it is derived. One of the goals for the 'Rumours of My Death' project was to specifically draw attention to works that have been largely buried in the public consciousness. *Lost in Track Changes* and *Hunted Down and Other Tales* go further, reproducing the source material alongside the remixes.

One of the governing principles behind all of if:book's various remix projects is respect: for the source material and its provenance and for the audience. These projects draw a clear distinction between openly using an existing work as a source to create something new and deliberately representing someone else's work as your own. Though some provisions for remixing have been made, current copyright law remains opaque and complex, largely because of its assumptions regarding the intent behind copying.

Works of remix contain layers of copyright protection: the rights that apply to the source material and the rights that apply to the act of remixing and any new work generated.

Prior to any creative engagement, a potential remixer is a member of the audience. Inherent in remix culture then is the notion that audience can become creator; that a remix can in turn become source material for another generation of works. if:book directly explored this chain of remix activity in *Lost in Track Changes*, in particular in the project's print edition that encourages further modification of the text. This blurring of the roles between audience/reader and creator/writer is reflected and reinforced by the use of Creative Commons licensing.

But even when working with material that explicitly permits remix, this layering effect of multiple rights holders creates interesting questions over a work's provenance and implications for ongoing modification. As demonstrated in our projects, a series of remixes can render a work where nothing remains from the original source. For how many iterations does the obligation to acknowledge the source remain? The consequences of this question are especially important when works are licensed for remixing and where such obligations may not be simply moral but also financial. At present, Australian copyright law provides no clear guidelines for a response to this question.

Remixing the Law

If a literary remix modifies its source material in a way that seeks to bring a new perspective, then is it possible to apply its techniques to existing copyright law? Can we creatively adapt the source material of copyright to establish a new version of the law that acknowledges the legacy of physical media while recognising the realities of digital media?

In considering how copyright can adapt to contemporary digital culture, it is worth first reflecting on its purpose.

One finding from if:book's experiments with the relationship between writer and reader and with the medium of expression is that copyright viewed through the narrow frame of 'protection' for original works is fundamentally at odds with digital culture. By placing a priority on the 'protection' of work at the expense of audience access and participation this expression of copyright leads to a restrictive and frustrating experience. At its most egregious, this approach treats the audience as criminals first, through punitive licensing agreements and user-hostile technologies such as digital rights management. Such moves succeed only in antagonising legitimate audiences, since they have proven ineffective against infringement. The expansion of skills, the blurring of traditional roles, and the play with medium that if:book explores would be impossible in a system predicated on protection first. If an artist's primary goal is the protection of intellectual property from bad actors, then the only sure-fire way to meet it is never to seek an audience nor allow your work to enter the public sphere.

So, rather than emphasising protection, a remixed copyright system should emphasise mutual understanding between artist and audience about rights and responsibilities for the work, clearly articulated and easily understood. Copyright should ensure that artists are recognised and remunerated appropriately for their work and that audiences can access, discuss, and share that work. While this does not infringe the capacity to buy and sell the rights for individual works, it does regard as ancillary the rights of any third parties.

Striking an appropriate and equitable balance between the rights of artists and audiences is a delicate, but not impossible task. Indeed, it could be considered a foundational principle of a remixed copyright law and one that applies as readily to physical media as it does to a digital environment where copying content, whether in part or in whole, has become a mechanically trivial act. This is a sentiment echoed by US Judge Thomas A. Higgins in the case *Bridgeport Music Inc v Dimension Films Inc*, which considered the unauthorised use of a two-second sample in a popular music recording: 'A balance must be struck between protecting an artist's interests and depriving other artists of the building blocks of future works.'[7]

Though conceived with digital media in mind, this approach does not dismiss other media through which creative work is distributed. Attempts to make digital works behave like their physical counterparts (artificially making the act of copying more difficult) in order to better fit existing copyright automatically tips the balance of rights in favour of the artist (or the rights holder) at the expense of the audience, just as wholesale permission to redistribute works without payment unfairly privileges the audience over the artist. Similarly, digital media is not a wholesale replacement for physical media — something *Hunted Down and Other Tales* as a born-digital print-only publication deliberately reinforces — and the systems and rules already in place for physical media do not need to be discarded.

Like any good remix, this approach would not necessarily be intended to replace what has come before it, but rather to change its focus and reset its priorities. Placing the relationship between artist and audience at the centre of copyright law makes the medium of that relationship a secondary consideration. It is flexible enough to accommodate ink on paper as readily as pixels on screen.

It also suggests a series of questions as a kind of litmus test for any proposed changes to the law. How does this change affect the balance of rights and responsibilities between artist and audience? If this change benefits third-party rights holders, does that benefit come at the expense of artist and audience rights?

---

7   Quoted in Rimmer, *Digital Copyright and the Consumer Revolution*, p. 137. Higgins found the sample was not significant enough to be considered an infringement; however, it is worth noting that this finding was rejected on appeal.

Works Cited

Australian Copyright Council (2014) 'Duration of Copyright (Information Sheet G023v17)', https://www.copyright.org.au/acc_prod/ACC/Information_Sheets/Duration_of_Copyright.aspx

— (2014) 'Mashups, Memes, Remixes & Copyright (Information sheet G118v04)', https://www.copyright.org.au/ACC_Prod/ACC/Information_Sheets/Mashups__Memes__Remixes___Copyright.aspx

Creative Commons Australia (2018) 'Learn About CC', http://creativecommons.org.au/learn/

Doctorow, C. (2008) *About Little Brother,* http://craphound.com/littlebrother/about/

Groth, S. (2016) *Hunted Down and Other Tales by Marcus Clarke* (Brisbane: if:book Australia).

— (ed.) (2015) *Memory Makes Us* (Brisbane: if:book Australia).

— (ed.) (2014) *Lost in Track Changes* (Brisbane: if:book Australia).

Rimmer, M. (2007) *Digital Copyright and the Consumer Revolution* (Cheltenham: Edward Elgar Publishing).

Simon Groth, http://simongroth.com

Stevenson, K. (ed.) (2012) *Willow Pattern* (Brisbane: if:book Australia).

Author's Note: Organisational and funding changes since if:book Australia's final projects in 2016 led to its online assets, data and projects being deleted. Though many of the websites mentioned in this chapter are no longer active, elements of their data have been preserved at the Internet Archive. It is a bitter irony that, more than eight years on from its bold charge to explore and investigate how technology was set to expand our conception of the book, if:book Australia's legacy is a collection of printed, bound pages.

APPENDIX:

CREATE POSITION PAPERS

1. Publishing Industry

Janis Jefferies, Academic

Current debates on the publishing industry tend to focus on digitization and on the transformation of products (books to ereaders, paper to screen) and this paper explores some of these debates. Certainly, in recent decades, the creative potential that stems from society has proven to be a key resource for innovation and for a more sustainable type of development. These new processes, which have been called 'social creativity', are turning out to be an unlimited source of innovation for social and economic aims. New cooperative and participatory practices have led to the emergence of new economic models that challenge the boundaries between what we have traditionally considered to be the public, private and common realms.

There are many small presses in the UK for example that are bridging the gap between writers, new writing and industry, seeking experimentation and innovation where the question of nurturing relationships and collaboration is the primary concern. Smaller presses like SALT, INFLUX or Gallery Beggar Press in the UK ('high-class boutique' presses) who publish up to twelve title a year (SALT) or four (INFLUX) face the same challenges: large or small, risk versus money, good editors as good readers and no book sells itself, authors are always key. Interestingly, some do delve into the dead zone of previously published books; for example Simon Crump's, 'My Elvis Blackout' (first published by Bloomsbury in 1998) was republished as an ebook by Gallery Beggar Press in 2012. Digital classics (Denton Welch) are built out of Twitter fan bases to provide a groundswell for reissue. This may not be the future as digital rights are now tied in with contracts from the very outset. The impact of Amazon and the promotion of the 99p sell (Cheaper than Chips is what it has been called) has a huge impact on the book world, writers and publishers alike.

Writers

It is of some interest to the Nesta workshop in September 2014 and this paper that the feature in *The Guardian* newspaper (Saturday 23 August 2014), written in the light of a survey by the Authors' Licensing and Collecting Society undertaken in 2013, reported that among professional authors (defined as those who dedicate the majority of their time to writing) the median income was £11,000.

'What Are Words Worth Now?', a survey of almost 2,500 working writers, commissioned by the Authors' Licensing & Collecting Society (ALCS) and carried out by Queen Mary, University of London has found that increasingly few professional authors are able to earn a living from their writing.

In contrast to the sharp decline in earnings of professional authors, the wealth generated by the UK creative industries is on the increase. Statistics produced by the Department of Culture, Media and Sport in 2014 show that the creative industries are now worth £71.4 billion per year to the UK economy (over £8 million per hour) and the UK is reported as having 'the largest creative sector of the European Union', and being 'the most successful exporter of cultural good and services in the world', according to UNESCO.

Commenting on the findings of the survey, Owen Atkinson, Chief Executive of ALCS said:

> These are concerning times for writers. This rapid decline in both author incomes and in the numbers of those writing full-time could have serious implications for the economic success of the creative industries in the UK. If writers are to continue making their irreplaceable contribution to the UK economy, they need to be paid fairly for their work. This means ensuring clear, fair contracts with equitable terms and a copyright regime that support creators and their ability to earn a living from their creations.[1]

---

1 'What Are Words Worth Now? Not Enough', 27 July 2014, https://www.alcs.co.uk/news/what-are-words-worth-now-not-enough

Nonetheless, one Irish writer, Julian Gough, is funding his new novel by offering backers the opportunity to receive postcards from Las Vegas bearing whiskey stains, lipstick and bullet holes. Gough, according to *The Guardian* feature, has dubbed his 'economic-slash-literary experiments' Litcoin. The idea came about when he found that he did not have enough money to make one final research trip to Las Vegas, where the novel is set. A Kickstarter campaign was set up for $25. So far the campaign has raised $7,300.

Also in *The Guardian*, Alison Flood reports that Gough has been contacted by a Swiss think-tank: 'charity is at a dead end. I want to create a model that benefits writer and reader. So if I can help invent some kind of […] new asset, new currency, that funds the writers I love, and that also gives their readers an interesting, very personal, physical asset that might even be worth something one day, so everybody wins, then I'd be pretty happy.'[2]

British authors and larger UK publishers have further condemned as 'deeply worrying' reports that Amazon is now pressing for improved terms from publishers in the UK, as its showdown with Hachette in the US continues to be played out in public.

According to Benedicte Page[3] Amazon is putting publishers under 'heavy pressure' to introduce new terms. In the same article, it is reported that these include the proviso that 'should a book be out of stock from the publisher, Amazon would be entitled to supply its own copies to customers via its print-on-demand facilities', and that 'books cannot be sold for a lower price than Amazon's anywhere, including on a publisher's own website. For many writers and publishers, this is a form of assisted suicide for the book business, driven by the idea that publishers are unable to run even the most basic operations efficiently'.

The Society of Authors chief executive Nicola Solomon called the print-on-demand clause 'deeply worrying', and said that Amazon was 'already far too dominant in dictating ebook prices'. 'No one company should have such dominance or be the principal commercial driver of an entire industry', she said.

---

2   Alison Flood, 'Julian Gough Launches "Litcoin" Kickstarter to "Remodel the Economics of Reading"', *The Guardian*, 19 August 2014, https://www.theguardian.com/books/2014/aug/19/julian-gough-litcoin-kickstarter-economics-reading-postcards

3   Benedicte Page, 'Amazon pressing for new terms in UK', *The Bookseller*, 23 June 2014, http://www.thebookseller.com/news/amazon-pressing-new-terms-uk

Although it is publishers who are currently feeling squeezed by Amazon, Solomon said the negotiations also 'threaten' published authors. 'Despite increasing profits, publishers are increasingly under pressure: they say, rightly, that even bestsellers tend to sell fewer copies than in the past (now readers have such a wide range of choice); their budgets will be under further pressure if they have to concede larger discounts to Amazon and pay for "services". Authors will suffer as publishers claim that paying large advances is increasingly risky and, of course, authors are traditionally paid less on print books if publishers concede high discounts. On ebooks they are paid a proportion of net receipts so higher terms for Amazon will result in less money going to authors', said Solomon.

The changes, she said, 'highlight one wider, and growing, trend across all publishing and bookselling. Namely, that the author is the only 100% essential component in the creation of a book. But retailers are taking a larger chunk of any income, and publishers are taking a larger chunk of any income, so the share of income which makes its way to the author is forever shrinking.'

In the UK a number of publishers spoken to as part of *The Bookseller*'s investigations into the Hachette dispute said Amazon was also now putting them under 'heavy pressure'. According to the sources, new demands include adjusting terms so that ebooks and physical book terms have parity; the adjustment is said to be in the direction of 'p', which traditionally attracts a higher percentage for the retailer compared with 'e'. Amazon is also understood to be targeting academic terms, which have historically been more favourable to the publisher. The retailer also wants to impose a ceiling on the digital list price of ebooks in preparation for 2015 when the retailer will have to begin imposing the standard 20% rate of VAT on digital titles. The UK chancellor George Osborne has confirmed that ebooks will be taxed from the consumer's European member state from 1st January 2015. A little-noticed section of last week's budget announcement confirmed that from the start of next year, ebooks and other e-services including broadcasting and telecommunications will be taxed in the European member state in which the consumer is located, as opposed to where the book is sold from. The move is set to ensure that ebooks are taxed 'fairly and helping to protect revenue,' the chancellor said. The decision was originally announced in 2013's budget and means a loophole that allows companies like Amazon, Kobo and Barnes & Noble to sell ebooks to the UK from Luxembourg will be closed. In the UK, ebooks attract a 20% VAT whereas Luxembourg charges a much lower 3% VAT. Official estimates suggest the move could raise an extra £300m for the Treasury, according to *The Guardian*.[4] However, consumers are also concerned the new rule will mean rising costs of downloads of music, DVDs and ebooks.

UK-based retailers that sell ebooks such as Waterstones, The Book People and E-books by Sainsbury's are likely to welcome the decision because it levels the playing field between them and larger multi-nationals such as Amazon and Kobo. Between January 2013 and January 2014, twenty new ebook readers have been introduced into the marketplace. In addition to these, the number of other mobile devices with ebook reading capabilities, such as tablets, laptops, and game consoles, have grown twenty-fold. These readers, along with the breakneck million-a-month pace being set by Apple's iPad, are driving the ubiquity of digital reader access for every possible piece of written material that becomes available.

Within five years, some will reach prices as low as fifteen pounds, maybe less. They will become as commonplace as calculators and virtually everyone will have one, or so it has been predicted.[5]

Readers

Readers, while welcoming the new generation of electronic reading devices, still buy predominantly paper copies of books. Time and again the conversation leads to blanket statements about 'the end of books' while little attention is paid to the vast potential for new hybrid forms of text, and the fundamental shifts in the writing-reader axis that the new technologies are enabling. Attributing too much agency to technology is often tantamount to the abdication of responsibility, and we are concerned with broadening the discussion toward notions of ethics, collaboration, property and creativity. It is interesting to note then that

---

4   Rowena Mason, 'George Osborne Closes Tax Loophole on Music and Book Downloads', *The Guardian*, 23 March 2014, http://www.theguardian.com/music/2014/mar/23/george-osborne-tax-loophole-music-downloads
5   https://fcforum.net/en/sustainable-models-for-creativity/how-to-manual/#writing

high-street book chain Waterstones saw a jump of five per cent in sales of paper books — and said that demand for Amazon's Kindle ebook reader, which it sells, had 'disappeared, to all intents and purposes'. Reports of the death of the paper-and-ink book may have been greatly exaggerated after ebook readers slumped and paper books made a strong return in Christmas 2014. Waterstones now plans to open more bookshops in the coming year.

Bookshop chains such as Borders in the US closed in the face of commercial pressures including rivalry from ebook readers such as Kindle — and tech sites predicted that ebooks would spell an end to the paper-and-ink version. However, commercial decisions by Waterstones UK chief executive James Daunt have shown how bookshops can flourish in the electronic age.

Speaking to the Financial Times, Douglas McCabe of Enders Analysis outlined how 'The rapid growth of ebook sales has quite dramatically slowed and there is some evidence it has gone into reverse.'[6] Daunt has credited the recent sales figures to the ability of local stores to respond to local tastes. This confirms the publishing strategy of Influx Press, an independent publisher formed in London by editors Gary Budden and Kit Caless, starting life in 2012 with the publication of *Acquired for Development By... A Hackney Anthology*. Since then they have published a number of titles, such as *Life in Transit* by poet Sam Berkson, *Marshland: Dreams and Nightmares on the Edge of London* by Gareth E. Rees and *Above Sugar Hill* by Linda Mannheim.

All their books explore in some way the idea of 'place': 'we are committed to publishing innovative and challenging site-specific fiction, poetry and creative non-fiction from across the UK and beyond.'

A Meeting of Text and Technology

Penguin Random House, the world's largest publishing house, is exploring new ways to tell stories through technology. Wanting to take this to the next level they have invited creative individuals, developers, entrepreneurs and designers, as well as global tech hubs, innovation labs, and universities to explore the technological and creative possibilities around one of their best known authors, Stephen Fry. This

---

6   *Financial Times*, 6 January 2015.

is *YourFry* — a collaborative global project to reinterpret the words and narrative of Stephen's brand new memoir, *More Fool Me.* As a technology enthusiast with over seven million followers, Stephen Fry is following on from the success of his prestigious Guardian-Media-Innovation-Award-winning MyFry app to push the tech boundaries even further for his latest autobiography. Stephen Fry himself set out the creative objectives of YourFry globally on 25 September 2014, streamed via a WeTransfer video message.

Stephen Fry and Penguin's YourFry project has been created to ask questions about the nature of how we create and publish autobiography in the digital environment. The web is responsive, interactive and chaotic — what if the conventional autobiography is thrown open to the web? What might the results look like, what form might they take?

The digital revolution is transforming the ways that people create and distribute art. Inexpensive, professional-quality technologies of creation, like digital cameras and camcorders, photo- and video-editing software, MP3 and digital music recording and manipulation, and even word-processing, make it possible for many people to create art with high production quality. The Internet gives creators a means of low-cost distribution. This combination of digital creation and online distribution is extremely powerful. Online artistic production, supported by digital technologies, enables artists to create works and distribute them to diverse audiences, and to receive feedback. A potential effect of online distribution is the blurring of artistic boundaries, in some cases, between producer and consumer; in others, between amateur and professional. Moreover, the relative ease of digital creation and online distribution and feedback may lead to production by the masses that rival production for the masses. User-generated-content practices encapsulated in Web 2.0 are changing businesses (Anderson 2006, Kelly 1999) and consumption patterns (Abercrombie 1998, Jenkins 2006). The concept of the 'prosumer' was foreshadowed by Toffler (1980), who suggested that, as technology advances, the distinction between the producer of culture and the consumer of it would blur or merge. Rose (2011) discusses the way today's consumers expect to see their favourite stories interlinked across 'platforms' (television, film, Internet). Jenkins (2007) goes further and argues that consumers are no longer consumers.

They, or at least certain more advanced consumers, are 'loyals', 'media-actives' or 'prosumers' or, in Jenkins' favourite term, 'fans' (Jenkins 2007). These active consumers play an important role, both culturally and economically. Indeed, Jenkins (2007) argues that 'fandom is the future': 'fandom represents the experimental prototype, the testing ground for the way media and cultural industries are going to operate in the future.' Jenkins emphasises an active consumer, in contrast to a 'passive' one, but he still focuses on the consumer side of the prosumer. The producer aspect of the prosumer is less well understood. Internet-based distribution and feedback channels ('creative hubs') are often funded largely or completely by creators themselves. But for more expensive projects, such as making a film or a web series (web-based television series, with multiple 'webisodes'), the Internet provides alternative funding mechanisms, including crowd-funding via 'peer-to-peer' finance with 'small contributions from a large number of sources, rather than large amounts from a few' (Baeck 2012: 3).

Creativity and innovation are supposed and proposed to be key drivers of the economy, particularly when subsumed under the 'creative industries': the transformation of the publishing industry, the writer/reader move to prosumer and the merging of text and technology (as in YourFry) are no exceptions.

So what do you do if you have a novel to write? Go to Twitter, and tweet about the work you're not doing, of course. Artist Cory Arcangel's new book is a compilation of those who couldn't resist tweeting the words 'working on my novel'. *Working On My Novel*[7] is a compilation of tweets, found on twitter by searching for the phrase 'working on my novel', and retweeted by Archangel's account of the same name. On the other hand, taking Publication Studio as a starting point, an open discussion about print-on-demand, sustainable publishing methods and alternative networks for independent and artist-led publishing, held at Raven Row (London) with Louisa Bailey, Ami Clarke, Arnaud Desjardin, Louise O'Hare and Eva Weinmayr revealed the thriving creative industries that independent publishers are pursuing.[8] The social life of books is as important as the ideas of producing publics who attend events and participate in the ways in which books are

---

7   http://www.coryarcangel.com/news/2014/07/working-on-my-novel/
8   http://www.ravenrow.org/events/publication_studio_/

made in different formats and on different sites. In February 2015, for example, the launch of Publication Studio, London opens with the live production of a Plastic Words publication, sampling the contents and output of its events. Printing (using the contemporary craft of laser printing) and binding will occur simultaneously at Raven Row and in the original Publication Studio in Portland, Oregon. Here there is convergence between independent galleries and project-based activities that are forming a strategic alliance with new forms of publishers, distribution and dissemination that even the art magazines like *Frieze* (see 'The Map is the Territory', issue 148, 2012) are getting excited about. Three Letter Words, run by Kate Phillimore and Louise O'Hare of Publish and Be Damned, is a non-profit organisation dedicated to the discussion and support of artist-led publishing through an annual fair, artists' dissemination projects and an online magazine. Working with the London Bookshop Map, there are plans to develop a user-generated distribution channel for publishers to be able to share content, link to on-the-ground distributors such as independent bookshops and galleries, reach a much bigger audience of collectors and enthusiasts, and connect to each other — effectively creating a global, 24/7, artist-led book fair. They have started the task of digitising the Publish and Be Damned Public Library/archive, which contains over 2,000 publications, uploading and tagging images from them to be freely accessible and searched online.

The point here that on the one hand the debates in the commercial publishing industries are fraught with corporate competition and anxiety over profit margins whereas the flourishing independent small-scale artist-based publishers and small presses are showing how other models of production and distribution can challenge the standard languages of conventional financial models. Most impressive of all is how new reading publics are generated. A favourite example is Banner Repeater, which is an artist-led reading room and project space, founded by Ami Clarke in 2009, situated on Platform 1, Hackney Downs railway station, London E8 1LA.

The reading room holds an archive dedicated to artists' printed material and is home to Publish and be Damned's public library. It provides an important bibliographic resource that all visitors to BR can browse. The bookshop holds a selection of artists' publications for sale.

The project is driven by its location, like a number of initiatives with a local sensibility, dedicated to developing critical art in the natural interstice the platform and incidental footfall of over 4,000 passengers a day provides. This is achieved by rush-hour opening times that attract commuters, and an open door policy maintained six days a week.

The emphasis on multiple points of dissemination, via pamphlets and posters published from the site and the other free material distributed, online activities, and the siting of the archive of artists' printed material as a public library; a resource that can be utilised by both local community and visitors in a working station environment, remain vital to Banner repeater's success.[9]

18 January 2015

---

9 http://www.bannerrepeater.org/un-publish and http://www.bannerrepeater.org/press

2. Is the Current Copyright Framework fit for Purpose in Relation to Writing, Reading and Publishing in the Digital Age?

Laurence Kaye, Solicitor

This is not a new question. I remember taking part in a debate on the same subject in 1994 at 'Cyberia', one of London's original Internet cafes — remember them? That was four years before Brin and Page published their algorithm for Google's first search engine and nearly ten years before Facebook, Twitter and social media appeared.

The fact that we are still debating this subject is revealing. Some people take the view that copyright is a dodo, belonging to a 'read only' world that cannot come to terms with a world of linking, sharing, mixing and mashing. From that perspective, copyright has been dying a lingering death since the Internet first appeared in the early 1990s.

I reject that view. Copyright is inherently format- and platform-neutral. Copyright exists in literary, audio-visual, artistic and other works in whatever digital, analogue or other forms in which they are expressed. It is ideas that fuel creativity and innovation. Copyright does not protect ideas, but only their expression.

Change driven by 'digital' — technologies, networks, platforms and tools — is complex and multi-factorial. It affects everything, from the law and business models through to social, cultural and political norms. These changes aren't synchronised. Technological change outpaces everything. It raises questions for others to answer. Sometimes the law seeks to anticipate or at least keep pace with technological change. In other cases, it is playing 'catch-up'. That's often the job of the courts. For instance, the ease of creating and redistributing perfect digital copies of copyright content raises questions about how the laws of copyright and free movement of goods and services are reconciled when applied to online marketplaces for pre-owned digital content.

The point is that working through these issues and finding balanced solutions takes time. Perhaps the immediacy and instantaneous nature of online communications makes it hard for us to have patience. The fact that we are still working on solutions in the copyright field doesn't mean that those solutions can't be found. Rather, adaptation and adjustment simply take time.

I am not complacent nor am I arguing that everything in the copyright garden is perfect. In the UK, a number of changes to copyright exceptions will be introduced following the Hargreaves Review. At a UK and European level there is a framework in place for orphan works. There are also a number of initiatives to improve rights management, including the Copyright Hub here in the UK. And that highlights the biggest challenge: how to make the management of copyright permissions as easy as 'click to buy' when you shop online.

The copyright framework is fundamentally Darwinian. It never stands still. It is always adapting. Sure, some would prefer to dispense with it or to dilute it through ever wider exceptions, compulsory licences and a shortening of the term of protection for copyright works.

But readers need professional authors of literary, artistic and audio-visual works to create works they can enjoy in whatever form they want. Copyright is the facilitator of the value chain that exists between authors and readers. For everyone in between, including publishers, their reward depends on the value that their authors on the one hand and the readers on the other perceive them to add. A perfectly Darwinian solution!

So the copyright framework is and will continue to adapt, whatever the new technologies and indeed forms of work. In my view, the real focus of work is not the framework per se but the management of rights, especially through the 'machine-to-machine' communication of rights.

3. Is the Current Copyright Framework fit for Purpose in Relation to Writing, Reading, and Publishing in the Digital Age?

Richard Mollet, Publishers Association

The current copyright framework, that is to say the underpinning structure of exclusive rights and exceptions, most emphatically is fit for purpose in the digital age. Moreover, digital technology is so superlatively beneficial to copyright that it borders on the absurd to suggest that copyright should be abandoned or radically weakened in reaction to it. However, that is not to say that every single strut, plank and adornment that is attached to the underlying structure is perfect. Like any system of law, changes and small adaptations have to be made from time to time.

The copyright framework can trace its lineage back to 1710 and during this time its robust and flexible nature has coped admirably with the advent of numerous new technologies. Digital tools are simply the latest in a long line of new ways to communicate and reproduce. The copyright framework is totally indifferent to the medium in which works are being conveyed. Fundamentally core to copyright is the granting of exclusive intellectual property rights to the creators of works, which as well as returning just rewards for their talent and endeavour are the ignition spark of economic activity by others, be they publishers, record labels or film studios. Those exclusive rights can be shaved, trimmed or expanded as befits contemporary mores, but the moral, legal and economic logic that underlies their existence is unshakeable.

It is a commonplace to say that digital technology has been hugely transformative to our society and economy. In western societies at least, even the most Luddite technophobe is touched by the digital transformation in some way or other, in spite of their resistance. Given this sometimes overwhelming rate of change it is understandable that some conclude that the only response is to redesign core aspects of our legal framework. Similarly it is understandable for some to conclude that laws need to be rewritten given their belief that the Internet is, to borrow the coinage, 'a vast copying machine'. Their logic would appear to be that since the acts of reproduction and distribution have become so facile, then any laws that seek to restrict or prevent such acts are axiomatically obsolete.

These reactions, whilst just about comprehensible, are both wrong and they are so because they fail to apprehend properly what copyright and intellectual property laws are there to do. Copyright merely grants rights to the creators of works; it does not take rights away from other people. Moreover, copyright does not confer rights on anyone other than the creator of a work. Nor does copyright arise simply from that which is technically possible. These are vital distinctions and it is the failure to grasp them that leads opponents of the copyright framework down their false trail.

Technology as an Enabler of Copyright

By setting out and granting exclusive rights, copyright law establishes where and in what circumstances the creator can legitimately assert ownership of their work — their property — and thereby assert the right to control what happens to whatever they have created. These rights are, rightly, circumscribed, by time and other conditions on use. What digital technology does is greatly enhance the creators' ability to exploit these rights. It does so in remarkably positive and innovative ways: it makes reproduction quicker and cheaper; distribution more targeted; communicating to the public global; processing remuneration more efficient. Digital devices and services are the steroids of the creative world, and they are injected directly into the veins of the body of copyright law. In these ways, digital technology is the perfect partner to copyright.

But of course, as well as enhancing the ability of creators and producers to exploit their rights, digital technology increases the opportunity for others to exploit works too, even when they do not have the right to do so — in other words, infringing them. The Internet may be a 'vast copying machine' (although its other attributes are more important) and, just as in the pre-digital world where we had only small-scale copying machines, on occasion the copying that goes on will be against the wishes of the creator of the work. Such infringement of copyright is, sadly, a given in any system. But again, copyright works precisely because it establishes clearly what sort of copying is permitted and which is not. In a world in which works can be reproduced so easily it is vital that the creator of a work has a strong and fixed reference point from which to determine what is right and what is not. The alternative view — that there are no such things as 'infringing copies' and that anything that takes place on this galactic-scale photocopier is fair game — is nonsensical in any context in which recognition and reward is to be paid to the creator.

It should also be noted that digital technology provides some excellent solutions to creators keen to monitor and prevent the infringement of their work. The Internet is not so much a double-edged sword as a Swiss Army knife, with any range of tools available to help tackle infringement.

Opponents of copyright, I suspect, see the world the other way around. They maintain that where the copyright framework does not give rights to creators it gives them instead to users. So, for example, where a creator does not have the right to prevent copying of a work for the purpose of instruction, then — they would maintain — the person doing the copying has the right to do so. This is a false perception. One can search the various international treaties, directives and national laws in vain for any language that confers such rights. Copyright exceptions may provide the permission for use, and sometimes a defence for the infringer, but do not provide them with a *right* to perform an act.

Copyright is not unique in this respect: in no areas of law is a right subject to a tug-of-war between its beneficiary and the population at large. By analogy, consider the Representation of the People Act. Where a person is deprived of their right to vote because they become a member of the House of Lords, that right is not distributed around the general electorate. I do not experience a micro-increase in my enfranchisement because the newly ennobled James Palumbo has lost his. So equally, a user does not begin to acquire the right to do something at the point at which the creator's right is curtailed under copyright. Surely, a user has *abilities* to do things and the copyright law acts as a guide to when doing such things is legal or not. But the user is not in possession of the same class of exclusive right as that held by the creator.

To put it bluntly, when a work enters the public domain the exclusive right in it expires; it does not transfer to others, it evaporates.

Rights are Based on law not Technology

This leads on to a further sense in which copyright opponents misapprehend the nature of copyright. They say, in terms, 'because digital technology has given me the ability to do something I therefore have the right to do it; but copyright laws are depriving me of exercising that right.' In this formulation (most often rehearsed in the 'right to read is the right to text-mine' debate), rights are acquired by an individual not by dint of the law but by dint of technology. A right is therefore held to be something that is attached to an ability.

The absurdity of such a world view becomes obvious in thinking through its logical consequences. An owner of a Formula 1 car does not have the right to travel the streets at 200 miles per hour; the owner of a mobile-phone-blocking device does not have the right to roam railway carriages shutting down others' conversations; in futurology, the owner of an invisibility cloak would not have the right to enter unobserved into other people's homes. The ability to do something does not confer the right to do it. Rights are generated by laws not by technology. To argue the converse hints at a rather unsavoury 'might is right' approach.

The Real aim of Copyright

'Ok', may say the copyright opponent (again to put words into their mouth), 'I agree but you are begging the question — your argument is precisely why I want to change the copyright framework in order that it *does* give me the rights commensurate with my digitally enhanced technical abilities'.

At which point we must return to the crux of what the copyright framework is there to do. Its ostensible aim is to facilitate the creation of useful works by providing rewards and incentives to creators. It is difficult to maintain an argument that such incentivisation would be maintained, let alone boosted, by a legal framework that removed from the creator the ability to control the reproduction of the work. Harder still to argue that companies like publishers, for whom copyright provides the incentive to invest, could remain engaged. Such a shift in the balance of rights away from creators would actually achieve nothing, other than to diminish the creator's economic and social standing. Hence, the challenge back to the copyright-curtailer is therefore the simple one of asking why they should benefit at the expense of the creator.

It is insufficient for them to say that they are not harming rights-holders' economic prospects, nor even that their acts of infringement might even somehow enhance them. For one thing, it is a rather patronising attitude of the infringer to suggest that the creator and their publisher doesn't know what's good for them, and that actually freely distributing their work to all and sundry would be a better thing in the long run. For another, it is self-aggrandising of the non-creator to claim a right at the creator's expense. This is true even if their activity did somehow redound to the creator. A good follow-up question to *cui bono* is often 'why should it be you?'.

Natural justice demands that there be a basis for a right. Moral logic requires there needs to be a reason for a person to enjoy domain over property. In most areas of life this right arises following the exchange of money on the basis of implied contract. When it comes to the creation of works, it is a long-held view (from John Locke and others) that the product of a person's talent and labour is justifiably theirs to control. What countervailing right could a user possibly point to? Some reach for freedom of speech. An important right to be sure, but nowhere in the annals of rights theory or practice is it a trump card: rights, when in conflict, must be balanced. In any case, it is notable that this most popular line of argument self-consciously eschews tussling over property rights. The proponent of the free-speech argument makes no claim for ownership over the work to which they assert the right to give vent; rather they take the debate on to different turf.

It would appear then that the advocates of rebalancing exclusive rights away from the creator have no strong basis for their claims. There is nothing in their locker that can outbid the intense moral connection between the creator and their right. And as we have shown, even an argument for rebalancing fails on these terms. Yes, it may be possible to trim some of the creator's exclusive rights, but these shavings do not plop into the hands of the user, rather they disappear.

Conclusion

Copyright is fit for purpose in the digital age for three main reasons: it is sufficiently flexible to adapt to any new technology; digital technology is particularly beneficial for the exercising of copyright; and copyright provides the ability to determine which digital usages are permissible and which not.

Those who argue that copyright prevents digital-age users from exercising their rights as users are simply misunderstanding the word 'right'. Similarly, those who argue that copyright prevents digital-age users from exercising their abilities are misunderstanding the concept of rights.

Fundamentally, copyright ensures that creators get rewarded for the great things that they create. Long may it prosper.

4. History of Copyright Changes 1710–2013

Rachel Calder, Literary Agent

Changes to the law of Copyright

The Act, or Statute of Anne passed in 1710 was heralded as an 'Act for the Encouragement of learned Men to compose and write useful Books'. It had replaced a system in which the Stationers' Company had a virtual monopoly on legal printing by issuing licences to printers that were designed to keep a tight control of the press. Early pressure for the right to prevent the copying of works came from printers and publishers and not writers, who had no ways of organising themselves or lobbying for better terms. The 1710 Act gave an exclusive fourteen-year period to books registered with the Stationers' Company, renewable for another fourteen years if the writer still lived. One of the most important aspects of the Act was not just the exclusive period but also that the grant of rights was assignable and could be passed to someone other than the writer or creator on terms to be agreed. The Act also gave the writer or copyright holder a right to redress should the copyright be misused or misappropriated. However, the main beneficiaries of this early Act were not usually the writers but the printers and booksellers to whom the rights were assigned, usually for an outright fee. In some cases, the writer even had to pay for the production and publication as well. If the title went on to be a runaway hit, the writer would not benefit again financially until the term of the licence expired and had to be renewed. The 1814 Act developed the term further to twenty-eight years or the author's lifespan, whichever was the longer, and this was then lengthened further in the 1842 Act to forty-two years or the author's life plus seven years, whichever was the greater. The international Berne Convention of 1886 (a document to which the USA did not become a signatory for another hundred years until 1989) agreed its term as the author's life plus fifty years, forcing the subsequent 1911 Act to include the same minimum term. Now the term has settled at the author's life plus seventy years.

The first Act in 1710 was devised for books and the book trade, but throughout the nineteenth century the subsequent Acts widened the remit to include lectures, engravings, dramatic works and designs. The twentieth-century changes added cinema and broadcasting, computer programmes and games. The passing of each new Copyright Act followed years of heated debate about where the balance of benefit should lie, with the creators or the producers/distributors, with the writers or the book trade and wider industries. From a twenty-first century point of view, extending the term can look like a benefit for the creators, but if the writer had to assign the title to the printer or bookseller for an outright fee, the common practice in the nineteenth century, the extended period is only of benefit to the producer of the book, not the creator. The balance between the individual and common good has always been delicate and it will remain so, but history has shown that the legislation is flexible and up to the task, and is constantly under review.

Although during the eighteenth and nineteenth centuries it was usually the booksellers, printers and publishers who made greater financial gains from the sale of books, creators and writers did eventually benefit too. The book trade and creative industries of the time lobbied Parliament and gained legal protection for the works they produced and invested in, but it was really only in the twentieth century that it became more common for contracts to include royalties for copies sold and percentage splits for rights sales. Being a literary agent myself, I like to think that it was the emergence of literary agents at the end of nineteenth century that ensured that writers, the original creators, were finally paid what was due to them but it is clear that this would have been impossible to achieve without the legislative framework to protect the creators' work.

Anyone who wants to know more about the historical perspective of copyright reform can read books and journal articles by several writers including Catherine Seville, John Feather, Mark Rose and Iain Stevenson.

5. Is the Current Copyright Framework fit for Purpose in Relation to Writing, Reading, and Publishing in the Digital Age?

Max Whitby, App Publisher

The regulatory framework controlling the publication, copying and distribution of content evolved in a technological and commercial environment very different to the digital landscape in which we now find ourselves. Our copyright laws were shaped in an age when IP was published in physical form, copying cost money and distribution was far from free. In that context it made practical sense to restrict the right to copy in order to protect the livelihoods of authors and publishers, who had to make a considerable investment in order to reach market.

Today it still costs time, creative inspiration and skilled effort to generate valuable IP. That much has not and is not likely to change. And the financial and creative investment involved remains something that the copyright framework should continue to protect and encourage, so that artists may eat and their audiences may continue to enjoy their output. But attempting to implement this protection through the blunt instrument of controlling the right to make and distribute copies of a work no longer makes sense.

As the digital pioneer Stewart Brand remarked in the early days of the information revolution: 'Information Wants To Be Free'. Another way to express this thought is that the ability to discover and communicate information (particularly the sort of protected information that is considered intellectual property) is a fundamental strength of our digital society. It is the engine driving the generation of ideas. We seek to stop this process (for example by attempting to prevent copying) at our peril.

Savvy authors and publishers know that free distribution of their copyright work is often an excellent thing. In crude commercial terms, piracy can sometimes be considered a highly effective form of marketing. Of course this depends on enough people being willing at some point to pay for content. But often discovery comes about through exposure to the free stuff. The challenge to digital publishers is to give away enough to encourage wide distribution. And then to offer real persuasive value in the form of additional content, enhanced functionality and community engagement that comes with purchase.

Let me give an example from my own app-publishing company Touch Press. On several occasions in the past year we have chosen to give away part or even all of one of our titles freely in order to reach a substantial new audience. The most spectacular example is our children's app Barefoot World Atlas. Apple selected this as one of their favourite apps of all time and invited us to give it away free for a week to celebrate the fifth anniversary of the iTunes App Store. We happily agreed and in seven days the app was downloaded four million times, vastly increasing our installed base. Now we are about to release a major update that will offer this expanded audience a range of additional content via in-app purchase.

So what needs controlling is the right to make money from copyright work: in other words to charge an audience. A shift in the legal framework towards this goal will continue to protect the fountain of innovation, without paradoxically blocking the free flow of ideas. The price of such a change will be to oblige authors and publishers to deliver real value and convenience to their audience in those things they choose to charge for.

November 2013

List of Illustrations

Chapter 1

1.1 *How It Is In Common Tongues*. Image provided by the authors, CC BY 4.0. 25

1.2 *How It Is In Common Tongues*. Image provided by the authors, CC BY 4.0. 26

Chapter 8

8.1 Millar and McCrea, *Crisis* #31 (1989), pp. 17/5–6. 187
8.2 Brown, *Yummy Fur* #21 (1990), p. 18/6. 194
8.3 Brown, *Yummy Fur* #20 (1990), pp. 5/1–4. 195
8.4 Sim, *Church & State Vol. I* (Windsor, Ontario: Aardvark-Vanaheim, 1989), p. 421. 197
8.5 McCloud, *Understanding Comics* (*Understanding Comics: The Invisible Art*, Northampton, MA: Kitchen Sink Press, 1993), p. 25/6. 200

Chapter 10

10.1 Screenshot of J. R. Carpenter, *Mythologies of Landforms and Little Girls* (1996), http://luckysoap.com/mythologies 249

10.2 Screenshot of J. R. Carpenter (1998–present), http://luckysoap.com 251

10.3 Screenshot of J. R. Carpenter, *Fishes & Flying Things* (1995), http://luckysoap.com/butterflies/parasite.html 253

10.4 Screenshot of Judy Malloy, *Uncle Roger* (1986), http://collection.eliterature.org/3/works/uncle-roger/ 255

10.5 Fig. 10.5 Screenshot of J. R. Carpenter, *CityFish* (2010), http://luckysoap.com/cityfish 257

Chapter 14

14.1	Proof copy of *Hunted Down and Other Tales* (ISBN: 9780994471925) alongside an original copy of Clarke's 1871 title *Holiday Peak and Other Tales*.	380
14.2	The 'drunk' text from *Hunted Down and Other Tales* mirrors the narrative as its characters become increasingly intoxicated.	381
14.3	The authors meet to discuss progress during the 24-Hour Book (left), Bronwen Blaney of On Demand Books presents the first copy of *Willow Pattern* (ISBN: 9780987251435) from an Espresso Book Machine.	385
14.4	Writer Kate Pullinger and participants recording memories at the first *Memory Makes Us* event in Brisbane, 2013.	386
14.5	Home page of book database willowpatterns.net, and a still from *I Will Say This Only Once*, a database remix by Pascalle Burton.	389
14.6	Pages from *Lost in Track Changes* (ISBN: 9780992373733) showing wide margins, 'track changes' layout, and remixed story layout.	390
14.7	Sample page from A [[Non]] *Guardian Age*, by Mez Breeze.	391
14.8	Tweet from @HenrySavery during the 2015 Brisbane Writers Festival.	392
14.9	Progression of 'advertisements' through *Hunted Down and Other Tales*, from original nineteenth-century copy to contemporary buyer recommendations and customer reviews.	393

Index

aaarg.org 35, 42–44, 53–54
academic 1, 3–5, 7–8, 10–13, 44, 47, 54, 65, 76–77, 92–93, 101, 110–111, 120, 146–147, 150, 158, 182–185, 188, 190–192, 196, 204, 206–210, 214–217, 243–244, 246, 249, 262, 270, 273, 284, 309–315, 317–324, 327–333, 337, 339, 349, 352–353, 361, 365–367, 369–371, 408
academic publishing 3, 8, 77, 93, 120, 182, 184–185, 216, 312–314, 337, 349, 371
Actor Network Theory (ANT) 81–82
Adema, Janneke 1, 13–14, 65
Aesop 258, 261
aesthetic 7, 24, 27–28, 274, 277
Africa, African 235–237, 322, 334
Afterall 36, 40, 59
Ahmed, Sara 300
Alliance of Independent Authors 117
Amazon 84, 91, 102, 124, 130, 167, 406–410
amplification 14, 91, 96, 100–101, 103
anthropology 309–311, 315–316, 323, 325
appropriation 8, 13–14, 67, 81–83, 110–111, 120, 192, 243, 245, 248, 250, 260–263, 272–273, 275–278, 316, 328, 330–332, 334–336, 338–340, 348, 351–353, 355–357, 359, 363, 367, 370, 372, 395, 399
Artecubano 47–48
article processing charges (APCs) 10–11, 93, 185
Artificial Intelligence (AI) 13, 21–22, 29
artists 1, 3–6, 9, 12, 14, 24, 27, 33–38, 44, 47–49, 51–52, 55–58, 99, 109, 141, 146, 153, 164, 170–171, 181–182, 191, 195–196, 243, 246, 248, 252–253, 259, 267, 271–274, 276–282, 284, 291, 293, 296–297, 332, 334, 348, 362–363, 384–385, 387, 399–400, 411–414, 427
arts 1, 34, 36, 38, 40, 47, 52, 55, 61, 142, 154–155, 204, 216, 236, 251–252, 258–260, 268, 284, 310, 312, 317, 319–321, 325, 327–328, 338–339
Arts Council England (ACE) 39–40, 136, 230
arXiv 93, 101
Asia, Asian 136, 229–230, 233, 235–237, 239
Association of Authors' Agents (AAA) 107–108
Atkinson, Owen 66–68
Australia, Australian 133, 235, 257, 324–325, 327, 334, 336, 379, 381–382, 385–386, 389, 391–398, 401
author 4, 7–8, 10, 13–15, 21–22, 24–27, 50, 65–81, 85, 93–96, 99, 103, 105–125, 129–131, 133, 137, 141–144, 146–147, 149–152, 158, 160, 163–166, 168–169, 172–173, 175, 181–182, 184, 188, 190, 194, 204, 215–216, 229, 231, 235–237, 240, 243–244, 247–248, 250, 252, 254, 256, 259–260, 262, 268, 271, 273–274, 279, 282, 284, 288–289, 292, 295, 298–299, 301, 314, 320–324, 326–328, 330, 337–339, 349–351, 354–359, 362, 365–366, 369, 371, 381–382, 385–394, 396–397, 405–408, 410, 416, 424, 427–428
Authorea 326–328

authorship 13–14, 21, 28, 52, 69–75, 77–80, 82, 85, 244, 263, 267–268, 271, 273–275, 279–282, 287–290, 293–294, 297–298, 300, 310, 312, 315–316, 318–327, 329–332, 334, 338–339, 351, 353, 355, 358, 364–365
Authors' Licensing & Collecting Society (ALCS) 65–72, 80–81, 85, 94, 149–151, 406

Bailey, Louisa 48, 50, 412
BAME 136, 229–239
Banff Centre, The 252–253, 258
Barnes, Julian 133
Barnes & Noble 272, 409
barriers 9, 39, 92, 206, 232, 365
　barriers to access 9, 206
　price barriers 9, 92
Barthes, Roland 351–352
BBC 46, 108, 203
Beckett, Samuel 13, 24, 27–28
　How It Is 13, 24–28
Belfast 182, 192
Benjamin, Walter 295
　'The Author as Producer' 295
Benkler, Yochai 94, 103
Bergvall, Caroline 246–247
Berlin Declaration on Open Access to Knowledge in the Sciences and Humanities (2003) 332, 365–366
Berne Convention (1886) 424
Bethesda Statement on Open Access Publishing (2003) 333, 365–366
Bhaskar, Michael 1, 14, 91
　The Content Machine 96
Black 136, 229–230, 233, 235–237, 239
Blackman, Malorie 231
Blake, Carole 106
borrowing 14, 248, 383, 391, 418
Brazil 240, 295, 336
Brisbane 381, 385–386, 392
Bristol 35, 247
British Library 2, 208
Brown, Chester 193–195

Brown, Wendy 69, 182, 232
Bruguera, Tania 37–38, 50–52, 54, 58–59
Budapest Open Access Initiative 365–366
Burrell, Robert 206, 208
Butler, Judith 293, 313

Cambridge 232, 237
Canada, Canadian 8, 35, 39, 133, 249, 252, 257–258, 348–349, 368–372
Canelo 1, 94
career 3, 93, 95–96, 111, 133, 156, 158, 160, 163, 165, 168, 172, 175, 234, 236, 238, 314
Cariou, Patrick 276, 278–279
　Canal Zone 276, 278
Carpenter, J. R. 1, 14, 243, 249–251, 253, 257
　'CityFish' 257–258, 261–262
　Fishes and Flying Things 253–254
　Mythologies of Landforms and Little Girls 249, 258
Carr, Nicholas 94
Castro, Fidel 36–37
Cayley, John 1, 13–14, 21
censorship 33, 37, 41, 284, 287, 293
Centre for Copyright and New Business Models in the Creative Economy 54, 181
Chapman, Neil 291
China, Chinese 134–135, 239
citation 3, 217, 243, 248, 331
Clarke, Cat 171–172
Clarke, Marcus 379, 392–393
　Hunted Down and Other Tales 379–381, 392–393, 398, 400
class 3, 233, 237, 239, 278, 405, 420
Coelho, Paolo 119
　The Alchemist 119
Coleman, Allison 206, 208
Coleman, Gabriella 299
collaboration 44, 74, 78
collective 13, 104, 112, 122, 146, 261, 267–268, 270–271, 291, 294, 296–297, 299–300, 332

College Art Association (CAA) 4, 283
Collins, Wilkie 193
comics 4, 164–165, 181–183, 185, 188, 191–193, 195–196, 198–201, 209, 215, 237
Comics Grid, The 182–183, 192, 208, 210
CommentPress 328
commodification 72, 81, 85, 349, 367
commodity 80, 262, 280, 309, 337
commons 13, 23–24, 27, 313–314
communication 9, 12, 74, 206, 217, 245, 286, 325, 327, 347, 351, 361–362, 365, 416
community 7, 35, 42–43, 46, 54, 75, 92, 111, 119, 135, 137, 183–184, 237, 256, 294, 328, 332–334, 336–338, 359–361, 366, 385, 414, 428
competition 6, 11, 92, 100, 103–104, 202, 214, 233, 239, 270, 300, 413
Coney Island 258, 262
control 29, 33, 41, 77, 91, 97, 99, 117, 120, 124, 130, 164–166, 170, 173, 241, 260, 274, 280, 284, 291, 325, 336, 354, 357–358, 363, 365–366, 418, 421, 423, 427–428
Coombe, Rosemary J. 72–74
'copyfight' 2–3, 8–9
copying 3, 6, 23, 82, 169, 192, 193, 198, 199, 200, 201, 205, 206, 208, 210, 287, 356, 369, 370, 371, 383, 384, 397, 398, 400, 418, 419, 423, 427, 428. *See also* plagiarism
copyright 1–9, 12–15, 19, 22–23, 29, 43, 45, 54–55, 66–68, 72–75, 80–81, 83–85, 93, 97–98, 105–106, 108–109, 111, 116–117, 141–150, 152–156, 158–165, 167–175, 181–185, 188, 190–193, 196, 198, 200–204, 206, 208–210, 214–216, 259, 267–269, 275–276, 278–279, 282, 284, 290, 294, 309–310, 312–321, 325–327, 330–340, 348–352, 355–356, 358–359, 365–372, 379, 381–385, 394–400, 406, 415–425, 427–428

Copyright Designs and Patents Act 1988 (CDPA) 192, 198, 201, 203, 209
Cornell, Joseph 250
cost 6, 10, 40, 49–50, 52–53, 77, 92–93, 95, 99, 109–110, 185, 214, 232, 240, 285, 322, 329, 339, 366, 383, 396, 409, 411, 427
Craig, Carys 72–74, 80–81, 83–85, 268, 288
CREATe 1, 5, 8, 142, 181–183, 403
creation 29, 68, 71, 74, 78–79, 96–97, 100, 170, 246, 260–261, 280, 283, 291, 318, 324, 329–331, 335, 340, 348, 350–351, 353–354, 358–359, 362, 364, 369, 386, 389, 396, 408, 411, 421
Creative Commons licenses 10, 75, 93, 120, 327, 337, 364, 395, 398
creative practice 1, 7–9, 12–14, 35, 141–142, 146–147, 149, 153–154, 156, 158–159, 162, 172–173, 283, 312, 316, 338, 340, 348–349, 361, 365, 371
creativity 1–3, 5–9, 12–14, 19, 23, 28, 35, 43–44, 65, 68–74, 79–86, 104, 109, 121–122, 132–134, 141–142, 146–147, 149, 152–156, 158–160, 162, 172–174, 194, 236, 238, 241, 260, 262, 268, 275, 282–283, 287, 296, 310–314, 316–318, 321, 324, 326, 331, 334, 336–340, 347–372, 385–388, 394, 396, 398, 400, 405–406, 409–412, 415, 418, 424, 427
creator 6–7, 67, 69–70, 72–73, 81, 105, 141–143, 146–148, 154–155, 158, 174, 268, 319, 321, 328, 350, 357–358, 360, 363, 369–370, 384, 396, 398, 406, 411–412, 417–424
Cuba, Cuban 13, 33–39, 41–42, 44–48, 50–51, 54–55, 59–61
Cuban-American 33, 59
culture 3–5, 7, 14, 22–24, 27–30, 60–61, 69–74, 80–81, 84–85, 91, 94, 98, 101, 125, 136, 161, 171, 188, 210, 233–237, 239, 243–244, 248,

255, 260, 263, 268, 271, 273, 281, 283–284, 286–287, 289, 296, 298, 309, 311–313, 315–317, 319, 321, 323, 325, 330–338, 340, 347–349, 352–355, 357–358, 361–363, 366–368, 371, 382, 384–385, 391–392, 396, 398–399, 406, 411–412, 415
Curham, Siobhan 112
Dear Dylan 112
Currie, Christopher 391–392
The Tweets of @HenrySavery 392
Curtis Brown 107, 114–115

Dadaist 248, 387
Deazley, Ronan 1, 4, 181, 185
Deleuze, Gilles 291
Proust and Signs 291
democracy 35, 55–56, 75, 247
Department of Culture, Media and Sport (DCMS) 5, 57, 283
Derrida, Jacques 252
Paper Machine 252
design 40, 47, 49, 339, 380–381, 388, 390
Diamond, Beverley 324, 331–332
Dickens, Charles 193, 393
Great Expectations 193
digital 1–3, 6–7, 14, 21–22, 27–28, 35, 38, 41–42, 48–49, 53, 60, 67–68, 70–71, 78–80, 82–85, 92, 95, 102, 104, 108–109, 114, 117, 133–137, 143, 146, 154, 160–161, 165–166, 170, 183, 199, 206, 208, 215, 217, 233, 243–248, 250–254, 256, 258–263, 285, 288, 311, 313–315, 328–330, 337–339, 347–349, 358, 361–364, 367–368, 372, 380–385, 387–389, 392, 399–400, 406, 408–409, 411, 415–420, 422, 427–428
digital literature 78
digital publishing 67, 252, 256, 262
Digital Rights Management (DRM) 117, 256
digital technological protection measures (TPM) 363–364, 371–372

Dimita, Gaetano 65
dissemination 29, 96, 110, 114, 122, 206, 208, 214, 216–217, 259, 287, 290, 295, 310, 318, 325, 331, 334–335, 338, 348, 350, 355, 364, 366, 372, 413–414
diversity 12, 52, 101, 136, 160, 230–235, 238–241, 246, 259, 310–311, 317, 322, 333, 411
Dockray, Sean 42–43, 53–54, 61, 290
Doctorow, Cory 93, 384
Drucker, Johanna 78–79, 245
Dryden, John 98–100
Ducasse, Isidore-Lucien (Le Comte de Lautréamont) 247–248, 260
The Songs of Maldoror 248
Duchamp, Marcel 196
Box in a Valise 196
Duchampian 281

earnings 7, 65, 66, 67, 94, 110, 142, 147, 148, 149, 150, 151, 152, 156, 157, 159, 160, 163, 167, 168, 172, 173, 174, 406. *See also* income
ebooks 130, 157, 166, 170, 259, 408–410
economic 2–3, 6–8, 10, 13, 22, 34, 50, 60, 68–70, 72, 81, 85, 92, 99–101, 137, 141–142, 146, 148, 152–154, 156–157, 161, 163–165, 167–169, 172–175, 184, 214, 217, 268, 274, 281, 313, 318, 320–322, 337, 340, 347–351, 353–354, 359–361, 368, 405–407, 417, 421
ecosystem 96, 132, 137
editing 4, 27, 36, 41, 82, 93, 123, 130–131, 217, 267, 288, 327, 385, 388–389, 411
editors 40, 42, 48–49, 54, 76–77, 109, 114, 131, 134, 235, 285, 320, 328, 385, 388, 405, 410
e-flux 38, 54
embargo 34, 45, 51, 61, 185, 314
Emerson, Lori 78–79, 254, 256
Writing Interfaces: From the Digital to the Bookbound 254

Enlightenment 74, 361
entertainment 95, 104, 124, 259, 360
Ernst, Max 251
ethics 1, 3, 12–13, 70, 75–76, 80, 85–86, 106, 310, 312–313, 316–317, 339, 409
  of care 75–76, 80, 85–86
ethnicity 229, 230, 231, 232, 234, 235, 236, 237, 240, 311, 359. *See also* race
ethnomusicology 309–321, 323–324, 330–332, 334, 336–337
ethos 55, 76, 364
European Comic Art 184, 188
European Commission 10, 141
European Information Society Directive 2001 203
European Union (EU) 46, 108, 145, 327, 371, 406
Europe, European 10, 99, 108, 141, 184, 188, 203, 247, 309, 311, 335, 356, 371, 406, 408, 416
Eve, Martin Paul 11, 318, 321–322
exchange 33, 35, 45, 61, 71, 74, 81, 278, 281, 349, 365, 421

Facebook 45–46, 59, 61, 84, 94, 118, 143, 155, 415
fair dealing 8, 193, 196, 198, 202–205, 208–210, 214, 349, 369–372, 396
fair use 4, 22–23, 192, 276–277, 279, 283–284, 396
Feld, Steven 334
feminist 1, 4, 12–14, 72, 74, 76, 86, 288, 300, 323, 349
Figshare 327–328
filtering 96, 100, 123, 130
Finch Report 2012 206
Fitzpatrick, Kathleen 269, 271, 328
  Generous Thinking 269
Flood, Alison 119, 407
Foucault, Michel 72, 288, 310, 320–321
  Foucauldian 80
France, French 35, 98, 248
Francke, Andrea 289
Fraser, Helen 203, 231, 233

freedom 11–12, 34, 50–51, 54, 114, 185, 214, 395, 421
free labour 3–4, 50, 84
free speech 34, 421
Frieze 60, 413
Fry, Stephen 410–411
funding 9–11, 34–35, 38–40, 52–54, 57–58, 60–61, 66, 92–93, 110, 120, 122, 137, 142, 144, 158, 160–161, 184, 205, 213, 231–232, 239, 250, 259, 263, 293, 314, 318, 334, 337–339, 401, 407, 412
Fusco, Coco 33–34, 38, 54
future 1, 5, 10, 13–14, 27, 105–106, 115, 117, 124–125, 133, 145, 149, 167, 173, 183, 217, 229, 239–241, 259, 276, 278, 295, 320, 325, 336, 340, 351, 360, 381, 385, 400, 406, 412

Gagosian, Larry 276, 278
Gaiman, Neil 137
gender 3, 298
Genova, Lisa 121
  Still Alice 121
Germany, German 66, 257–258, 295
Gibson, Johanna 65, 81, 83–85
Goldsmith, Kenneth 82–83, 272
Google 5, 39, 84, 262, 415
government 2, 5, 11, 38, 41–42, 45, 47, 52, 56–58, 97–98, 144, 184–185, 208, 213–215, 263, 283, 286, 293, 337, 339, 350, 360, 367
graphic 48, 184, 188, 192, 254
Greece, Greek 261, 286, 354
Green Party 143–147
Groth, Simon 14–15, 379

Haaften-Schick, Lauren van 277
Hachette 238, 407–408
Hagedorn, Katherine 324
Hargreaves, Ian 5–6, 8–9, 15, 416
Harnad, Stevan 321–322
HarperCollins 231, 238–239, 241
Harris, Thomas 237
Harvard University 240, 382

Havana 33–38, 41, 44, 46–50, 52, 56–60
  Havana Biennial 35, 38
  Havana Times 47
  Havana University 36, 44
Hayles, N. Katherine 22–23, 78, 245
Hesiod 248, 260
Hindley, Victoria 4
Hocking, Amanda 131
Hodder, Clare 116
Holden-Brown, Heather 108, 110, 124
Hood, Mantle 318–319
Howe, Daniel C. 13–14, 21
human 22, 24, 27–29, 69, 78–79, 82, 84, 112, 171, 261, 268, 311, 325, 349, 351–353, 359, 362, 366, 368
humanist 70–71, 83–84, 269, 323
humanities 1, 204, 215–216, 259, 310, 312, 317, 320–321, 327–329, 338–339

ideology 4–6, 29, 75–76, 170, 172
if:book Australia 379, 381–382, 385–389, 394–395, 398–399, 401
income 14, 60, 65, 66, 68, 94, 95, 117, 142, 144, 148, 149, 150, 151, 152, 156, 158, 159, 160, 161, 162, 163, 164, 165, 166, 168, 172, 173, 175, 230, 334, 406, 408. *See also* earnings
India, Indian 236–237, 239, 313
Indigenous 312–313, 315, 324–325, 331–336, 338–340, 361
individual 7, 15, 68–70, 72–74, 106, 111, 116, 122, 142, 150–152, 154, 157, 172, 181, 193, 195–196, 201, 207, 246, 267, 270, 274, 283, 288, 294, 297–298, 300, 313–314, 319, 327, 332, 336, 348, 350–351, 353, 355–357, 359, 384, 387, 399, 420, 424
inequality 11, 150–152, 298
information 34–35, 42, 54, 74, 82, 102, 104, 109, 112, 116–119, 122, 124, 183, 188, 192, 206, 255, 259–260, 314, 328, 330, 333–334, 337, 350, 352, 357, 361–364, 366–367, 369, 372, 383–384, 427
In Full Colour 230, 241
innovation 2–3, 6, 9–10, 24, 81, 84–85, 254, 260, 326, 348, 351–352, 354, 360, 362–363, 365, 368, 371, 405, 410, 412, 415, 418, 428
intellectual property 2, 6, 8–9, 13, 21–23, 28–29, 34, 43–45, 68–72, 74, 80–81, 83–84, 92–93, 95–96, 100–101, 108, 143, 147, 152–153, 164, 172, 174, 244, 268–269, 282–283, 285–286, 293, 312, 314, 320, 324–326, 330, 336–337, 339–340, 347–352, 354–361, 363–368, 370, 381–382, 384, 399, 417–418, 427
intellectual property law 6, 13, 74, 84, 244, 348–352, 354–360, 363, 366–368, 418
intellectual property rights 2, 68, 70, 74, 83, 147, 269, 325, 339–340, 360, 417
Internet 3, 23–24, 27–28, 35, 38, 41–42, 44, 91–92, 94, 135, 190, 208, 252, 254–255, 263, 314–315, 328, 332, 354, 361–364, 366, 382–384, 388, 401, 411–412, 415, 418–419
Internet Archive 208, 401
invention 3, 256, 350–351, 355, 368
iPad 256, 409
iPhone 60, 256
Ireland, Irish 106, 314, 407
Italy, Italian 60, 257

James, E. L. 121
  Fifty Shades of Grey 103, 121
Jancou, Marc 280–282
Janke, Terri 334–335
Jaszi, Peter 351
Johnson, Philip 65
JSTOR 44, 314

Kean, Danuta 12, 229
Keay, John 158
Kelly, Susan 270–271, 296–297
Kember, Sarah 1, 9, 12, 84

Kheria, Smita 1, 7
Kindle 92, 130, 410
King, Stephen 118
Koons, Jeff 278

labour 3–4, 12, 50, 68, 76–77, 84, 92, 182, 208, 294, 322, 353, 357, 383, 421
Larsen, Mel 230, 235
Lassiter, Luke E. 322–323
Lecercle, Jean-Jacques 244
  A Marxist Philosophy of Language 244
legal 1, 4, 14, 22, 29, 53, 61, 72, 74, 94, 106–111, 114, 116–118, 123–125, 145, 153–154, 168, 174, 196, 208, 268, 274–276, 278, 280, 282, 285–288, 321, 325–326, 335, 339, 348–350, 353, 355–356, 358–359, 361, 364–365, 367–371, 383–384, 395–396, 417–418, 420–421, 423–424, 428
Lessig, Lawrence 73, 93, 362
Letterists 248, 260
Levine, Sherri 273–274
library 11, 35, 43–44, 53, 191, 216, 270, 290–294, 365, 371, 413–414
Lissitzky, El 252
literary 13, 21, 27–28, 65, 83, 85, 97–99, 106–107, 111–112, 114, 123, 130, 134, 137, 155, 193, 196, 204, 229–231, 235–238, 243–244, 247–248, 250–252, 258–260, 262, 299, 351, 365, 379–380, 387–391, 396–397, 399, 407, 415–416, 424
Literary Agency, The 114. *See also* Swift, Rebecca
Literary Platform, The 1, 255
literature 24, 36, 47, 78, 82–83, 98, 119, 135–136, 148–149, 169, 174, 215, 243, 246, 248, 250, 254, 256, 258, 260, 272, 317, 351–352, 357, 366, 381, 387–388, 397
Little, Brown Book Group 238, 271
Liu, Alan 259–260
  The Laws of Cool: Knowledge Work and the Culture of Information 259
Llópiz, Julio César 48, 50, 56
London 2–3, 33–36, 38–39, 42, 44, 46, 48–50, 52–56, 58–61, 65, 97, 232, 234–235, 237, 250, 283, 291, 295, 406, 410, 412–413, 415
love 6, 46, 119, 162, 166, 182, 185, 248, 254, 256, 259, 385, 407

machines 21, 78–79, 82, 102, 208, 254, 269, 288, 293, 384, 416, 418–419
magazines 4, 8, 13, 34–35, 37, 41–43, 47–50, 54–55, 58–60, 136, 243, 250, 413
Malkani, Gautam 237
  Londonstani 237
Malloy, Judy 254–255
  Uncle Roger 254–255
Mantel, Hilary 133
  Wolf Hall 133
marketing 60, 92–93, 96, 103, 106, 114, 122, 131, 134, 137, 236, 367, 428
Mars, Marcell 53, 290
mass media 4, 92
materiality 78–79, 244, 250, 291
Mattering Press 4, 75–77
McCloud, Scott 199–200
  Understanding Comics 199–201
McIntyre, Sarah 143–144, 147
methodology 66, 154, 243–244, 246–247, 318
Milton, John 97–100
Mollet, Richard 8–9
money 6–7, 40, 92, 94, 100, 109, 118, 124, 134, 144, 151, 159, 161–162, 165–167, 231, 243, 259, 322, 332, 383, 405, 407–408, 421, 427–428
Montreal 253, 258
moral 7, 14, 22–23, 57, 73, 209, 268, 335, 350–351, 355–356, 398, 417, 422
moral rights 7, 14, 22–23, 335, 355–356
multimedia 41, 259, 327

music 9, 14, 41, 45, 56, 59, 109, 142, 154, 160–161, 171, 204, 217, 244, 309–311, 313–315, 318–321, 323–324, 327–328, 330–332, 334–337, 339, 348, 356, 368, 387–388, 391, 400, 409, 411
musicology 311, 313, 339

narrative 9, 71–72, 82, 84, 86, 182, 196, 199, 249–250, 255, 324, 380–381, 389, 411
Nesta 2, 406
Nettl, Bruno 313, 339
newspapers 4, 48, 102, 119, 134, 144, 196, 201, 237, 393, 406
New York 34, 38, 59, 102, 240, 258, 271, 273, 280, 328, 348
New Yorker Magazine 285
New York Times 102, 240
Noland, Cady 279–282, 294
   Cowboys Milking 280

Obama, Barack 50, 61
object 24, 69–73, 76–77, 80–82, 84, 217, 245, 251, 258, 267, 270, 296, 338, 358
O'Hare, Louise 13–14, 33, 412–413
online 7, 9, 35–36, 40, 42, 47, 49, 53–54, 58, 61, 92, 102, 119, 121, 123, 131–136, 150, 155, 161, 166–167, 170–172, 181–182, 198–199, 207–208, 247, 254, 256–257, 262, 290–291, 298, 313, 328, 337, 363–365, 367, 385–386, 388, 393, 401, 411, 413–414, 416
Open Access (OA) 1–4, 8–14, 70, 74–75, 85, 92–93, 101, 110, 120, 182, 184–185, 205, 309–310, 312–318, 320–322, 326, 329–335, 337–340, 349, 361–362, 364–367, 371–372
   Open Access movement 14, 74
Open Book Publishers 207–208, 313
Open Library of the Humanities 93, 101
openness 3, 10–12, 75, 92, 315, 332, 337–338

original 7, 13, 22, 24, 27, 70, 73, 79–81, 142, 154, 164, 173, 181, 183, 203, 214, 244, 268, 271, 273–274, 277, 292, 351–352, 380–381, 383, 388, 391, 393, 397–399, 413, 415, 424
originality 24, 73, 82, 244, 268, 273, 275, 279, 351, 353
Other, Otherness 81, 104, 108, 162, 229, 237–238, 290, 293, 313, 320, 322, 367
Ovid 248, 260
Owen, Lynette 66, 106
ownership 5, 22–23, 29, 49, 53, 58–59, 70–74, 80, 98, 100, 111, 119, 147–148, 157, 164–165, 175, 191–192, 196, 198, 208, 210, 238, 262, 275, 282, 291, 309, 312–314, 316, 320, 325, 327, 330–336, 356, 361, 364, 370, 394, 416, 418, 420–421
Oxbridge 229, 232, 235

Paquete Semanal, El 35, 41–42, 45, 60
payment 94, 141, 164, 174, 215, 400
peer review 3, 11, 93, 101, 120, 184, 328, 330–331
Penguin Random House 94, 103, 107, 231, 233, 239, 241, 410–411
permission 4, 10, 37, 47, 58–59, 92, 116, 161, 182, 184–185, 188–193, 198, 208, 210, 214–216, 262, 284–285, 287, 320, 326, 387, 396, 400, 416, 419
photography 58, 193, 243, 248, 257–258, 262, 271, 273–274, 276, 278, 280, 311, 321, 356
piracy 45–46, 73, 81, 93, 97, 117, 119, 271–272, 286–287, 289, 293, 367, 383
Piracy Project 286–291, 293–294, 297
plagiarism 247, 260, 271. *See also* copying
platforms 34–35, 43, 48, 91–92, 94, 101, 118, 121, 124, 130, 132, 135, 137, 143, 217, 245, 252, 256, 263, 290–291, 311, 327, 329–330, 388, 411, 414–415

poetry 1, 78, 82–83, 235, 387, 389, 391, 410
policy 3, 5, 7, 10, 12, 14, 50, 61, 66, 81, 141, 143–147, 150, 154, 191–192, 205, 283, 291, 300, 311–312, 314, 318, 325, 337, 370–371, 414
politics 3–4, 9, 12, 22, 35, 69, 75–77, 98, 170, 273, 275, 285, 293, 295–297, 321, 347, 351, 353–354, 361–362, 368, 415
posthuman 70, 78–81, 83, 85–86
postmodern 22, 323, 390
power 22–23, 29–30, 33, 54, 103, 107, 119, 134–135, 233, 281, 285, 321, 323, 330, 352, 354, 362
practice 1, 3, 7–9, 11–14, 21–23, 27–29, 35, 45, 49, 70, 76, 81, 85–86, 107, 111, 115–116, 141–142, 146–147, 149, 152–156, 158–164, 170, 172–174, 230, 238, 245–246, 248, 250, 262, 267–271, 283–284, 286, 288, 290, 292–300, 310–318, 320, 322, 326, 330–331, 333, 335–340, 347–349, 353, 355–356, 360–361, 365–368, 371, 398, 405, 411, 421, 424, 427
price 9, 50, 92, 94–95, 130, 280–281, 337, 379, 407–408, 428
 price barriers 9, 92
Prince, Richard 96, 271–279, 281–282, 287, 289, 294
private 4, 9, 12, 41, 43, 45, 53, 61, 72, 204–206, 261, 268, 278, 280, 283, 327, 357–359, 361, 363–364, 366, 370, 394, 405
professional 9, 57, 66, 91, 94, 96–97, 100–101, 112–114, 122, 125, 133, 146, 149–151, 154–155, 160, 162, 164, 166, 168–169, 175, 184, 232, 238, 270, 298, 353, 406, 411, 416
profitability 239–240
Project, The 23–24, 27–28
public 4, 8–10, 12, 35, 38, 40–42, 45, 52–53, 57, 83, 92, 98, 100, 146, 160, 183, 205–207, 209, 214, 232–233, 235, 241, 253, 257, 259, 270, 276, 283–285, 291, 322, 326, 334–335, 350, 355, 357–359, 363–367, 370, 386, 389, 391, 394–395, 397–399, 405, 407, 413–414, 418, 420
publication 42, 47, 49, 94, 99, 107, 110–111, 113–114, 123, 137, 144, 146, 157, 160, 167, 173, 182–185, 188, 202, 207, 215–217, 237, 240, 243, 249, 263, 270–271, 278, 314, 319–320, 326, 349, 366, 393, 397, 400, 410, 413, 423, 427
Publication Studio 35, 49, 412–413
Public Library of Science 93, 101
publisher 1, 3–6, 8, 12, 14, 53, 91–94, 96–109, 111–115, 120, 122–124, 130–131, 133, 135–137, 148, 156–157, 165–171, 181, 183–185, 188–191, 196, 207–210, 216–217, 230–241, 244, 248, 252, 254, 256–257, 259–260, 262, 270–271, 276, 288, 292, 295, 298, 313, 317, 320, 324, 329, 331, 335, 337–339, 358, 366, 369, 396, 406–408, 410, 412–413, 416–417, 421, 423–424, 427–428
Publishers Association (PA) 5, 8, 106, 108, 192, 202, 206, 209–210, 216, 230, 238
publishing industry 2, 76, 97, 124, 130, 133–135, 168, 229, 244, 254, 262, 382, 405, 412

Queen Mary, University of London 65, 406

race 3, 229, 236, 237. *See also* ethnicity
Ranciere, Jacques 292
 Ignorant Schoolmaster 292
readers 4, 13, 15, 21, 23, 28–29, 42, 76, 78, 103, 109, 112, 118–119, 121, 123–124, 130–132, 134–137, 144, 172, 188, 192–193, 195–196, 199, 208, 229–230, 236, 244, 249, 252–253, 255–256, 261, 263, 288–289, 292, 298, 313–314, 322, 330, 380–390, 394, 398–399, 405, 407–410, 412, 416
Readers Project, The 13, 21, 23, 28–29

relationality 13–15, 70, 73–75, 80–81, 83–86, 287, 348–349, 351–354, 357, 359–362, 364–367, 369–370, 372
 relational creativity 348–349, 353, 360, 364, 367, 369–370, 372
remix 14–15, 73–74, 82–83, 260, 348, 379–380, 387–391, 393, 395–400
research 2, 4, 6, 8–12, 27, 35, 44, 65–66, 69, 92–94, 109, 111–112, 142, 147–148, 152–154, 156–157, 163, 172–174, 182, 184–185, 188, 196, 198, 202–206, 208, 210, 213–217, 230, 237–241, 243, 245, 270, 276, 284, 286–288, 298–299, 309–314, 318–319, 321–326, 328–329, 331, 334, 337–340, 349, 352, 354, 366–367, 370, 372, 407
responsibility 3–4, 67, 79, 85–86, 104, 107, 109–111, 115–116, 122–125, 188, 216, 241, 310, 312, 326, 333, 336–337, 409
reuse 10, 81–82, 92–93, 328, 395
rights 2, 6–7, 9–10, 13–15, 22–23, 40, 66–72, 74, 80, 83–84, 98, 105–106, 108–109, 115, 117, 119, 124–125, 135, 142, 147, 155–157, 159–162, 164–175, 188, 190, 210, 215, 268–269, 280–282, 284, 310, 312, 317, 319, 325–326, 329, 331–332, 335–337, 339–340, 349–350, 355–360, 363–365, 368–372, 382, 384–385, 394, 396, 398–400, 406, 416–424
Rochester, Sophie 1, 14, 129
Romantic 288, 348–349, 351, 353–354, 361
Rose, Mark 72–73, 268, 356, 411, 425
Ross, Orna 117–118
Rowling, J. K. 144
Royal Literary Fund 158
Rushdie, Salman 107
 Satanic Verses 107
Russia, Russian 119, 252
Ruth, Jan 7, 118

sales 40, 46, 95, 100, 103, 119, 130–131, 148, 157, 160–161, 165–166, 171–172, 214, 217, 243, 259, 274, 278, 280, 359, 410, 413, 424
Salinger, J. D. 271–272, 281
 The Catcher in The Rye 271
Sarmiento, Sergio Muñoz 277–278
Savery, Henry 392
 Quintus Servinton 392, 397
Scotland, Scots 8, 149, 166
self-publishing 91, 93, 95, 101, 103, 111–125, 130–133, 135–136, 247, 259, 291
Shakespeare, William 98–100, 248, 260
sharing 3, 10, 14, 35, 41–44, 53, 61, 104, 106, 110–111, 114, 116, 118, 122, 132, 147–148, 170–172, 230, 240, 250, 283–284, 290–291, 293, 310–314, 316–318, 320–321, 327–339, 349, 362–364, 367, 369, 384–385, 395, 399, 408, 413, 415
Sicot, Catherine 35–38, 41, 47–48, 57, 59, 61
Sim, Dave 182, 193, 197
 Cerebus the Aardvark 193
 Church & State 193, 196–197
social 2–4, 8, 14, 36, 72, 74, 77, 80, 94, 102, 116, 123, 131–132, 144, 146, 153, 155, 209, 229, 231, 241, 243, 267–268, 270, 273, 278, 286–287, 293, 296, 310–312, 317, 326–327, 330, 338–339, 347–349, 351, 353–355, 357, 359–361, 364, 367–368, 386, 405, 412, 415, 421
 media 94, 102, 116, 123, 131–132, 144, 146, 155, 241, 311, 386, 415
Society for Ethnomusicology (SEM) 312, 314
Society of Authors (SoA) 105–106, 108–109, 115–116, 120, 133, 149–150, 407
Society of Young Publishers 231–232
Solomon, Nicola 52, 133, 407–408
Sotheby's 280–281
source 71, 108, 131, 144, 149–150, 158–159, 165, 172, 232, 243, 246, 252, 256, 258–259, 263, 329, 351,

364, 366, 380, 387–388, 390–391, 395–396, 398–399, 405
Soviet Union 34
Spain, Spanish 35
Spinosa, Dani 78
Spivak, Gayatri 300
Spread the Word 136, 230, 238, 240
Statute of Anne 1710 141, 355–356, 423
Stewart, Kevin 116, 427
Supreme Court of Canada (SCC) 349, 369–372
sustainability 40, 48–50, 70, 86, 124, 313, 318, 320, 329–330, 340, 405, 412
Swift, Rebecca 98, 114. *See also* Literary Agency, The
Swijghuisen Reigersberg, Muriel 14, 309, 324
Szilak, Illya 250–251

Tate galleries 4, 28, 57, 59
Taylor & Francis 189–190, 210
technology 2–3, 5–6, 9, 67, 77–79, 84, 92, 101–102, 107, 109, 112, 117, 137, 268, 355–356, 362, 381, 383–385, 401, 409–412, 417–420, 422
text 8, 13, 24, 27–28, 34, 36, 43–44, 61, 73–74, 76, 78–80, 82, 84, 91, 95–96, 98, 102, 119, 182–183, 189, 243–248, 250–251, 253, 256, 258, 261–263, 270–271, 284, 286–288, 290, 292, 295, 297–300, 313, 315, 318–319, 321–324, 328–330, 334, 338, 348, 351–353, 356, 362–364, 366–367, 369, 371, 379–381, 386–388, 390, 393–394, 397–398, 409, 412, 420
theft 23, 172, 384
theoretical 70, 273, 275, 295, 312, 318, 355
theorists 78, 94, 295, 362
theory 22, 43, 46, 48, 78, 81, 93, 96, 100, 154, 250, 268, 311, 315, 323, 350, 353, 357, 421
Titon, Jeff Todd 312, 336
Tonson, Jacob 96–101, 103–104

Toronto 36, 38, 258
 University of Toronto 38
Trade-Related Aspects of Intellectual Property (TRIPS) Agreement 357, 359–360, 363
Turcotte, Joseph 13–14, 72–74, 347
Twitter 118, 155, 256, 392, 405, 412, 415

UK Research Integrity Office (UKRIO) 325–326
UNESCO 37, 333, 406
United Kingdom 2–6, 8, 10–12, 24, 35, 38–39, 48–49, 56–57, 59, 65–68, 70, 95, 97–99, 101, 104, 106, 123–124, 129–130, 133, 136, 141–143, 147–150, 152, 154, 159, 163–164, 169, 172, 184–185, 192, 206, 208, 210, 213, 216, 229–232, 234, 236, 238–241, 247, 257, 260, 283, 296, 325–327, 338, 355–356, 405–410, 416
United States 4, 33–36, 45–46, 50–53, 55–56, 59–61, 95, 102, 104, 117, 123–124, 133, 167, 192, 236, 240, 257–258, 271–273, 279–280, 283, 322, 324, 332, 334, 356–357, 360, 386, 396–397, 400, 407, 410
University of the Arts London (UAL) 39–40, 52–53, 283, 291

value 5, 6, 7, 8, 11, 12, 23, 28, 68, 69, 70, 71, 72, 73, 74, 76, 79, 84, 85, 96, 100, 101, 102, 103, 136, 142, 147, 152, 161, 163, 165, 168, 170, 173, 174, 183, 184, 217, 234, 269, 276, 281, 282, 295, 314, 321, 326, 388, 416, 428. *See also* worth
version 38, 42, 44–45, 59, 117, 119, 159, 166, 181–185, 207, 249, 258, 289, 292, 314, 387–388, 393, 399, 410
Virgil 99, 260

Ware, Chris 182, 196
 Building Stories 196

Wark, McKenzie 248, 260–261
   The Beach Beneath the Street: The Everyday Life and Glorious Times of the Situationist International 248
Waterstones 131, 409–410
Wattpad 135
wealth 23, 30, 68, 96, 98, 278, 283, 320, 333, 406
Weinmayr, Eva 1, 14, 267, 412
Williams, Raymond 2
   structure of feeling 2
Wise, Gordon 107–108, 115
Woodley, Caroline 39–40, 59
Woodmansee, Martha 351
works 7–9, 11, 13–15, 21–22, 24, 27–29, 35–36, 40, 43–46, 48–52, 55–56, 60, 67, 69–70, 72–77, 80–82, 92–93, 95, 97–100, 102, 105–106, 108–112, 114–120, 122–124, 131, 133–134, 141, 144, 148, 152, 155, 157–158, 160, 162, 164–168, 170–172, 174, 181–183, 185, 188, 190–196, 198, 200–204, 206–210, 213–217, 231–232, 235–238, 241, 243–244, 248–250, 253–261, 263, 267–272, 274–275, 277–285, 287–289, 291, 294–295, 297–299, 311, 313–314, 316–317, 320–329, 332–333, 336–337, 340, 348–350, 352–353, 355–360, 362–367, 371–372, 380–392, 394–400, 406, 411–412, 415–421, 423–424, 427–428

World Trade Organization (WTO) 357, 359
worth 13, 68–71, 80, 86, 91, 93, 95–96, 100–104, 144, 152, 169–170, 184, 202–203, 298, 339, 351, 383, 397, 399, 406–407
writers 1, 5, 6, 7, 9, 14, 28, 29, 33, 35, 40, 44, 45, 47, 49, 65, 66, 67, 68, 69, 70, 78, 83, 91, 94, 95, 98, 99, 100, 105, 106, 114, 119, 123, 124, 130, 131, 132, 133, 134, 135, 136, 137, 141, 142, 143, 144, 146, 147, 148, 149, 150, 151, 152, 154, 155, 156, 157, 158, 159, 161, 162, 163, 164, 165, 166, 167, 168, 169, 170, 171, 172, 173, 174, 175, 188, 229, 230, 232, 233, 234, 235, 236, 237, 239, 240, 241, 243, 244, 245, 252, 254, 256, 259, 262, 263, 272, 291, 293, 298, 328, 352, 367, 381, 382, 385, 386, 387, 388, 389, 390, 394, 396, 398, 399, 405, 406, 407, 412, 423, 424, 425
Writing the Future 136, 230, 231, 232, 233, 234, 235, 237, 238, 239, 240, 241

YouTube 109, 132, 135, 315
Yummy Fur 194, 195

Zittrain, Jonathan 382, 384

This book need not end here...

Share

All our books — including the one you have just read — are free to access online so that students, researchers and members of the public who can't afford a printed edition will have access to the same ideas. This title will be accessed online by hundreds of readers each month across the globe: why not share the link so that someone you know is one of them?

This book and additional content is available at:
https://doi.org/10.11647/OBP.0159

Customise

Personalise your copy of this book or design new books using OBP and third-party material. Take chapters or whole books from our published list and make a special edition, a new anthology or an illuminating coursepack. Each customised edition will be produced as a paperback and a downloadable PDF. Find out more at:

https://www.openbookpublishers.com/section/59/1

Like Open Book Publishers

Follow @OpenBookPublish

Read more at the Open Book Publishers BLOG

You may also be interested in:

Privilege and Property
Essays on the History of Copyright
*Edited by Ronan Deazley, Martin Kretschmer
and Lionel Bently*

https://doi.org/10.11647/OBP.0007

Digital Humanities Pedagogy
Practices, Principles and Politics
Edited by Brett D. Hirsch

https://doi.org/10.11647/OBP.0024

The Digital Public Domain
Foundations for an Open Culture
*Edited by Melanie Dulong de Rosnay
and Juan Carlos De Martin*

https://doi.org/10.11647/OBP.0019

Text and Genre in Reconstruction
Effects of Digitalization on Ideas, Behaviours, Products and Institutions
Edited by Willard McCarty

https://doi.org/10.11647/OBP.0008

www.ingramcontent.com/pod-product-compliance
Lightning Source LLC
Chambersburg PA
CBHW062025290426
44108CB00025B/2784